DAILY LIFE OF

THE
NUBIANS

The Greenwood Press "Daily Life Through History" Series

The Age of Charlemagne
John J. Butt

The Age of Sail
Dorothy Denneen Volo and James M. Volo

The American Revolution
Dorothy Denneen Volo and James M. Volo

The Ancient Egyptians
Bob Brier and Hoyt Hobbs

The Ancient Greeks
Robert Garland

Ancient Mesopotamia
Karen Rhea Nemet-Nejat

The Ancient Romans
David Matz

The Aztecs: People of the Sun and Earth
Davíd Carrasco with Scott Sessions

Chaucer's England
Jeffrey L. Singman and Will McLean

Civil War America
Dorothy Denneen Volo and James M. Volo

Colonial New England
Claudia Durst Johnson

Early Modern Japan
Louis G. Perez

Eighteenth-Century England
Kirstin Olsen

Elizabeth England
Jeffrey L. Singman

The Holocaust
*Eve Nussbaum Soumerai
and Carol D. Schulz*

The Inca Empire
Michael A. Malpass

Maya Civilization
Robert J. Sharer

Medieval Europe
Jeffrey L. Singman

The Nineteenth Century American
Frontier
Mary Ellen Jones

The Old Colonial Frontier
James M. Volo and Dorothy Denneen Volo

Renaissance Italy
Elizabeth S. Cohen and Thomas V. Cohen

The Soviet Union
Katherine B. Eaton

The Spanish Inquisition
James M. Anderson

Traditional China: The Tang Dynasty
Charles Benn

The United States, 1920–1939: Decades of
Promise and Pain
David E. Kyvig

The United States, 1940–1959:
Shifting Worlds
Eugenia Kaledin

The United States, 1960–1990: Decades of
Discord
Myron A. Marty

Victorian England
Sally Mitchell

World War I
Neil M. Heyman

DAILY LIFE OF

THE NUBIANS

ROBERT STEVEN BIANCHI

The Greenwood Press "Daily Life Through History" Series

GREENWOOD PRESS
Westport, Connecticut • London

Library of Congress Cataloging-in-Publication Data

Bianchi, Robert Steven, 1943–
    Daily life of the Nubians / Robert Steven Bianchi.
        p. cm. — (The Greenwood Press "Daily life through history" series)
    Includes bibliographical references (p.) and index.
    ISBN 0–313–32501–4 (alk. paper)
        1. Nubians—Social life and customs. I. Title. II. Series.
    DT159.6.N83B527   2004
    939'.78—dc22   2004013208

British Library Cataloguing in Publication Data is available.

Library of Congress Catalog Card Number: 2004013208
ISBN: 0–313–32501–4
ISSN: 1080–4749

First published in 2004

Greenwood Press, 88 Post Road West, Westport, CT 06881
An imprint of Greenwood Publishing Group, Inc.
www.greenwood.com

Printed in the United States of America

The paper used in this book complies with the
Permanent Paper Standard issued by the National
Information Standards Organization (Z39.48–1984).

10   9   8   7   6   5   4   3   2   1

Every reasonable effort has been made to trace the owners of copyright materials
in this book, but in some instances this has proven impossible. The author and
publisher will be glad to receive information leading to more complete acknowl-
edgments in subsequent printings of the book and in the meantime extend their
apologies for any omissions.

For my mother and father

Contents

Preface

My initial interests in Nubia were actually imposed on me by the late Bernard V. Bothmer, who as chair of the Department of Egyptian, Classical, and Middle Eastern Art at The Brooklyn Museum, organized the first modern international loan exhibition devoted to the arts of ancient Nubia. Preparations for this exhibition, *African in Antiquity. The Arts of Ancient Nubia and the Sudan,* were already in progress when I joined his staff on New Year's Day in January 1976, at which time Floyd Lattin had already been entrusted with the lion's share of its administrative details. Shortly after my arrival, Mr. Bothmer added aspects of this exhibition to my curatorial duties so that by the summer of 1978, I found myself immersed with myriad curatorial responsibilities, which culminated in the actual installation of the objects themselves. And although Professor Bothmer and I did not always agree on their actual placement and juxtapositions, my judgment prevailed in the majority of cases.

I went on to train the docents and staff in New Orleans in preparation of its tour there from May 19–August 12, 1979, and supervised both the installation and final deinstallation of the exhibition in The Hague's Gemeentemuseum in the late summer and winter of 1979 with the able assistance of Anthony Melillo. I can still vividly recall those snowy November days on which I accompanied the return of the loans from Warsaw and Berlin as a courier.

As a result of that exhibition, I gained a firsthand knowledge of the objects themselves and a familiarity with the literature with which I have attempted to keep abreast. In the interval between the opening of that exhibition in Brooklyn and the appearance of this book, I have occasionally written about Nubian subjects for both popular and academic audiences and was honored with the presentation of a *karadj,* or ceremonial wedding basket, by the Nubian Association of Alexandria in 1992 for my lecture series in that city to its commercial members and youth group. My first children's book, *The Nubians. Peoples of the Ancient Nile,* was written, in part, as a response to that organization's request for a volume about their ancient Nubian heritage that might be read and consulted by the young men and women of their community.

My discussions of Nubian culture, which rely on examples of ancient Egyptian art, are informed by the view that that art was a canonical undertaking making manifest the ideology of the elite who co-opted craftsmen for its creation. Within this canonical enterprise, which is decidedly different in its visual vocabulary and stylistic conventions than are those encountered in Western art, the ancient Egyptians were concerned with visual clarity rather than with allusions of reality. It is for this reason that I eschew all attempts to read ancient Egyptian art literally as a replication of reality. This volume, devoted to the daily life of the ancient Nubians, is not, therefore, the appropriate forum in which to review art criticism of this nature. The reader who wishes to explore these avenues of art history and appreciation are directed to the bibliography where references to my earlier essays on these issues may be found.

I traveled to some of the Nubian regions repeatedly in the 1990s under the auspices of Archaeological Tours of New York City due to the kindness of Linda Feinstone. The sites visited and impressions gained have been valuable for contributing to my verbal descriptions throughout this volume. I am indebted to my daughter, Kyria Marcella Osborne, for reading and rereading successive drafts and for making valuable suggestions for increasing the text's readability and clarity of ideas.

It is only from the year 664 B.C.E. with the establishment of Dynasty XXVI that ancient historians can more narrowly date events in ancient Egyptian and Nubian history because of the synchronisms afforded by recorded events in Greek and later Roman history. As a result, almost all of the dates in this volume are approximate and are expressed as either B.C.E. (before the common era) or C.E. (common era), rather than as B.C. and A.D., respectively. I have employed B.P. (before the present) for cultural horizons appearing before approximately 10,000 B.C.E. Nevertheless, dates provide a framework within which to appreciate the longevity of the ancient Nubian cultures discussed in this volume. For convenience, therefore, the dates employed are those found in the handy 1999 volume of J. von Beckerath. One must also understand that most of these dates are approximate and that scholars disagree about the relative chronological positions of several historically prominent ancient Nubians. In order to illustrate the complexities of these circumstances, we have used the biography of the elite Nubian woman, Katimalo, as a case study.

I have quoted extensively from ancient texts to enable students to gain a contextual idea about the types of subjects treated. Where appropriate, I have cited the source of the translation, but here state that for reasons of internal consistency or clarity I have in some instances emended the published translation. In the interests of consistency, I have taken the liberty of replacing the noun "Negro" with "Nubian" in all of the translations that I quote in which that noun appears. Each quotation is followed by the volume and either the paragraph (§) or page number from which the translation is either taken or adapted. A list of the abbreviations used can be found at the back of this volume on pages 273–274. In order to ensure internal consistency, the spellings of proper nouns may have been changed in order to conform to the spellings employed throughout this volume.

Of the many individuals who have assisted me on this project, I wish to thank in particular Dorothea Arnold, Charles Bonnet, Edda Bresciani, Nadine Cherpion, Silvio Curto, Peter Der Manuelian, Anna-Maria Donadoni-Roveri, Richard A. Fazzini, John A. Larson, Angelika Lohwasser, Geoffrey T. Martin, Bernard Mathieu, Dimitri Meeks, David O'Connor, Jacques Reinold, Stephan Seidlmayer, Friederike Seyfried, Patricia A. Spencer, and Dietich Wildung. I wish to record my gratitude to Sidney Burnstein, the late Nicholas B. Millett, Steffan Wenig, and Janice Yellin, all of whom have continuously been engaged with me over the years in discussions about Nubian issues.

Robert Steven Bianchi
Tampa, Florida

Introduction

Today, interest in the antiquity of Africa appears to be exclusively concerned with ancient Egypt. To be sure, network and cable telecasts on ancient Egyptian themes, both documentary and fiction, habitually draw impressive audience share in the ratings. Additionally international loan exhibitions of ancient Egyptian works of art perennially attract more visitors than do other types of shows. All this attention on ancient Egypt obscures the fact that the antiquity of the African continent is so much more than the civilization of ancient Egypt alone. A cultural minister of an African nation–state once remarked to me in London over a quarter century ago that the civilizations of Africa can stand on their own and do not require linkages with Egypt to justify their value. Indeed, the significant, ancient civilizations that developed to the south of the Egyptian city of Aswan and that are generally referred to as "Nubian" have received little or no popular presentation here in the English-speaking world precisely because of this Egyptocentric bias in modern popular approaches to the antiquity of Africa. This Egyptocentric approach is ostensibly so all pervasive that the organizers of the 1995 exhibition, *Africa: The Art of a Continent* bundled the presentation of ancient Egypt and Nubia into one chapter in its accompanying catalogue. In order to redress this seeming imbalance in the treatment of Africa's antiquity, the editors of this series have invited me to submit the following volume on the Daily Life of the Ancient Nubians.

My acceptance is consistent with more progressive museological approaches to ancient Egypt and Nubia. So, for example, during my tenure as a Fulbright-Hayes Fellow to a divided Berlin in the late 1970s, I experienced for the first time the installation of galleries in a Western museum devoted exclusively to the arts of Nubia. The Royal Ontario Museum in Toronto, Canada, and The British Museum in London, England, have since followed suit, and the Museum of Fine Arts in Boston, Massachusetts, maintains a department of Ancient Egyptian, Nubian, and Near Eastern Art within the umbrella of its Department of the Art of the Ancient World. The government of Egypt has even inaugurated a Museum of Nubian Art in Aswan, in the region of the traditional common border between ancient Egypt and Nubia. There are, moreover, five ancient, architectural monuments, originally erected in Nubia, which have subsequently been dismantled and reerected in Berlin, Leiden, Madrid, New York, and Turin. The cumulative weight of this little-known Nubian presence in the West must be shouldered by a wider audience, one that is not confined to specialists and limited to their continuing, and significant, research.

Concomitant with the innovative museological focus of those aforementioned institutions is the observation that education, at least in the United States, has undergone a revolution of its own during the past quarter of a century or so. One clamors for modifications or additions to literary canons so that these lists are more representative of world literature in general and less gender restrictive. A heightened awareness of the world in which we now live has prompted an interest in multiculturalism. Enlightened individuals acknowledge that the study of cultures other than their own exposes one to articulated differences, which promotes dialogue rather than maintains mute isolation. It is, therefore, within the ambit of these progressive tendencies that the following is offered.

There is, moreover, another dimension to these tendencies, particularly in America, where Black Studies programs have been in place for some time. Racially tendentious positions regarding the ethnicity of the ancient Egyptians themselves have often radically divided communities and have led to the adoption of baseline curricula promoting an essential Black African nature of the ancient Egyptians in some American public school systems. Martin Bernall's *Black Athena* (1987) caused a firestorm in that regard and in and of itself generated a veritable cottage industry of support and dismissal. The question of the ethnicity of the ancient Egyptians remains contentious, but the Nubians are Black African peoples. As such, their cultures, in and of themselves, deserve to be presented to a wider audience in keeping with the imperatives just outlined. This need for a wider, popular dissemination of Nubian civilization was particularly recognized in 1992 by the Nubian Tradition Committee of the Archaeological Society of Alexandria, Egypt, whose executive committee invited me to deliver a series of lectures to their children in an effort to keep their history alive.

Just as my first popular book on the subject, *The Nubians: People of the Ancient Nile* (1994) was intended for young readers, this volume, *Daily Life of the Nubians,* is intended as an introduction for both college and university undergraduates and the interested, informed reader. It would, however, be unfair to pigeonhole the volume for a niche audience. Although *Daily Life of the Nubians* can adequately serve as a general historical overview, its value for ancient art and architecture, cultural anthropology, and costume cannot be overlooked. The engines driving my narrative are archaeological and inscriptional. I have relied for the earlier periods of Nubia's history on the archaeology of the region and have distilled my narrative from publications primarily in French and German, which may be unfamiliar to my intended audience. In an effort to bridge the gap between our time and that of the ancient Nubians, I have also relied on English translations of ancient texts, most of which were written in ancient Egyptian. The volume serves, therefore, as a ready reference to those sources. Throughout, I have included discussions and, in some instances, reinterpretations of Nubian works of art, and have included for illustrations some of their more significant, but less readily available, monuments. I have striven to record in each chapter what can be fairly stated about the diet and fashions of the Nubians. That diet changed over time, as did the fashions represented in their art and reflected in material recovered from excavations.

In organizing the material, I have benefited enormously from my first exposure to Nubia in 1976 and from my initial physical contact with the works of art themselves during the installations of the exhibition, *Africa in Antiquity: The Arts of Nubia and the Sudan* in Brooklyn and at Den Haag in The Netherlands. Most recently in October 2003, I had the opportunity of viewing and studying the objects and accompanying catalogue of the extraordinary exhibition *Nubia: Los reinos del Nilo en Sudán,* in Madrid, Spain, mounted by the Fundación "la Caixa" of Barcelona.

Chronology and nomenclature (chapter 1) are of paramount importance in discussions about the Nubians. It is for that reason that I begin my narrative with a thumbnail chronological sketch extending back in time to the period around 300,000 B.P. I then devote some attention to the nouns by which the Nubians were anciently and modernly named so that the reader can understand the nuanced differences between Kushite and Aethiopian, for example. This chapter continues with a discussion of geography, introduced by the caveat that oftentimes scholars are uncertain about identifying any given geographical location with a place name recorded in the written record. With time, place, and names introduced, the initial chapter then deals with selected early European travelers, the central role of the Egyptian dams at Aswan in fostering investigations of Nubia, and Nubian studies in a nonpolemical context.

The Earliest Nubians (chapter 2) relies almost exclusively on the archaeological record and begins by focusing on the period from about 40,000–10,000 B.P. Settlements and cemeteries are passed in review in an effort to demonstrate the emergence of an elite and a progressively more stratified society increasingly dependent on agriculture and animal husbandry. Here and in the following chapters one will find sections dealing particularly with diet and dress providing the reader with an opportunity to image the Nubians as real people in the mind's eye.

The Neolithic Revolution (chapter 3) is presented by an analysis of data from cemeteries, from which inferences about the emergence of chieftains are drawn. Pottery and clay figurines are discussed at length, with some reinterpretations offered, before considering the issue of continuity and disjunction in Nubian culture, a question that will be addressed as well in subsequent chapters.

The A-Group Nubians (chapter 4) provide one with the earliest, clearly definable cultural horizon, indebted to the pioneering efforts of George Andrew Reisner. The interfaces between the Nubians of this period and the contemporary Egyptians are surveyed with special attention focused on the Qustul incense burner with related discussions about Nubian petroglyphs, or rock art, and ceramics. The fall of Nubia during this period and the concomitant rise of Egypt is presented by quoting from the ancient sources.

The Nubians of the C-Group culture (chapter 5) is based on the archaeological record and their peaceful coexistence with an Egyptian military presence in Nubia explained. Various military campaigns are presented. Of particular importance is the appearance of tattoos for the very first time on the African continent, and its impact on Egypt is assessed.

The Nubians of the Kingdom of Kerma (chapter 6), the earliest and longest-lived of any African civilization south of Egypt, are next treated with focus on the city of Kerma itself. The archaeological record divides the history of this kingdom into three phases with particular attention paid to the Classic Kerma Period and its powerful elite members. The architecture of the site is presented in some detail, with particular attention paid to the two *deffufa*s, or massive mud-brick edifices. The arts flourished at Kerma, particularly with regard to personal adornment and ceramics.

The fall of Kerma is presented, and Nubia during Egypt's New Kingdom (chapter 7), discussions of the phenomenon of cultural assimilation, and depictions of Nubians in ancient Egyptian art. A great deal of attention is devoted to Egyptian military campaigns against the Nubians, but these records paint a picture of Nubian prosperity, the wealth of Africa in general, and population and seem to be the result of suppressing sporadic revolts rather than expressions of prolonged campaigns. The chapter includes discussions of the Egyptian administration of Nubia, Egyptian-style temples there, and the apparent dominance of Egyptian religious tenets. The introduction of new place names prompts a geographic discussion, which includes a consideration of the land of Punt.

Nubia during the Ramesside Period of the Egyptian New Kingdom (chapter 8) focuses on Egyptian exploitation of Nubian gold and the need for wells in its procurement, military campaigns, and the wealth of Africa. Of particular note is the discussion of a numen, resident in the matrix of natural rock, within Nubian culture.

Nubia during the Third Intermediate Period and the Rise and Fall of Dynasty XXV (chapter 9) begins with an assessment of the role of the God Amun in both Nubia and Egypt and the critical role played by the site of Gebel Barkal in the formation of the Nubian state. Thereafter biographies of known Nubian monarchs associated with the Kushite Dynasty of Egypt are presented, with special attention given to Piankhy, his reputed piety and administration, and to Taharqa. Presentation of Assyrian-Egyptian relations creates the backdrop against which the fall of Dynasty XXV and the subsequent rise of the native Egyptian Dynasty XXVI are sketched. Nubian theology as well as questions about a Nubian matriarchy are passed in review. The chapter concludes with an examination of Nubian temples and art, particularly sculpture in the round.

Nubia during the Napatan Period (chapter 10) begins by examining the dismantling of the Nubian administration of Egypt and the subsequent rise of the Napatan Dynasty deep in the Nubian heartland of Africa. Egyptian punitive campaigns are presented and assessed as are the threats of marauding tribes. Attention is focused on Nubian architecture and sculpture—both in the round and two-dimensional relief—of the period. There are extensive discussions of various aspects of Napatan Nubian costume and accessories.

Nubia during the Kingdom of Meroe (chapter 11) represents the final chapter of ancient Nubia's history, during which period the earliest dated inscriptions written in Meroitic are dated. That language is discussed and the difficulties of translation presented by analyzing texts. The nature of Nubian government with its apparent "king, queen, and prince" as well as viceroy is discussed, as are facets of the economy. The role of processions in religious ceremonies and investiture are presented as are political relationships with the contemporary Egyptian dynasty of the Ptolemies. The revolt of the Meroites under Augustus and the subsequent diplomatic settlement with its advantageous terms conclude the historical section. This is followed by a discussion of Nubian temples, particularly the speos and Temple of Dendur now in New York City, and sculpture, with attention on the composite ba-birds. Presentations of Meroitic pottery and jewelry as well as the issue of scarification are included. Suggestions are then offered regarding the eclipse of the Kingdom of Meroe in terms of the Roman Empire and rise of the Kingdom of Axum.

Chronology

All dates are approximate.

1,500,000–100,000 B.P.	Acheulean Era	
300,000 B.P.	Paleolithic Period (Old Stone Age)	
40,000 B.C.E.	Neolithic Period	
5500 B.C.E.	Neolithic Agricultural Revolution	
3700–2800 B.C.E.	The A-Group Culture	
	3700–3250 B.C.E.	Ancient Phase
	3250–3150 B.C.E.	Classic Phase
	3150–2800 B.C.E.	Final Phase
2300–1600 B.C.E.	The C-Group Culture	
	2300–1900 B.C.E.	Ancient Phase
	1900–1600 B.C.E.	Second Phase
2500–1500 B.C.E.	The Kingdom of Kerma	
	2500/2400–2050 B.C.E.	Ancient Kerma Period

	2050–1750 B.C.E.	Middle Kerma Period
	1750–1500 B.C.E.	Classic Kerma Period
1550–1069 B.C.E.	Nubian Cultures Contemporary with New Kingdom Egypt	
	1550–1292 B.C.E.	Dynasty XVIII
	1292–1185 B.C.E.	Dynasty XIX
	1186–1069 B.C.E.	Dynasty XX
1000–275 B.C.E.	The Rise of the Kingdom of Napata	
	785–760 B.C.E.	Alara
746–653 B.C.E.	Egypt's Nubian Dynasty	
	Kashta	
	Piankhy	
	Shabaka	
	Shebitqo	
	Taharqa	
	Tantamani	
275 B.C.E.–350 C.E.	The Kingdom of Meroe	
	Ergamenes I (Arkamni-Qo)	
	Ergamenes II (Arkamani II)	
	Adikhalamani	
	Amanikhabale	
	Natakamani	
	Amanitore	
	Amanimalel	
	Amanishakheto	

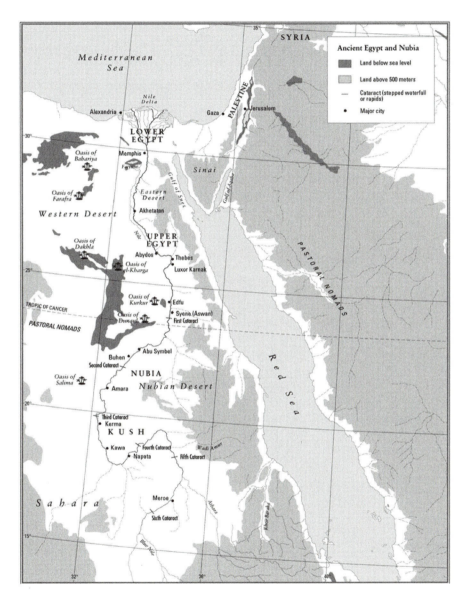

Nubia in the northwest quadrant of the African continent with Egypt to the north and neighboring regions to the east.

1

The Nubians: Ancient Peoples of the Nile

Who were the ancient peoples inhabiting the regions south of the modern Egyptian city of Aswan in the northeast quadrant of Africa? What do we know about their cultures, which were contemporary in date with the rise and fall of ancient Egypt's civilization? By what name or names were these peoples anciently known? What can the archaeological record tell us about their daily life? Answers to these questions are complex.

What follows, therefore, is an attempt to pass in review the ancient designations of these Black African peoples with a view toward clarifying existing confusion for the general reader, while at the same time providing a synopsis of how these peoples have been regarded from the vantage of Western scholarship. It is important to stress that for most of their history, the peoples who are the subject of this book did not develop a written language of their own. In the early Iron Age of the first millennium B.C.E., they adopted the prevailing notational system of the ancient Egyptians and only developed their own system of writing, termed Meroitic, late in their history. Although strides are being made in its decipherment, and many passages in the preserved inscriptions in that language can be transliterated, translated, and understood, our knowledge of Meroitic is still imperfect. As a result, one must carefully evaluate what other ancient peoples—not only the Greeks and Romans but also both Assyrians and Hebrews as well as the ancient Egyptian themselves—had to say about these Black Africans. Because the Nubians themselves did not write those accounts, one must exercise caution when citing those records as evidence for historical truths. Nevertheless, as one school of criticism correctly observes, all comments, even negative ones, when placed into the appropriate context, can be revealing. Egyptian accounts of the numbers of Nubians killed or captured in campaigns, for example, serve as indices for population density, and accounts of pillaging or plunder reveal the extent of Nubian wealth. The content of those records must, of course, always be analyzed in light of the archaeological record.

NUBIA AND THE NUBIANS

I'm using *Nubians* and *Nubia* when referring to these Black African people and their homeland throughout the book. These nouns are imprecise but appropriate because the Ancients used these nouns themselves.

The word *Nubia* appears relatively late in the region's history, appearing in the ancient lexicon in the third century B.C.E. Its etymology is disputed. The popular notion linking it with an ancient Egyptian noun *nebu*, meaning "gold," is based more on current cultural matters than solid research. A more plausible explanation for the noun *Nubia* argues that the word is related to and derived from "Noubai," a Nubian people who appear rather late in the history of Africa. Be that as it may, *Nubian* and *Nubia* primarily convey the geographic location of a people rather than their ethnic background or makeup. One should be aware of the fact that there are thriving communities of individuals who refer to themselves as Nubians still resident in Egypt, and who, although possessed of Egyptian citizenship, nevertheless consider themselves heirs to the ancient Nubians discussed herein.

A CHRONOLOGICAL OVERVIEW

The history of Nubia can be traced back to the Paleolithic Period, or the Old Stone Age, some 300,000 years ago. Advances between 40,000 and 10,000 B.P. set the stage for the emergence of Nubia's Neolithic cultures. By the sixth millennium B.C.E., the Nubians had developed agriculture and pioneering contacts with Egypt further to the north. Such contacts were to characterize Egypt–Nubian relationships for the remainder of ancient Nubia's history. Because the Nubians developed their own written language rather late, historians have by necessity linked the history of Ancient Nubia to that of Ancient Egypt, from whose written record we have derived much if not most of our knowledge of the early Nubians.

In broad strokes, the major historical epochs of the ancient Nubians can be charted as follows:

Approximate Date	Nubian Culture
3700–2800 B.C.E.	The A-GROUP CULTURE
2300–1600 B.C.E.	The C-GROUP CULTURE
2500–1500 B.C.E.	The KINGDOM OF KERMA

1550–1069 B.C.E.   The Nubians contemporary with the Egyptian New Kingdom

1000–653 B.C.E.   The rise of the KINGDOM OF NAPATA and EGYPT'S NUBIAN DYNASTY XXV

1000–275 B.C.E.   The KINGDOM OF NAPATA

275 B.C.E.–300/350 C.E.   The KINGDOM OF MEROE

NEHESIU AND AETHIOPIANS

During the course of their New Kingdom (Dynasty XVIII–XX [about 1550–1069 B.C.E.]), the ancient Egyptians had recourse to several nouns and phrases by which they referred to the Nubians. One of the phrases current at that time was "the Nehesiu with burnt faces." The Egyptian proper noun, *Nehesiu*, in this context, connotes a Southerner, that is, one who lives south of the border of Egypt. The phrase "with burnt faces" refers to skin color, because the Nubians' complexions were generally darker than their Egyptian contemporaries. This ancient phrase was not conceived as a racial slur, because the degree of melanin varies among the Black Africans even today as one travels across the continent. The proper noun *Nehesiu*, the *Nubians*, served as a generic term, and was commonly

Portrait of the Kushite Pharaoh Taharqa. ALEA.

employed by the Egyptians to include all Black Africans. The modern personal name *Phineas* is etymologically derived from the root of this ancient Egyptian noun, which is also found in Semitic languages. The modern name means "the Southern one," which anciently may have connoted an African in general or a Nubian in particular.

The adjective *Aethiopian,* on the other hand, appears among the earliest written designations of these peoples in Greek contexts. It is frequently encountered in the epic poems of the Greek poet Homer, whom tradition maintains was active in the eighth century b.c.e. Homer calls the Nubians "Aethiopians," a Greek noun that is the literal translation of the ancient Egyptian phrase "burnt faced." The designation "burnt face" in Homer and the Greeks appears to have more to do with geography as a determinative of one's complexion than with race. Homer and his Greek contemporaries regarded the Aethiopians as the peoples living closest to the sun by virtue of their perceived proximity to the earth's equator. Their faces were, therefore, burnt by the scorching rays of the sun. This Greek interpretation is in keeping with the Egyptian interpretation. In an ancient Greek or Roman context, then, the word *Aethiopian* may be generically applicable to the Nubians, but that word has not been adopted for use in this volume to avoid any confusion with its homonym, Ethiopia, a modern nation-state.

KUSH AND THE KUSHITES

The ancient Egyptians referred to a region, located south of the third cataract of the Nile River, in which the Nubians dwelt, as Kush, most often in the phrase "vile Kush" or "wretched Kush." Within such a context, this phrase is not a racial slur. Throughout the history of ancient Egypt there are numerous, well-documented instances that celebrate Nubian–Egyptian marriages. A study of these documents, particularly those dated to both the Egyptian New Kingdom (after 1550 b.c.e.) and to Dynasty XXV and early Dynasty XXVI (about 720–640 b.c.e.), reveals that neither spouse nor any of the children of such unions suffered discrimination at the hands of the ancient Egyptians. Indeed, such marriages were never an obstacle to social, economic, or political status, provided the individuals concerned conformed to generally accepted Egyptian social standards. Furthermore, at times, certain Nubian practices, such as tattooing for women and the unisex fashion of wearing earrings, were wholeheartedly embraced by the ancient Egyptians.

The phrase "vile/ wretched Kush" must, consequently, be regarded as a marker of difference, particularly in nationalistically Egyptian historical inscriptions recounting military campaigns waged by the Egyptians against their neighbors. Indeed, in the inscription on the Kubban stela of pharaoh Rameses II (about 1279–1213 b.c.e.) the epithet is transferred to the title, "king's son of Kush," assigned to the chief administrator of Nubia.

"As for the country of Akita, this is said concerning it," said the king's-son of wretched Kush.... (ARE 3: §292)

Within such a context, the ancient Egyptians were simply attempting to divide the inhabitants of their known world into 10 distinct groupings, one comprising the Egyptians themselves. They could, thereby, readily wage a war of propaganda against their foes whom they then divided into nine traditional divisions, of which the Nubians, like the Syrians, Libyans, or peoples of the Aegean, formed a part.

As a result of this ancient Egyptian practice, neighboring civilizations, such as the Assyrians and the Persians, termed the Nubians "Kushites" and their homelands "Kusu" and "Kushiya," respectively. This ancient distinction notwithstanding, modern scholarship has adopted the proper noun *the Kushites* as a designation for the Nubians, particularly during that period of their history when Nubians ruled over most of Egypt for about a century as pharaohs in their own right during Dynasty XXV shortly after 720 B.C.E.

NAPATA AND THE NAPATANS AND MEROE AND THE MEROITES

In like manner, the Nubians may be referred to as "the Napatans" during that period of their history when their capital was at Napata and as "the Meroites," when their kingdom was ruled from Meroe. Each of these cultural horizons is discussed at length later in its own respective section.

THE GEOGRAPHY OF NUBIA

Today, automobiles are often equipped with Global Positioning Systems, and automobile clubs and other organizations routinely provide detailed road maps to their members containing specific information about routes, their lengths, and estimated time of travel to particular destinations. It is, therefore, somewhat disconcerting to begin this narrative with the observation that one simply cannot be certain about numerous facets of ancient geography as they impact on the study of the daily lives of the ancient Nubians. This geographic imprecision reflects the paucity in the archaeological record of topographical information from which a cartographer might develop a map of ancient Nubia. To be fair, however, one must stress that the ancients often did refer to specific geographic regions by name, but scholars are often in disagreement about where to situate any of these named regions on a map. As a result, the reader is here forewarned that theories and countertheories abound in the literature about localizing a great many Nubian place names. So, for example, the phrase "Ta-sety," literally, "the land of the bow," could be anciently applied to both the area around Aswan as well as the region of Edfu, which comprised the First Nome, or province, of Upper Egypt. In other contexts, this phrase refers to Nubia itself, as seen, for example, in certain titles borne by Nubian queens of Dynasty XXV and later who are styled, "Mistress of Ta-Sety."

In some instances it has proven difficult to equate an anciently attested place name with an actual archaeological site or geographic region. This observation obtains for "Ta-nehesy," "the land of the Nehesy-Nubians," who, as peoples, were either settled south of Aswan or roamed as nomads in the same area. Similarly, the Classical Greeks developed their own partitions of Aethiopia into several regions.

MODERN NAMES AND ANCIENT PLACES

One can, nevertheless, gain an enhanced sense of place by describing modernly recognized topographical features and the names of cities and rivers located within them in an attempt to correlate this data with the geography of ancient Nubia as preserved in the archaeological record. This correlation can begin by considering the northeastern quadrant of Africa in which the modern nation-states of the Arab Republic of Egypt and the Democratic Republic of The Sudan are located. The most familiar geographic feature topographically uniting these two polities is the Nile River. Using the Nile River to help visualize the geography of ancient Nubia has the added advantage of referring to that river's cataracts, of which there are six between Khartoum and Aswan. These cataracts are geological intrusions of igneous granite into the prevailing stratified sandstone. As the Nile cuts its channel, its waters remove the former at a more rapid rate than it does the latter, causing the granite, thus exposed, to form rapids, or white water, which are termed cataracts. One can now use the Nile River and its six cataracts as convenient points of reference for an understanding of Nubia's geography.

UPPER AND LOWER NUBIA

In antiquity, the first cataract at Aswan marked the southern border of Egypt. Beyond lay Nubia. And in keeping with conventions whereby Egypt is divided into two regions, Upper and Lower Egypt, so, too, is Nubia likewise divided into Upper and Lower Nubia. The designations "upper" and "lower" are keyed to the direction of the Nile's flow so that Lower Nubia is *downstream* in relation to Upper Nubia.

Lower Nubia Lower Nubia, therefore, is generally situated south of Aswan in the area bounded by the first and second cataracts and includes the modern city of Wadi Halfa, on Egypt's southern border with The Sudan. As a result of the construction of the Aswan High Dam, most of this area is presently beneath the waters of Lake Nasser. In antiquity, Lower Nubia was a barren land, but early European travelers in the nineteenth century were taken by the awesome beauty of its stark sandstone cliffs. Some scholars would identify the ancient place name "Wawat" with southern Lower Nubia and "Irtjet" with northern Lower Nubia. In Classical times, a stretch of the Nile some 90 miles in length and extending to the south from Aswan was often referred to as the "Dodekaschoinos," "the twelve schoinoi," a schoinos being an ancient Greek linear measurement of approximately 7 1/2 miles in length. The Dodekaschoinos served as a buffer zone between the Roman Empire and the Kingdom of Meroe in the late first century B.C.E. Many of the Nubian temples, dismantled in advance of the creation of Lake Nasser, rising behind the Aswan High Dam, have been given as gifts by the Egyptian government to nation-states in recognition of their services to the UNESCO-sponsored Nubian archaeological project. A gateway from Kalabsha is in Berlin; the Temple of Taffeh in Leiden; the Temple of Debod in Madrid; the Temple of Dendur in New York City; and the Speos, or rock cut shrine, of Ellyhesia in Turin.

In antiquity during the fourth to the sixth centuries C.E., Lower Nubia was home to two Nubian cultural horizons, termed the Ballana and Nobadia cultures, respectively. The southern frontier of Lower Nubia was at Batn el-Hagar, the Belly of Rocks.

The region from Batn el-Hagar to the fourth cataract of the Nile comprises Upper Nubia. Within this region is the **Upper Nubia** Dongola Reach, the most fertile stretch of the Nile River south of Thebes. Here, too, is located Kerma, one of early Nubia's most powerful kingdoms, which flourished during the early Bronze Age. The later Nubian site of Pnubs is located in approximately the same place.

The area between the fourth and fifth cataracts is desolate, the banks of the Nile River barren. Nubian sites are few and far between, with only a handful, such as Abu Hamed and Kurgus identified to date. In ancient times, this desolate region was traversed via trading routes crisscrossing the Bayuda Desert.

To the south of the fifth cataract the Atbara and Nile Rivers converge, and further on along the Nile lies Meroe, capital city of one of ancient Nubia's most prosperous realms, which ruled the region until the fourth century C.E. Because of the configuration of the Atbara and Nile Rivers, the region in which Meroe is located was anciently regarded as being surrounded by water; this region was consequently, but incorrectly, referred to as The Island of Meroe. Here is found the Shendi reach of the Nile River and the Butana, in which have been excavated many of the storied sites of the Meroitic Kingdom, such as Naqa and Musawwarat es-Sufra. In the period before the eighth century B.C.E., scholars suggest that this region may perhaps have been "Irem" and "Miu," referred to in the ancient texts. Its seasonal rain belt fostered a savanna, densely wooded in places, which provided habitat for giraffes, elephants, lions, and leopards. The region provided the Nubians with ebony, ivory, animal skins, and incense.

To the west of the Nile one finds the sites of Darfur and Kordofan, both dated to the Medieval Period, but archaeological exploration has uncovered evidence, however slight, of C-Group, Kerma culture, and Meroitic cultural horizons as well. To the east, the savanna extends to the foothills of modern Ethiopia. Here, some have suggested, was the Land of Punt, whose myrrh was so highly valued by the Egyptians of the late Bronze Age.

MEROE AND AKSUM

The Kingdom of Meroe flourished until the fourth century C.E., after which the Nubian state appears to have become fragmented into a number of smaller principalities. Throughout the course of the first millennium, however, contacts were established with the Kingdom of Aksum to the south and the peoples of the Arabian Peninsula across the Red Sea to the East. In antiquity, the southern frontiers of Nubia appear to have been slightly to the south of Khartoum, the modern capital of the nation-state of The Sudan, which was founded at the juncture of the White and Blue Niles. Further to the south, the sites of Sennar and Gebel Moya revealed Nubian activity; names of Nubian kings of Dynasty XXV are likewise attested in this area.

NUBIA REVEALED

The lasting impact of Greece and Rome on Western civilization is due in no small part to the observation that, although Latin is a dead language and modern Greek bears only a slight relationship to ancient Greek, Western scholars have always been able to translate these texts into modern languages. The West has never lost its ability to read, comment on, and understand ancient Greek and Latin. Knowledge of texts in both of those languages provided early historians with the basis of their interpretations of the Nubians.

SOME EARLY EUROPEAN EXPLORERS

Educated at Harrow and having studied oriental languages, James Bruce (1730–1794) was among the first Europeans to visit Nubia. In 1722, Bruce was able to identify the ruins of Begraweya with the site of ancient Meroe and subsequently published the results of his voyages to this part of Africa in his *Travels,* the first edition of which appeared in 1790.

Almost a century later, the initial phases of a more systematic study of Nubia began as the result of a military campaign. Mohamed Ali (ruled 1805–48), initially the Ottoman governor of Egypt whose coup d'etat established him as sole ruler of Egypt, launched an offensive against The Sudan in 1821 with a view toward annexing the region and incorporating it into his realm. His military objective was the Funji Kingdom, of which

Sennar was the capital. Numerous scholars followed in the wake of his victory, and they began to document Nubia's cultural history in accordance with the period's established norms. Rather than excavating with trowel and brush, these scholars concentrated on visible, architectural ruins, which they drew (because the camera had not yet been sufficiently developed) and measured.

Frédéric Cailliaud (1787–1869) was a mineralogist by profession who, after arriving in Egypt, was commissioned by Mohamed Ali to locate the emerald mines described by several Arabic historians and was among the first to publish detailed accounts of Nubia. His monumental *Voyage à Méroé*, comprising four volumes of text and three folio volumes of plates, appeared between 1819 and 1926.

Karl Richard Lepsius (1810–1884), trained as a scholar and well versed in several languages including the newly deciphered Egyptian hieroglyphs, led what has been described as the best-equipped expedition ever to travel to Egypt and the Sudan up to that time with the expressed purpose of surveying the monuments and collecting objects. His monumental *Denkmäler* (1859), devoted to the results of his campaign of 1842–1854, is undoubtedly the largest Egyptological work ever produced. Its 12 vast volumes contain 894 folio plates, and its accompanying five volumes of text were compiled posthumously and appeared between 1897 and 1913. These and several other significant academic advances in the study of

The site of Naga in Nubia as recorded by Richard Lepsius. Reprinted from Richard Lepsius, *Denkmäler I*, 141 (1844).

Nubia were short-lived, however, because the Mahadist Revolution (1881–1898) virtually closed the area to outside travelers and scholars.

Renewed academic interest in Nubia began almost immediately after the quelling of the Mahadist Revolution, but that interest was driven by a need to balance modern technological innovations with the imperatives of archaeology. A pattern was about to be established that was to characterize the twentieth century's approach to Nubian archaeology and would culminate in the international effort to save the Nubian temples. This pattern was inaugurated between 1898 and 1902, when the first of the Aswan dams was erected to create a reservoir ensuring a supply of water and to generate hydroelectric power. This "cork in a bottle's neck" was 30.5 meters in height and 27 meters wide at its base. Many sites in Lower Nubia were in danger of being flooded as a result of the reservoir created, and several would be forever lost.

In 1907, the Egyptian government decided to increase the size of this dam by adding another 5 meters to its height. That decision prompted the first (1907–1911) of several archaeological campaigns to rescue the region's antiquities. More than 40 Nubian cemeteries were excavated as a result, and the artifacts found therein were the basis for establishing a relative chronology for many Nubian cultural horizons. That chronology is still, with slight modifications, accepted and universally employed in Nubian studies.

Further work was carried out on this Aswan dam between 1929 and 1932, which now reached a height of 42 meters and a length of 2441 meters. The capacity of the reservoir was so great that sites between the Wadi es-Sebua and Adindan were in danger of being flooded and lost. As a result, a second archaeological campaign (1929–1934), spearheaded by British archaeologists, was launched. Among the significant and lasting results of this effort was the recovery of important objects and data from excavations at Qustul and Ballana.

AL-SADDAL-ALI (THE ASWAN HIGH DAM) AND THE UNITED NATIONS EDUCATIONAL AND SCIENTIFIC ORGANIZATION (UNESCO) PROJECT TO SAVE THE NUBIAN MONUMENTS

As if history were about to repeat herself, the Egyptian government in 1959 decided to erect the al-Saddal-Ali, the present Aswan High Dam, which became operational on January 15, 1971. The resulting reservoir, Lake Nasser, is one of the world's largest artificial lakes, measuring some 500 kilometers in length with an average width of 10 kilometers. Its waters overflowed the Nile's original banks between Aswan in the south and Dal, just north of the second cataract. UNESCO launched an international appeal to save the Nubian monuments, based on the two previous efforts, which likewise mobilized the archaeological community, but this time the campaign was enormous in scope and financially expensive. The rock cut temples of Rameses II at Abu Simbel became the poster-child for the campaign. It has often been remarked that no comparable area of the world has received such intense archaeological attention over such a period of time, as that part of Nubia explored under the auspices of UNESCO during this campaign. And although much of Lower Nubia was surveyed and excavated, and several of its more imposing monuments were dismantled and either moved to higher ground or given as gifts of gratitude by the Egyptian government to nation-states contributing to the salvage effort, much of Lower Nubia today still remains under the waters of Lake Nasser, drowned forever, and beyond the reach of archaeologists.

The UNESCO campaign to save the Nubian monuments was also characterized by a downside because very little was done to assist the Nubians, whose ancestral homelands were also being inundated by the ever-rising waters of Lake Nasser. Resettlement villages were erected far from the banks of the Nile River, and the rhythm of life enjoyed by the Nubians was fatally interrupted. Millennia-old traditions were being lost, the ancestral language was being forgotten, and the quality of life was beginning to deteriorate. The plight of the modern Nubian peoples recounted by archaeologists and reiterated in personal conversations is a condemnation of UNESCO policies, which placed the safety of monuments above the well-being of human beings.

THE NATIONAL CORPORATION FOR ANTIQUITIES AND MUSEUMS (NCAM)

Today, archaeological activity in The Sudan with a view toward furthering our knowledge of ancient Nubia continues apace. The National Corporation for Antiquities and Museums (NCAM) is the Sudanese department currently cooperating with more than 20 foreign missions whose members are conducting fieldwork in various parts of The Sudan. New areas of the country, particularly in the south and the west, are being examined for the first time. The climate for international collaborative efforts of this sort has never been more cordial.

THE HISTORIOGRAPHY OF NUBIA

It was commonplace to employ the cultural achievements of one's own civilization as a yardstick against which the achievements of another could be measured and evaluated. For the ancient Greeks, the Nubians were regarded as the most righteous of individuals, living in a simpler, nobler world than the one in which they found themselves. To the Greeks, the Nubians epitomized the concept of "the noble savage." The Nubians also acquired a reputation for being the world's most accomplished magicians, although in at least one ancient Egyptian tale, *The Romance of Setne*

Khamwas and Si-osire, recently dated to Dynasty XXV, when the Nubians ruled as pharaohs in their own right, a master Nubian magician is trumped by a native Egyptian.

But, just as in some quarters aspects of ancient Egyptian civilization were judged inferior to aspects of the culture of Greece of the fifth century B.C.E., so, too, aspects of Nubian culture were considered inferior when yardsticks of ancient Egyptian art were applied to them. The banal Egyptian phrase, "vile/wretched Kush," the stereotypical representations of Nubians among the Nine Bows in ancient Egyptian art, the absence of a Nubian language until relatively late in their own cultural history, and their seemingly complete assimilation into Egyptian culture in certain earlier periods contribute to a prevailing negative assessment of Nubian culture.

NUBIAN STUDIES IN A NONPOLEMICAL CONTEXT

In some quarters, this apparent denigration of Nubian culture was regarded as a form of white racism. In order to present an alternative view of Nubian culture, a form of what some scholars have termed "black racism" evolved whereby certain Africanists claimed Nubia as the metaphorical egg from which all subsequent Western European arts, sciences, and philosophies hatched.

In a postmodernist academic environment, some would argue that all versions of history are equally true and equally defensible, although such a position encourages polemic rather than resolution. It seems preferable, therefore, not to compare and contrast civilizations with a simplistic objective of determining which is inferior and which superior. The more valuable social exercise is to allow the cultural records of each specific group to speak for themselves by allowing the data to be examined without recourse to another culture's filtering lens. One needs to see the Nubians for themselves, without the drive to apologize for certain social customs, for example, the practice of massive human sacrifice during the Kerma Period, and without recourse to excuses for putative shortcomings in, for instance, the stylized character of the art of the Napatan Period. With the recent change of the millennium, scholars must recognize that civilizations have to be understood on their own terms so that notions of cultural superiority and inferiority are made to yield to an appreciation of significant articulated differences. Thus we may gain an enhanced understanding of a multicultural worldview.

2

The Earliest Nubians

Attempts at reconstructing the remote periods of Nubia's history are thwarted by the spotty archaeological record. Many regions are still virtually unexplored, and some are now known to lie outside the areas intensively explored by the UNESCO-sponsored campaign to save the Nubian monuments. Continued archaeological investigation over time will doubtless change the picture painted below, but our immediate task is to draw a sketch of the early history of Nubia as it is now generally accepted. It must be remembered that archaeologists are faced with a daunting task in developing this sketch. The following remarks are to be understood within the context of this developing sketch and concern themselves with the Paleolithic, or Old and Stone Age, up to the time of the Neolithic Revolution.

THE ROLE OF THE ARCHAEOLOGIST

These modern archaeologists are not horseback riding, bullwhip snapping heroes engaged in knock-'em-out battles with evil adversaries as cinema and television have portrayed them. Quite the contrary, they are highly trained women and men who spend untold hours laboring under the hot sun in meticulously surveyed trenches using mason's trowels and small brushes to uncover the material remains of the past.

Archaeological excavations in Nubia are generally concerned with (a) settlements, defined as permanent locations within which a population lived, (b) their religious centers, generally confined to a temple or complex of sacred structures, and (c) the cemeteries in which the Nubians were buried.

NUBIA BEFORE 40,000 B.P.

One can begin this survey of early Nubian cultures by remarking that the homelands of the Nubians are located in West Africa, to the west of the Rift Valley, which many anthropologists claim is the birthplace of hominoids. That there should be no apparent connection between the fossil remains of these ancestors and the subsequent emergence of the earliest Nubian cultures should come as no surprise. In fact, the earliest artifacts of any cultural horizon associated with the ancient Nubians are the hand axes of the Paleolithic Period, or Old Stone Age, which are suggested to date to the period of about 300,000 B.P.. These hand axes are only slightly different from other bifacial hand axes of the Acheulean Era (1,500,000–100,000 B.P.) found at other Paleolithic sites. As the Paleolithic Period came to a close about 40,000 B.C.E., the Nubians had developed the technology to produce stone blades and microliths, or small flint instruments. As these lithics, or stone tools and implements, demonstrate, the Nubians were proficient hunters, who were particularly fond of the auroch or wild bison; they were also accomplished fishermen, given their proximity to rivers.

NUBIA IN THE PERIOD FROM 40,000 TO 10,000 B.P.

It has often been remarked that civilizations in the ancient world developed along river valleys—the Egyptian on the Nile, the Mesopotamian between the Tigris and Euphrates Rivers, and the Indian Mohenjo-Daro on the Indus River. One should be reminded that the same pattern emerges for the Nubians, whose earliest settlements were focused in the valleys of the Atbara and Blue Nile Rivers. The lithic remains, defined as implements generally crafted from flint such as points for spears, attest to the importance of these rivers for Nubian life because they provide evidence for a well-developed fishing industry. One should not, however, suggest widespread cultural diffusion on the basis of the similarities these lithics share with others associated with the Maghreb (an Arabic term for the three nation-states of northwestern Africa, Morocco, Algeria, and Tunisia), the Levant (the Syria–Palestine region), or Central Africa.

By the eighth millennium B.P., the climate of the northeast quadrant of the African continent was beginning to change as the Nile River valley was gradually transformed into a steppe landscape extending some 500 miles farther to the north than the desert landscape one now associates with the region. Here, archaeologists have identified both stable settlements and seasonal camps, not only in Khartoum at the site of the Khartoum hospital, but also at Saqqai, near the sixth cataract.

In order to explain the development of Nubian society during this period, scholars have relied on drawing cultural analogies with the perceived development of contemporary emerging Egypt, farther to the north. In both regions, hunting and fishing were accompanied by the gathering of fruits and plants. Society was also being stratified, as individuals began to specialize in particular tasks.

SETTLEMENTS

Settlement archaeology, although desirable, is almost nonexistent because the settlements themselves have not been preserved. The earliest of these Nubian settlement sites have all but disappeared because of human intervention in the form of building over earlier remains and quarrying ancient sites to obtain soil rich in phosphates used to fertilize modern agricultural endeavors. Wind and water erosion have compounded the problem. These factors have destroyed whatever architectural features may have been associated with these early sites. To date, virtually no workshops, trash heaps, or shelters of any kind have been identified that can be associated with these early cultural horizons. As a result, scholars can only guess about the appearance of Nubian architecture during these early periods. Because the structures of this period were erected before the widespread use of stone, Nubian architecture of this early period probably utilized more perishable materials such as wattle-and-daub, mud brick, reeds, animal hides, and other perishable materials, but the most common type of dwelling was most probably constructed of the hides of hunted animals or gathered reeds and/or grasses.

In attempting to identify these early settlements, archaeological surveys are often conducted. These surveys entail the arduous task of actually walking over the terrain. In so doing careful examination of surface finds such as broken pieces of pottery and the like may yield promising results. In Nubia, very early settlements have been identified in just such a manner. The painstaking work is labor intensive and costly but may occasionally reveal the remains of a hearth, containing a wealth of floral and faunal data that, when properly analyzed, provide information about climate and diet.

CEMETERIES

Most of our information about the lives of these most ancient Nubians, therefore, derives from their cemeteries. In excavating these cemeteries, the archaeologist's mandate is not necessarily to find artifacts, but rather to measure, record, photograph, and assess the disparate data that an excavation reveals. The processes involved are complex. The archaeologists map out three-meter squares (the metric system is preferred to that of feet and inches for such scientific work) and meticulously excavate, often digging no more than a few inches below the surface, in order to recover artifacts, the positions of which are rigorously recorded and plotted. Soil removed from the archaeological trenches is thoroughly studied by means of a series of scientific processes. The intention is not only to recover fragmentary artifacts, which might have initially escaped the eye of the excavator, but also to isolate floral and faunal remains, which are often too small to be seen by the naked eye. The dimensions of tombs and their locations relative to one another in any given cemetery often reveal societal stratification. The grave goods found within them suggest indications of status among the population whose skeletons are also subjected to forensic examination.

Archaeologists have, therefore, been more successful in locating cemeteries, some of which were anciently in close proximity to now-vanished settlements. The graves and their contents are relatively better preserved than the objects associated with settlements. Careful assessment of the size and location of these graves and of their contexts enables scholars to suggest ways in which Nubian society developed in these remote times. A great deal of care must, however, be exercised in the interpretation of these data, because similarities between certain objects recovered from the early Nubian sites with like objects found elsewhere in Africa are insufficient reasons for positing widespread cultural interconnections.

Having understood some of the archaeological processes by which data is amassed for analyses, we can now turn our attention to how that data may be understood.

THE EMERGENCE OF A NUBIAN ELITE

Nubian society became more and more stratified during this period, with an advantaged elite comprising a relatively small percentage of the population, enjoying social, economic, and political privileges. The emergence of the Nubian elite can be suggested to have occurred in the following manner. As society became more complex, individuals were obliged to devote their time and energy to specific tasks. The development of agriculture required settlements, and these demanded materials from which the structures, however ill defined they may be for an archaeologist, were to be erected. The materials necessary for making the implements used by farmers in the performance of their tasks had to be obtained and crafted into the desired tools. The crops had to be planted, harvested, processed, and stored. If one now simply adds to this equation the observation that the crops, once harvested, had to be transported in order to be exchanged, one can readily gain an appreciation of the levels of organization necessary to keep such a society on track. The same observations hold true for the domestication of animals and the associated need for animal husbandry. It is within this context that the Nubian elite emerged.

The presence of this elite can be detected in the archaeological record, particularly in cemeteries. Here, elite graves are generally larger in size and more abundantly appointed with grave goods. These grave goods often contain power-facts, artifacts associated with status such as mace heads, which served as symbols of authority.

ANIMAL HUSBANDRY AND AGRICULTURE

The foregoing generalizations are based on data obtained from just two Nubian regions, one area located in the central Sudan, extending from the Atbara River to a distance of about 100 kilometers south of Khartoum, and the second from Wadi Halfa at the modern border between Egypt and The Sudan southward to the area between the third and fourth cataracts. The climatic changes, discussed earlier, continued to occur so that by the second half of the sixth millennium B.C.E., Nubia was becoming increasingly desiccated, or desert-like. In addition, cultural distinctions are observable between Lower Nubia and the central Sudan during this period. Whereas the Lower Nubians remained for the most part hunters and gatherers, the Nubians in the central Sudan began to domesticate animals such as oxen, goats, sheep, and even dogs. Zoologists contend that these animals are not indigenous to the Nile Valley and must have been introduced into Nubia either by the arrival of populations from the Sahara or via contact with those peoples. It is impossible to gauge, given the limited state of our knowledge, whether these contacts resulted in other transformations of Nubian society. The transition to animal husbandry appears to have been gradual. At Kadero, some 20 kilometers north of Khartoum, a rarely encountered rubbish heap at the edge of the settlement yielded the intermingled bones of both wild and domesticated animals.

The domestication of these animals seems to precede by almost a millennium the introduction of agriculture, although the approximate date of its inauguration in Nubia is difficult to determine for the following reason. Excavations of sites have yielded ceramic vessels associated with millet, but the millet recovered is not of a form botanically distinguishable from wild millet. The indistinguishable character of these grains leaves the question about whether the millet was harvested from planted fields or gathered in the wild. One is on somewhat firmer ground with respect to barley, which is suggested to have been grown in Nubia by the mid-fifth millennium B.C.E. Its cultivation is based on indirect evidence, namely in the form of grinding stones discovered in several Nubian sites of the period, such as at Kadero. Here the evidence also suggests the emergence of an early African pastoral society in which the raising of livestock was supplemented by hunting and fishing.

DIET

Discussions of the cuisine and diet of the ancient Nubians are hampered by the almost complete absence of contemporary texts on these subjects, but the increasing analyses of previously ignored floral and faunal remains unearthed during archaeological excavations have contributed to our better understanding of the Nubian diet during this early period.

Before about 10,000 B.C.E., the Nubians relied on the Nile River as a source of life. On the basis of the presence of hand axes, one can suggest that they hunted animals, which came there for water. These included the giraffe, wild ass, and zebra, which were doubtless hunted for their hides, as well as the large wild ox, together with the horned antelope, gazelle, and ibex. On the basis of scenes on Egyptian tombs of Old Kingdom, attempts were made, though ultimately unsuccessful, to domesticate antelope, gazelle, and ibex. These wild animals are also depicted as alternative food sources, allowing one to suggest that the Nubians, too, consumed them.

The presence of excavated fish bones suggests that the Nubians also fished and fowled the water birds in the river's marshes. They lived in temporary shelters of perishable materials. As hunter-gatherers, the early Nubians doubtless foraged for edible plants. It has been suggested that these included melons, the fruity meat of which was prepared as a kind of soup and served within the rind itself. It is suggested that some of these fruity soups served as pharmaceuticals as well.

Excavated, brown-colored vessels, which served as cooking pots, suggest the development of a cuisine, perhaps with specific recipes. The use of the shells of mussels for the incising of designs on other types of pottery from the period suggests that the Nubians had contact, either directly or via intermediaries, with the Red Sea. One may, therefore, suggest that seafood was perhaps part of their diet as well.

TOOLS AND WEAPONS

Hand in hand with the development of agriculture and animal husbandry are technological advances achieved in lithics as more types of stone tools and implements were added to the repertoire. Simple tools and weapons continued to be produced from quartz pebbles found lying on the terraces of the rivers. When struck, the splintered flakes produced surfaces suitable for cutting and scraping. Remarkably, the quartz pebbles were so abundant and the labor necessary for crafting these tools so nonintensive, that archaeologists suggest they were discarded after being used only one time. Technological advances enabled the Nubians to work other types of materials such as obsidian, or volcanic stone, and sandstone, which appears to have been the medium reserved for grinding stones, cosmetic pallets, and millstones.

Small arrowheads and blades fitted to wooden handles for use as either sickles or ax heads were more carefully crafted and are characterized by worked edges. Furthermore, higher quality polished tools for axes, various blades, as well as cosmetic palettes with grinding stones now become more common. The limited appearance of mace heads used as weapons and symbols of power and authority indicate the presence of an elite whose numbers were represented by a statistically small percentage of the population.

These early Nubian craftsmen also used other materials for the creation of artifacts. Bone and ivory were crafted into spears and harpoons, fish-hooks and needles, knives and axes, and even finely decorated handles.

POTTERY

In Nubia, one encounters the earliest known examples of pottery. Hand made and thin walled, these large format vessels were initially decorated with wavy lines, the later examples relying on patterns of dots. Similarly crafted and decorated ceramics are encountered throughout the southern Sahara from Morocco to the lakes of East Africa, but these correspondences, as we have repeatedly stated, cannot confirm that all of these pottery-making societies are members of one and the same homogeneous culture.

The Nubians crafted some of the oldest pottery vessels known on the African continent. In fact, scholars suggest that Nubians were creating pottery as early as perhaps the fifth millennium B.C.E., well before the period in which they developed agriculture. From these beginnings, the Nubians went on to distinguish themselves as potters, creating in the process some of the African continent's most technically and aesthetically accomplished ceramics.

The ubiquity of the potsherds, the broken fragments of clay, or pottery, vessels recovered, and their sheer cumulative weight, measured in tons rather than pounds, attests to an active production during this period. Some of these shards have been recovered in debris associated with Nubian settlements of the period. Despite their quantity, when studied these shards indicate that the repertoire of forms in which the Nubian potters excelled was rather limited, but did include flasks and flat dishes.

DRESS AND ACCESSORIES

On rare occasions, the teeth of hippopotami were used for the creation of cosmetic boxes, and these are contemporary with very early forms of Nubian jewelry crafted of stone, ivory, bone, and shell. These forms include armlets, bead necklaces, pendants, and even earrings. Due to the scant nature of the archaeological evidence, one is imperfectly informed about the clothing of the Nubians of the Paleolithic Period.

TERRA-COTTA, OR BAKED CLAY, FIGURINES

Some of the figurines in baked clay from these early periods exhibit a network of incised lines. These lines have been interpreted as indications of clothing, body art, or tattoo. Because of the absence of both human remains and corroborating evidence from other sources, the interpretation of these incised lines on these figures is moot. They may well represent clothing, as well as tattoo, attested first in Nubian contexts, or even body painting, which the Nubians of this period are said to have practiced. Body painting and the use of either malachite or galena for the painting of one's eyes in this period was imbued with symbolic value and did not merely serve, as in contemporary society, as cosmetic enhancements of one's appearance. If one can apply a cultural analogy from ancient Egypt, eye painting created a symbolic barrier across which potentially malevolent forces could not travel. The ancients believed that these forces could enter the body via the orifices of the head, and of those, the eyes provided the easiest entrance. On the basis of cultural analogies with African societies today, one can impute to the Nubian practice of body painting religious and symbolic meanings. Cosmetic palettes, therefore, serve as one of the indices of decorum by which elite members of the Nubian community may be distinguished from others.

The appearance of snakelike forms on a terra-cotta figurine in Brooklyn has been interpreted as evidence of tattoo. Whereas this might well be the case, the incised lines may also represent details of a costume or body painting. One cannot, therefore, be dogmatic in the interpretation of such motifs.

On the other hand, these same figurines are crafted with telling attention to detail. One such figurine has her hair bound in a pigtail. This style and its longevity would become identifiable as a typically Nubian coiffure during the course of the New Kingdom, when Egyptian texts would describe the Nubians as "the pig-tail wearers." The appearance of this hairstyle presumes the attendant accessories such as combs and perhaps hair clips, but none of these implements is so far attested in the archaeological record.

3

The Neolithic
Revolution

As so often happens in archaeology, scholars have no way of predicting the eventual chronological sequence of areas being excavated. It is for this reason that the area designated as Cemetery A at el-Kadada is actually more recent in date than Cemetery C. Of the 100 of these burials investigated, scholars can detect evidence for the so-called Neolithic Revolution during which time a sedentary lifestyle with agriculture, animal husbandry, and craft specialization became a fixed feature of Nubian life. One recognizes an unusually large number of graves loosely packed together over a short period of time. This overlapping appears to be intentional because any single burial might be surrounded by as many as a dozen additional burials, each one cut into and partially destroying the original single burial. Scholars suggest that such agglomerations may be an early form of a family mausoleum. Remarkably, there are no skeletal remains of children associated with this cemetery. On the contrary, one finds child burials on the top of the settlement mound where the bodies were placed in large, partially destroyed ceramic vessels just below the surface. The average age at death for these interments appears to be six years or less. One suggested reason for the localization of these child interments within the settlement mound is that the youths may not have been considered full-fledged members of the community as a whole and may not yet have performed specific rites of passage.

NUBIAN SOCIETY AS REFLECTED BY THE DATA
RECOVERED FROM CEMETERIES

**The Two
Cemeteries at
Kadero**

We now turn our attention to specific cemeteries because the graves and their contents provide valuable information about the nature of Nubian society during the Neolithic Period.

The cemetery of Kadero is instructive in this regard, because the 160 graves excavated to date, although only representing a small percentage of the total number of interments, reveal both the growth of the settlement's population and its stratification. Ten percent of the excavated graves belong to the elite members of the population, and that number includes not only men but also women and children. One can suggest that these elite graves belong to members of the same ruling family whose authority was passed down from one generation to the next.

These graves are designed as simple pits, excavated relatively deeply into the earth in relation to the nonelite graves. The grave goods found therein include ivory jewelry, shells from the Red Sea, malachite, stone tools, thin-walled pottery vessels, and weapons such as mace heads. The clay vessels with red polish or incised patterns of Kadero represent Nubia's first technological advance in pottery and command a place of honor among African ceramics in general because of their high degree of artistic achievement. The presence of Red Sea shells and malachite suggests a developing trading network, the mechanics of which are still imperfectly understood, but the presence of mace heads suggest that the male members of the ruling family were emerging as rulers over the group and were instrumental in maintaining these mercantile contacts.

**The Cemeteries
of El-Kadada**

A slightly different situation obtains for the late Neolithic site of el-Kadada in the region of Shendi, about 180 kilometers south of Khartoum. Although the settlement mound of el-Kadada, dated to the second half of the fourth millennium B.C.E., occupies an area of several hectares (a metric unit used in scientific notation instead of acres, each hectare measuring 10,000 square meters) and contains layers of strata indicating different periods of occupation that are over a meter deep in some sectors, all building foundations and virtually all of the associated artifacts have been destroyed by subsequent activity on the site.

The site's two cemeteries, one on the northern slope and the second at the southern foot of the settlement mound, and their respective contents are indicators of changes in Nubian social structure effected by economic factors brought about by the gradual drying of the climate. These changes occurred over two successive and identifiable cultural phases, which exhibit no perceptible disjunctions, indicating that the Nubians of el-Kadada during this period developed their own internal responses to their changing ecological circumstances.

Archaeological surveys suggest that the area designated as Cemetery C contains approximately 3,000 burials of which only about 200 have been presently investigated. Routinely, each grave was a simple pit, round or oval in outline, measuring between 0.8 and 2 meters in diameter. The earth removed during its excavation was then returned to the pit to cover the interment. These pit-graves do not appear to have had any architectural adjuncts, although the possibility does exist that they may have possessed a superstructure built of perishable materials. The corpse was laid on a mat, but apparently without preference for either a right- or a left-handed side and with a similar disregard for its orientation within the pit. Likewise, the elite graves were not confined to specific locations within the cemetery but appear to have been randomly placed among nonelite graves.

Because of the physical condition of the skeletons, determining gender proved to be impossible so that one could not ascertain whether certain

A Nubian chieftain's tomb. Courtesy of Jacques Reinold, French Sector of the Antiquities Organization of the Sudan, Khartoum.

grave goods were gender specific. The finds within specific graves did, however, suggest the presence of an elite. Their grave goods included artifacts of stone and bone found in the vicinity of the hands and ox horns occasionally found beneath the head. All other grave goods in these elite burials were arranged around the body.

Some of the tombs of the elite contained two or even three burials, one on top of the other, but great care was taken in these interments so that the upper burials neither disturbed nor destroyed the burial immediately beneath it. These multiple interments have been interpreted as evidence of human sacrifice, a custom that will characterize the funerary rites of the later Nubian epochs, particularly during the Kerma culture. As such, they proclaim a very pronounced hierarchical division of Nubian society.

THE EMERGENCE OF CHIEFTAINS

Excavations above the third cataract in an area of about 50 kilometers in the Wadi el-Khowi in the Kadruka district, which commenced less than two decades ago, present a somewhat different picture of Nubia in the Neolithic Period, but the evidence for settlements is extremely difficult to assemble because they had anciently developed along old beds of the Nile River. Over time, these had been seriously eroded by the wind and are now being destroyed by modern agricultural projects, which irrigate with motorized pumps.

On the other hand, the cemeteries have been spared, in part because they lie on mounds, and the relative depths of their burial shafts have contributed to their preservation. Thirty cemeteries have been identified, and these range in time from the sixth to the fourth millennium b.c.e. Although the average number of graves in any one cemetery is about 150 burials, each of a handful of cemeteries contains well over 1,000 interments. It is important to realize that the individuals interred in these graves, which are relatively homogeneous and in use for a relatively short span of time, belonged to a tightly knit population group, whose number was not very large.

The graves found on the highest point of any mound are of particular interest, and Tomb 131 of Kadruka Cemetery 1 provides the key for our understanding of the social hierarchy of Lower Nubia. The tomb itself is situated on the highest point of the mound and possesses a particularly deep shaft. It contained the mortal remains of an adult male, estimated to have been about 40 years old at the time of death. Other graves were laid out concentrically around his grave, which served as the center. All of the graves were provided with what one might term "deluxe" artifacts associated with the Nubian elite. The slopes of this mound were designed to accommodate graves containing a large proportion of female burials.

It is clear that the male in Tomb 131 of Kadruka Cemetery 1 stood at the head of his tribal community of Nubians, for whom he doubtless served as chieftain. Society was stratified with the chieftain and a relatively small, elite class at the top, whose members enjoyed social, political, and economic advantages. Evidence from the cemeteries would suggest that membership into this elite class of Nubians was hereditary, and that they enjoyed specific funerary rites denied to other members of society. Craft specialization developed along with animal husbandry and agriculture, and an intricate network of trade, the mechanics of which are difficult to define, evolved, judging from the varied materials associated with the grave goods of Neolithic Nubian cemeteries. One may, therefore, well imagine that as the Neolithic Period drew to a close, several powerful chieftains established their authority over relatively small domains and attempted to extend their power over their neighbors. This inter-Nubian competition was, however, to fade in the face of the advancing military might of Egypt.

THE DIET OF THE NUBIANS DURING THE NEOLITHIC PERIOD

The Neolithic Period (after 10,000 B.C.E.) witnessed the transition of Nubian society from one of hunter-gatherers to that of settlements occasioned by the domestication of animals and plants. The development of Nubian agriculture may be regarded as part of the Neolithic Revolution in general. Around 5500 B.C.E. sheep and goats appear to be among the earliest beasts domesticated by the Nubians, together with the dog, developed to herd these flocks. Because these animals do not appear to be indigenous to the homelands of the Nubians, scholars suggest that there may have been social intercourse with individuals from the Sahara to the north, which may have resulted in their introduction. Be that as it may, Nubians in the vicinity of Khartoum appear to have pioneered the animal husbandry of cattle, whose importance as both an index of wealth and social status was to dominate all subsequent Nubian cultural horizons. The presence of these animals, therefore, suggests that the meat and milk of these animals became staples of the Nubian diet.

Evidence for the development of agriculture is more difficult to interpret. It is clear that during the sixth millennium B.C.E. the climate of the northeastern quadrant of Africa grew progressively drier, but whether this was a catalyst for the subsequent development of agriculture is moot. The presence of millet in Nubian cultural horizons of this period indicates that this cereal played a role in their diet as well, but scholars are presently unable to determine whether that millet was wild or domesticated, the two strands appearing morphologically so close as to preclude classification. In time the Nubians cultivated both barley and wheat as well as peas and lentils.

The data recovered from the trash heaps of the site of Kadero, about 20 kilometers north of Khartoum, portray the gradual agricultural transformation of Nubia during this period. If certain petroglyphs can be securely dated to this period, one can suggest that these Nubians also hunted the rhinoceros and elephant, which figure as prominent motifs in their rock art. Although there is evidence for the Nubian use of the hides, ivory, and bones of these mammals, it is, perhaps, possible that these animals were also sources of food.

Bones of both wild and domesticated animals, particularly sheep and goats, suggest that hunting and animal husbandry coexisted together with fishing. Fragments suggested to be millstones argue for the presence of edible plants, but whether these included domesticated millet is moot. It is, nevertheless, clear that the Nubians were cultivating barley by the middle of the fifth millennium B.C.E. Archaeological excavations have revealed countless grinding stones at many Nubian sites, which suggest an ever-expanding agricultural basis. With the passage of time, the number of stone blades for insertion into wooden handles for use as sickles for the harvest of domesticated grains also increased.

Nevertheless, one must stress that the farming techniques pioneered by these early Nubians are fundamentally African and may have had their impact on the emerging agricultural practices of their contemporary Egyptians. In Egypt as in other African river basin cultures, seed is sewn in October after the floodwaters of the rivers, including the Nile, have subsided. This differs from the agricultural practices of other contemporary cultures of the Ancient Near East, where seed is planted in the fall before the arrival of the winter rains. One must also stress that the types of crops planted by the Nubians, particularly indigenous African cereals such as sorghum, were initially not suitable for cultivation in Egypt proper because of their differing ecological requirements.

The number of apparent special-purpose vessels excavated at such sites as Kadruka and now in Khartoum indicates an expanding Nubian cuisine. These include bowls with a single spout and others with two spouts, one at each end, a hemispherical bowl that served as a sieve because it is perforated with a network of holes, and a number of plates. These vessels suggest that soupy gruels and more solid foods were part of the diet. These vessels include flasks in which liquids were stored, suggesting that the Nubians had developed one or more beverages, the ingredients for which are not presently known.

POTTERY VESSELS OF THE NEOLITHIC PERIOD

The earliest Nubian ceramics of the Neolithic Period are hand made, with rather coarse, unpolished surfaces. Their decoration displays a degree of creativity in the choice and application of their designs. Some are characterized as wavy-lined ware in which a rippling network of wavy, parallel lines was incised into the vessel by pressing and dragging a tool, suggested to have been the spine of a fish, across its surface. The repertoire of decorative motifs increased with time. Combinations of wavy and parallel incisions in association with dots and dashes, suggested to have been made by a pointed stick or bone, were introduced and replaced thereafter with more geometric designs impressed into the wet clay using shells, fingernails, and the like. The latest of these exhibit smooth surfaces, suggestive of a degree of polish. The blackened surfaces of several indicate their use as cooking vessels. One suggests that this pottery was multifunctional, serving both the quotidian and ritual, primarily funereal needs, of Nubian society.

At some point in time during the Neolithic Period, the Nubians appear to have assigned particular types of vessels to specific functions. Utilitarian vessels were restricted to a limited number of types such as plates, bowls, and flasks, ostensibly for foodstuffs and liquids. The design of the bowls, hemispherical in profile, was to be a long-lived one in Nubian ceramics with variations appearing in every major cultural epoch through the end of the Kingdom of Meroe. So-called bell-shaped vessels, with flaring lips tapering into tear-shaped bottoms, designed, it would appear, to be held in the hand and without any means by which they could stand erect on their own, were reserved exclusively for funerary use.

Vessels of both types are hand made of fired clay, brick red in color. Their smooth surfaces, some the result of polishing, are decorated with thin, delicate networks of incised lines, suggested to have been made by impressing and dragging a comblike implement with very thin teeth over the surfaces. Occasionally one finds scratched and dotted patterns as well as triangles and meander patterns. During the course of the Late Neolithic Period, the Nubians also created a bichrome ware, on which the white, linear decorative patterns stand out from the black fabric of the walls of the vessel itself. The shapes include plates, bowls, and ladle-like vessels, the walls extending into a large, protruding and tapering appendage, which served as a handle.

More significant is the observation that statistically rare bell-shaped vessels, characterized as nonfunctioning because of their impractical shape, appear to be associated exclusively with cemeteries rather than settlements. These particular vessels appear to have been associated with mortuary rites, perhaps offering ceremonies. Their rarity strongly suggests that they were used exclusively for selected members of the elite population, who may have enjoyed rituals not shared with others. These bell-shaped vessels consistently exhibit either smooth or polished surfaces, onto which either scratched or dotted patterns in meandering or triangular motifs may be added. Some of these examples appear to anticipate the so-called Ripple Ware associated with the later Nubian A-Group. One encounters examples of painted pottery as well as vessels carved from stone.

TERRA-COTTA, OR BAKED CLAY, FIGURINES

The most interesting of the artifacts recovered from these Nubian sites of the Neolithic Period are undoubtedly the female figurines, usually made of fired clay and more rarely of sandstone. Commonly, but perhaps incorrectly, termed fecundity idols, these statuettes are designed as extremely formal abstractions, which barely reveal their gender. These statuettes will now be discussed in terms of the broader category of "fertility figurines."

The profusion of female figures in most cultures of the ancient Near East during the Neolithic Period is not necessarily indicative of the existence of putative matriarchies, as has been often suggested in the past. One now comes to realize that with the transformation of society from that of hunter-gatherers to a more sedentary way of life, male members of the elite became the principal leaders of society. The skeletal remains of graves of this period confirm this. The largest and most lavishly appointed of these elite burials are habitually associated with a male skeleton.

Specialists may also call the predominantly female characteristics of these early images into question on analogy with reinterpretations of European Prehistoric idols. In their view, the manipulation of several of these so-called European Stone Age idols provides the individual manipulating them with different views, some of which are evocative of male genitalia. Indeed, one cannot dismiss out of hand the androgynous character of almost all of these idols. Two baked clay effigies, now in the National Museum in Khartoum, were excavated at the Nubian site of el-Kadada and are datable to the Neolithic Period. Both are clearly female depictions designed as a head, neck, and torso. The pubic mound and

A terra-cotta figurine in the National Museum, Khartoum.

pelvis have been designed as an abstract, rounded form that was intentionally finished and deliberately excluded the depiction of the legs and feet. If rotated ninety degrees, the abstract forms superficially resemble equally abstracted and stylized male genitalia, suggesting that these figures may have each been designed as androgynous.

A sandstone effigy, now in the National Museum of Khartoum, was excavated at Nubian Kadruka and is datable to the Neolithic Period as well. There is no reason a priori to describe this figure as female inasmuch as all anatomical detail save for the head have been avoided. The only details are in fact incised lines, which are gender unspecific. These include several horizontal lines at different levels where one wishes to see eyes and another at the very top, interpreted as a hairline. There are also a series of more faintly incised vertical lines. Taken together, this incised linear network is genderless. One is more compelled to identify this idol as male owing to the absolute suppression of female breasts and pubic mound-pelvic region. Indeed, its overall columnar shape is phallic, a formal observation that reinforces its identification as a depiction of a male figure.

There are, of course, distinctly designed female effigies of the period, such as the unmistakable idol, again of baked clay in the Khartoum collections, that was likewise excavated within a cemetery at el-Kadada. Her head appears to have been broken off at the level of the neck, but the treatment of the breasts, pubic region, and thighs are such that some have interpreted the figure as being pregnant. Her arms are purposefully truncated.

All of these figures, aside from the sandstone idol from the Neolithic Period, wear elaborate coiffures and the so-called pregnant idol has the remains of a pigtail between her shoulders. They are additionally decorated with a series of incised lines arranged into patterns or impressed into the clay before firing. The significance of these lines is disputed; some scholars suggest that clothing is thereby indicated, whereas other scholars maintain the designs are tattoos (see following). Received wisdom interprets these effigies as fecundity figurines suggestive of a matriarchy, but the androgynous nature of many of these idols and the known hierarchy of Neolithic Nubian society with male members assuming primacy precludes its acceptance.

Two avenues of investigation remain. On the one hand, these figurines may have been placed into the tomb to accompany the deceased in the Hereafter on analogy with the sacrificed victims so prevalent in elite tombs of the Kerma culture. Such an interpretation is in keeping with later Nubian practice, adapted from the Egyptians, whereby figurines interred with the deceased are surrogates, which can be magically animated to serve the tomb owner.

On the other hand, a religious interpretation appears to be preferable. The arguably androgynous design of the majority of these figurines suggests that they represent the male and female principles of creation united in one and the same figure. Their union, if subsequent religious beliefs can be here invoked, established the creation of the world because the male and female principles of procreation were in equilibrium. The interment of such figurines in elite graves would, therefore, suggest resurrection in the Hereafter on the basis of human procreation.

THE DRESS AND ACCESSORIES

The evidence still remains meager for the Neolithic Period, but some general observations about this epoch can be made. Excavations at sites dated to the Neolithic Period have brought to light bone and ivory needles. This suggests the existence of the craft of sewing, almost exclusively of the hides of the animals, which were hunted. These sewn hides may have sheathed wooden frameworks serving as shelters or served as clothing. This clothing, the designs of the individual garments of which are sketchy at best, were accessorized with jewelry created from stone, ivory, bone, and shell, indicating that already at this very early date the Nubians recognized the appeal of products that would later feed the appetite of the ancients for luxury products from Africa. The appearance of elements crafted of shells from mollusks native to the Red Sea also indicates the geographic distances the Nubians or their intermediaries traversed to obtain these exotic materials.

The Nubians also seem to have favored cosmetics. Palettes and grinding stones from several sites with traces of either malachite or galena suggest that the Nubians were probably lining their eyes with this material, on a model known from the later Egyptian practice depicted in vignettes on the walls of their tombs. There is additional evidence to suggest that these early Nubians also colored their teeth with malachite.

Axes and mace heads must have been displayed in life as in death as indices of decorum, particularly by the leaders of the oligarchies as symbols of their power and authority. This is suggested primarily by the morphology of the disk-shaped mace heads, which are so thin in profile as to have precluded their actual use in war. These have been found in tombs of elite individuals, who may have also carried them about in real life on ceremonial occasions.

CONTINUITY OR DISJUNCTION

We have been employing the proper noun *Nubians* throughout this volume as the generic designation for the African peoples who are the subject of this book. The evidence discussed earlier from Cemetery C at el-Kadada indicates that a local population effected the transition from one cultural phrase to the next. The same situation obtains for a local Nubian cultural horizon, termed the Abka, the material remains of which appear to span the entire millennium and eventually develop into the A-Group culture. Such patterns of cultural continuity should not obscure the simple fact that the Nubians, like other African peoples, were seldom a homogeneous group of individuals. In fact, the central pillar of African life in general is the enormous diversity of her peoples. In the early periods that here concern us, there is evidence for the existence of several different groups of individuals, all of whom are for convenience termed Nubians, but who in all probability may have possessed differing customs and who perhaps spoke dialects of the same or even different languages.

So, for example, in the middle of the fifth millennium B.C.E. in the region of the second cataract of Lower Nubia, archaeologists have identified three different groups of Nubian peoples who practiced a hunter-gatherer economy. Two of these groups appear to be indigenous in origin, but the third seems to have migrated into the area from regions much further to the south because its dotted, wavy line ceramics are similar to those identified with ceramics associated with the Early Khartoum Neolithic. As our story unfolds, other distinctive groups of Nubians will become evident as well.

4

The A-Group Nubians

Under the direction of the Frenchman Gaston Camille Charles Maspero (1846–1916) in his capacity as head of the Egyptian Antiquities Service, the American George Andrew Reisner (1867–1942), a Harvard-educated Egyptologist, led the first intensive effort to document Nubian cultural horizons in response to the danger posed to her archaeological sites as a result of the construction of the first of the dams at Aswan. Because the history of Nubia was virtually unknown at the time, Reisner devised an ingenious system whereby he assigned letters of the alphabet as labels for the various chronological sequences of Nubia's history, which his excavations revealed. These designations—A-Group and C-Group—remain valid and form the foundations for ancient Nubian studies.

Reisner's investigations were confined to Lower Nubia to the south of Aswan in the area between the first and second cataracts. Here he identified the chronologically earliest artifacts as belonging to the Nubian A-Group culture. Reisner's classification has been refined but not replaced over time, so that currently scholars recognize three chronological phases within the A-Group: the Ancient (about 3700–3250 B.C.E.), the Classic (about 3250–3150 B.C.E.), and the Final (about 3150–2800 B.C.E.). Current research also suggests that the system of elites, headed by a male chieftain, which was already a fixture of Nubian society from the middle of the fourth millennium B.C.E., continued to be the norm throughout the history of the A-Group. The evidence from the local Abka culture of the Neolithic Period would also indicate that Nubian civilization of the A-Group developed internally, at least in some regions, without response to outside stimuli.

Reisner's localization of the Nubian A-Group in Lower Egypt appears to be confirmed by more recent excavations in the area between the second and fourth cataracts. Here at the sites of Kerma and Kadruka, south of the third cataract, a Nubian culture, contemporary in part with the A-Group and sharing some of its cultural characteristics, but possessing sufficient differences to warrant its own cultural designation, developed. This recently identified condominium is provisionally labeled the "Pre-Kerma culture."

SETTLEMENTS

Several Nubian settlements dating to the time of the A-Group phase have been identified and excavated. Most of the dwellings appear to have been small huts or other flimsy shelters. At Afyeh, archaeologists unearthed a stone structure with alluvium, or the soil deposited by a flooding river, used as a type of mortar. Its interior rooms were rectangular in plan, suggesting that this particular building served as the headquarters of an elite chieftain.

At the site of Kerma, silo-pits were likewise discovered, but these were surrounded by circular huts measuring between 4.3 and 4.7 meters in diameter. Here, as at Afyeh, there was only one rectangular building discovered, deep below which was found a stratified area containing a hearth and 180 pits, three of which still had storage jars in situ. It would appear, therefore, that the elites of both the A-Group and Pre-Kerma culture shared certain cultural norms.

THE BURIAL CUSTOMS

The Nubians of the A-Group culture, in turn, continued to inter their deceased in cemeteries, the graves of which appear to develop logically from those already in vogue during the late Neolithic Period. Graves of the A-Group culture exhibit two designs, one directly related to the pit graves of the earlier period in which the deceased was interred in a pit dug into the earth, generally circular in shape, on a mat accompanied by grave goods. A nascent tumulus, a man-made hill of earth and rubble, was then raised over the pit. The second design was that of a modified pit, in which a rectangular chamber was dug into the pit's floor, deeper on one side to accommodate the body, again arranged in a contracted position and accompanied by grave goods. Often a stone slab, resting diagonally from the wall to the floor of the pit, covered the opening into the rectangular chamber. Archaeologists have debated whether the superimposed bodies found within these graves represent either human sacrifices, a ritual known to have been practiced in Neolithic Nubia, or the subsequent reuse of the tomb for another burial. Their consensus favors sacrifice.

The circular design of the graves recalls both the design of storage silos and circular huts, with diameters ranging from 4 to 5 meters, which characterize the settlements of this period. Rather than seek a thematic link in the use of such a design to suggest that the graves were "houses" for the dead, the ubiquitous use of the curvilinear is perhaps to be attributed, rather, to the limited technology of the period.

Within these graves, whether they take the form of ovals, circles, or rectangles, the corpse, again in a contracted position, is generally placed on a mat on the floors. On occasion, the deceased may be dressed in leather garments, less frequently in ones of linen. Accessories include necklaces and bracelets, rarely pottery figurines, and an array of pottery. In fact, Nubian A-Group pottery is clearly distinguishable from contemporary ancient Egyptian vessels.

Superimposed burials, that is, one above the other in the same grave as encountered earlier in some burials within Cemetery C at el-Kadada, may indicate a continuance of a specifically Nubian burial practice, but commentators question whether the appearance of such agglomerations in an A-Group context are the result of human sacrifice. Nevertheless, the graves in A-Group cemeteries reveal a quantifiable social hierarchy in terms of their shape, location within the cemetery, and grave goods found within so that one can readily identify members of the elite.

NUBIA AND PREDYNASTIC EGYPT

In order to understand the dynamics operative in Nubia in the period between about 3700–2800 B.C.E., one must take into account developments in contemporary Egypt during that civilization's Predynastic Period. The Egyptian evidence will then serve as a cultural analogy for explaining developments in Nubia.

In both Predynastic Egypt and Neolithic Nubia, cemeteries are indices of the social status of those interred within them. The larger the grave and the more opulent its offerings, the higher the social status of the individual. Because many more Predynastic cemeteries have been excavated in Egypt than in Neolithic contexts in Nubia and because these excavations have been conducted from the Delta to Upper Egypt, one can reconstruct the political history of Egypt during the Predynastic Period as follows. Local elites, headed by chieftains, gradually gained control of small areas. In time, these chieftains began to extend their authority over neighboring polities, or organized political entities. In the century around 3200 B.C.E. several chieftains in Upper Egypt had so successfully consolidated their realms and extended their authority over their neighbors for many miles that larger principalities emerged. These vied with one another for more universal rule over ever-increasingly larger and larger regions until the kinglets of the Upper Egyptian city of This managed to gain military control of Upper Egypt and extend their own authority from Aswan northward to Memphis. Their successors continued to wage a series of military campaigns against competing elites in the Delta, some of whom had likewise extended their authority over larger and larger geographic areas. Upper and Lower Egypt were finally unified around 3200 B.C.E. during an epoch designated as Dynasty 0, a conventional label indicating that the era of Egyptian prehistory had come to an end and pharaonic Egypt with its hieroglyphic system of writing was about to begin.

NUBIAN–EGYPTIAN TRADE

As the kinglets of Upper Egypt were attempting to establish their authority in Upper Egypt, they were certainly aware of the presence of their Nubian neighbors to the south. Early international mercantile relations were doubtlessly established between individual leaders of Egypt and certain chieftains of Nubia's A-Group culture. The objective of such contacts was to funnel the wealth of more southerly Africa into the hands of the Egyptian elite, who would in exchange barter characteristically Egyptian products. During the Classical and Final epochs of the A-Group's history, the Nubians south of Aswan must have established a pattern of social interaction among themselves that enabled them to control trade routes. Received wisdom suggests that the Nubians of the Pre-Kerma culture, resident south of the third cataract, obtained gold, ivory, ebony, incense, and animal skins from their neighbors even further to the south and established a trading chain whereby these luxury articles were passed to the Nubians of the A-Group. They in turn bartered these goods with the Egyptians for beer, wine, oils, and cereals, suggested by the presence of large Egyptian-style storage vases discovered in A-Group archaeological contexts. So, for example, at the site of Khor Daud researchers discovered over 500 silo pits dug into the earth, each containing storage vessels of Egyptian manufacture.

Additionally these Nubians received copper weapons and tools manufactured in Egypt. It is further argued that the Nubians exploited the mineral resources of the eastern desert to satisfy Egyptian demands for semiprecious stones as well as the resources available from the Red Sea. Also, the Nubians relied heavily on the value of their cattle as a precious medium of exchange. In addition their milk was often used in divine offerings to Nubian deities, particularly in the later periods when milk was associated with the lion god Apedamek in the Meroitic Period.

The degree and extent of these mercantile contacts can be gauged by the presence of extraordinarily deluxe objects in certain tombs of elite chieftains of the A-Group, some of which may be considered royal gifts from Predynastic Egyptian leaders to their elite Nubian counterparts. One such object is a mace, the pear-shaped stone head of which is attached to a lavishly decorated handle, covered with gold and adorned with a series of animals, found at Sayala. The style of the animals and of the motifs, par-

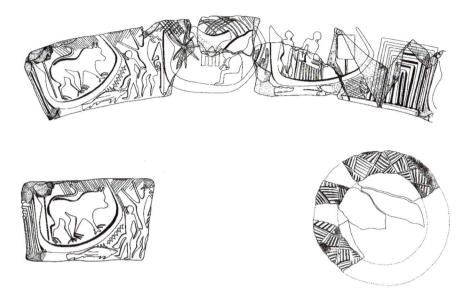

The limestone incense burner from Qustul. Courtesy of the Oriental Institute of the University of Chicago.

ticularly that of an elephant with serpents underfoot, betray an Egyptian provenance for the object because this is a motif encountered on other power-facts of contemporary Egyptian origin and manufacture.

No single example of Nubian art has caused such a furor in recent times as a stone vessel with relief decoration from Grave 24 of Qustul's Cemetery L, which is now in the collections of the Oriental Institute of the University of Chicago. The heated debate that raged in academic circles in the late 1970s and 1980s about the significance of this object has now subsided, but it is worth recapitulating here because of the heated emotions that often accompany discussions of Nubian art.

This limestone object appears to have been a vessel with a flat rim decorated with hatched triangles. Its body was designed as a series of vignettes in sunken relief, that is, they were carved into the body of the vessel, as were the examples of rock art carved in the stippled silhouette style. The individual motifs consist of a palace façade and three boats. There is a male figure standing behind a cabin on the first boat with a crocodile, now consisting only of its head, in the water below. The presence of the second vessel is suggested by its preserved prow and stern, behind which appear to be three disparate motifs, namely, a harpoon, a goat standing on its hind legs, and a male figure wearing a loin cloth. This figure has been composed, apparently, to interact with the third vessel because he both faces it and raises one arm in its direction. This vessel bears a quadruped, the scale of which is larger than that of any figure except for the vessels themselves. Beneath the vessel is a fish pierced by an implement, tentatively identified as a harpoon. The entire top of the scene is framed with a series of thin diagonally running incised hatchings.

It has long been recognized that the material from which this vessel, suggested to have served as an incense burner, is crafted is a limestone indigenous to Egypt. It has been further established that the fragments that have been modernly joined to form the present vessel were discovered over a relatively large area in the vicinity of the Grave 24, suggesting to some that the object was purposefully destroyed, either to prevent its misuse by others or as part of a funerary ritual. The large quadruped is tentatively identified as a baboon, but a comprehensible narrative for the vignettes in their entirety has proved elusive.

There is no doubt that the Qustul vessel is a deluxe object and one that could only have belonged to an elite leader of Nubia's A-Group oligarchy, perhaps the king of the city itself and its surrounding region. From these observations, at least one scholar proclaimed that the vessel was created in Nubia rather than in Egypt, and extrapolated from that assertion that the Nubians not only pioneered the development of sunken relief sculpture but also were responsible for the formulation of early indices of royal decorum, which were subsequently adopted by the Egyptians of the Early Dynastic Period. The resulting controversy, initially passed over a detailed study of the Qustul incense burner itself, soon degenerated into a vigorous debate about the primacy of Nubia in the formation of the emerging Egyptian state.

In the intervening period of time, the controversy has disappeared, notably because the Egyptian character of the Qustul incense burner has been firmly established. The vessel can now be shown to be an Egyptian product imported into Nubia, as evidenced from comparison with numerous slate palettes, mace heads, and stone vessels in the material culture of contemporary Egypt. There is no comparable corpus of stone in the material culture of the A-Group Nubians. The archaeological evidence further suggests that the Egyptians were responsible for the destruction and eventual disappearance of the A-Group culture. This archaeologically suggested set of circumstances becomes difficult to reconcile if the Nubians of the period were the actual progenitors of pharaonic civilization, as initial interpretations of the Qustul incense burner suggested. It is advisable, therefore, to regard this object as a royal Egyptian gift, sent to a chieftain of Qustul, in order to cement mercantile relationships between the two courts. And although Qustul does seem to have been an important Nubian chiefdom at this period, attempts by some to describe its more lavishly supplied burials as royal tombs is ill advised.

It is interesting to note in this context that no such royal gifts have yet been excavated in Pre-Kerma culture cemeteries, the graves of which, in fact, contain almost no genuine Egyptian artifacts. This marked absence of Egyptian objects in the material remains of the Pre-Kerma culture strongly reinforces the suggestion that the Egyptians were dealing directly and exclusively in their mercantile relations with their A-Group Nubian counterparts. Lower Nubia emerges during this period as a buffer zone between Egypt proper and the regions of Africa further to the south.

PETROGLYPHS, OR ROCK ART

Early relief sculpture in Nubia is often linked to petroglyphs, rock art, incised, or more rarely painted, into the living rock, although certain purists would prefer to remove the painted images from this corpus altogether. One survey of Nubian rock art, now over a quarter of a century old, inventoried 4,700 examples. Visitors to the site of New Kalabsha immediately south of the Aswan High Dam can see numerous examples, cut from the living rock during the UNESCO campaigns to save the Nubian monuments. Most scholars would site Nubian relief sculpture within the larger context of African rock art in general, particularly as it relates to that of North Africa, of which there are approximately 500,000 petroglyphs identified in Algeria's Tassali Region alone, and a few would argue further that a study of cultural interconnections between these diverse regions would eventually provide data for a chronology of rock art.

Attempts at narrowly dating any of these images, however, have proved to be exceedingly difficult, especially because there are no viable scientific tests that can be applied to the carvings to suggest their age or to distinguish them from the geologic age of the living rock in which they appear. Most of these examples of Nubian rock art, suggested to date from the earliest periods, are rendered in two distinct styles, both of which rely on stippling. One group simply represents the contours of the object depicted, using the stippling technique in a linear way. A representative example is a figure, identified as that of an elephant, now in Berlin. The second group relies on a silhouette technique, whereby the entire image is stippled into the rock, as seen in a depiction of a rhinoceros, also in Berlin. Both of these images were designed in accordance with design tenets, seemingly very similar to those governing contemporary Egyptian two-dimensional representations. The rotation of planes, evident in the design of the ears of the rhinoceros, and the extremely abstracted, simplified profile of the elephant adequately demonstrates this similarity. Because the dating of such examples cannot be absolutely certain, one cannot posit with assurance directions of influence. As a result, these examples cannot be used as evidence for the primacy of Nubian aesthetic concerns and their antedating of Egyptian stylistic conventions.

Scholars have, nevertheless, attempted to suggest a chronology on the basis of the subject matter of the petroglyphs themselves. One such attempt arranges certain examples of Nubian rock art across a five millennia range from the eighth to the third millennium B.C.E. The construct is based on the assumption that the motifs depicted reflect developments within Nubian culture that developed from earlier hunter-gatherer to later pastoral economies. Consequently, the earliest of these categories are representations of animals, such as those described earlier, which are rarely depicted in association with human figures. The observation that the change of climate and the alteration of the natural habitat of these beasts caused them to retreat to the south and disappear from the Egyptian landscape is one of the reasons for establishing the early date for these representations.

The images of the second, or intermediate, stage almost exclusively depict female figures richly attired to the virtual exclusion of animal and other motifs. This suggestion is based on the perceived predominance of female figures in the early Nubian Neolithic Period, the validity of which has already been challenged (see earlier discussion).

The final stage of Nubian rock art is suggested to be contemporary with the A-Group culture, because it includes images of animals such as long-horned cattle, other bovines, and donkeys, which were known to have been domesticated by this period. The images assigned to this period also include male figures and hunting dogs, another domesticated animal that now became increasingly popular. The interrelations between Nubian and North African rock art are often affirmed because of the observation that the breeding of this specific species, represented in the latest phases of Nubian rock art, was introduced into the Nile Valley from the regions of the Sahara.

Nevertheless, it remains to be demonstrated whether the introduction of domesticated species was accompanied by the concomitant adoption by the Nubians of visual means of expression from other cultures. Such putative linkages between the subject matter of Nubian rock art and other aspects of Nubia's material culture remain uncertain; some assumptions may even be disputed. So, for example, the suggested extinction of certain African animals does not obtain. Many of the species represented were still to be found in their natural habitats in the Nubian deserts in historic times.

Attempts at dating rock art by an analysis of the animals depicted are habitually foiled because exacting studies reveal that the hoped for similarities between motifs in rock art and those found in other cultural expressions remain elusive and unsupportable. The same frustration holds true from a study of the depictions of boats in these petroglyphs. A recent study suggests that the designers of the vessels in the rock art of the Wadi Gash, located some 60 kilometers from the Nile River, employed such a mixed iconographical repertoire of forms as to be virtually useless for chronological inferences. Although these examples are from an alleged Egyptian Prehistoric context, roughly contemporary with the Nubian A-Group culture, the interfaces with regard to the appearance and use of flat-bottomed boats by both groups is not without its impact on the assessment of Nubian petroglyphs of the period.

Nevertheless, continuing study of the interconnections between other examples of early Egyptian and Nubian rock art have produced some interesting results. Human figures with arms raised up over their heads in an arc are depicted in the silhouette, stippled style at various sites in Egypt and Nubia. These appear to be so morphologically similar as to suggest that they are not only roughly contemporary in date but are also indebted to a common model. Such figures and their accompanying gesture are reflected in baked clay, Egyptian images of the Predynastic Period, some of which appear to have beaked, birdlike faces. One commentator suggests that these are depictions of the deceased in a blessed state in the Hereafter, based on the admittedly superficial resemblance of the gesture to the later Egyptian hieroglyph and motif of the upraised arms, denoting the "ka," or soul of the individual.

The present state of the study of rock art of the earlier Nubian cultural horizons, therefore, is highly speculative. As a result, one can certainly entertain the suggestion that some of these vignettes are contemporary with the Neolithic Period and A-Group culture, but their meaning(s) and function(s) can only be established after their dating is more certain, as one has just seen.

CERAMICS

The Nubian ceramic production of the A-Group culture is distinctive and readily distinguishable from contemporary Egyptian vessels. All the examples continued to be hand made, with technically accomplished polished surfaces adorned with a series of abstract patterns, which scholars assume mimic the designs of contemporary baskets, woven from grasses. The repertoire of forms was exponentially increased so that virtually every type of vessel is represented from closed to open forms. All are hand made, meticulously polished, and often decorated with motifs imitating basketry. Black-topped red ware, created in oxygen-reducing kilns, ripple ware, the surfaces of which are characterized by an irregular pattern of subtle hills and valleys and which is evocative of an earlier type of pottery, and a ware crafted from a fine tan-colored Nile silt with decoration applied in red pigment form the large part of the repertoire, the forms of which include bowls, cups, and neckless jars.

A characteristic fabric is brick red in color and is designed with a black mouth and interior, created in an oxygen-reducing kiln. A conical vessel from Gezira Dabarosa, now in Khartoum, features a series of hatched, interlocking triangles, clearly evocative of basketry design, whereas a second from Saras, also in Khartoum, with its pronounced black lip, is burnished to form a subtle, undulating pattern on its surfaces.

Popular as well was a light- to pale-brown-colored fabric, created from very finely levigated Nile silt, with such extremely thin walls, measuring between 3 to 5 millimeters, that the fabric has been named eggshell ware. Its surfaces are highly polished, and the fabric is painted, inside as well as out, generally with geometric patterns. A good example is a jar without provenance, now in Cambridge, that features seven rows of inverted red triangles joining tapering, cojoined ladder motifs at its bottom. The triangles are rare, however, as decorative motifs; interlocking segments of a circle, crosshatched banding, herringbone patterns, and spiral swirls are the more common devices.

A second example, evoked as evidence for dating petroglyphs to this period (see earlier), is problematic in that the vessel itself is of Egyptian manufacture, but its two lug handles were purposely removed. There is no direct evidence, however, about whether the handles were removed by craftsmen in a Nubian or Egyptian atelier, and the same equivocation applies to the ethnicity of the painter, who added six animals to the vessel's surfaces in red paint in a linear style. As a result, the painting on this vessel cannot be used in establishing any criterion by which to judge putatively contemporary petroglyphs. Nevertheless, clearly demonstrable appropriations of Egyptian works by Nubian ateliers are perhaps more widespread than generally acknowledged, as the presence of an Egyptian storage jar of typically Naqada II design found at Aksha and now in Khartoum reveals. The incised bull was subsequently added, perhaps by a Nubian atelier. The appearance of unaltered Egyptian ceramic vessels, such as the storage jar found at Qustul and now in Chicago, suggests the intensity of trade between the two regions and places the Nubian appropriation of these Egyptian vessels, perhaps used as containers for exchanged commodities, into context.

RELIEF SCULPTURE

Despite the difficulties inherent in establishing a chronology for Nubian petroglyphs of the preceding period, scholars maintain that the stippled-silhouette technique was still employed by the Nubians of the A-Group culture, as the ascription to that period of an example of a hump-backed, long-horned bull in Berlin demonstrates. The technique of the stippled, linear design of the contour is suggested to have been transformed during the course of this period into a deep incision, which in most instances is both bold and assured. The artisans appear to have mastered the use of the tool to such a degree that they could create a compelling image by using just a few simple lines. A vignette in Munich from the region northwest of Korosko is representative of this technique. This assured, brisk linear style has been compared to a distinctive calligraphic style used in the decoration on some of the vessels of the period. The rendering of the bulls and antelopes painted on a squat vessel from Dakka, now in Munich, tend to support such a dating for the Korosko example.

SCULPTURE

Idols in baked clay continued to be made, again by hand, by the Nubians of the A-Group culture. These tend to be the same size, about 4 inches in overall height, as the examples from the Neolithic Period and are similarly embellished with a series of incised lines or patterns. All of these continue to be designed in a stylized, abstract manner in which arms, hands, legs, and feet, are either summarily indicated as truncated forms or not indicated at all.

An example excavated at Dakka is a more abstracted version of the type. Its legs are designed as an undifferentiated conical form, its arms are truncated, and the breasts, made separately, have been applied to the torso. A second example from Halfa Degheim is less abstract. Its conically shaped feet are each indicated but without knees and feet. The arms meet in the middle of the chest under the breasts, but lack distinctly formed hands and have no fingers. The lower abdomen, sides of the buttocks, and thighs are decorated with a unified pattern of curvilinear, almost concentric, incisions, which imply either clothing, tattoo, or fat folds suggestive of steatopygia. The exceptionally long necks of both figures terminate in heads in which incision is employed to represent the eyes, but the overall effect is phallic in the extreme and confirms the observation that these figures were intentionally designed as androgynous figures, supporting the religious interpretation that such idols were interred to insure the resurrection of the deceased as explained earlier. This interpretation seems to be confirmed by the fact that the Dakka figure was found in a grave containing the skeleton of a child of undetermined sex because of its young age.

The Nubians of the A-Group culture may have also created sculptures on a much larger scale, if the baked clay image of a hippopotamus, now in Chicago's Oriental Institute Museum, which measures over seven inches in length, is any indication. The sculpture was excavated in an elite grave of late A-Group date at Qustul, which was exceedingly richly appointed. One can only speculate about its meaning because its date indicates that there were already close interconnections between the Nubians and the Egyptians. One wonders whether prevailing Egyptian religious beliefs were the impetus for this object's ultimate interment.

COSTUME AND ACCESSORIES

In certain respects, the costumes and accessories of the Nubians of the A-Group culture find their correspondences in the immediately preceding Neolithic Period and suggest a degree of cultural continuity.

The Nubians of this period continued to hunt, fish, and fowl, but also placed great value on the raising of cattle, on the model provided by the modern Maasai. The hides of these herds were cured and dyed for manufacture into clothing. The presence of the antelope as a motif on vessels of the period and on petroglyphs putatively of the same date suggests that their hides were also used for such garments. More rarely, the Nubians of the period wore linen garments, but either the bolts of cloth or the garments themselves had to have been imported into Nubia from Egypt because flax, from which linen is derived, was not natively cultivated during this period. The leather garments were either simple loincloths in a short and long style or phallus sheaths for men, which were worn separately, not together, if one can trust later depictions of the phallus sheath. These could be secured around the body with belts, which like the leather garments, might be decorated with a network of beads either of bone or imported faience sewn into geometric patterns.

There is evidence that the Nubians also wore a leather cap. The appearance of the cap at this time indicates the longevity of certain fashion statements, because a similar cap was also worn by Nubians during the Kerma culture. Both of these are evocative of a cap still worn by Nubians today.

The accessories of the Nubians were rather simple in design. These included bracelets, which often incorporate seeds, strung as if they were beads. Luxury materials such as ostrich egg shell and ivory were crafted into armlets and necklaces, which might also be designed from stones. Beads were by far the most popular form of decorative element in the jewelry of the period, and those made of faience represent imports into Nubia from Egypt. Finger rings are known, but are rare. The presence of palettes suggests the continuing use of cosmetics, which may have also been used in life, in order to accompany the styling of hair, as the presence of both combs and hairpins suggests. Nevertheless, certain articles of the Nubian toilette continued to serve as indices of decorum. Graves of elite members of the Nubian oligarchy at Sayala, for example, were buried with cosmetic mirrors made of a mica, cosmetic palettes (indicating the practice was unisex), and two ceremonial maces, the handles of which were gold sheathed. One presumes the weapons were used in life as parade accessories. To date there is no evidence for the use of ear, lip, or nose plugs during this period.

DIET

The accelerated mercantile interactions between the Egyptians and the Nubians during the course of the period of the A-Group culture (about 3250–2800 B.C.E.) witnessed the exchange via barter of Africa's natural resources by the Nubians for typically Egyptian products. These exchanges were to have their impact on the diet of the Nubians. Cattle, which were always a measure of wealth among the Nubians, as among the modern Maasai today, served the medium of exchange in this barter economy of the period. The Nubians, consequently, bartered their cattle for Egyptian staples, which included beer and wine, as well as cereals and vegetable oils, which were now introduced into the Nubian diet. These same Nubians continued to hunt, fish, and fowl and may have continued to eat the flesh of the antelope, an animal that is the frequent subject of their vessels and of petroglyphs suggested to date to this period. They also expanded the repertoire of crops grown, which now increased to include wheat, barley, peas, and lentils. Melons continued to be a feature of their diet as well.

THE FINAL PHASES OF THE A-GROUP CULTURE

At some point in time during the Final Phase of the A-Group culture the mercantile condominium that had been established between the Egyptians and the Nubians was dismantled. That dismantling is ascribed to numerous factors, one of which was certainly changes in the climate that caused the drying up of one or more arms of the Nile River, forcing Nubians of the A-Group to abandon their settlements there. These climatic changes contributed to a depopulation of the area, which was accompanied by a more aggressive Egyptian military presence in the region. Some scholars have interpreted a tablet associated with the Egyptian pharaoh Aha of Dynasty I (about 3007–2975 B.C.E.) as an early commemoration of a victory over the Nubians. Although this interpretation is not universally endorsed, the evidence for such campaigns seems to be unequivocal regarding the subject of a rock carving from Gebel Sheikh Suliman, now removed and in the collections of the National Museum in Khartoum. This scene was probably created during the reign of one of Aha's immediate successors, Djer (about 2974–2927 B.C.E.). This monument appears to be a record of an Egyptian raid against the Nubians in the vicinity of the second cataract. By the end of Egypt's Dynasty I (about 2850 B.C.E.) Lower Nubia no longer appears to be actively trading with Egypt; the importation of Egyptian goods and products appears to have been arrested, but military activity appears to have accelerated. The closing years of the Final Phase of the A-Group culture witnessed the virtual disappearance of the Nubians of the A-Group. Having lost control of Lower Nubia, her inhabitants appear to have retreated to the desert or regions beyond the third cataract.

NUBIA DURING THE THIRD MILLENNIUM B.C.E.

One of the most frustrating aspects confronting scholars dealing with ancient Nubia is just how empty the archaeological record appears to be at certain intervals. This is certainly the case for most of the third millennium B.C.E. from the apparent disappearance of the Nubians of the A-Group culture to the appearance of the Nubians of the C-Group culture. The gap between these two Nubian cultural horizons may be filled by evidence found in the ancient Egyptian archaeological and epigraphic records, but that evidence is decidedly jaundiced, often propagandistic in nature because it reflects an ancient Egyptian ideology that regarded the Nubians, as indeed all of Egypt's neighbors, as both alien and unfamiliar.

Nevertheless, a study of these ancient Egyptian documents reaffirms the observation that Nubia was not a monolithic state. This is evident from the numerous toponyms, or place names, employed in the autobiographies of the ancient Egyptians who traveled into Nubia on various missions in which they report contact with several different chieftains, each apparently ruling separate domains. The lack of geographic specificity in these accounts renders the identifying of any named Nubian territory moot, but these same sources are replete with references to the types of African goods and products which the Egyptians relied on the Nubians to supply.

A survey of these same Egyptian documents, written over time, suggests that Egypt's foreign policy vis-à-vis Nubia changed. At times it was aggressive; at other times mercantile and peaceful. The evidence also indicates that the Nubians occasionally fought against one another and that on at least one occasion these conflicts were resolved by Egyptian intervention, apparently unilateral in nature. It is to a consideration of those documents that we now turn our attention.

EGYPTIAN ACCOUNTS OF NUBIA DURING THE EGYPTIAN OLD KINGDOM

The archaeological picture of Nubia presented earlier may now be compared to the picture of Egypto–Nubian relations preserved in the records of the ancient Egyptians. Within this context it should, therefore, come as no surprise to learn that the earliest accounts of Egyptian contact with Nubia should be military in nature. A passage in the Palermo Stone, referring to events of Egypt's Dynasty IV (about 2614–2479 B.C.E.), may be understood in terms of Egyptian foreign policy at the close of the Final Phase of the A-Group culture when an Egyptian military presence in Lower Nubia was the norm. This campaign is suggested to have occurred during the reign of pharaoh Sneferu, the first king of Dynasty IV.

Hacking up of the land of the Nubian
   Bringing of 7,000 living prisoners, and 200,000 large and small cattle [ARE I: §146)

In addition to documenting a punitive campaign against Nubia, this passage, however hyperbolic it may be, indicates that certain regions of Nubia were densely populated. The number of captives may be compared to estimates of contemporary populations in Egypt, one such suggesting that there were about 870,000 inhabitants in the land at the beginning of Egypt's history in Dynasty I, and that number increased only slightly to 1.2 million at the height of the Old Kingdom's population explosion. Significant as well is the mention of cattle, an important measure of Nubian wealth, which was already recognized under the barter system of the A-Group culture.

There is at least one indication from Dynasty VI (about 2322–2191 B.C.E.) that the diverse groups of Nubians provided the Egyptians with mercenaries in their campaigns against other foreigners.

His majesty made war…in the midst of the [strongholds] among the Irthet-Nubians, the Mazoi-Nubians, the Yam-Nubians, among the Wawat-Nubians, among the Kau-Nubians….

His majesty sent me at the head of this army and of the Nubians of these countries…. [ARE I: §311–312]

These forces were pressed into service in campaigns against the Asiatic Sand-Dwellers, who were doubtless threatening Egypt's eastern frontier. The distances traversed were great, ancient sources claiming, for example, that the round trip between Egypt and the Yam-Nubians consumed seven months.

In addition to supplying troops, the Nubians during the Old Kingdom offered the Egyptians assistance in other areas and at times seem to have consented to personal appearances at official Egyptian state occasions. One such occasion was a visit by pharaoh Mernere of Dynasty VI to the region immediately south of the first cataract.

The coming of the king himself standing behind the hill-country while the chiefs of Mazoi, Irthet and Wawat did obeisance and gave great praise…. (ARE I: §317)

The purpose of this royal visit was doubtless to lend authority to the subsequent engineering endeavor to dig canals enabling river traffic to negotiate the waters of the first cataract in order to transport more effectively Aswan granite blocks for this pharaoh's pyramid. The Nubian chieftains supplied the timber for these vessels.

His majesty sent [me] to dig five canals in the south and to make three cargo boats and 4 [tow]boats of acacia wood from Wawat. Then the Nubian chiefs of Irthet, Wawat, Yam, and Mazoi drew timber therefore, and I did the whole thing in one year. (ARE I: §324)

Other contemporary autobiographies indicate that the Egyptians on occasion did prefer to blaze their own trails deep into Nubian territories in order to obtain the desired products for themselves.

The majesty of pharaoh Mernere, my lord, sent me together with my father, the sole companion and ritual priest, [named] Iry to Yam in order to explore a road to this country. I did it in only seven months and I brought all [kinds of gifts] from it. (ARE I: §333)

PATTERNS OF EGYPTIAN–NUBIAN TRADE DURING
THE OLD KINGDOM

During the course of the Egyptian Old Kingdom military hostilities between the Egyptians and the Nubians seem to have halted and were replaced by more mercantile endeavors. A fragmentary Egyptian autobiographical text of Dynasty V (about 2479–2322 B.C.E.) mentions

The Malachite-country...
  Punt, 80,000 measures of myrrh, [6,000]...of electrum, 2,600 [...] staves.... (ARE I: §161)

These products, particularly malachite, which is attested earlier among the grave goods at Kadero of the A-Group culture, lend credence to the suggestion that the Nubians pioneered the mining of these minerals in the regions south of Aswan. The mention of electrum, a naturally occurring alloy of gold and silver, is understandable in this context when one considers that Nubians supplied Egypt with much of its gold throughout its long history. The mention of Punt is problematic. Researchers are still unable to reach an accord about the location of this incense-rich land. They remain divided in their opinion about whether it was a region controlled by the Nubians or one with which they traded to obtain myrrh. One must, however, bear in mind that the ancient Egyptians habitually reached Punt via the Red Sea.

Such repeat visits to the lands of the Nubians involved the Egyptians more directly in their affairs. As a result of one such expedition, the Egyptians discovered, apparently without forewarning, that certain Nubian tribes were in conflict. This autobiographical account indicates that the Egyptians unilaterally intervened to bring the conflict to an end.

His Majesty now sent me a third time to Yam; I went forth from...upon the Uhet-road, and I found the chief of Yam going to the land of Temeh to smite Temeh as far as the western corner of heaven. I went forth after him to the land of Temeh, and I pacified him, until he praised all the gods for the king's sake. (ARE 1: §335)

The chieftain of the Yam-Nubians was apparently delighted with the outcome and duly acknowledged the assistance received by presenting the Egyptians with cattle and providing an escort for their return to Egypt.

Now when I had pacified the chief of Yam...below Irthet and above Sethu, I found the chief of Irthet, Sethu and Wawat...I descended with 300 asses laden with incense, ebony, heknu, grain, panthers...ivory, [throw sticks] and every good product. Now when the chief of Irthet, Sethu, and Wawat saw how strong and numerous was the troop of Yam, which descended with me to the court, and the soldiers who had been sent with me, (then) this [chief] brought and gave to me bulls and small cattle, and conducted me to the roads of the highland of Irthet....(ARE I: §336)

Autobiographies of expeditions to Nubia during the reign of pharaoh Pepy II, the last monarch of Dynasty VI, are characterized by a remarkable shift of emphasis. On the one hand, peaceful, mercantile relations between the two regions continued, often described in amusing, anecdotal ways. So, for example, a wall of the tomb of the same Harkhuf, mentioned earlier, purports to be a copy of a letter sent to him by this pharaoh, in which the monarch acknowledges Harkhuf's return from Yam with many Nubian products, among which was a dancing dwarf, suggested to be a pygmy.

... thou has descended in safety from Yam with the army which was with thee. Thou hast said [in] this thy letter that thou hast brought all great and beautiful gifts which Hathor, mistress of Imu, hath given to the ka of the King of Upper and Lower Egypt Neferkare (= the prenomen of Pepy II)...thou hast brought a dancing dwarf of the god from the land of spirits.... (ARE I: §351)

The inscription ends with a royal admonition to Harkhuf directing him to transport the dwarf to the court safely on a vessel by ensuring that he is watched day and night lest he fall into the Nile River.

The location of Yam has long occupied archaeologists, and some have even hesitatingly identified this toponym in the above inscription of Harkhuf with the realm of Kerma, just south of the third cataract on the east bank of the Nile River in the rich Dongola Basin. Others even suggest Yam may be an earlier name for the region later known as Irem.

The ancestors of the Nubians of the Kingdom of Kerma were already settling into this area about 2500 B.C.E., and their presence, together with that of the Nubians of the C-Group culture, who became established in Lower Nubia at a slightly later date, reveal just how difficult it is to unravel inter-Nubian relationships during this period and weave those relationships into the complex picture of Nubian-Egyptian relations. Each of these two Nubian cultural horizons, the C-Group culture and the Kingdom of Kerma, will be treated separately later.

Be that as it may, other Egyptian autobiographies of the period likewise record the peaceful interaction of the Egyptians with their Nubian neighbors to the south, but these are punctuated by reports of punitive military campaigns.

The majesty of my lord sent me to hack up Wawat and Irthet...I slew a great number there consisting of chiefs' children and excellent commanders.... I brought a great number of them to the court as living prisoners.... (ARE I: §358)

This account continues, and it is interesting to note that safety becomes a dominant concern, clearly mentioned. It is a concern not found in autobiographical inscriptions of earlier date mentioning voyages and expeditions to Nubia.

Now, the Majesty of my lord sent me to pacify these countries. I did so ... I brought the two chiefs of these countries to the court in safety, bull and live [goats] which they ... to the court, together with the chiefs' children and the two commanders .... (ARE I: §359)

I went forth with my lord ... to Kush, and ... to Punt [11] times. I was brought back in safety after I had visited these countries. (ARE I: §361)

The autobiography of Sabni, who also lived during the reign of pharaoh Pepy II of Dynasty VI, is instructive on many levels. Although the beginning of the account is lost, one can determine that Sabni's father, Mekhu, had participated in an expedition to Nubia and there met his death, reinforcing the concern for safety so clearly articulated in contemporary autobiographies. Sabni then sets out for Nubia on his own initiative, privately raising the necessary resources from his own estate. These include Egyptian products expressly ear-marked as gifts. Sabni's expedition apparently engaged in military action of some sort, and he returned with an array of luxury products for which Nubia was famed.

[Then I took] a troop of my estate, and 100 asses with me, bearing ointment, honey, clothing, thenet-oil and ... of every sack, in order to [make presents [in] these countries [and I went out to] these countries of the Nubians. (ARE I: §366)

I pacified these countries (ARE I: §368)

I descended into Wawat and Uthek and I [sent] the royal attendant with two people of my estate as ... bearing incense and clothing .... 3 cubits long, one tusk, in order to give information that [my best] one was 6 cubits long; one [hide], ... and all kinds of gifts from these countries (ARE I §369)

I went forth to Memphis bearing the gifts of these countries .... (ARE I: §372)

The autobiography of Sabni's Nubian adventures invites speculation about several issues. That Sabni should apparently set out of his own accord may be indicative of the crumbling of Egyptian royal authority at the end of the Old Kingdom, although his enterprising spirit is not only recognized by the crown but also rewarded, as one learns at the end of his account. Whereas it may be true that the gradual dissolution of the Egyptian bureaucratic apparatus, which accompanied the fall of the Old Kingdom, may in part be responsible for the sporadic Nubian attacks against Egyptian expeditions into their regions, one asks whether these conflicts might also reflect a change in the demographics of Nubia herself. This suggestion is not idle inasmuch as recent archaeological exploration has demonstrated the influx of two different groups of Nubian peoples in the period between 2500 and 2300 B.C.E. The first group includes the Nubians whose descendants would develop the Kingdom of Kerma in the region south of the third cataract. A second group of Nubians were beginning to resettle Lower Egypt in the regions between the first and second cataracts at the very point in time that the Egyptian Old Kingdom was coming to a close. The unavoidable conclusion is that the events were related. The weakening of Egyptian authority in the region invited the resettlement of the area by the Nubians, who are identified as belonging to the Kingdom of Kerma and the C-Group culture, respectively.

5

The C-Group Nubians

As we have seen, a combination of factors both climatic and bellicose forced the Nubians of the A-Group culture to abandon their ancestral homelands of Lower Nubia in the region between the first and second cataracts. Their exodus from this area was gradually accompanied by an intensified Egyptian presence, a process that culminated in the later part of the Old Kingdom in the form of actual Egyptian pockets along certain trade routes and, it is suggested, in particular mining areas that had formerly been under the control of the Nubians of the A-Group culture. This Egyptian infiltration of what had formerly been Nubian-held territory prevented the Nubians from initially reestablishing themselves in these regions, particularly because the Egyptians founded settlements in many of these areas. Such is the case at Buhen, in the neighborhood of Wadi Halfa, where sealing impressions bearing the names of Egyptian kings of Dynasty IV and Dynasty V have been discovered. With the passage of time, settlements such as Buhen developed into fortresses.

Strangely enough, however, in areas such as Buhen archaeologists have uncovered evidence of an indigenous Nubian people who were contemporary with the Egyptian Old Kingdom and whose remains have been found between the second cataract and Aniba. The pottery assemblages associated with these Nubians suggest linkages between the A- and C-Group cultures, but it is presently not possible to establish any direct relationship with certainty. Complexes of like artifacts have been recovered in other gold-mining regions in the eastern desert and the hills of the Red Sea. The weight of this evidence suggests that these Nubians have affinities with the C-Group, although their precise relationship, again, remains difficult to define with precision.

The first clearly identifiable horizons of C-Group Nubians, whose culture is divided into an Ancient (about 2300–1900 B.C.E.) and a Second Phase (about 1900–1600 B.C.E.), appear around 2300 B.C.E., contemporary in date with Egypt's Dynasty VI. This established presence presupposes a period of development presently of indeterminable length during which time the C-Group Nubians presumably entered into the region on an exploratory basis, seeking specific areas in which to establish future settlements. Such a process seems to indicate that the C-Group Nubians either met no Egyptian resistance or that the Egyptians acquiesced to their presence. In this regard, it should be remembered that a nomarch, or provincial Egyptian governor from Moalla, near Thebes, records in his autobiography the sending of Egyptian grain to relieve a famine in Wawat, which seems to have occurred during the middle of the Ancient Phase of the C-Group culture.

ARCHITECTURE

Before the widespread use of stone, Nubian architecture utilized more perishable materials such as wattle-and-daub, mud brick, reeds, animal hides, and other perishable materials. The settlements have left their marks in the landscape where they appear as mounds, built up over time by the successive construction in the same place by subsequent generations. The actual structures have vanished with the passing of time, but evidence for hearths, particularly from the Neolithic Period, survives.

SETTLEMENTS

The Nubians of the C-Group culture initially did continue to live in circularly designed structures. These took the form of stone-floored edifices framed with wooden or other pliant poles and sheathed with hides, wattle-and-daub, or other material. There is also evidence of structures relying on a central pole, which have been alternatively described as either huts or tents. Gradually mud brick gained currency as the building material of choice, and settlements became larger in size, such as that of this period at Wadi es-Sebua, which occupied a natural rise in the landscape covering an area of 40 meters.

THE FORTS

The ever-increasing presence of the C-Group Nubians was apparently not regarded as a threat. Their communities enjoyed a degree of independence, and their material remains have even been found as far south as Kerma below the third cataract. Some of these Nubians may even have served as mercenaries in the Egyptian army, although their combined fighting strength was not sufficient to challenge Egypt's military might. Nevertheless in the Second Phase the C-Group Nubians constructed forts. At Wadi es-Sebua, the elevated Nubia settlement covered an area of some 40 acres, defended by a fortified enclosure entered via three gates. The enclosure contained openings at regular intervals through which archers might loose their arrows. The settlement at Areika, although different in layout, also functioned as a fortress, measuring 8 meters in length and 30 in width.

As these structures reveal, the C-Group Nubians devoted particular attention to architecture. In the Archaic Phase, at both Sayala and Aniba, the settlement was characterized by round houses framed with poles on foundations of large slabs set vertically into the earth. These were apparently sheathed with perishable materials or perhaps cloth and/or leather judging from other archaeological evidence suggesting the presence of other contemporary structures identified as either tents or huts. During the Second Phase of the C-Group culture settlement architecture began to rely on unbaked bricks. Many more houses were erected in each settlement than in those of earlier epochs, and these were of more complicated design with irregular areas suited to the multifunctional purposes to which these edifices were put.

The settlement of Areika appears to have been designed as a rectangularly shaped fortress from the very beginning. During its apparently long period of occupation, its architects employed a variety of materials including mud, mud brick, and stone.

FUNERARY ARCHITECTURE

Throughout this period, the graves of Nubia have proved to be more lasting, partly because they were originally excavated into the earth and were almost immediately thereafter covered over at the time of the interments. In the early periods these were simple pits dug into the earth. Oval or round in circumference, they varied in diameter from just under 3 feet to over 6 feet. From the observation that the deceased was placed on a mat, scholars suggest that superstructures, constructed of the same or similar perishable materials, were erected over the pit grave, although no traces survive. With the passage of time, changes in the graves' dimension and location, as well as in the differing quantity and quality of the grave goods within, become indices of social status by which one can gauge the gradual emergence of the Nubian elite and the development of its oligarchy. Accompanying this stratification of Nubian society were the introduction of ritual meals and libations, which over the course of time appear to have become fixed features of Nubian funerary rites.

The Nubians of the C-Group culture continued to develop the circular pit as the preferred design of their graves. Elsewhere, graves, either round or oval in design, were excavated to a depth of up to 2 meters. The position of the body within the grave and its orientation appear to have become codified, with the choices limited to either a contracted or flexed position, the corpse resting on its right side, its head oriented toward the east. Personal accessories were few and, if present, simple and crafted almost exclusively of bone or stone. Occasionally the corpse was attired in leather clothing, embellished with geometric designs fashioned of bone or beads of faience, a glazed material.

The most significant innovation of the C-Group culture in funerary architecture was the introduction of burial mounds that were to become specifically associated with Nubian funerary rites. This innovation is contemporary in time with Egypt's Dynasty VI, when the Egyptians were simultaneously trading and warring with the Nubians. By the final stages of the C-Group culture, the deceased was interred in a rectangular pit excavated into the earth. This was often closed with a stone slab and covered with a circular tumulus, the outer walls of which were constructed of stone with a rubble-filled interior. On occasion, a nascent form of a vault, constructed of stone, was used to close the rectangular grave, but this, too, was covered with a tumulus of the same type just described.

Some tombs, approaching 16 meters in diameter, were designed with attached chapels, rectangular in plan, which were wreathed with the skulls of oxen decorated with painted red and black dots. The presence of such structures suggests an organized funerary praxis, the details of which remain unknown, but which seem to be shared with other Nubian cultures. So, for example, the Nubians of the roughly contemporary Pan Grave culture, who interred their deceased in shallow, "crepe/frying pan" like shaped graves, employed the skulls of gazelles, which have been finger-painted black and red using soot collected from a fire and red ochre. These may have had an apotropaic function, warding away evil when placed over entrances to their huts or tents or when associated with their graves, but there is no scholarly consensus on this issue.

Those members of the C-Group culture dwelling in the vicinity of Kerma developed their own local variations of these characteristically Nubian funerary practices, no doubt inspired to do so by their Kerma culture contemporaries. In these archaeological contexts, then, one finds the same gravel-lined circular tombs but with the addition of a corresponding circular superstructure, also gravel-filled, erected from a single circle of sandstone stelae, or upright slabs resembling modern, undecorated tombstones.

During the Second Phase of this culture, the design of the graves changed. It became rectangular, its walls occasionally lined with vertically placed stones or bricks. Despite the meager appearance of the unfired brick employed in the construction of some of the burial chambers, the interments could be quite opulent and spectacular. Often the deceased was placed on a bed, accompanied not only by sacrificed animals, but also by archery equipment, often found in association with daggers and axes.

Human and animal figurines of mud and baked clay are also found, but in greater quantities in individual burials than heretofore encountered.

The most elaborate of these burials of the C-Group culture were equipped with circular chapels, the largest measuring some 16 meters in diameter, erected to the east of the tomb's superstructure. These were in turn wreathed with the skulls of oxen decorated with a series of red and black dots. In some cemeteries, the tombs of the elite, characterized by their relatively larger size, might be grouped together in discrete areas of the cemetery in an effort to emphasize the hierarchical organization of Nubian society of the C-Group culture.

SCULPTURE

From a strictly formal perspective, some of the baked clay idols of the C-Group culture appear to be linear descendants of those of the preceding Neolithic and A-Group cultures. Two such are distinctly female idols excavated at Shirfadik and Aniba. The feet of both are abstractly designed and roughly conical in shape with either a depression or incised line separating one leg from the other, which are truncated and, thereby, without the feet and toes. The arms are likewise schematic and very short, as if they ended at the elbow. The long necks continue to be a stylistic feature of the group, and these are provided with separately made and subsequently attached heads, often with beaklike noses and short, horizontal slits for eyes. The ball-like heads are often divided by three incised lines framing the face, the hair on the crown of the head rendered as linear incisions, whereas that on the sides are indicated by deeper incisions or depressions. The neck, torso, and conical legs are habitually decorated with an incised network of lines, often in wave or triangular patterns. These have been interpreted as either clothing, tattoos, or jewelry.

Because of the practice of making the heads separately and then attaching them to the bodies, heads without bodies have often survived. Two from Aniba are remarkable in their design, which is so abstract as to appeal to modern sensibilities. The incised lines that frame the hairline create a rectangular face in which the bridge of the nose is raised from the surface as a subtle plane, a series of horizontal slits suggests the eyes, and mouths have been indicated by the manipulation of the clay to form a small, everted rise, itself scored with a horizontally incised line. It is interesting to observe that the eyes of these figures are rendered in a stylistically similar way to the eyes on the sandstone effigy of the Neolithic Period. Divorced from their bodies, these heads appear to be imbued with no gender-specific indices by which they can be identified as either male or female. The coiffures and treatment of the faces seem to subscribe to an aesthetic of unisex. It is extraordinary to observe that this same gender nonspecificity is operative in the design of heads of Meroitic ba-statues (following), which, in like manner, seem to share a unisex coiffure.

On rare occasions, the appearance of pendulant breasts, often decorated with a series of impressed holes, indicate that the idol is female. In most cases, however, these figures of the C-Group culture appear to be either androgynous or perhaps male. Whereas most of the figurines are designed with swelling hips, the area of the genitalia receive no special articulation to suggest either the presence of a pubic mound or male genitalia. Furthermore, the chests are, in most instances, rendered without prominent breasts, which, in some cases, are indicated by impressed circles, as is the navel. An earlier commentator used the rather infelicitous phrase, "flat-chested woman," to describe such figures, which indicates a seeming reluctance to admit the possibility that some of these figurines may in fact have been created as male effigies. The function(s) of these idols are moot, but must relate to the funerary cult of the deceased in whose graves they have been found.

A more remarkable effigy in baked clay, now in the Museum of Natural History of the University of California, Los Angeles, was excavated at Askut and represents an animal-headed human figure, designed in conformity to the idols just described, but with the portion beneath the hips broken off and missing. The arms are truncated, the chest without indication of any kind for the breasts, and the integral head shaped to resemble that of a sheep. This remarkable effigy, which is almost 4 inches in height, was found in a chamber that contained a shrine. This context permits one to interpret this effigy as an early and unequivocal idol of a Nubian god, suggested to be Amun, based on the later association of the ram with that god. It would seem to anticipate the ram-headed granite idol, 60 cm. tall, representing Amun, which is dated to the Napatan Period. It was found at Gebel Barkal and is now in the collections at Khartoum.

The Nubians of the C-Group culture also created a veritable herder's wealth in the form of baked clay images of cattle, sheep, and goats. Some approach 6 inches in length, and all were found in graves. These are abstractly designed with little indication of detail for the hair or parts of the head such as the mouth and nostrils. The designs do capture the essence of the animal depicted, such as the majestic sweep of the long-horn cattle or the prominence afforded the dewlap in other bovine images. On occasion the goat sports a beard, and at least one depiction of a sheep (see following) was designed with a spherical headdress. On occasion a single grave might contain both a statuette of a sheep and a bull, as found at Aniba. Various interpretations of these animals, which reflect the herds of the Nubians in life, have been proposed. These range from symbols of wealth to be perpetuated in the Hereafter, to potentially animated provisions for eternity, surrogates for animals sacrificed during mortuary rites, and the like.

POTTERY

The material culture of the Nubians of the C-Group culture is best represented by its figurines in baked clay (see earlier) and by its ceramic pro-

Hemispherical bowl with depictions of cattle. Courtesy of the
Oriental Institute of the University of Chicago.

duction. Of these, the red-polished, black-topped wares are, perhaps, the
most well known. Because this fabric appears throughout the history of
the C-Group Nubians and each example conforms to a uniform technique,
it is impossible to arrange its production chronologically. Most of the vessels are either hemispherical or ovoid bowls.

Spherical, sometimes described as ovoid, jars with either short cylindrical or concave necks, dominate a second classification of C-Group ceramics, the fabric of which is a coarse, reddish-brown clay. These are often
decorated with combinations of incised zigzags, hatched triangles, lozenges, and other geometric designs. Occasionally these vessels are decorated with incised depictions of birds, perhaps to be identified as
ostriches, and horned animals such as goats, ibexes or antelopes, and cattle. On rare occasions, one encounters isolated human figures, which, save
for the emphasis on the hips, are otherwise gender unspecific, as are some
of the baked clay statuettes of this period.

The most accomplished classification of Nubian C-Group ceramics is
polished, incised ware, which exhibits several subgroups. One classification of these categories consists primarily of open forms such as dishes
and the ubiquitous hemispherical bowls. Fired in oxygen-reduction kilns,
the fabric appears black to gray-black in color, the brick-red examples having been improperly fired and not intentionally produced. The exterior
surfaces of these vessels exhibit a range of geometric motifs, all created

with incision, into which a white pigment has been introduced to render the design more visually comprehensible. Of all of the Nubian ceramics created by the C-Group this one classification is acclaimed as the most beautiful. These include hemispherical bowls and jars, the walls of which have become blackened in oxygen-reducing kilns, but whose incised geometric designs have been filled with a white paste.

A second classification of this fabric, primarily encountered in hemispherical bowls, relies on deeply incised lozenges, arranged horizontally, and motifs floating on the surface, with modifications at the foot and lip,

Detail of a troop of Nubian bowmen from an elite Egyptian tomb at Assuit. ALEA.

the latter often set off from the body by two incisions forming a band, which sets off the lip proper, articulated with impressed triangles. The lozenges themselves are filled with red and yellow pigment.

A third classification consists of similarly designed hemispherical bowls with a lip, likewise decorated with impressed triangles, set off from the body of the vessel by a band formed of two lines horizontally incised into the vessel's circumference. A herd of animals, designed as silhouettes, either completely devoid of interior embellishment, or adorned with short, densely packed dashes grouped together in rows of twos or threes, randomly filling the field of the beast's silhouette, are the principal motifs. These are rare and restricted to a few cemeteries, such as that at Adindan, whence the two examples just discussed, in Chicago and Cairo, respectively, come. The animals are highly stylized and generally lack zoological detail altogether. Were it not for the appearance of horns, slightly projecting over the heads of some of the animals, one could scarcely identify them as cattle. They are shown in strict profile, with only a single front and rear leg, and lack all indications of eyes, snout, and muzzle. Their conception stands outside the design tenets of the contemporary baked clay menagerie of farm animals and does not relate to any image encountered in the petroglyphs. The purpose and function remain to be elucidated.

DRESS AND ACCESSORIES

The cultural record of the Nubians of the C-Group suggests a degree of continuity with the preceding cultures insofar as costume and accessories are concerned, but these fashions are, understandably, a bit more developed and sophisticated. This difference demonstrates not only technological advances, but also societal stratification indicating the presence of a relatively more affluent, but still statistically less numerous, Nubian elite.

The loincloth in both a short and long version continued to be a staple of the Nubian wardrobe of this period. Such garments continued to be made of cured and dyed leather, more rarely of imported Egyptian linen. These could be decorated with sewn-on beads, arranged in geometric patterns. A model of an elite troop of 40 Nubian archers, doubtless auxiliaries or mercenaries, discovered in an Egyptian elite tomb at Assiut in Middle Egypt and dated to this period provides a very good visual impression of one aspect of this Nubian wardrobe. The Nubians are wearing short kilts, better described as loincloths, which are painted red to indicate that the leather was dyed. These are belted with one end passing down the front of the body between the legs to about the level of the knees. The belts and loincloths are decorated with geometric motifs, recalling the actual bead-networks sewn onto these garments. White hairbands complete their costume. Their left hands carry bows and their right a brace of arrows.

Bracelets and necklaces continued to be a popular accessory. Some examples of bracelets in calcite exhibit a C-shaped section. This stone, from which the Qustul incense burner was also crafted, is not native to Nubia, so one must ask whether the material alone was imported into Nubia and worked there, or whether the finished bracelet was itself imported. Bracelets, necklaces, and the like continued to rely on beads. Faience, a glaze material, became more and more common in these accessories, but it was imported from Egypt and not manufactured locally. A two-stranded necklace, from Aniba now in Leipzig, is composed of ostrich eggshell and mother-of-pearl, both deluxe materials, indicating a continuing Nubian knowledge of the sources of African deluxe materials and an ability to exploit them. Needlelike and spatula-shaped pendants strung on the second, or bottom, string of this Aniba necklace are perhaps to be understood as amulets. Another deluxe necklace was found at Uronarti. It consists of 141 spherical amethyst beads together with an equal number of gold, truncated-cylinder beads, the gold and amethyst being typically Nubian luxury materials mined locally. The focal point of this necklace is a single amethyst scarab in Egyptian style. Other accessories included anklets and finger rings, which gained in popularity.

Coiffures were styled with combs, hair rings, and hairpins made of ostrich shell or ivory, bone, or stone. Hair ornaments specific to the Nubians of the late stages of this period are pincer-shaped hair clips, the design of which resembles a modern keyhole. Most are made of mother-of-pearl but examples in ivory are known, and earlier were misidentified as earrings. When worn the hair was drawn through the slot and bunched in the hole. These hair clips appear to have been worn exclusively by women and show signs of wear. Several are broken and were anciently repaired by boring holes in both pieces and fastening them together by means of a thread or wire passing through them. This type of repair is also attested for personal accessories of the Kerma Period.

One is imperfectly informed about the appearance of these coiffures, which must have required relatively long hair for their effect. The coiffures depicted on the baked clay figurines of the period as well as in contemporary Egyptian two-dimensional representations of Nubians, particularly women, represent them with short coiffures, generally closely cropped curly hair. The Nubians are suggested to have further adorned their hair with the addition of a single or double ostrich feather. As an index of decorum, certain members of the elite were accompanied in death, and perhaps also in life, by ostrich feather fans.

Palettes for the grinding of pigments continued in use. Their designs are simple geometric forms such as circles, ovals, and rhomboids. In keeping with practices current in the immediately preceding period, these ground pigments were used for the eyes and for body painting.

The bow and arrow may likewise have been indices of decorum in life as well as in death, if one's interpretation of the bow- and mace-wielding Nubian chieftain, wearing a version of an Egyptian white crown fronted by a uraeus on a stela from Buhen, is any indication. Archers' equipment features prominently as grave goods of the period as do daggers and axes, which may have been worn in life in belts.

With the increased presence of the Egyptians of the Middle Kingdom in Nubia, particularly in garrisons in the fortresses to the north and south of the Nile River's second cataract, numerous opportunities for cultural exchange between the two groups were presented. As a result, some Nubians adopted prevailing Egyptian fashions. This seems to be the case with the Egyptian kilt, belted in a variety of styles, which is worn by a group of statues created in Upper Egypt, said to be representations of Nubians. The identification is open to debate, inasmuch as the images are not inscribed. Nevertheless, other depictions of individuals, identified as Nubians by either inscriptions or other supporting data, in Egyptian style habitually represent them in Egyptian costumes and accessories. The most common garment for men is the Egyptian kilt, made of linen and, therefore, almost always painted white, because the nature of ancient Egyptian dyes was ineffective on linen, which has no natural mordant with which to hold the coloring. The accessories might include necklaces, armlets, bracelets, and sandals, but these were so common to both the Egyptian and Nubian wardrobe that no conclusions may be drawn about the tradition to which these accessories belong. Nubian women are often similarly accessorized and are generally shown wearing the Egyptian linen sheath, again white, which at the time of the C-Group culture was designed with its shoulder straps forming a trapezoidal design at the intersection of the horizontal bodice, which, if one can trust the representations, left both breasts exposed.

NUBIAN BODY ART IN THE FORM OF TATTOO

On the basis of modern cultural analogies with contemporary African tribes together with the presence of cosmetic palettes in their graves, scholars have suggested that the ancient Nubians practiced body art in the form of painting and/or tattoo. It is clear that the Nubians painted their eyes, initially at any rate, for religious purposes in order to deter malevolent beings from entering the body via the eyes, its most vulnerable portal. The network of incised lines on the baked clay figurines of all of the Nubian cultural horizons discussed to this point have been variously interpreted as schematic indications of costume or fat folds and evidence for either body painting or tattoo. Because of the complete absence of any corroborating evidence, all such identifications are arguable, but not demonstrable.

The first incontrovertible evidence for tattoo on the African continent comes in the form of actual tattoos preserved on the mummified skin of women discovered in Egypt. One such individual, Amunet by name, served as a priestess of the goddess Hathor during Egypt's Dynasty XI, which is roughly contemporary in time with Nubia's C-Group culture. Her mummy was found at Deir el-Bahari in Western Thebes.

The mummy of Amunet was in an excellent state of preservation. Her tattoos comprise a series of abstract patterns of individual dots or dashes randomly placed on the body with apparent disregard for formal zoning. An elliptical pattern of dots and dashes was tattooed on the lower abdomen beneath the navel. Parallel lines of the same pattern were found on her thighs and arms. A second mummy, identified as belonging to a female dancer of the period, was decorated with dots composed into diamond-shaped patterns on the upper arms and chest. In addition, the tattoo on this second female mummy exhibited a remarkable cicatrix, or intentional scarification, across her lower abdomen just above the pubic region. This incision, whether made by knife or cautery, does not invade the muscles of the abdominal wall and thus cannot be explained as surgery or a wound. A third female mummy, contemporary in date with these two, displays similar tattoos.

Because tattoo does not appear to have been part of the native Egyptian cultural tradition until the time of the Middle Kingdom, scholars are inclined to attribute its introduction into Egypt by the Nubians themselves, particularly because it can be demonstrated that Amunet and the two other anonymous females from Dynasty XI can be associated with Nubia. That they may have been Nubians themselves is quite possible, although the process of mummification removes all traces of melanin by which their ethnicity may have been confirmed.

Nevertheless, excavations of C-Group graves at the Nubian site of Kubban in 1910 brought to light fragments of a hapless tattooed female Nubian mummy, who was a contemporary of Amunet and her peers. The tattoos on this anonymous Nubian woman correspond closely to those found on Amunet and the other two mummies. Such tattoos, created by grouping dots and/or dashes into abstract geometric patterns, demonstrate the longevity of tattoo in ancient Nubia, as recent excavations at Aksha demonstrate.

Here, excavators have brought to light a number of mummies of both adolescent and adult women with blue (or blue-black) tattoos in precisely the same geometric configurations as those found on the three mummies from Egypt and the one from the C-Group culture. The archaeological context of the Aksha mummies places them in the fourth century B.C.E. That such dot-and-dash tattoos persisted in Nubia in an apparently unbroken tradition for almost 2,000 years speaks for the longevity of ancient Nubian cultural norms and against its suggested disjunctive characteristics.

One suggests that the tattoos on these Nubian women were applied by repeatedly piercing the skin with one or more fish bones, which were used to drive in the pigment, perhaps lamp black to judge from the blue-black colors of the preserved tattoos themselves. All of the Nubian mummies with tattoos known to date are female, suggesting that this practice was gender specific. Because of the funereal nature of the tattooed mummies from Nubia, one is not fully informed about the significance or meaning of the tattoo among Nubian women, although cultic associations cannot be altogether excluded. In Egypt, Amunet was a priestess of Hathor, goddess of the revel, drunkenness, and dance in ritual contexts associated with religious procreation and rebirth, cosmic creation, and harmonic renewal. The second tattooed female has been identified as a dancer as well, an occupation that accords well with the personnel needs of the cult of Hathor. One can suggest, therefore, that tattoo was used, at least in Egypt, if not also in Nubia, in such religious contexts.

From these origins, tattoo continued to be used by the ancient Egyptians of the New Kingdom, but it was exclusively reserved for women. During this period the flash, or design of the tattoo, was virtually limited to images of Bes, a protective genii of the Egyptian pantheon who was particularly associated with pregnant women, birthing mothers, and their neonates. The image of Bes figures prominently on one or both thighs of naked women, primarily serving as handles for mirrors. In Egyptian ritual contexts, the disk of the mirror came to represent either the sun or the moon, which as celestial spheres, rose and set or passed through phases, respectively, providing analogies for these same cosmic cycles. It is interesting to note that at least one of the later Nubian mummies from Aksha of the fourth century B.C.E. was also tattooed with a Bes image.

DIET

One suggests that the basic diet and cuisine of the Nubians of the C-Group culture did not differ significantly from those of the preceding A-Group culture. This diet must, however, have been modified because of the continued presence of Egyptians in Nubia, particularly in the fortresses north and south of the Nile River's second cataract. Clay sealings from such Egyptian settlements are suggested to have sealed Egyptian foodstuffs in either vessels or sacks. In addition, the Egyptians are known to have sent relief in the form of their own grain to alleviate a Nubian famine.

The introduction of new pottery types, notably in the form of footed vessels, suggests a further development in Nubian cuisine insofar as its preparation was concerned. Whether the Nubians continued to exploit the sea fare of the Red Sea, based on the use of mother-of-pearl for a certain type of hair ornament, is moot, but possible.

THE NUBIANS OF THE C-GROUP CULTURE AND THE EGYPTIANS

The dynamics of C-Group Nubian society were such that its members were apparently able, in a remarkably nonthreatening manner, to interact with the Egyptians as well as with the Nubians of the Kerma culture, despite their decidedly militaristic characteristics of dwelling in fortresses, serving as mercenaries, and to judge from certain complexes of grave goods, being accomplished bowmen. A painted, wooden troop of Nubian archers, some 40 in number, advancing in four rows on a separately made pedestal was discovered in the tomb of an elite Egyptian named Mesehti at Assuit in Egypt and is dated to the period around 2000 B.C.E. The skill of the Nubians as archers was apparently long-lived. As recently as the Islamic Period in the seventh century C.E., an Arabic commentator could state that he never saw a people who were sharper in war than the Nubians, who were fond of fighting with arrows. Their ability to hit the mark is reflected in one of the Egyptian epithets applied to the Nubians. They are called "the pupil smiters," indicating that they could routinely loose an arrow into a human "bull's eye."

As their population increased, the Nubians of the C-Group culture were well disposed toward the Nubians of the Kerma culture, aspects of whose funerary practices were incorporated into their own. It should come as no surprise, then, to learn that the material culture of the C-Group Nubians contained imports of both Egyptian and Kerma culture manufacture in addition to their own local productions. Of that production, none is more universally esteemed as the most beautiful of all Nubian wares than one classification of C-Group pottery vessels consisting of hemispherical bowls and jars, which have been described in more detail previously.

The C-Group Nubians, then, may be regarded as occupying an intermediary position between the Nubians of the Kingdom of Kerma, further to the south, and the Egyptians to the north. One can imagine the southern frontier of Egypt established in the region of the first cataract in the vicinity of Aswan. The region to the south as far as the second cataract served as a buffer zone, apparently under the administrative control of Egypt but one within which the C-Group Nubians lived and exercised a degree of independence. This buffer zone was subsequently fortified by the Egyptians to the south and north of the second cataract, where remains of massive Egyptian strongholds were established during the course of Dynasty XII (about 1976–1793 B.C.E.). The region to the south of these forts stretching to the third cataract appears to have been extremely inhospitable for the Egyptians and formed a vast frontier within which were, nevertheless, established settlements associated with the Kingdom of Kerma as, for example, at Sai. The Nubians of the Kingdom of Kerma flourished in the region just south of the third cataract and, in fact, tolerated the presence of C-Group Nubians within their domains. In the subsequent history of international Nubian–Egyptian relations, the role of the military is a decisive factor. As a result, these conflicts will be briefly sketched before discussing the Nubians of the Kingdom of Kerma, whose kings defeated the Egyptian armies and established a Nubian kingdom that lasted for approximately 1,000 years.

Portrait of Pharaoh Amenemhet I. The Metropolitan
Museum of Art, Museum Excavations and Rogers
Fund, 1908. (08.200.2) Photograph, all rights reserved,
The Metropolitan Museum of Art.

THE NUBIAN CAMPAIGNS OF THE EGYPTIAN PHARAOHS

It is, therefore, to an examination of the nature of these military campaigns that one now turns. That the city of Kerma should be fortified by an enclosure wall and ditch should come as no surprise because large urban complexes of this period throughout the entire Middle East were so constructed. That the Egyptians should have erected massive forts just to the north and south of the second cataract contemporary in time with the rise of the Kingdom of Kerma should also come as no surprise because other contemporary cultures similarly fortified their own frontiers. The question arises, therefore, about whether the presence of these two types of fortifications can be interpreted to suggest that relations between Kerma and Egypt were habitually bellicose in nature. Are we to infer that a state of war existed between Egypt and Kerma during the course of the Middle Kingdom, when Egyptian records are replete with references to military campaigns against the Nubians? In order to answer this question, a survey of those Egyptian documents follows.

The Egyptian military campaigns against the Nubians are contained in documents that must be understood against the background of the Egyptian forts themselves. Buhen and Mirgissa are located, respectively, south to north before reaching the second cataract, whereas Semna is found on the west bank and Kumma on the east bank of the Nile River just beyond the second cataract, Uronarti being to their north. Semna and Kumma are foundations of pharaoh Sesostris III (about 1872–52 B.C.E.) and are featured prominently in inscriptions associated with his own Nubian campaigns.

The plan of the fort at Buhen is here taken as representative of these structures in general. Its design, rectangular in ground plan, is bastioned with walls projecting at an angle and provided with crenellations with a main gate located in the center of its long wall and provided with apertures, or openings, at regular intervals for archers. The structure was surrounded by a deep ditch. In other words, the design of this defense structure is similar in many respects to the defense system fortifying the city of Kerma itself. Communication between this network of Egyptian forts was doubtless by a system of signals clearly visible to the naked eye. The exact nature of these structures is provided by excavations at Mirgissa, where stockpiles of spears, javelins, arrowheads, and stone knives had been neatly stored for future use, suggesting that Mirgissa served as an armory.

The collapse of the Old Kingdom plunged Egypt into the first (about 2145–2020 B.C.E.) of three intermediate periods precipitating the rise of competing elites warring for control over the country. These competing Egyptian elites also waged war against the Nubians, but the motivation for these campaigns is difficult to ascertain. Some of these campaigns against the Nubians, dated to Dynasty XI (about 2119–1976 B.C.E.), may be regarded as episodes in the Egyptian dynastic struggles of the period, whereas others appear to be specifically waged against the Nubians. Moreover, one cannot overlook the fact that the C-Group Nubians served as mercenaries in the Egyptian armies and that at least one local Egyptian governor reported the dispatch of Egyptian grain to alleviate a famine in Nubia during the First Intermediate Period. This picture is further complicated by the suggested interpretation of the following passage from *The Prophecy of Neferti*. This is a literary composition known from a single manuscript of Dynasty XVIII date (about 1550–1292 B.C.E.), set in the time of Dynasty IV, in which the sage whose name appears in the work's title predicts the rise of the Middle Kingdom.

Then a king will come from the South
Ameny, the justified, by name,
Son of a woman of Ta-Sety, child of Upper Egypt.
He will take the White Crown

He will wear the Red Crown
He will join the Two Mighty Ones,
He will please the Two Lords with what they wish,
....
Rejoice, o people of his time,
The son of man will make his name for all eternity! (AEL I: 143)

Although another example of Egyptian fiction, clearly composed as a prophecy after the event, scholarly consensus maintains that its narrative may contain a germ of historical truth. The mother of the future king is undoubtedly a Nubian, and research has unequivocally established that her son's name, Ameny, is in fact that of Pharaoh Amenemhet I (about 1976–1947 B.C.E.). If this tale is taken as historical evidence, Amenemhet I, the founder of Dynasty XII, may be shown to be of Nubian descent. The complexities raised by these issues often thwart precise interpretations of the military accounts, which are our primary concern. The problems of interpretation are further compounded by the lack of corroborating, contemporary evidence.

One begins, therefore, with evidence from the Nebhetep-Montuhotep I of Dynasty XI (about 2119–2103 B.C.E.) in the form of fragments of worked blocks from his temple at Gebelein in Middle Egypt.

Binding the chiefs of the Two Lands, capturing the South and the Northland, the highlands and the two regions, the Nine Bows and the Two Lands...Nubians, Asiatics, and Libyans. (ARE I: §423H]

These campaigns appear to form part of the larger operation aimed at the reunification of Egypt by securing her frontiers.

A very fragmentary inscription of one of his successors, Nebkhrure-Montuhotep II (about 2046–1995 B.C.E.), found among a series of reliefs near Aswan mentions

...and ships to Wawat. (ARE I: §426)

Despite its brevity, this snippet may well be interpreted as a reference to an expedition against the Nubians, although the lack of context renders precision impossible. It may well be that this putative campaign forms a part of the continuing Egyptian effort to secure its borders during the battles for reunification, as is suggested by the context of a slightly later graffito in the Wadi Hammamat dated to the reign of Amenemhet I (about 1976–1947 B.C.E.), the founder of Dynasty XII.

...then my lord the King of Upper and Lower Egypt appointed me to the position of..... I went down with his Majesty to...., in twenty ships of cedar [which] he [led] coming to.... He expelled him from...Nubians..., Asiatics fell; (ARE I: §465)

An inscription at Korusko, located in Nubia between first and second cataract and dating from the reign of this same pharaoh, contains one of the first explicit references to a campaign waged specifically against the Nubians during the Middle Kingdom.

Year 29, of the King of Upper and Lower Egypt, Sehetepibre (= prenomen of Amenemhet I), living forever. We came to overthrow Wawat… . (ARE I: §472)

Its location in Nubia is significant and may indicate the actual location of the confrontation.

The campaigns appear to intensify during this reign, although one must recognize that the following extract from *The Teaching of Amenemhet* is a posthumous literary composition, not an historical document, and the in-tandem mention of pharaoh's triumph over beasts and Nubians may simply be a literary device intended to enhance the monarch's stature.

All that I commanded was correct.
I [captured] lions, I took crocodiles,
I [seized] the people of Wawat,
I captured the people of Mazoi. (ARE I: §483)

During the course of Dynasty XII (about 1976–1793 B.C.E.) Egyptian references to campaigns against the Nubians become more explicit, and the earliest of these are associated with the Nubian wars of pharaoh Sesostris I (about 1956–1910 B.C.E.). The first is the caption at the top of a relief found at Wadi Halfa, which depicts this monarch in the company of Montu, the Egyptian god of war.

Montu, Lord of Thebes, [says]I have brought for thee all countries which are in Nubia beneath thy feet, o great god. (ARE I: §510)

The noun translated here as Nubia is the phrase Ta-pedjet, literally, "the land of the bowmen/archers." It appears to be without geographic overtones.

A second inscription dated to the reign of this same monarch links a campaign against Kush, here qualified by the adjective "wretched/vile," with the procurement of gold.

I passed Kush, sailing southward, I advanced the boundary of the land, I brought all gifts…then his Majesty returned in safety, having overthrown his enemies in wretched Kush.
     I sailed southward to bring gold ore for the majesty of the King of Upper and Lower Egypt…I brought the gold…. (ARE I: §519 and 520)

The same linkage between a military operation and the procurement of luxury items from Nubia is found in an inscription dated to the reign of his successor, Amenemhet II (about 1914–1876 B.C.E.).

...and I forced the Nubian chiefs to wash gold. I brought malachite, I reached Nubia of the Nubians. I went, [overthrowing], by the fear of the Lord of the Two Lands. I came to Heh, I went around its islands, I brought away its produce. (ARE I: §602)

Scholars suggest that the toponym, or place name, Heh is perhaps to be situated in the vicinity of Abu Simbel.

The Egyptian forts, which must have played significant roles in these campaigns, were apparently subject to routine inspections, to judge from an inscription dated to the reign of Sesostris II (about 1882–1872 B.C.E.).

...[the courtier] Hapu came in order to make an inspection in the fortresses of Wawat. (ARE I: §616)

Because these Egyptian fortresses were clustered in and around the second cataract, it would appear to follow that this region was called Wawat by the ancient Egyptians, as this text suggests.

Pharaoh Sesostris III (about 1872–1852 B.C.E.) seems to have initiated several engineering and architectural projects in Nubia. These include the digging of canals and the erection of fortresses. It is interesting to note that in keeping with Egyptian cultural conventions, each of these projects bore a specific name. The first two deal with the digging of canals in order to utilize the Nile River more fully during the course of these campaigns.

He made [it] as his monument for Anukis, the mistress of Nubia...making for her a canal, whose name is "Beautiful-Are-the-Ways-of-Khekure (= prenomen of Sesostris III).... (ARE I: §644)

His majesty commanded to make the canal anew...when his majesty proceeded up-river to overthrow wretched Kush. Length of this canal, 150 cubits, width 20; depth 15. (ARE I: §647)

During the reign of Sesostris III, there seems to be an apparent increase in the number of campaigns against Nubia as well as in their intensity. These were accompanied by the construction of a fortress south of the second cataract. That at Uronarti is named in the following inscription.

Stela made in Regnal Year 16...when the fortress [named] Repulse-of-the-Troglodytes" was constructed (ARE I: §654)

The Egyptian noun here translated "Troglodytes" by convention is a generic, pejorative designation applied by the Egyptians since the time of the Old Kingdom to several of their neighbors. The translation attempts to capture the sense of the Egyptian word, but should not be literally interpreted and applied to the Nubians of the Kingdom of Kerma. The fortress of Semna was similarly named.

Repulse-of-the-Troglodytes (ARE I: §654)

The purpose of these fortifications is explicitly stated in the First Semna Stela.

Southern boundary, made in Regnal Year 8, under the majesty of the King of Upper and Lower Egypt, Khekure,...in order to prevent that any Nubian should cross it, by water or by land, with a ship, (or) any herds of the Nubians; except a Nubian who shall come to do trading in Iken, or with a commission. Every good thing shall be done with them, but without allowing a ship of the Nubians to pass by Heh, going downstream, forever. (ARE I: 652)

The toponym Iken has not been geographically identified.

The majority of inscriptions dated to the reign of Sesostris III simply record the fact that military operations against Nubia were undertaken, as seen, for example, in the following three texts.

His majesty journeyed to overthrow Kush.... (ARE I: §653)

...Sesostris III journeyed to overthrow wretched Kush in Regnal Year 19 (ARE I: §661)

Then I made ready at his side, (and) my majesty caused that I be appointed to be an "attendant of the ruler." I furnished sixty men when his majesty proceeded southward to overthrow the Troglodytes of Nubia. Then I captured a Nubian...(ARE I: §687)

Sesostris III even characterizes the Nubians.

Regnal Year 16...his majesty's making the southern boundary as far as Heh. I have made my boundary beyond that of my fathers...since the Nubian hearkens [to] the...of the mouth; it is answering him which drives him back; when one is eager against him, he turns his back; when one slinks back, he begins to be eager. But the Nubians are not a people of might, they are poor and broken in heart. My majesty has seen them; it is not an untruth. (ARE I: §657)

Such characterizations must be regarded against the broader background of Egyptian propaganda levied against the Nubians during this period, particularly in the form of execration texts, many of which were excavated at Mirgissa. Inscribed on pottery or clay figurines, generally in the shape of prisoners, these objects were created with the purpose of being broken so that via a process termed "sympathetic magic" the individual depicted or named would be believed to suffer the same fate. Two versions of a standardized version of these inscriptions appear to have been developed during the course of the Middle Kingdom, with specific reference to the Nubians.

[Every rebel of this land, all people, all patricians, all commoners, all males,] all eunuchs, all women, every chieftain, [every Nubian, every strongman, every messenger], every confederate, every ally of every land who will rebel in Wawat, Zatju, Iretit, Yam, Ianekh, Masit, and Kau, who will rebel and who will plot by saying plots or by speaking anything against Upper Egypt or Lower Egypt forever.

Every Nubian who will rebel in Irit, Wawat, Zatju, Yam, Kaau, Iankh, Masit, Mdja, and Meterti, who will rebel or who will make plots, or who will plot, or who will say anything evil. (MAEMP 139)

It is within this context that the characterization of the Nubians by Sesostris III is to be understood. He then continues by recounting episodes of the campaign.

I captured their women, I carried off their subjects, I went forth to their wells, I smote their bulls; I reaped their grain, and set fire thereto.... (ARE I: §658)

One of the primary objectives of these campaigns, as had been the case for earlier ones, was to procure Nubian gold.

My majesty commands that thou shalt...make monuments...with the gold which he (the god Osiris) caused my majesty to bring from Upper Nubia in victory and triumph.... (ARE I: §665)

Despite the apparent wealth of this documentation and the unavoidable conclusion that the Egyptians did engage in military expeditions against the Nubians, perhaps even against those of the Kingdom of Kerma, there is no evidence for the motivation of these bellicose activities. The inscriptions habitually refer to campaigns into specified regions, naming Heh, Iken, Mazoi, and Wawat as well as Nubia and Kush. The Nubians are occasionally referred to by the generic designations either Ta-pedjet or Troglodytes. The only specific architectural feature referred to in any of these texts are "wells." There is never any mention of sacked cities, looted temples, or the like. What is one to make of all of this? I do not think that a case can be made for a perpetual state of war between these two kingdoms. On the contrary, I would tend to support an alternative suggestion. Namely, these Egyptian military activities were of secondary importance, merely serving as a forceful means of protecting the mercantile interests of the Egyptians in the area in order to ensure a continuous importation of gold among other products from Nubia into Egypt. The Egyptian forts and Kerma, the fortified capital of the Kingdom of Kerma, are visual legacies of the military might of both realms placed into the service of their mercantile endeavors. I would prefer to regard both as equal partners in a mercantile condominium that funneled the riches of Africa into the treasure cities of Egypt. The Egyptian forts embracing the second cataract and the city of Kerma nestled beyond the third cataract simultaneously rose and flourished. They also simultaneously perished.

The suggestion of earlier scholars that armies from the Kingdom of Kerma ended the Egyptian military presence in Nubia by ultimately storming and sacking the forts along the second cataract is no longer tenable, but the possibility exists that these same forts were eventually captured and held by the Nubians of Kerma. As Egypt's central authority atrophied during the Second Intermediate Period (about 1794–1645 B.C.E.) and her military strength weakened, the Nubians of the Kingdom of Kerma apparently occupied Lower Nubia. As a result, a revisionist view is gaining momentum that posits that the Egyptian forts and the city of Kerma itself were simultaneously destroyed by the military conflicts occurring at the end of the Second Intermediate Period and continuing into the early years of Dynasty XVIII. The Egyptian reoccupation of Nubia toward the end of this period probably witnessed the destruction of Kerma and the abandonment of its cemeteries. The Nubian people were not annihilated, but were apparently so acculturated to the intensive Egyptian presence during the New Kingdom that their own ethnic identities and markers of identification were subsumed beneath an impenetrable veneer of Egyptian culture.

6

The Nubians of the Kingdom of Kerma

Because certain relationships between the Nubians of the C-Group, Pre-Kerma, and Kerma cultures are still imperfectly understood, discussions of some of the material remains associated with the C-Group culture have been incorporated into the following discussions dealing with aspects of art creating by the Nubians during the Kingdom of Kerma. This approach is supported by recent archaeological investigation, which suggests that the competing elites, established in the Pre-Kerma culture at sites such as Kerma and Kadruka, south of the third cataract, were eventually united into a kingdom between 2500–2400 B.C.E. by powerful chieftains, just a century or two before the establishment of C-Group Nubian settlements. The earliest tombs of this period were dug near preexisting Pre-Kerma culture settlements, whereas the main urban complex of this emerging kingdom was founded at a distance of about four kilometers away, adjacent to the Nile River's main artery. One is justified in designating this emerging urban complex a town, because its extent is greater than that of any earlier or contemporary settlement found in Nubia to date. Its size demands conceding that it must have served the kingdom as its capital.

From these beginnings, the Kingdom of Kerma was to emerge as one of the greatest of all African kingdoms to date, and it was one of the longest-lived, having survived for almost an entire millennium. The total extent of its territory cannot be precisely defined, but it did at the very least encompass the regions stretching from the fourth cataract in the south to the Batn el-Hagar in the north. In some circles, the Kingdom of Kerma has taken on epic proportions because of its putative ability to defend itself successfully and repeatedly against Egyptian military assaults, but this supposition will be examined later. There is, however, no doubt about the fact that its kings exercised absolute authority. Their tombs together with the accompanying funerary offerings bear witness to their power and status within the community they ruled.

THE SITE OF KERMA

Early European travelers, arriving at the site of Kerma, were overwhelmed by two large earthen structures, the western one of which was habitually but incorrectly described as a governor's fortified residence. These are now recognized as immense religious structures to which the noun *deffufa,* etymologically derived from an ancient Nubian word for any fortified structure erected of unfired brick, is applied. Continuing excavations at the site by a team of Swiss archaeologists led by Professor Charles Bonnet continue to illuminate fascinating aspects about the site and the culture of the Kingdom of Kerma, and the French scholar Dr. Birgit Gratien has established the following chronology for the kingdom based on her intensive investigations of the cemeteries on the island of Sai, upstream from the second cataract. According to her schema, there are three definable phases associated with this particular Nubian cultural horizon, which she names and dates as follows: Ancient Kerma (about 2500/2400–2050 B.C.E.), Middle Kerma (about 2050–1750 B.C.E.), and Classic Kerma (about 1750–1500 B.C.E.). Her focus on the cemeteries is instructive because other archaeologists have maintained that the cemeteries and their contents are the best indices for tracing the developments within the Kingdom of Kerma. Changes in funerary practices, for example, are most discernible in the eastern necropolis at Kerma. These developmental changes occur in the north before being gradually adopted by the Nubians to the south. This sequence may then explain why certain Kerma culture burial practices were incorporated into those of the C-Group Nubians of Lower Nubia.

THE ANCIENT KERMA PERIOD

During the Ancient Kerma Period, the earliest tombs are designed as round structures, averaging 1 meter in diameter, characterized by long slabs of sandstone arranged in concentric circles in a mixture of alluvium and quartz pebbles. To the east of many of these tombs, archaeologists have discovered in undisturbed contexts still *in situ* bowls or basins having intentionally been placed upside down. Such a placement argues in favor of an established funerary rite. This is confirmed from excavations on the western site of these same tombs in areas in which straw and evidence of liquid libations have been found, which are thought to reflect other rites associated with the sealing of the tomb. The use of liquid libations in honor of the deceased was to become a fixed feature of Nubian funerary practice. As recent as the early Christian Period, the tombs of Nubian bishops buried at Faras were provided with pierced holes through which the funerary libations could reach the deceased.

The graves themselves may be either oval or circular and of depths measuring between 1 and 2 meters. As was the case with certain C-Group burial rites adopted from Kerma, the bodies were either contracted or flexed on the right-hand side with the head oriented toward the east. This was to become the canonical arrangement for all such Kerma interments until the end of its history. Unlike bodies in related C-Group burials, however, those in Kerma contexts were often placed between leather covers. Either a loincloth or long skirt knotted at the bottom was common, and these funerary garments were often found in association with leather or linen with which the upper body was wrapped. Small beads of faience, a type of glazed material, or of shell were finely stitched into the leather, arranged in geometric patterns, again recalling embellished funerary garments associated with the C-Group culture. Sandals often covered the feet, decorated with patterns of incised lines. As in C-Group burials, jewelry when worn was modest and consisted of finger rings of wood or bone, often found in place on the hands; earrings of hard stone or wood; necklaces with beads of faience, ostrich eggshell, rock crystal, and calcite occasionally associated with pendants. Of particular interest is the presence in these Kerma culture burials of small leather bags habitually found on the pelvis, which generally contain a clay seal, a bone pin, and quartz tools. Ostrich feather fans are the most frequently encountered form of grave goods aside from the personal accessories just described and pottery vessels. The latter are mainly in the form of bowls and basins, their profiles tapering to a point. The potters favored a red-colored clay fabric with black mouths and interiors, the exteriors incised or impressed with geometric decorations, which might be accentuated by the addition of red paste. One can compare these examples with the black ware of the C-Group, the impressed decoration of which was filled with white paste.

A reliable indicator of the accelerated development of the Ancient Kerma Period is again provided by the cemeteries because rather early on tombs become much larger, some attaining dimensions of about 8 meters. These are abundantly provided with relatively more grave goods than the tombs of smaller dimension. Their accompanying mounds increase proportionally in height, surrounded by a ring of stones with alluvium serving as mortar, their centers filled with white pebbles shaped into a dome. Similar tombs in the south of the kingdom are often wreathed with ox skulls, a practice once again reaffirming the primacy of the south in funereal innovation, and recalling the C-Group custom of wreathing their tombs with the skulls of oxen decorated with a series of red and black dots. The sheer number of these skulls is staggering; an estimated 1,000 to 1,400 have been associated with the burial of a single individual, presumably a king. These animals are thought to represent sacrifices on the occasion of a royal funeral. As is habitually the case in all Nubian cemeteries, the graves provide ample documentation of social stratification and the marked presence of an elite. The corridor and burial of one elite tomb contained a combined area of 490 square meters.

MIDDLE KERMA PERIOD

Cemeteries continue to provide the indices for an understanding of the Nubians of the Kingdom of Kerma, and in the Middle Kerma Period the burials become more complex in design and ritual. The burials included enormous quantities of choice cuts of meat, accompanied by jars and bowls containing a variety of additional foodstuffs. Some male bodies were buried with arrow-filled quivers and daggers placed into their belts. The modest personal accessories of the Ancient Kerma Period now give way to jewelry of gold and silver, arranged along the head and upper chest of the deceased in such a predictable fashion that modern grave robbers, after locating a tomb, simply dug holes into the corresponding location of these zones of the body and, thereby, effectively and efficiently snatched away the valuables.

Chapels or oratories now appear on the western side of the superstructures, and these, judging from the seal impressions found next to some of their entrances, were places for well-organized worship thought to be practiced at regular intervals.

Sacrifice also played a role, as the practice of interring entire herds of either sheep or goats with the deceased reveals, although their total number in any one tomb was generally about six. They were apparently always buried alive with their bodies facing east. These animals were subjected to a specific ritual before interment to judge from the observation that their horns were pierced for the suspension of beaded pendants. A disk-like headdress of ostrich feathers was additionally placed on their heads. There is an extended discussion of this phenomenon following, in the section dealing with Nubian Rock Art.

In addition to these herds of either sheep or goats, there is evidence for human sacrifice, perhaps linked in some way to the same practice documented in the Neolithic Period. The position of the heads of these hapless individuals, always facedown, is the index of their fate. There appears not to have been any distinction made between sex or age with regard to these sacrificial victims. In one instance two women together with two children were sacrificed. Sacrifice continued to be practiced by Nubians of later periods as part of their funerary rituals. In later periods both dogs and cats were sacrificed as well as the traditional animals. Such a practice has been described as a sign of the power and authority of the Nubian ruler.

Toward the end of the Middle Kerma Period human sacrifices as funeral rites increased whereas the sacrifice of herds of sheep and goat decreased.

Model of Kerma, reconstructed. Courtesy of Charles Bonnet.

A Nubian kar. ALEA.

It appears that entire families, including the very young, were assembled and sacrificed close to the principal burial, which was habitually that of a male, who was laid out on a wooden bed, the feet of which were hoof-shaped, recalling the design of Egyptian furniture.

THE CLASSIC KERMA PERIOD

One can state with emphatic justification that the earliest true kingdom south of Egypt to develop on the African continent was that established by the Nubians of the Classic Kerma Period. The culture of this period is characterized by developed and complex religious and political systems, with an absolute monarch at the head of the elite. Although the names of these great Nubian kings are lost, the extent of their authority and their privileged status can be gauged by their funerary establishments.

These leaders of Nubia's elite were interred in gigantic mounds, some measuring between 80 and 90 meters in diameter, a size that approaches the length of an American football field. Designed to retard wind erosion, their construction incorporates mud-brick walls, within which was con-cealed a burial chamber, accessible via a central corridor. Excavations of one such corridor revealed several hundred skeletons, one tomb contain-ing 322 victims, each in a contracted position and placed either directly on the bare earth or on either hides or mats, all sacrificed, it is surmised, to accompany the king into the Hereafter. The body of the king was laid out on a bed, similar in form to those still used today in homes in both Nubia and the Sudan. It is interesting to observe that the Egyptian tale, *A Dispute Over Suicide,* which some suggest was composed about this time, de-scribes funerary rites in which the corpse is not laid to rest on a bier in accordance with Egyptian practice but rather on a homely bed. This appears to be a reflection of this characteristically Nubian practice, which was long-lived. So, for example, the presence of a bed burial in Tumulus 101 at Sesebi reveals that the practice continued into Christian times.

The funerary beds of the Kerma culture were sumptuously decorated with either ivory or copper inlays in their footboards, their design lacking head boards altogether. Funerary paraphernalia, generally piled high at the foot of this funerary bed, might include a headrest, model boats, and an infinite repertoire of vases crafted in faience, stone, and clay. It is inter-esting to observe that elite and nonelite members of society might wear skullcaps decorated with applied ornaments made of mica, a soft, white stone containing particles that glisten in the light.

The Nubians of the Classic Kerma Period appear to have been a deeply religious people, to judge from the two enormous religious structures that dominate one quarter of the city of Kerma. These are the Eastern Deffufa and Western Deffufa, which so impressed nineteenth-century travelers. Constructed of unfired brick, each contains two long narrow rooms joined by a small corridor. The interiors were sumptuously appointed, some of the long walls being encrusted with faience titles covered with gold leaf, whereas the short walls and corridors were adorned with wall paintings depicting boats, animals, and so-called scenes of everyday life, to appropriate a term employed by archaeologists for describing similar scenes in Egyptian tombs. The transference of the term is not inappropriate inasmuch as some of these painted vignettes evoke scenes in contemporary Egyptian tombs of the Middle Kingdom (about 2000–1750 B.C.E.), including depictions of fishing in the marshes, navigation on the river, and even fighting bulls. Noteworthy of emphasis is the western wall on which the decoration is almost exclusively confined to the depiction of animals— giraffes, oxen, and hippopotami. These are rendered in a painting style that is so archaizing, or old fashioned, that it is evocative of a much earlier period of representation. The depictions invite comparison with the earliest depictions of animals in Nubia, particularly on rock art. These lavishly adorned walls served as foils for magnificently crafted furniture found within these edifices.

In order to gain a deeper appreciation of the material culture of the Classic Kerma Period, one must turn to the cemeteries and the contents of the graves within them. Of those goods, the pottery is accorded primacy, most of the forms of the repertoire of which are finely crafted. These include red wares with polished interiors and exteriors and black mouths. Other examples are completely black or of reddish-brown or buff fabrics. Their designs may be impressed or incised, the decorative repertoire confined to geometric designs such as triangles, chevrons, and zigzags.

Of all of ceramic production of the Classic Kerma phase none is more highly regarded by connoisseurs than a variety of black-topped red ware, the exteriors of whose wafer-thin hand-made walls are often adorned with a blazing silver-colored metallic band, masterfully achieved during the firing process.

The Nubian potters were not the only skilled craftsmen at Kerma. Metalworkers excelled in the manufacture of weapons of war such as daggers, swords, axes, and knives of all sorts. They also manufactured objects for daily use such as razors, tweezers, and mirrors. Remains of their bronze kilns have been found within the main temple of Kerma, demonstrating the Nubian origin of these implements. These craftsmen labored together with others who worked stone and bone, which were crafted into tools and implements. Leather tanners, crafters of ivory, and carvers of hairbreadth-thin mica ornaments contributed to the material wealth of Kerma.

The deeply religious predilections of the Nubians of the Classic Kerma Period are again emphasized by relationships between structures in the various urban quarters of the city. In one sector, the architectural focus rests on a religious edifice, first consecrated in this location on the site about 2500 B.C.E. At that time the settlement was dotted with tents and huts. Storage areas for foodstuffs appear to have been holes cut into the earth, the sides of which were protected with a coating. Over time this

house of worship was enlarged, constructed of unfired brick, and surrounded with walls of wood and mud. As this structure was built and
rebuilt, so, too, did the settlement grow and its architecture evolve. A
degree of urban planning is suggested by the fact that certain areas of the
city of Kerma were earmarked for specific functions. So, for example, religious buildings eventually developed within complexes bearing slight,
but unmistakable, correspondences with contemporary Egyptian religious complexes.

In the center of Kerma, the Western Deffufa appears to have served as
the main temple. Because it was reconstructed repeatedly over time, each
successive rebuilding period obliterating early phases, it is virtually
impossible to document its stages of transformation from one period to
the next. In the end, however, the Western Deffufa emerged as the tallest
building, dominating the landscape as do church bell towers and minarets
of mosques. It was surrounded by a complex of secondary chapels, but the
designs of these, too, had been repeatedly transformed over time. Within
were excavated both workshops and storerooms, containing raw materials. It has been suggested, therefore, that these complexes were associated
with the international mercantile interests of the Nubians and may, therefore, have served as kinds of warehouses in which goods were transferred
and stored. It would appear, therefore, that manufacturing in Kerma, as in
Egypt, was often the domain of temples.

The city of Kerma had other edifices as well. In keeping with the function of architecture to articulate societal differences, structures identified
as the residence considered to belong to either the elite priests or kings
were segregated from other dwellings in the community by a wall,
thought to have reached 5 meters in height. In addition, there were large
bakeries set against the city's fortified enclosure wall on its eastern side,
the bread suggested to have been prepared for use as offerings.

A second specialized quarter of the city of Kerma appears to have developed about 50 meters to the south of the Western Deffufa. This section of
town was dominated by a huge hut with a conical roof, which, like the *deffufa*, dwarfed the shorter buildings in its vicinity. Like the *deffufa*, it, too, was rebuilt time and again, as were the circular huts, measuring 4.3 to 4.7 meters in diameter, with which the conical-roofed edifice
was associated. The religious nature of this structure appears to have survived in later times when an Egyptian hieroglyph, read *kar*, appears in the
form of just such a round, conically domed structure reflected in a monument in the Museum of Fine Arts, Boston. This sector of the town site also
contained storerooms. The archaeological evidence from this sector of the
city, particularly with regard to the organization and the orientation of the
complex associated with the conical-roofed building, suggests that this
is the district in which the royal residence would have been located,
although admittedly recent archaeological activity has unearthed what
appears to be a second palatial complex further to the west. This newly

discovered complex contains not only apartments and storerooms with silos, but also a large audience hall as well. Its main building is oriented in such a way that its axis is centered on that of a temple and important chapel, giving one the distinct impression that the palatial complex is metaphorically under the protection of the religious buildings, a suggestion that once again underscores the religiosity of the Nubians in Kerma.

Other inhabitants of the city of Kerma appear to have resided in houses of irregular layouts that were clustered in four discrete "residential" districts. Of different sizes, these houses are characterized by courtyards and gardens.

The entire city was encompassed by fortified walls surrounded by a ditch, as were the Egyptian forts described earlier. Although this once impressive feature has all but disappeared from the landscape, archaeologists have still been able to identify and visitors see preserved remains of both its bastions and foundations, constructed of stone together with either baked or unfired brick.

Two other distinct and separate areas have been provisionally explored to date. The first, to the southwest of the main city of Kerma in the direction of the Nile River, appears to have been a secondary town, or suburb, which, like the city proper, was completely fortified in antiquity. This settlement with its huge number of chapels and attendant workshops was provisionally associated with the funerary rites for the kingdom's dead monarchs. Closer to the Nile River is a third settlement, which may have served as the port for the city of Kerma.

The continuing Swiss excavations at Kerma are significantly clarifying aspects of its material culture, which in turn are elucidating aspects of the city's history. Clearly, the monarchs of the Kingdom of Kerma oversaw an administrative mechanism that contributed to Kerma's dominant role in the exchange of goods not only between North and South, but also between East and West. The appearance of so many Egyptian objects within the material culture of Kerma invite speculation about their presence, given the prevalent bellicose nature of their relationship. These Egyptian objects may have reached Kerma in one of three ways, namely, as gifts, on the order of the Sayala mace, as the result of barter, or as booty taken in military campaigns. Continued investigation may ultimately suggest the answer.

THE ARCHITECTURE OF THE KERMA CULTURE

With the arrival of the Nubians of the Kerma culture the architecture of both tomb and settlement reveal how traditional designs were modified. The earliest graves of this culture, which are still oval or circular in plan, might reach a depth of 2 meters. The deceased was arranged in either a contracted or flexed position, invariably on the right side with the head facing east, an

Funerary Architecture

orientation that was to be rigidly observed throughout this period, and generally placed between leather covers rather than as earlier upon a reed mat. The superstructure was constructed of blocks of sandstone arranged in concentric circles, the outer up to a meter in diameter, its interior filled with alluvium and quartz pebbles. Associated with these superstructures were bowls and/or basins found upside down, indicating the performance of libations in honor of the deceased.

As the power and prestige of the elite members of the Kerma culture increased, so, too, did the decorum of their tombs. Some were 8 meters in diameter, ringed with stone blocks using alluvium as a kind of mortar, which served as a wall, the center of which was filled with carefully selected white pebbles. One side of the superstructure was appointed with the skulls of cattle. Proportionate with their increased prestige, the funereal rituals accompanying the interment of the elite became more complex. Elaborate chapels were attached to the western side of these superstructures for the performance of periodic rites of commemoration. Entire herds of animals were now routinely sacrificed on their behalf, as were human beings, identified by their facedown position within these funerary complexes.

The elite rulers of the Classic Kerma Period were interred in enormous tombs. Tumulus K III, one of the largest known, is circular in form, with a diameter of almost 90 meters. This tomb covers an area of almost 6 1/2 square meters. Its tumulus is preserved to a height of over 2 meters.

A corridor, aligned with the diameter of the circular design, bisects the tumulus and is about 2 meters wide, oriented in an east to west direction. A number of passages intersect the central corridor, those to the south assumed to be contemporary with the initial interment, those to the north somewhat later in date, perhaps either dug by grave robbers because archaeological evidence reveals that the tomb was plundered, or to serve subsequent interments. The burial chambers consist of two vaulted rooms, each originally sealed by a wooden door. Their walls, lined with mud brick, were plastered, whitewashed and lavishly painted, but only the motif of an Egyptian winged sun disk had survived when this particular tomb was entered by the excavators.

Forty-five sacrificial victims were found within the corridor, but their number may have been considerably greater, the loss attributed to the looters, ostensibly in search of treasure. The corpse of the tomb owner was arranged in the flexed position, his head resting on his right hand, and placed upon a funerary bed, surrounded by sumptuous offerings. The entire complex was covered by a man-made tumulus reinforced with mud-brick walls, its interior constructed of layers of sand and pebbles. There is archaeological evidence to suggest that there were 38 subsequent burials within the subterranean maze of passages and small compartments, but the relationships between these individuals and the principal tomb owner remain unknown. In keeping with the practice of animal sacrifice as a funerary ritual, one of these large tombs contained almost 1,400 skulls of cattle; this marks the burial place of one elite member of this society. The cemetery of Kerma also included over 10 one-room structures in additional to two large brick buildings. These are suggested to have been both mortuary chapels and focal points for the celebration of funerary rites.

The development of the urban settlement at Kerma has been systematically studied. In the beginning, the settlement appears to have flourished because of the site's religious associations. This circumstance recalls that of Napata, which rose to prominence as a Nubian capital because it was in the shadow of the national sanctuary of Amun at Gebel Barkal, the Holy Mountain. This early place of worship was protected by a circumvallation of wood and mud, with tents and huts within. Early houses were square in plan and consisted of a single room and courtyard. The subterranean storage silos of the earlier period are here replaced by silos, still circular in design, but raised off the ground.

The City of Kerma

The settlement of Kerma developed in tandem with its religious establishments. The nucleus of the town in the second half of this period revolved around a complex of religious structures, the design and layout of each resembling a classical Egyptian temple, discussed later. Ancillary buildings reserved for chapels, some of which were converted to other uses such as manufacturing or warehouses, were erected in close proximity. A residence for either the king or chief priest was erected in the same area but was sequestered from the other buildings by its own circumvallation rising to a height of some 5 meters. Bakeries were purposefully erected at the eastern side of the town so that what a modern terms "industrial pollution" would not affect the settlement proper.

At some remove from this sector of the town was a large building, circular in plan, with a conical roof, the height of which dominated the townscape. It may have served as Kerma's royal audience hall. It, too, was surrounded by a series of smaller huts, some almost 5 meters in diameter. A series of buildings that functioned as storerooms in this sector suggest that perhaps this, too, was the location of an elite residence.

The residential quarters of the town featured domestic residences that were not laid out in accordance with any strict urban plan but that did seem to respect the four main arteries leading into the settlement. Of differing dimensions, most featured interior courtyards, perhaps developed from the architecture of the C-Group culture, and gardens. Eventually, the entire town appears to have been surrounded by both moatlike ditches and a circumvallation, constructed of stone and brick, both mud and fired. The design of this defensive system recalls the design of contemporary Egyptian fortresses in Nubia.

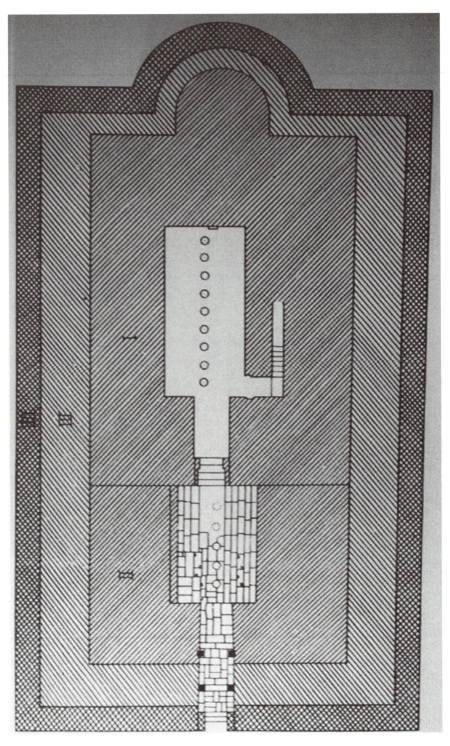

Kerma, Ground plan of Deffufa K XI. From *Africa in Antiquity,* vol. 2, by Steffen Wenig (Brooklyn: The Brooklyn Museum, 1978), p. 35, figure 12.

Kerma, part of the scene painted on the western wall of the entrance to Deffufa K XI. Photograph, © 2004 Museum of Fine Arts, Boston.

The **Deffufas** *of City of Kerma*

Two of Kerma's most interesting structures are the *deffufa*s, designated K II and K XI on archaeological site maps of Kerma. The noun *deffufa* is Nubian and refers to any type of massive edifice, usually a fortress, of mud brick. The plan of K II, or the Eastern Deffufa, is instructive. The rectangular ground plan is characterized by a solid massif of mud brick. This envelopes two rectangularly shaped rooms, oriented lengthwise along the medial axis of the massif. A narrow rectangular corridor on the south end leads to the first of two rectangular rooms. The first is joined to the second by a similarly narrow corridor, shorter in length than the entrance corridor but aligned with it on the axis. The floors of these two chambers were dressed with stone on which rested eight stone column bases in a row, four in each room. These two colonnades were aligned with the central axis of the corridors. There was a second story, long since destroyed, but whether the colonnade was structural to support the second story or merely decorative remains uncertain. The interior of this *deffufa* was originally stuccoed, whitewashed, and painted with designs in red, yellow, blue, and black.

Deffufa K XI is remarkable in that it is, to date, one of the few mud-brick buildings at Kerma, the exterior of which is sheathed in a stone, here sandstone, veneer. Moreover, the northern short side of this structure is apsidal in plan. The building was subjected to several renovations or stages of construction. In its final state its ground plan conforms generally to that of K II, but its two chambers are of different dimensions. The interior or northern chamber is both larger and supplied with an L-shaped passage located at its northeastern corner containing steps that are thought to be the passageway to the now missing second floor. There is also a colonnade in each chamber, aligned with the central axis, with an estimated five columns in the southern and nine in the northern chamber.

The interior of this *deffufa* was more lavishly decorated than the interior of K II. That decoration consists of wall paintings, some recalling contemporary Egyptian themes with their Nilotic subjects of fishing and sailing, as well as a painted frieze in registers depicting giraffes, hippopotami, Nubian cattle, and a fleet of ships. The walls were additionally decorated with faience tiles and inlays, some enhanced by the addition of gold leaf.

When excavated their interiors yielded fragments of Egyptian stone stelae, sculpture, and vessels, but these articles provide no clues about the function(s) that these massive structures served. Scholars now dismiss the earlier suggestion that the *deffufa*s were staging areas for the temporary housing of the dead elite in preparation for interment in one of the tumuli. This suggestion, based in part on the observation that the thick walls would maintain a relatively cooler temperature conducive for delaying the decomposition of the corpse, has now been dismissed because neither the interior decoration nor the objects found within can be interpreted in support of such a position. The identification of other areas of the town site as locations of elite residences would seem to preclude the function of the *deffufa*s as palaces. One might argue that their massive walls and the deluxe nature of the Egyptian articles found within indicate that the *deffufa*s were treasuries and/or workshops, but this suggestion also requires demonstration.

Whatever their function(s), the design and plan of both of the *deffufa*s at Kerma are unique in Nubia and remain without parallel in contemporary Egyptian architecture. They serve as a testament to the architectural creativity of the Nubians of this period.

The Sculpture of the Kerma Culture   The material culture of the Kingdom of Kerma, which lasted for approximately 1,000 years, represents a high-water mark for the ancient Nubians. The material excavated within the *deffufa*s and elsewhere suggests the flow of products into the capital from as far away as the Syria-Palestine region and the islands of the Aegean and perhaps also from the Mycenean mainland beyond.

Effigies of both humans and animals in baked clay appear to disappear from the cultural record. That disappearance suggests that the Nubian reliance in this period on actual human and animal sacrifices to accompany their elite interments enabled them to dispense with surrogate statuettes.

On the other hand, there seems to have been a profusion of animal sculpture in glazed quartz, a technique apparently pioneered by the Nubians of the Kerma culture because it is apparently without parallel in contemporary Egypt. Most of this sculpture is in a lamentably fragmentary state, but the head of a ram, now in the Museum of Fine Arts, Boston, reveals an animal naturalistically modeled in broad planes incorporating linear adjuncts for the articulation of details such as the eyes and muzzle. Faint traces of the glaze are still preserved, and these may enable the mind's eye to reconstruct the original appearance of such masterpieces of African art.

The Nubians of the Kerma culture excelled in the manufacture of faience, a material related to glass but fired at a lower temperature, with the result that the colorants within the matrix percolate to the surface and there are fused, creating the shining surfaces that are characteristic of this fabric. The Nubians of the period often gilded their mold-made faience objects and used them as adjuncts to decorate architectural interiors. An assemblage of such inlays from Deffufa K II, now in the Museum of Fine Arts, Boston, reveals the magnificence of this type of embellishment. The figure of the striding lion, with the flecks of glittering gold still attached,

A baked clay figurine of a ram prepared for sacrifice. Courtesy of Universität Leipzig, Ägyptologisches Institut/Ägyptisches Museum.

attests to the splendor of the material culture of the elite Nubians of this period. Faience was also used to decorate clothing, as suggested by a plaque with a scorpion in raised relief, in Khartoum. Intentionally pierced, the holes were the means by which the piece was sewn onto a garment. Faience fragments in the form of cattle's feet, in Leipzig and Khartoum, originally formed the feet of beds on which some members of the Kerma community were laid to rest. The mind boggles when one considers the skill necessary to create such a large piece of furniture, the component parts of which must have certainly been independently crafted and later assembled.

The most characteristic types of objects found at Kerma and that are again unattested elsewhere in Africa are the veritable menageries and botanical gardens created from mica, some individual examples of which reach 4 inches in height. These include real animals, such as the giraffe, lion, and avian, as well as mythological beasts drawn from ancient Egypt's pantheon, such as Taweret, a composite beast that is part crocodile, hippopotamus, and human. Most of these are paper thin in depth and open worked in lace-like patterns. They were found in tombs where they appear to have been exclusively sewn onto the caps and other garments of the deceased, perhaps as apotropaic devices to ward off evil. These are related to corresponding articles carved in ivory, which exhibit perhaps a wider range of forms and were used exclusively as inlays in wooden furniture, principally beds, for the same purpose.

NUBIAN PETROGLYPHS OF THE C-GROUP AND KERMA CULTURE

One of the more perplexing aspects of Nubian petroglyphs resides in the interpretation of certain depictions of the ram, an animal habitually associated with the god Amun in Nubian contexts, and its putative cultic relationship to seemingly similar North African depictions. An interesting baked clay statuette from Aniba, now in Leipzig, has been interpreted as a statuette of an ovine. It is distinguished from other animal sculptures of the C-Group culture because of its distinctive, rounded headdress, which is decorated with a series of holes, suggested to have originally held ostrich plumes. The headdress appears to be almost identical to reconstructions of that associated with the physical remains of ovines excavated at cemeteries at Kerma. One such animal, from Tomb 81, appears to have had such a round-shaped, ostrich-feather headdress affixed to its head via a pierced hole in each horn through which a cord, the ends of which were decorated with a beaded pendant, passed. The ovine was apparently ritually adorned in such a fashion in preparation for its ritual sacrifice on behalf of the deceased. One scholar, struck by this apparently identical motif in two contemporary Nubian cultures, has sought to find its corre-

Vessel with relief decoration in the National Museum, Khartoum.

spondence in the rock art of North Africa. To that end, he had adduced a series of petroglyphs from the Atlas Mountains including western Algeria (see earlier) in which sheep are depicted in the same or similar head-dresses. The conclusion drawn reaffirmed a diffusionist interpretation of the transference of this motif from one region to the other.

A further examination of this evidence suggests that the 80 or so North African images so interpreted belong to a different species (*Ovis longipes*, not the Nubian *O. palaeoaegypiaca*) and can, for a number cogent reasons, be dated almost two millennia later than the Nubian examples of the C-Group and Kerma cultures. They are, therefore, posterior rather than anterior or contemporary with the Nubian. Nevertheless, the North African sheep seem to be depicted in some vignettes as if they are to be sacrificed by male figures wielding axes. Given these similarities, one may suggest that the Kerma culture was responsible for the attiring of sheep for sacrificial, funerary purposes. This practice was apparently known by the Nubians of the C-Group, who created their own version in the form of at least one baked clay image and bequeathed the practice to others, if one's reading of the limited number of these North African petroglyphs has been properly interpreted. The survival of this practice in Africa is not surprising, given the documented survival of other aspects of ancient Nubia's culture in more recent times.

THE RELIEF SCULPTURE OF THE C-GROUP AND KERMA CULTURE

Petroglyphs continued to be created, and some have been assigned to this period based on the perceived correspondences between their design elements and those found on certain classifications of pottery created by the Nubians of the C-Group culture. The most common motif in both appears to be bovines. Once again, stylistic correspondences between motifs of known date within Nubia have been used as the criteria by which the petroglyphs of the area have been dated. The same arguments are employed to date other examples of Nubian petroglyphs to the Kerma culture.

The second millennium B.C.E. witnessed repeated expeditions in the Red Sea, possibly to reach Punt. Egyptians and Nubians alike must, therefore, have gained a knowledge of the Arabian coast, lying on the other side of the Red Sea, and perhaps also to the regions beyond. It is interesting to observe in this connection the appearance of petroglyphs in North Yemen in Wadi Šaih, which are uncannily evocative of vignettes in the Dakhleh Oasis depicting human figures finding their closest parallels in the androgynous baked clay figurines of the C-Group culture. The Yemeni examples similarly have truncated limbs, place an emphasis on corpulent hips, and are designed with long necks on which are set disproportionately large heads. The similarities are striking enough to warrant further investigation, but cannot presently be evoked as evidence for any diffusionist theory.

A second classification of relief sculpture from the Kerma culture takes the form of raised relief decoration on certain classifications of pottery (see following) and on stelae. A theriomorphic vessel, the spout of which is in the form of a horned animal, suggested to be a goat, is now in Khartoum but was found at Kerma. The vessel is characterized by thin walls with a modeled male figure wearing an indistinct garment, most likely an Egyptian kilt with central flap, rather than a kilt with a phallus sheath, because the latter was traditionally worn by itself. The figure appears to be leading an animal, which was destroyed when the vessel was anciently broken, and has been identified as a herdsman. The other side of the vessel bears a raised six pointed rosette, which some suggest represents the rear quarters of an indistinct animal, and there are the remains of a six legged crocodile on the rim. A second pitcher of the same fabric, also in Khartoum, has a monkey sitting on its spout and a large crocodile on the belly, designed as if about to attack the simian. Other vessels are more whimsical in design, including a pitcher, again in Khartoum, which is theriomorphic in shape, recalling an ostrich or other avian, despite the fact that it has three legs, and no head; it is however provided with rudimentary wings and a tail, applied as raised adjuncts.

Whether or not the Nubians of the Kerma culture created other examples of relief sculpture in addition to petroglyphs and these raised motifs

Vessel with a long spout. ALEA.

on their ceramics is moot. The proportions and summary design of an archer in sunk relief on an uninscribed, sandstone stela from Buhen, an Egyptian fortress, has been attributed to a Nubian craftsman, because its archaeological context suggests a date within the Second Intermediate Period when the fortress may have been under Nubian control. The subject, an archer, is shown wearing a flaring, Egyptian style kilt and what appears to be the white crown fronted by a uraeus. He holds a bow in his far hand and a mace in his near hand. If the identification of this figure as a king of Kerma can be maintained, it would become an appropriate antecedent for the bronze archer-king of the Meroitic Period found at Tabo on the island of Argo and would demonstrate, once again, how long-lived certain Nubian traditions established during the course of the Kerma Period really were in Africa.

THE CERAMICS OF THE KERMA CULTURE

Among the objects created in Nubian ateliers of the Kerma culture, ceramics certainly rank as one of the most important classifications because these vessels represent an acknowledged high point of African art. The previous creations of both the Nubians and the Egyptians in this sphere pale in comparison to the Kerma examples. One scholar has attempted to quantify this prodigious output by dividing the pottery into 18 groups in which one can identify over 300 forms. These examples represent the unleashed creative genius of these Nubian potteries not only with regard to the shapes but also with regard to the decoration of their surfaces.

Technically accomplished, these vessels are, for the most part, character-ized by even more thinly uniform walls than the eggshell ware of the C-Group culture and may be compared in this respect to the eggshell ware of the later Kingdom of Meroe. The potteries of the contemporary Nubians of the C-Group and their geographical proximity to potteries of the Kerma culture may explain the similarities that some fabrics appear to share.

The most common vessels among these ceramics of the Kingdom of Kerma are the black-topped red polished wares. As is to be expected, their walls are exceptionally thin and their profiles very appealing to modern aesthetic sensibilities; they seem to unite form and function elegantly in an extraordinary display of artistically graceful and eminently functional shapes. This ware also exhibits a technical innovation in the form of an intentionally introduced zone, usually of mottled gray, which often appears to be a shimmering, metallic silver streaked band, brilliantly con-trasting in its effect with the dark black neck and lip and the rich, brick-red color of the body. The exterior surfaces and rims of this fabric are polished, and their interiors are generally, but not exclusively, black in color.

Tulip-beakers, characterized by truncated conical bodies with wide mouths and slightly open lips, hemispherical bowls, spouted vessels and the like represent the more commonly encountered shapes. Other exam-ples include ovoid pots with disproportionately long, slender spouts, equipped with applied handles in the form of falcons, each with a perfo-ration between its legs and tails for the insertion of a cord from which these vessels were suspended when stored.

On occasion vessels created in this fabric exhibit a great deal of whimsy, such as a long-spouted vessel that humorously recalls an image of an ostrich to a modern viewer. Abstractly designed, the rotund body of this vessel is equipped with rudimentarily attached clay adjuncts, recalling the use of similarly applied handles in the form of falcons on the example just discussed, positioned around this form to suggest wing tips and a tail, while the long-necked spout with slightly flaring lips without any detail whatsoever does in fact evoke the head and neck of the flightless avian. The vessel is supported by three legs, but this tripod does not diminish its overall zoomorphic impression. The gray-banded zone has been inte-grated into the design of the vessel.

The Kerma potteries also produced a variety of vessels in an entirely black fabric. These examples exhibit a wide variety in the thickness of their walls, raging from the relatively thin to the remarkably thick. Flasks, beakers, and cylindrical jars are the more commonly encountered types. Rarer are the less than 50 known examples of a distinctively shaped tall beaker, the profile of which is stepped, the lip gently flaring. Some of these appear to have been fitted with conical lids. The design of this type appears to be unique to the Kerma potteries, but its function and interpre-tation remain elusive. Some scholars, however, suggest that the stepped profile is an imitation of a series of cups, one nested within the other, that might enable the beaker to serve as a less-expensive substitute for an actual set of cups. The presence of a conical lid on some examples, however, would seem to preclude this interpretation.

The Kerma potteries also created a series of red polished wares. Flasks of medium size predominate, but the types created also include handled vessels, spherical containers, and small pots with long spouts.

The whimsy encountered in the design of the ostrich-recalling vessel of the black-topped red ware with a gray zone continued to be exploited by the Nubian potteries of the Kerma culture, particularly in their red polished wares. Among these amusing creations are a series of pitchers, the spouts of which are often in the form of heads of animals. One from Kerma, now in Boston, is designed as a large sphere, with a large mouth in its center, framed by a ribbed lip, which is drawn into the wide strap handle straddling the mouth's diameter. Just below the juncture of this strap handle and the body is found the head of a ram, with its surfaces polished as are those of the body of the vessel itself. Such vessels are often described as teapots, so-called because of their evocative shape. The heads of the hippopotamus and cow also serve as spouts for these teapots, the design of which can be quite complex, as seen in another example in which the spout is designed as a monkey squatting on the head of a bovine.

These red-polished ware teapots are additionally the only specimens of pottery from the Kerma culture decorated with relief, often as whimsically designed as the spout in the shape of a monkey crouching on the head of an ox. An example is a vessel from Kerma, now in Khartoum, the spout of which is designed as an entire monkey, seated astride the spout as if sitting in its natural environment. One side of this vessel is decorated with the image of a crocodile in relief, designed as if stalking the monkey as its prey. A second example, with like provenance and now also in Khartoum, is a more traditionally spouted teapot, its spout in the form of an animal's head, suggested to be that of a goat. The fact that its horns have been broken off and are now missing precludes certainty. The side of the head of this beast is decorated with an incised linear design of six bars formed into a starlike pattern. The attempt to interpret this motif as an abstracted quadruped's feet, tail, and head when viewed from the bottom is tempting, but lacks support. Two more incised lines, just behind this design, seem to mark the juncture of the neck and head. The principal decorative motif on the vessel's belly is an applied group, of which only the human figure survives. He has already been identified as a hunter, whose costume has previously been discussed. On the basis of the crocodile stalking the monkey on the first vase, one can suggest that a narrative of some kind unites the figure of this herdsman leading an animal with the animal-headed spout, but their thematic relationship is far from clear. These relief-decorated red-polished ware vessels may have, therefore, served as indices of decorum, particularly because they have tentatively been identified as containers for either wine or beer.

The Nubian potteries of the Kerma Period created unpolished redware vessels as well as drab wares. The latter fabric has been unceremoniously described as a coarse native product, because of its unpolished surfaces and irregularly applied decoration. This characterization is unfortunate, as an exceptional example of this type from Kerma, now in Boston, reveals. The vessel is a three-legged bowl of roughly hemispherical shape. It is decorated with a single row of impressed but irregularly spaced dots of differing diameter. Its underside as well as the areas serving as junctures from the legs to the body are articulated by irregular incisions, which to a modern observer appear to resemble the folds of an elephant's hide. The presence of the ostrich-vessel discussed earlier suggests that such an association may very well have been intended by its designer, a conclusion that is not necessarily incompatible with the alternate suggestion that the vessel is in the form of a drum. In either case the irregular incisions seems to evoke the skin of an animal.

The rich repertoire of forms created by the Nubian potteries of the period include so-called keel vessels with narrow, projecting tubelike rims; white ware vessels in both polished and unpolished varieties; as well as a white-filled incised fabric (see following). Additionally, the Nubian potteries of the period created a series of painted wares, which although not very numerous, are generally in the form of lidded baskets, incorrectly identified in some of the earlier literature as replications of circular Nubian architecture. Their palette is virtually restricted to white, red, and yellow with which the abstract designs are rendered. An example from Kerma, now in Khartoum, features a red body with black zigzags painted on a white slip. The apex and lower border of its conical lid is painted red, the top separated from the motifs below by a horizontal black line. In between these two red zones is an alternating pattern of white and yellow color fields roughly rectangular in shape and aligned with the lid's vertical axis. These are separated by lattice patterns alternately painted red and black.

Whether these Nubian potteries produced wares with painted figural decoration is moot. A single vessel, the only example known to date, designed as a typically Nubian keel vessel with tubelike rim, now in Boston, effectively depicts a combat between a male protagonist and two lions. The male figure is depicted wearing either a cap or sporting a closely cropped coiffure; he is wearing a form-fitting garment that has the appearance of swimming trunks, but its exact design is difficult to describe. The style is not particularly Nubian and seems rather to relate to a group of painted vessels, excavated at Aswan and now in the Egyptian Museum, Cairo, which appear to be of Middle Kingdom date. It is, therefore, quite possible that this vessel, from a Nubian context, was painted by an Egyptian. In this context one recalls a vase of typically Egyptian design, the handles of which were subsequently removed and the surfaces of which were embellished with painted decoration at a date subsequent to its manufacture.

COSTUME AND ACCESSORIES

The Nubians of the Kerma culture continued to wear costumes and accessories fashionable during earlier epochs and introduced new fashions of their own. In general one may state that they were more elaborately dressed than the earlier Nubians were.

The Nubian loincloth continued to be a staple of the wardrobe in the traditional cured, dyed leather with beads sewn into patterns. An innovation appears to have been the introduction of stamped patterns in the leather. This loincloth was, however, now secured by knotting across the stomach, as was the newly introduced skirt, designed in both a long and short version, often made of cloth adorned with a sewn bead network. In death, and perhaps also in life, the Nubians of the Kerma culture wore these garments beneath a leather or linen upper garment. These leather garments were now tailored of several pieces, carefully sewn together. They continued to be decorated with tiny beads of either shell or faience, which the Nubians could now create on their own, sewn in more sophisticated, finely designed patterns. Literal interpretations of depictions in the art of the period should be avoided until one understands more fully the artistic conventions in use. So, for example, it is unlikely that the individual depicted in raised relief on one of the so-called teapots of the period is wearing both a kilt and a phallus sheath, because fashion dictated that these garments were not worn as an ensemble.

The discovery of a faience plaque with a raised relief image of a scorpion suggests that some garments of the period may have been more lavishly embellished with appliqués of this type. The holes pierced through this plaque are the means by which it was sewn on to a garment. Although it is true that this article belonged to the garment of an individual sacrificed in accordance with a specific funeral ritual at Kerma, the plaque was broken in antiquity and repaired by the passing of a cord or wire through the holes, in the model of the repaired hair clips found in a C-Group grave. The repaired scorpion plaque suggests its use in life, because it is unlikely in the extreme that the Nubians of the Kerma culture would have re-entered burials in order to retrieve either the clothing or accessories of the deceased or the sacrificed. Sandals completed the costume, often with finely incised decoration in the leather. Both the living and the dead, elite and nonelite wore caps often adorned with animals or plant forms cut lacelike from mica.

Turning now to the accessories of the Nubians of the period, one can begin with a discussion of necklaces. An example from Kerma now in Khartoum is designed with 12 hollow, biconical beads of sheet gold and 50 spherical beads of carnelian. Carnelian, particularly as ball beads, is a common material for Nubian jewelry of the period, but gold is much rarer, the biconical beads of this article being one of the few necklaces with gold elements. Elements of other necklaces are of ostrich eggshell and rock crystal. Ball beads are a ubiquitous element of Nubian jewelry of the period and continue to dominate accessories into the fourth century B.C.E. Proof of their longevity is their appearance as decorative elements on pottery of the Kingdom of Meroe. Examples in faience, which were now routinely manufactured in Nubia, are numerous, some measuring as large as 1 1/2 inches in diameter, and are mostly blue or black in color. In addition, ball beads of the period are crafted of glazed rock crystal, quartz, gold, stone, and semiprecious stones. Another necklace from Kerma, now in Boston, is an adaptation by Nubian artists of Egyptian spherical, ribbed beads. These are greenish-blue faience in color and have been strung with red carnelian beads and a violet-colored amethyst element that may be amuletic. Although colorful, the present stringing of the elements suggests that their position in the necklace was not determined by a graduation of their size.

Finger rings might be crafted of either bone or wood, and earrings might likewise be made of wood or hard stones. Purses or handbags are also attested, but these take the form of leather bags, found in the pelvic area of the deceased, which might contain a clay seal, bone pin, or quartz tools. Ostrich feather fans are also attested.

One can suggest that walking about with a bow together with a quiver full of arrows or a dagger in the belt were indices of decorum, and the stela from Buhen suggests that the Nubians of the period may also have borrowed power facts from Egypt such as the mace and the staff, as well as royal insignia such as the white crown and royal kilt.

DIET

By the time of the Kerma culture (about 2500–1500 B.C.E.), the Nubians had developed extensive agricultural and animal husbandry practices. The discovery of what appear to be entire herds of either sheep or goats in tombs as well as quantities of choice cuts of meat, particularly from cattle, which continued to serve as an index of both status and wealth, point to these advanced practices. Innumerable bowls and jars, presumably containing stores of (plant-based) foodstuffs bear eloquent testimony to the abundance of their crops and the fecundity of their flocks. The variety of their ceramics tends to suggest a varied cuisine and perhaps the presence of etiquette for dining, at least for the elite.

7

Nubia during Egypt's New Kingdom: Dynasty XVIII

THE NATURE OF CULTURAL ASSIMILATION

It is an extremely difficult task to attempt to describe the Nubians during the course of the Egyptian New Kingdom, because their presence appears to have virtually evaporated from the archaeological record. This seeming disappearance has been variously explained. The Egyptian presence in Nubia during the New Kingdom in the aftermath of the military campaigns, described later, may have been so culturally overwhelming as to compel the Nubians to acculturate themselves to Egyptian norms. The result has been described as a wholesale Nubian assimilation into Egyptian society. This assimilation was so complete that it masked all Nubian ethnic identities insofar as archaeological remains are concerned beneath an impenetrable veneer of Egypt's material culture. Such an explanation must be entertained in terms of the broader impact of Egyptian culture on those of its neighbors. In the Kushite Period when Nubians ruled as pharaohs in their own right, the material culture of Dynasty XXV (about 750–655 B.C.E.) was decidedly Egyptian in character. In like manner, the Persian overlords of Egypt during both the fifth and later fourth centuries B.C.E. are hardly discernible within the material cultural record of ancient Egypt. The same obtains but to lesser degrees for the Ptolemies, particularly in the chora, or all of the regions of Egypt with the exceptions of Alexandria and a handful of other decidedly Greek cities established during their dynasty (305–30 B.C.E.). The inescapable conclusion is that Egyptian culture was itself such an all-encompassing sea that all foreigners entering it became so drenched that their own ethnic identities were washed away.

It is, therefore, understandable how this situation might occur. As we have argued, the material culture that has survived from Nubia in general and from ancient Egypt in particular is a visual reflection of their respective elites. These advantaged and privileged members of both societies were statistically in the minority, more so, it would seem, when it comes to the population of Nubia as a whole during the course of the New Kingdom. The policy adopted by the Egyptians with regard to certain Nubian princes by which they were educated, one might almost say indoctrinated, into the manners and customs of Egypt before being allowed to return to Nubia did much to foster the imposition of this Egyptian influence, particularly because Nubia's entire landscape up to the region of the third cataract was dotted with temples indistinguishable in style and decoration from contemporary temples erected in Egypt. The same observation obtains for the smaller number of typically Egyptian tombs in which these elite Nubian princes were interred.

On the other hand, the ancient Egyptians themselves depicted their Nubian contemporaries in the form of two-dimensional representations decorating both their tombs and temples. Indeed, the depiction in the ancient Egyptian visual arts of the Nubians, for example, in the Theban Tomb of Huy, Viceroy of Nubia (about 1333–1323 B.C.E.) during the reign of the pharaoh Tutankhamon or shortly afterward in the relief decoration of the Memphite Tomb of Horemheb, erected while he served as commander-in-chief of the former's army, reveal the appearance of these Nubians through the lens of the Egyptians. This visual evidence suggests that Nubian customs and traditions proved at least somewhat resistant to ancient Egypt's cultural deluge; those traditions were, however, modified in response to the Egyptian presence.

THE EGYPTIAN SECOND INTERMEDIATE PERIOD AND THE HYKSOS

What happened to the Nubians of the Kingdom of Kerma may be outlined by briefly tracing Nubia's history during the interval between the end of the Egyptian Middle Kingdom to the end of the Egyptian Dynasty XVIII. As if repeating a pattern inaugurated at the end of the Old Kingdom, the collapse of central authority at the end of Dynasty XII and into Dynasty XIII plunged Egypt into the second (about 1794–1645 B.C.E.) of its three intermediate periods, during which time, again, competing elites vied with one another for control of various regions. At the same time, for reasons that are variously explained, a demonstrable Canaanite people, conveniently termed the Hyksos, from the Egyptian phrase translating, "rulers of the desert uplands," established themselves in the Eastern Delta at Avaris, modern Tel-el-Daba, as continuing excavations by the Austrian mission have revealed. Whether these Asiatics gradually infiltrated into the Delta and after a time established their political presence or whether they suddenly gained control of the Eastern Delta as the result of a premeditated military campaign are contentious issues.

Hyksos' control in the eastern Delta, nevertheless, appears to have developed in tandem with Nubian control in Lower Nubia. It would appear that Nubian influence extended at least as far south as the Egyptian frontier at Aswan, which itself at times may have been under Nubian control, at least nominally. During the height of this, the Second Intermediate Period, Egypt was a stage on which international politics played a significant role. In the North, the Canaanite Hyksos may have been in direct diplomatic contact with Minoans from the Aegean Sea. The Hyksos were also in contact with the Nubians to the south.

THE RISE OF EGYPTIAN THEBES

A competing Egyptian elite was finally able to establish its military and political presence at Thebes and acutely sensed, at least as revealed in Egyptian propaganda of Dynasty XVIII (about 1550–1292 B.C.E.), a slight to their national pride because of the foreign occupation of what had formerly been Egyptian land and territories. This decidedly biased Egyptian view of these events must be carefully evaluated in light of the total absence of written versions of these same events by their enemies, the Hyksos and the Nubians. Nevertheless, the Egyptian pharaohs of Dynasty XVII (about 1645–1550 B.C.E.) appear to have been alternatively at war and at peace with their foreign neighbors to the north and south. Early in the dynasty there is evidence that the Hyksos and Egyptians had developed diplomatic contacts, recognizing each other's authority in their respective geographic spheres of influence. These ties appear to have been furthered by at least one dynastic marriage of a Hyksos princess to an Egyptian pharaoh.

THE EGYPTIAN WARS OF LIBERATION

As the dynasty drew to a close, however, the peace unraveled and for reasons that still remain opaque, these Egyptians from Thebes launched a series of military campaigns aimed at ridding their country of the Canaanites to the north and the Nubians to the south. Under the reign of the Egyptian pharaoh Seqenenre Tao II one learns that "the land of Egypt was in distress." In order to rectify the situation, he waged a brutal and savage series of campaigns, placing himself in the midst of the forays and suffering wounds such as a near fatal blow to the head caused by a Hyksos battle ax. Postmortem examinations of his surviving mummy reveal that this wound healed, and that Seqenenre Tao II returned to the field of battle.

His son and successor Kamose continued the campaign.

His Majesty spoke in his palace to the council of grandees who were in his suite: "I should like to know what serves this strength of mine, when a chieftain is in Avaris, and another in Kush.... (AHAE 190–1)

Evidence suggests that Kamose was successful in gaining control of trade along the River Nile, perhaps as far north as the city of Avaris itself. He also intercepted envoys in the western Oasis, according to an account on one of his surviving stelae. Their mission was to effect an alliance between the Hyksos and the Nubians by which the Egyptians would be caught in a pincer movement, forced to fight a war on two fronts in the North and South, simultaneously against Canaanite and Nubian advances. The capture of the envoys, according to the Egyptian sources, and the intelligence gathered is described in the following manner.

I captured a messenger of his [i.e., Apophis, ruler of Avaris] high up over the oasis traveling southward to Kush for the sake of a written dispatch, and I found upon it this message in writing from the chieftain of Avaris: "I, Aewoserre, the son of Ra, Apophis, greet my son the chieftain of Kush. Why have you arisen as chieftain without letting me know? Have you [not] beheld what Egypt has done against me, the chieftain who is in it, Kamose the Mighty, ousting me from my soil and I have not reached him—after the manner of all that he has done against you, he choosing the two lands to devastate them, my land and yours, and he has destroyed them. Come, fare north at once, do not be timid. See, he is here with me...I will not let him go until you have arrived." (AHAE 192)

The text of this stela implies military campaigns into Nubia, but there is no other compelling evidence for determining either their extent or achieved results.

THE MEDJAY, OR PAN GRAVE, NUBIANS

These sallies into Nubia are further compounded by the documented presence of another distinct group of Nubian peoples, alternatively termed the Medjay in the ancient Egyptian documents, or Pan Grave culture Nubians, by archaeologists, because of the characteristic shallow, oval configuration of their graves. Graves of this type have been discovered over a wide geographic area from Nubia as far north into Egypt as Saqqara.

The repertoire of grave goods associated with the Pan Grave culture is limited, but does include certain types of jewelry, such as two-stranded necklaces. These consist of faience disk beads threaded onto an upper and lower string, the strings themselves connected by a series of rectangular plaques, to the lower strand of which were attached rudimentarily formed pendants of ostrich eggshell and mother-of-pearl. These Nubians also appear to have favored earrings, worn in a pierced lobe and crafted of either silver or copper wire formed into hoops with overlapping ends or twisted in numerous spirals. It has been cogently suggested that the ancient Egyptian custom of wearing ear ornaments for the first time in their history during the Second Intermediate Period is due to their adoption of this Nubian practice, which during the course of the New Kingdom became an ancient Egyptian unisex fashion. That the Medjay are desert-Nubians is certain. Their presence has been detected in Old Kingdom contexts, but the Medjay are more frequently encountered as a distinct group during the Middle Kingdom when their designation, Medjay, appears among the named Egyptian foes in the Execration Texts of the Middle Kingdom. On the other hand, the Medjay like the Nubians of the C-Group culture interacted favorably with the Egyptians. In the case of the Medjay, they appear to be reliable allies and formed, therefore, part of the Egyptian army under Kamose in his campaigns against the Hyksos. Some have suggested that a Medjay contingent may have played a primary role in Kamose's interception of the Hyksos embassy en route to Nubia. Members of the Medjay community continued to be of service to the Egyptians of the New Kingdom, during which time they served in Egypt as the equivalent of policemen. They continued to serve in this capacity well into the reign of pharaoh Rameses IV (about 1152–1144 B.C.E.), during which time they accompanied an expedition into the Wadi Hammamat. They are listed in the personnel roster as follows.

Medjay gendarmes   50 men

(ARE 4: §466)

NUBIA DURING EGYPT'S DYNASTY XVIII

The Wars of Liberation initiated by the Theban pharaohs of Dynasty XVII continued to be waged by the pharaohs of the early Dynasty XVIII. Accounts of these and subsequent Dynasty XVIII military expeditions into Nubia are to be **The Military Campaigns** found in the autobiographies of Egyptian officials serving in the armed forces or in other administrative capacities. The earliest among these are preserved in the tomb of a naval officer, named Ahmose, whose mother was named Abana, at Elkab to the south of Thebes. The inscription appears to have been composed and carved by his grandson, Pahri, an accomplished draftsman. One learns that Ahmose's distinguished career spanned the reigns of three different Dynasty XVIII pharaohs, namely Ahmose I, Amenhotep I, and Tuthmosis I. He was apparently following in the career path of his father, who served under Seqenenre Tao II, the predecessor of Ahmose I.

Now after his Majesty had slain the Asiatics, he ascended to the river to Khenthennofer, to destroy the Nubian Troglodytes; his Majesty made a great slaughter among them. Then I took captives there, two living men, and three hands.... His

Majesty sailed downstream, his heart joyous with the might of victory, (because) he had seized Southerners and Northerners. (ARE 2: §14)

There came the enemy of the South; his fate, his destruction approached; the gods of the South seized him, and his Majesty found him in Tintto-emu. His Majesty carried him off a living prisoner, and all his people carried captive. I carried away two archers as a seizure in the ship of the enemy.... (ARE 2: §15)

The Nubian campaigns continued into the reign of Amenhotep I, and Ahmose, son of Abana, includes them within his autobiography as well.

I sailed with King Djeserkare (= prenomen of Amenhotep I), triumphant, when he ascended the river to Kush, in order to extend the borders of Egypt. His Majesty captured that Nubian Troglodyte in the midst of his army,...who were brought away as prisoners, none of them missing...I fought incredibly; his Majesty beheld my bravery...one pursued his people and cattle.... (ARE 2: §38)

Similar reports characterize the autobiography of Ahmose-pen-nekhbet, who also served under Amenhotep I.

I followed King Djeserkare (= prenomen of Amenhotep I), triumphant, I captured for him in Kush a living prisoner. (ARE 2: §41)

Such military action continued throughout the history of the dynasty. The epigraphical record associated with the campaigns of Tuthmosis I in Nubia are extensive. These consist of both royal commemorations and passages found in autobiographies of officials in his service. One such official commemoration takes the form of an inscribed royal stela found at the site of Tombos, just above the third cataract, in which Tuthmosis I celebrates a victory. One may tentatively suggest that this stela was erected in the vicinity of the victory gained.

...The southerners came down river...and all lands are bringing together their tribute...He [Tuthmosis I] hath overthrown the chief of the Nubians; The Nubian is helpless, defenseless in his grasp. He hath united the boundaries of his two sides, there is not a remnant among the Curly-Haired, who come to attack him; there is not a single survivor among them. The Nubian Troglodytes fall by the sword, and are thrust aside in their lands; their foulness, it floods their valleys; the...of their mouths is like a violent flood. The fragments cut from them are too much for the birds, carrying off the prey to another place.... (ARE 2: §70)

A somewhat more personalized account of these contemporary military engagements is preserved in the autobiographies of both Ahmose, son of Abana, and Ahmose-pen-nekhbet, respectively.

I sailed with King Ahkeperkare...when he ascended to the river to Khenthennofer in order to cast out violence in the highlands, in order to suppress the raiding of the hill region. I showed bravery in his presence in the bad water, in the passage of the ship by the bend . . . His Majesty was a furious threat, like a panther; his Majesty cast his lance first . . . their people were brought off as living prisoners. His Majesty sailed down-river with all countries in his grasp, that wretched Nubian Troglodyte being hanged head downward at the [prow] of the barge of his Majesty, and landed at Karnak.

I followed the king Akheperkare . . . I captured for him in Kush. . . . (ARE 2: §80 and 84, respectively]

The successful conclusion of one of these campaigns is celebrated in an inscription on the island of Sehel in the vicinity of the first cataract, as the triumphant Egyptian army of Tuthmosis I was about to cross the border and return to Egypt.

Year 3 . . . His Majesty sailed this canal in victory and power, at his return from overthrowing wretched Kush. (ARE 2: §76)

Preoccupation with Nubia also characterizes aspects of the foreign policy of the female-pharaoh Hatshepsut (about 1479–1457 B.C.E.), perhaps the most famous of all Egyptian women who ruled as monarch in her own right. In the suite of her coronation inscriptions at Deir el-Bahari in Western Thebes, the deities of Egypt promise that she shall

smite with the mace the Troglodytes; thou shalt cut off the heads of the soldiers. . . . (ARE 2: §225)

Her coruler and eventual successor, Tuthmosis III (about 1479–1425 B.C.E.), called by some the Napoleon of Egypt because of the extent of his military campaigns, led assaults against Nubia, the first occurring in Regnal Year 3. These continue intermittently until near the end of his reign in Regnal Year 50 and are all recorded in *The Annals* inscribed on the twin towers of his pylon at Karnak.

List of the countries of the south, the Nubian Troglodytes of Khenthennofer, whom his Majesty overthrew, making a great slaughter among them, [whose] number is unknown, and carrying away all their subjects as living captives to Thebes, in order to fill the storehouse. . . .
    . . . among the Nubians, given from chiefs and living captives . . . when wretched Kush, was overthrown. . . . (ARE 2: §646)

These triumphs over Nubia are celebrated in his *Hymn of Victory* in a somewhat hyperbolic fashion.

. . . have bound together the Nubian Troglodytes by tens of thousands and thousands. . . .

...I have come, causing thee to smite the Nubian Troglodytes.... (ARE 2: §656 and 660, respectively]

His successor, the sporting pharaoh Amenhotep II (about 1428–1397 B.C.E.), of whom it is said, "there is not one who can draw his bow," warred in Asia and apparently went through the trouble of transporting a hapless, captured Asiatic prince all the way to Napata so that he might serve as an object lesson for the Nubians.

Then the other fallen one was taken upriver to Nubia and hanged on the walls of Napata in order to cause to be manifest the victories of his Majesty, forever and ever in all lands and countries of the Nubians; since he had taken the Southern- ers...that he might make his boundary as far as he desired, none opposing his hands.... (ARE 2: §797)

Pharaoh Amenhotep III (about 1388–1350 B.C.E.) also campaigned in Nubia, as one of his stelae, erected at Konosso, reveals.

...Regnal Year 5; his Majesty returned, having triumphed on his first victorious campaign in the land of wretched Kush; having made his boundary as far as he desired.... (ARE 2: §845)

Reports of an advance into Nubia by this same pharaoh are recorded on a worked, granite block from a temple at Bubastis in the Nile Delta, which, if complete, might have been as extensive as *The Annals* of Tuthmosis III insofar as information about this Nubian campaign is concerned. The text, however, in its present state of preservation is damaged, and many of its passages are lacunose, or missing.

...Nubians...this army, while their hearts were [eager] to fight quickly...of the Nubians who fell, in order that my Majesty might know, because he did this...it was not commanded for them. His Majesty smote them himself with the baton which was in [his] hand...His Majesty commanded, that 124 men of the army be dispatched...living captives, which they found among them: Nubians, 113 cattle, male and female; 11 asses, male and females.... (ARE 2: §849–850)

Like his predecessor Tuthmosis III, Amenhotep III also recorded his tri- umph over Nubia by erecting a *Victory Stela* in Thebes for the edification of its inhabitants and administrators. In its accompanying vignette Amen- hotep III is depicted driving his chariot over fallen Nubians, captioned more fully than in the passage in the text proper that refers to this campaign.

...mightily in dragging them (in his chariot), annihilating the heir of wretched Kush, bringing their princes as living prisoners

...every country...wretched Kush...are at the feet of this Good God.... (ARE 2: §857 and 858, respectively]

Military campaigns continued into the end of the reign. The son and successor of Amenhotep III, Amenhotep IV, who changed his name to Akhenaten and transferred the capital from Thebes to Tel el-Amarna, even campaigned in Nubia. A fragmentary inscription from Buhen, with its parallel discovered at Amada, commemorates a campaign of Akhenaten against the Nubians in the region of Ikayta, perhaps as late as Regnal Year 12. The record is found in the autobiography of his Viceroy of Nubia, Djutymoses, who reports that this Egyptian punitive campaign was conducted in the Wadi el-Alliqui in retaliation for the pillaging of grain in the valley. He records his capture of some 145 Nubians and 361 head of cattle, but stresses that others were impaled. On other occasions, Nubian prisoners were routinely tied to the shafts of royal chariots, directly beneath the tail of a horse, with humiliating consequences.

These military operations were accompanied by engineering and architectural activities, foremost among which were the excavation and/or clearance and maintenance of canals for the transport of troops and cargo. The clearance of one **Canals and Forts** such canal, excavated earlier during the reign of Sesostris III of the Middle Kingdom, is recorded in an inscription dated to the reign of Tuthmosis I on the island of Sehel in the region of the first cataract.

Regnal Year 3…under the Majesty of the King of Upper and Lower Egypt, Akheperkera…. his Majesty commanded to dig this canal, after he found it [stopped up] with stones [so that] no [ship sailed upon it]. He sailed [downstream] upon it, his heart [glad, having slain his enemies]…. (ARE 2: §75)

The clearance of these canals also occupied Tuthmosis III, as this inscription, also found on Sehel, reveals. Having been cleared, it was renamed in his honor.

His Majesty commanded to dig this canal, after he had found it stopped up with stones [so that] no ship sailed upon it. He sailed downstream upon it…having slain his enemies. The name of this canal is: "Opening-of-this-Way-in-the-Beauty-of-Menkhepere (= prenomen of Tuthmosis III)-Living-Forever." The fishermen of Elephantine shall clear this canal each year. (ARE 2: §650)

The Egyptians of Dynasty XVIII reoccupied some of the forts that were operational during the Middle Kingdom and often, as at Semna, completely replaced the earlier brick structure with one constructed entirely out of stone. In the process the Egyptians were acutely aware of their own history and recognized significant pharaohs whose earlier efforts to secure Nubia were deemed worthy of commemoration. Here at Semna, Tuthmosis III paid homage to Sesostris III.

…Cause that there be engraved the divine offerings, which the King of Upper and Lower Egypt…Khekure (= prenomen of Sesostris III)…made…. (ARE 2: §170)

The Egyptians of Dynasty XVIII appear to have also founded forts anew in Nubia, such as this one erected during the reign of Tuthmosis I.

The lords of the palace have made a fortress for his army [named], "None-Faces-Him-Among- the-Nine-Bows-Together;" like a young panther among the fleeing cattle; the fame of his Majesty blinded them...his southern boundary is as far as the frontier of this land, [his] northern boundary as far as that inverted water which goes downstream in going upstream.... (ARE 2: §72–73)

As this inscription reveals, fortresses as well as canals were named.

Revolts Rather Than Prolonged Campaigns
Within the context of these architectural programs, then, and from an Egyptian perspective, Nubia appeared, superficially at least, to have been pacified, but throughout the period there are frequent mentions of Egyptian military campaigns. These appear to be punitive in nature, the objective of which was to quell periodic Nubian insurrections. These insurrections are characterized in the language by the word *revolt*, clearly indicative of an Egyptian military response to a Nubian threat against the established authority and prevailing status quo in the region.

One such rebellion is recorded in the autobiography of Ineni, who served under pharaoh Tuthmosis II; it is carved into a rocky outcropping on the road from Aswan to Philae.

One came to inform his Majesty as follows: Wretched Kush has begun to rebel, those who were under the dominion of the Lord of the Two Lands propose hostility, beginning to smite him. The inhabitants of Egypt are about to bring away the cattle behind this fortress which thy father built in his campaigns...in order to repulse the rebellious barbarians, the Nubian Troglodytes of Khenthennefer, for those who are there on the north of wretched Kush...his Majesty was furious thereat, like a panther...said his Majesty, "I will not let live anyone among their males...Then his Majesty dispatched a numerous army into Nubia on his first occasion of a campaign, in order to overthrow all those who were rebellious against his Majesty or hostile to the Lord of the Two Lands. Then this army of his Majesty arrived at wretched Kush...this army overthrew those barbarians; they did [not] let live anyone among their males...except one of the children of the chief of wretched Kush, who was taken away alive as a living prisoner with their people to his Majesty...This land was made a subject of his Majesty as formerly.... (ARE 2: §121–122)

The Nubians were in rebellion again during the reign of Tuthmosis IV, as one learns from his Konosso inscription.

One came to say to his Majesty: "The Nubian descends from above Wawet; he hath planned revolt against Egypt. He gathers to himself all the barbarians and the revolters of other countries...his Majesty proceeded to overthrow the Nubian in Nubia...he found all [his] foes scattered in inaccessible valleys.... (ARE 2: §826–829)

There was also a military sally launched against the Nubians on behalf of Amenhotep III by his Viceroy of Nubia, Mermose, in response to a revolt in Ibhet, which is recorded in an inscription at Semna. In this instance, the Egyptians also conducted a body count of the dead enemy, represented in this text by the tally of [severed right] hands.

The might of Nebmare (= prenomen of Amenhotep III) took them in one day, in one hour, making a great slaughter.... List of the captivity which his majesty took in the land of Ibbet, the wretched. Living Nubians, 150 heads; Archers 110 heads; Nubians (female) 250 heads; Servants of the Nubians 55 heads; Their children 175 heads; total, 740 living heads; hands thereof 312; grand total 1,052.... (ARE 2: §853–854)

In terms of the Egyptian perception of these revolts, one must ask whether all the campaigns waged in Nubia by the pharaohs of Dynasty XVIII were directed at the same group or groups of Nubians. The territory is vast, remote, and inhospitable. Might these military operations have been conducted over the course of Dynasty XVIII in distinctly different fields of operation, separated perhaps by very great distances from one another, and against very different groups of Nubians?

Nubians bearing tribute in a register from the Tomb of Rekhmire. The Metropolitan Museum of Art (31.6.40).

**The Egyptian
Administration
of Nubia**

The unequivocal objective of all of these military campaigns was doubtless an infusion of wealth into the Egyptian economy derived from the riches of Nubia and Africa farther to the south. That the importation of that wealth was the motivation for these military campaigns may be inferred from the autobiography of Harmini, whose only title preserved on a stela on which this account is recorded is "scribe." Although no pharaoh is named, one assumes that Harmini served under an Egyptian pharaoh during the early part of Dynasty XVIII.

I passed many years as mayor of Hieraconpolis. I brought in its tribute to the Lord of the Two Lands; I was praised...I attained old age in Wawat.... I went north with its tribute for the king.... (ARE 2: §48)

These early campaigns compelled the ancient Egyptians to develop an administrative mechanism whereby they might maintain their control over the regions of Nubia and ensure the uninterrupted importation of Africa's luxury goods. To those ends, they developed an office, namely that of a viceroy of Nubia. Such administrators bear titles such as the King's-son of Kush, the Chief of the Land of the South, the Overseer of the Southern Lands. These administrators were chosen from among the favorite courtiers of pharaoh and were not military men, but men versed in the mechanisms of the royal bureaucracy. Their field of competence reinforces the observation that the military campaigns of Dynasty XVIII into Nubia were not ends in and of themselves but were, as indeed they were during the Middle Kingdom, a means of achieving mercantile superiority in the acquisition of Africa's luxury goods. That superiority was the charge that the King's-son of Kush was expected to execute. He was assisted in his duties by a military officer, the Chief of the Archers of Kush, who served as second in command, again suggesting that the military served at the pleasure of the chief civil administrator, namely the King's-son of Kush, and not the other way around. The bureaucracy also included two lieutenant generals, one for the northern province of Nubia, suggested to reach as far as the third cataract and encompassing what some scholars have identified as Wawat, and his counterpart for the southern province of Nubia, Kush proper, representing minimally the territory under the control of the future kings of the Napatan Period. This bicameral, or two-part, division of authority may have been patterned on the Egyptian vizerate, a system of dividing the administration of the country into two departments, one for Upper and the second for Lower Egypt. There was an Egyptian presence as far south as Gebel Barkal, "the holy mountain of the Kushites."

One of the earliest individuals entrusted with this position is Thure, who served initially under Tuthmosis I (about 1492–1479 B.C.E.) and continued in office into the reign of Tuthmosis III (about 1479–1425 B.C.E.). He records his investiture, which occurred during the reign of Tuthmosis I in his autobiography, engraved on the southern wall of the Egyptian temple of Semna during the reign of pharaoh Tuthmosis III

The King of Upper and Lower Egypt, Akkheperkera (= prenomen of Tuthmosis I)…he appointed me to be King's Son of [Kush]…. (ARE 2: §64)

In addition to his other duties, Thure was charged with observing the form of the royal name to be employed when taking oaths, as recorded in his pharaoh's coronation decree, preserved on two stelae originally erected in Nubia at Wadi Halfa and Kubban, respectively.

…Cause thou that the oath be established in the name of my Majesty…. (ARE 2: §58)

On the office of the investiture of the Viceroy of Kush, we have the auto-biographical account of Huy, from his Theban tomb, who served in that capacity under the boy king, Tutankhamon.

The overseer…he says, "This is the seal from Pharaoh…who assigns to thee [the territory] from Nekhen to Napata…. King's-son of Kush…[take] the seal of office, O king's-son of Kush…the office is assigned to the king's-son of Kush from Nekhen to Karoy…. He accounts Khenthennefer, included under his author-ity…King's-son of Kush, governor of the southern countries…bringing in all the tribute…the arrival in peace…the chief of Miam, good ruler. The chiefs of Wawat. The children of the chiefs of all countries…. The chiefs of Kush, they say: "Hail to thee, O King of Egypt…give us the breath which thou givest. Men live by thy love…. Arrival from Kush bearing this good tribute of all the choicest of the best of the southern countries…by the king's-son of Kush, Huy. (ARE 2: §1022–1038)

Included in the decoration of this tomb are depictions of Egyptian officials serving in Nubia, several accompanied by their titles, such as the deputy of Kush, the mayor of Soleb, and several officials and priests associated with the Egyptian fortresses in Nubia.

The ultimate responsibility of the Egyptian viceroy of Kush is clearly and succinctly stated in the autobiography of Nehi, Viceroy of Kush in his speos or rock cut grotto, at Ellesiyeh.

Bringing tribute of the southern countries, consisting of gold, ivory, and ebony, [by]…the king's-son, governor of the south countries (ARE 2: §652)

It is, therefore, to these products that one now turns.

THE WEALTH OF AFRICA

Ebony was an important product, its importation used for the erection of ebony shrines to a variety of Egyptian deities. One such ebony shrine is described in a dedicatory inscription carved three times on the outside of its left side-panel. The dating of this particular shrine is problematic, but it doubtless belongs to the period contemporary with the early Tuthmoside pharaohs.

...The Lord of the Two Lands...he made [it] as his monument for his father, Amun-Re, making for him an august shrine of ebony of the best of the highlands.... (ARE 2: §126)

But the Nubians also provided the Egyptians with slaves, as specified in this passage of a coronation text from the time of the joint-rule of pharaohs Hatshepsut and Tuthmosis III.

...I filled it with [captives] from the south...children [of the chiefs] of Khenthennefer.... (ARE 2: §162)

The most extensive accounts of the Nubian campaigns by any pharaoh of any dynasty are contained within *The Annals* of pharaoh Tuthmosis III. Found inscribed on the inner sanctum of the Temples of Karnak, this record of over 200 lines provides a wealth of information. The following are extracts of those passages dealing with Nubia.

[Seventh Campaign] Regnal Year 31...impost of Wawat
[Thirteenth Campaign] Regnal Year 38...impost of Kush and Wawat
[Fifteenth Campaign] Regnal Year 40...impost of Kush and Wawat
When his Majesty arrived in Egypt, the messengers of the Genebteyew came bearing their tribute, consisting of myrrh,...10 male Nubian attendants; 113 oxen [and]calves; 230 bulls; total, 343; besides vessels laden with ivory, ebony, skins of panther....
[List of the impost of Wawat]: 5...of Wawat; 31 oxen and calves; 61 bulls; total, 92; besides vessels laden with all things of this country; the harvest of Wawat, likewise.
[Impost of Wawat]...13 male [Nubian] slaves; total 20; 44 oxen and calves; 60 bulls; total 104; besides vessels laden with every good thing of this country; the harvest of this place likewise.
Impost of wretched Kush: gold, 300...deben; 60 Nubians; the son of the chief of Irem.... total, 64; oxen [95; calves,] 180, total, 275; beside [vessels] laden with ivory, ebony, and all products of this country; the harvest of Kush likewise.
The [impost] of Wawat; gold, 254 deben; 10 Nubian slaves, male and female;...oxen, and calves [besides vessels laden with] every good thing of [this country]
Impost of wretched Kush; gold, 70 deben, 1 kikdet; slaves male and female...oxen, calves,...[beside vessels laden] with ebony, ivory, all the good products of this country, together with the harvest of [Kush likewise].
[Impost of Wawat]...34 Nubian slaves, male and female; 94 oxen, calves, and bulls; besides ships laden with every good thing; the harvest of Wawat, [likewise].

Impost of wretched Kush: gold, 100 [... +] beden, 6 kidet; 36 Nubian slaves, male and female; 111 oxen, and calves; 185 bulls; total, 306 [*sic*], besides vessel laden with ivory, ebony, all the good products of this country, together with the harvest of this country.

Impost of Wawat: [gold] 2,844 [deben, ... kidet]; 16 Nubian slaves, male and female; 77 oxen and calves; besides [vessels] laden with every good product of this country.

[Impost of Wawat]: gold, 3,144 deben, 3 kidet; 35 oxen and calves; 79 bulls; total 114; besides vessels laden with ivory.... (ARE 2: §406–527)

Elsewhere in the Karnak Temples, Tuthmosis III lists additional products received from Nubia, which include

...necklaces, amulets, and pendants of real electrum brought to his Majesty from southern country as their yearly impost.... (ARE 2: §654)

In reviewing this primary evidence, one concludes that the Egyptian presence in Nubia did not extend much further south than the third cataract. Their control of the Nile River at that point mandated a periodic cleaning of older and the repeated digging of newer canals, in one instance their maintenance being entrusted to the fishermen of Elephantine Island. Countless vessels must have crashed against the rocks of the three cataracts, their hulls broken to pieces, their cargoes and crews lost, to judge by the recording of "counting the boats." Despite the repeated references to Egyptian military campaigns, the level of Nubian opposition, judging by the extensive inventories of Nubian imports found in *The Annals of Tuthmosis III* alone, appears to have been insufficient to thwart the Egyptians from their extraction of tribute from the Nubians and their economic exploitation of the riches of Africa. These luxury goods included ivory, African woods such as ebony, perfumes, skins of leopards, feathers and eggs of ostriches, an array of exotic beasts including simians of various species and giraffes, and human beings as slaves. Such displays of Africa's wealth are interestingly enough paralleled in accounts of some of the Ptolemaic rulers of Egypt, particularly Ptolemy II Philadelphus (284–246 B.C.E.) and in the histories of some of the Fatimid rulers of Egypt (969–1171 C.E.), particularly with regard to their similar display of many of the same African beasts.

Attractive as these luxury items were, nothing was of more immediate concern to the Egyptians than unrestricted and unlimited access to Nubian gold, which poured into Egypt in such quantities that a Western Asiatic kinglet during the reign of Akhenaten could state that gold was more plentiful in Egypt than grains of sand in a desert. But its extraction was physically demanding and the plight of its miners deplorable by modern standards.

The bald accounting records of those annals fail to convey a real impression of the conveyance of these resources. The Viceroy Wesersatet records in his speos at Qasr Ibrim that 1,000 porters alone were required just for the transport of ebony on one occasion and that 50 men were required to present chariots crafted of Nubian woods. The organizational effort was enormous, and already during the reign of Tuthmosis III there is evidence of a gigantic customs house at Napata in which goods were presumably inventoried for receipt from Nubia prior to their export into Egypt.

NUBIANS IN EGYPT AND IN NUBIA

In their descriptions, Egyptian primary sources give the Nubians expressive names, often derived from their physical appearance. From some of these accounts we learn of particularly Nubian coiffures, because they are called "pigtail wearers" and "fuzzy haired." Their garments caused them to be designated as "animal-skin-wearers." The characteristically Nubian penchant for scarification resulted in the appellation "scar bearers." And the descriptive, "the Nehesy-Nubians with burnt faces," seems to anticipate by a millennium Homer's Aithiopians, "the burnt faces."

After the quelling of a Nubian rebellion in Regnal Year 1 of Tuthmosis I, the surviving son of a massacred Nubian chieftain was taken to Egypt as a hostage. There, he was raised at court, instructed in Egyptian customs, and perhaps even in its language, religions, and political system. Acculturated to Egyptian norms, he would eventually be returned to Nubia to serve in the administration as a converted ally of pharaoh. Such youths were routinely to become pages of the harem, often schooled with peer groups of Egyptian boys of similar age, all bearing Egyptian, not Nubian, names. Such was the case of the Nubian prince Hekanefer of Miam, himself a page in the royal harem. His tomb, north of Toskka, is decorated with consummately crafted hieroglyphs.

His is not an exceptional case. Prince Djuhtyhotep in particular was buried in a tomb erected at Tehkhet not far from Debeira, which was decorated with beautiful paintings in the pure style of contemporary Egyptian tombs at Thebes. His brother, Amenemhet, was interred in a pyramid just across the river. It is difficult to gauge what the lives of these individuals were like, but it is clear from the presence of their tombs that these princes were advantaged members of society and belonged to a Nubian elite.

Most of their contemporaries, however, were certainly disadvantaged because all power resided in the hands of the Egyptian officials administering Nubia. Their number provided the Egyptians with a vast pool of labor, including slaves. A passage in the building inscription of Amenhotep III implies that Nubians were resettled in foreign lands that he conquered, but whether as slaves engaged in building projects there or not is moot.

I cause thee to seize the Tehenu-peoples [so that] there is no remnant of them. [They] are building this fortress in the name of my Majesty; surrounded with a great enclosure wall reaching to heaven, settled with children of the chiefs of the Nubian Troglodytes.... (ARE 2: §892)

The Annals of Tuthmosis III even refers to slaves taken from Punt.

Nubians depicted in the Tomb of Huy. The Metropolitan Museum of Art
(30.4.21).

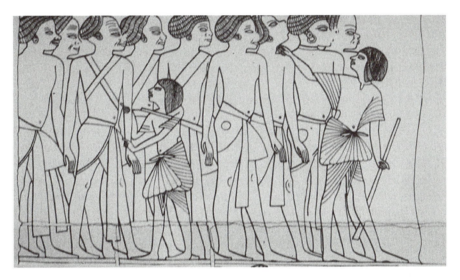

Nubians depicted in the Memphite Tomb of Horemheb. Courtesy of The Egypt
Exploration Society.

Marvels brought to his Majesty in the land of Punt.... 134 slaves, male and
female.... (ARE 2: §486)

The Egyptians realized the rigors of physical labor in Nubia, particularly the travail associated with the mining of gold. "If I lie, may my nose
and ears be cut off—or let me be sent to Kush!" Nubians served in other
capacities as well, including laborers of all kinds as well as soldiers and, in
the case of the Medjay, policemen. One can now profitably turn one's
attention to Egyptian depictions of the Nubians.

EGYPTIAN DEPICTIONS OF NUBIANS

The tomb of the boy-king, Tutankhamon, in the Valley of the Kings was filled with objects stereotypically representing Nubians as conquered foes of Egypt, for example, on his canes. Depicted with arms bound behind his back at the elbows, this Nubian's coiffure is arranged as a series of echeloned curls arranged in neat rows, his ears adorned with large hoopearrings. The use of Nubians for such motifs is long-lived in the New Kingdom and finds parallels in depicted heads of Nubians adorning statue bases and surrounds of royal boats and chariots. Two-dimensional representations of the pharaoh often depict him massacring handfuls of enemies, Black Africans noticeably among their number. Nubians are also shown led in chains before the Theban triad gods—Amun, Mut, and Khonsu. Their names are often strangely written in geographical lists as if to subdue them symbolically. On balance, there are perhaps statistically more surviving representations of Nubians as prisoners from the time of Tutankhamon than from any other single reign. This is due not only to the number of such motifs decorating numerous objects discovered in his own tomb, but also to the depictions of Nubians in tombs of officials who served in his administration, including both Huy and Horemheb. It is to these representations that we now turn.

Nubians are depicted in the Theban Tomb of Huy, that monarch's Viceroy of Nubia, particularly in two registers of a tribute scene. The nuances of their complexions are suggested by the use of different hues to depict skin tones. Some, for example, the kneeling figures to the right of the topmost register and the six figures to the far left, are coifed in variations of the hairstyle found on the Nubian cane from the Tomb of Tutankhamon. Their costumes vary, from the typically Egyptian consisting of gossamer linen garments, which are pleated, to Egyptian festive kilts. Some even wear Egyptian short-sleeved tunics tied at the neck. Occasionally these Egyptian garments are accessorized with bandoleers. In the group of six to the far left, five of whom are male prisoners whose taming stick, the *sheyba,* is attached to their wrists and necks, four wear loincloths of animal skins, but the fifth, standing at their head and doubtless intended to be their leader, wears the festive kilt of the Egyptian elite. The Nubians in the register beneath, all of whom are unfettered, sport a combination of Egyptian and Nubian style coiffures, but all are clothed in the fashionable, gossamer linen Egyptian, pleated garments. They bear their tribute in the form of circles of gold ingots on trays, luxury items in vessels, a giraffe, and a group of Nubia's justly famous cattle, their heads adorned with dummy heads of Nubians set between horns ending in human hands. Several individuals in both registers wear plumes in their hair.

Of particular note is the vignette in the center of the uppermost register, which depicts a Nubian princess dressed in the trendy Egyptian fashion of the day, complete with broad collar, and Egyptian wig, made of blonde hair, in an ox-drawn chariot driven by a charioteer. Whether the incongruity of arriving in such a conveyance at such a state occasion was meant as a slight to the amusement of the ancient Egyptians remains moot, but the unavoidable conclusion is that this particular princess has completely masked her Nubian ethnicity by utterly adopting foreign Egyptian style.

The process of acculturation evident in these depictions is also found in representations of Nubians in the Memphite Tomb of Horemhab, a contemporary of Huy. Of the two reliefs almost certainly from this tomb in Bologna, one depicts a presentation of Nubian captives. This worked block must be considered in conjunction with other depictions of Nubians still *in situ* in his tomb. Almost all of those individuals are represented wearing the Nubian wig and selectively hoop-earrings. All appear to be clothed in belted kilts on the order of those worn by the Egyptians themselves, some electing to wear a bandoleer over their bare chest. Some of these kilts include a so-called apron in the front with one end of the belt reaching to a point between the knee and ankle. The spotted decoration on these longer belts and bandoleers may indicate that they are crafted from skins of exotic animals, which is also the material from which at least one other kilt worn by a Nubian in these representations appears to have been made as well.

But the most significant aspect of these representations of Nubians resides in their scale relative to that of the Egyptians who serve as their guards. It has been long noted that the relative scale of objects depicted in Egyptian art cannot be taken as an index of the relative size of the same objects in real life. In Egyptian art, the size of one object relative to another in the same composition is an artistic index of importance: the larger an object is, the relatively more important its role within the scene. It is, therefore surprising and somewhat unusual to discover that the Nubians, in these scenes in the Memphite Tomb of Horemhab, are habitually depicted as being taller than their Egyptian guards, reversing one of the canonical indices of hierarchy in ancient Egyptian art. The reason for this reversal is self-serving and rooted in the vocabulary of propaganda. It would be of little consequence for a victorious general to make light of his foe, denigrating his prowess in battle or his physical strengths. To do so would diminish his own victory. If, on the other hand, the victorious general magnified the foe in any way, his ultimate victory would appear to be that much more impressive. The artists of the Memphite Tomb of Horemheb have reversed the canonical index of relative scale for exactly this purpose—to aggrandize the Egyptian domination of Nubia. The visual impact of these scenes is even more compelling when one realizes how relatively few in number and virtually unarmed, save for an occasional cudgel, these slender Egyptians are in the presence of the vastly superior numbers of powerfully built, taller Nubians. The message is clear. This artistic conceit appears to have been pioneered by the ancient Egyptians and recalls the lauding of the Gauls by Julius Caesar in his *De Bello Gallico*, praise of the enemy, which likewise magnifies their defeat at his hands.

EGYPTIAN TEMPLES

It is difficult to evaluate the lasting success of such campaigns. The fact that military operations against the Nubians were undertaken in virtually every successive reign of Dynasty XVIII may lead one to question their effectiveness. On the other hand, the Egyptians seem to have believed that they had indeed pacified the region, because many of the royal records preserve mention of several architectural projects, primarily in the form of temples, which the Egyptian pharaohs raised to their deities deep in Nubia. One such temple was erected at Soleb, south of the third cataract, by Amenhotep III. It is designed as a jubilee temple, ostensibly honoring the Egyptian state god, Amun-Re, himself a solar deity and a dominant religious figure in the heart of Nubia, where he is also venerated as a god and associated with the ram. But the temple is dedicated as well to the cult of the deified, but living, Amenhotep III.

The lengthy inscription that records his architectural activities here was carved on a stela erected in that pharaoh's mortuary temple in Western Thebes, where it was subsequently effaced by Akhenaten, but restored by Sety I of Dynasty XIX. In it he describes this temple with these words.

I made other monuments for Amun…I built for thee thy house of millions of years…Khammat [being the name of this temple], august in electrum.… it is finished with fine white sandstone; it is wrought with gold throughout; its floor is adorned with silver; all of its portals are of gold…I cause the chiefs of wretched Kush to turn to thee, bearing all their tribute on their backs.… (ARE 2: §890–891)

Clearly, the temple at Soleb, a universally acclaimed masterpiece of Egyptian architecture, could not have been constructed in a hostile environment. Its erection demanded an expenditure of financial resources and manpower over a given period of time.

Egyptian architecture, like so many other aspects of pharaonic culture, was symbolic and magically activated. In general, an ancient Egyptian temple can be considered a theme park in which the pharaoh (in theory as the chief priest of the land but in practice via the clerics who served as his surrogates) during the performance of his daily and annually recurring festivals, ritually reenacted the creation of the cosmos and the maintenance of cosmic order.

In order to make these religious concepts manifest for both the elite and the illiterate agrarian population in general, the Egyptian temple, erected in stone, was regarded as the primeval mound from which creation arose. As a result, a temple was entered by a gateway, termed a pylon, the two tall trapezoidal towers separated by an intervening negative space. This twin-towered design of the pylon was the mystical horizon from which and into which the sun rose and set, respectively, during its diurnal journey across the heavens. The pylon might be equipped with tall flagstaffs of cedar from which were suspended pennants. The fluttering movement of the pennants by the wind was regarded as a sign of a divine presence within the temple.

The ground plan of a typical temple was rectangular, longer than it was wide. This rectangle was composed in its simplest design as a series of alternately opened, or unroofed, and closed, or roofed, spaces, each becoming smaller in size as one proceeds from the entrance to the rear. In addition, the floor of each successive room or space rose while the height of the ceiling from the floor in those roofed spaces decreased. Passing through this space was a psychological experience, enabling the celebrants to shed gradually an awareness of this world in order to focus on the godhead resident in the inner sanctum, the smallest and darkest room found at the end of the rectangle. The proportionally decreasing space architecturally reinforced the hierarchy of the priesthood because only those of progressively higher status were permitted to make their way toward the inner sanctum, entrance into which was theoretically restricted only to the person of pharaoh.

The entire temple was surrounded by a circumvallation of mud brick. Erected in sections, these walls now exhibit a horizontally wavy pattern of their horizontal courses. Although prosaic commentators attribute this wave to the slumping of lower course of mud brick under the weight of the cumulative courses above them, the wave pattern was perhaps intentionally designed to reflect the ripples of the watery abyss from which the mound of creation appeared on the very first day of creation. The circumvallation also served to isolate the godhead from the profane.

The basic tenets of the ancient Egyptian creation myth posited the existence of a watery abyss in which the forces of creation were nascent. On the dawn of the first day, termed in Egyptian "the first occurrence," the first rays of the rising sun struck the watery abyss and in so doing caused a mound of earth to arise immediately. Some scholars regard this mythological description as connected with the natural phenomenon whereby the annual inundation of the Nile River could not cover the tops of ancient tells, the presence of which amid the waters of the river's flood may have contributed to the development of this myth. The polyvalent nature of ancient Egyptian religious beliefs was such that alternate explanations could be accommodated within its unitarian embrace of seemingly contradictory elements, which were always integrated into the system.

In the performance of rituals associated with celebrating the creation of the cosmos, one can well imagine pharaoh, or his surrogate, sequestered within the narrow confines of the dark inner sanctum. With the dawning of the sun, its rays would penetrate the inner sanctum, the architectural design of which included fenestration for just such purposes. The rays of the sun would metaphorically strike a cultus, either a statue, a shrine, or the like which, via a series of set ministrations, would become animated. It might then be carried in procession, moving into ever-increasingly larger spaces, because the line of march was toward the temple's entrance until it emerged from the pylon itself to continue on its processional way.

The stone from which the temple was formed became a metaphor for the matrix of the mound of creation. It stood, created, within a precinct surrounded by the wavy pattern of the circumvallation, a concrete metaphor of the risen primeval mound within the watery abyss.

In time, the Egyptians ascribed symbolic properties to stones, the red of granite and the brown of aged quartzite being possessed of solar associations. The outer walls of the temples, particularly the exterior wall of the pylon, were habitually decorated with military-themed scenes in which pharaoh, always triumphant, felled or presented captive prisoners to the deities of the temple. Such scenes validate the observation that Egypt was a theocracy, its pharaoh serving simultaneously as chief priest. These scenes emphasize the relationship of pharaoh with the deities because the enemy symbolized the forces of chaos, either real or imagined, which pharaoh was obliged to keep in check.

Scenes within the temple habitually involve those described in a Latin phrase as *do ut des*, expressing the reciprocal relationship enjoyed by pharaoh and the deities. The pharaoh gave articles of the real world—jewelry, incense, land, and the like—to the deities so that they might bestow upon pharaoh intangible desirables—happiness, a long life, a peaceful reign, and the like. These scenes were habitually brightly painted and, when they appeared on doorways, for instance, might be further enhanced with the addition of inlays of faience and other materials such as semiprecious stones and even clad in part with gold, silver, electrum, and/or copper or bronze. The purpose of such secondary materials in temple architecture was not decorative. These secondary materials symbolically represented the mineral and floral wealth of the earth. When so incorporated into the fabric of the temple as primeval mound, the temple was possessed of all the earth's natural resources, further reinforcing its symbolic value as a surrogate for the cosmos.

The nuances of such symbols were clearly understood by the Nubian elite during the course of the Egyptian New Kingdom. Their Egyptian-designed and decorated tombs reveal that they themselves had been thoroughly integrated into the fabric of ancient Egyptian life. All of these lessons were not lost on the Nubians of Dynasty XXV, who continued to erect temples designed in accordance with Egyptian architectural plans and imbued with these same cosmic, symbolic values. Statements by the Nubian pharaoh Taharqa claim that members of the Egyptian elite "from the whole land" together with "the wives of the princes of Lower Egypt" came to Nubia with the expressed purpose of both constructing Egyptian-style temples and instructing the Nubian elite on their attendant rituals and ceremonies. Such temples continued to be a feature of the material culture of the Nubians right through the Meroitic Period.

EGYPTIAN RELIGIOUS DOMINANCE IN NUBIA

All along the Nile River in Nubia, temples in Egyptian architectural orders decorated in accordance with Egyptian design tenets and inscribed in hieroglyphs dotted the landscape. These are found at sites such as Sesebi where the Theban triad was venerated, at Kawa where Akhenaten founded a Gem-pa-aten temple, at Dakka and at Tabo on the island of Argo where Tuthmosis III founded sanctuaries, at Faras where Hatshepsut dedicated a temple to Hathor, and within the former fortress of Buhen, where she erected a temple later usurped by Tuthmosis III, at Kalabsha, Qasr Ibrim, Semna East, Sai, Amada, Wadi es-Sebua, Kuban, Aniba, and at Sedeinga, in the vicinity of Soleb. All of these are indistinguishable from their Egyptian counterparts in the Nile Valley and Delta. The preponderance of so many monuments in so purely an Egyptian idiom is often cited to demonstrate the complete adoption by the Nubians of Egyptian norms during the course of Dynasty XVIII.

The Egyptians in Nubia, statistically less numerous than the Nubians themselves, included individuals in the administrative staff of the viceroy, other civil servants and priests (particularly needed to staff the ever-increasing number of Egyptian temples being erected in Nubia), officers and soldiers, and merchants. Their presence resulted in the administration of Nubia for the colonial glory and aggrandizement of Egypt. Egyptian norms prevailed in the economic and social structure of Nubia. The Egyptian language was the only written language. These advantaged members of society lived together in villages thought to be larger than those in which contemporary Nubians lived. These villages replaced earlier fortresses, although their name, menenou, "fortresses," was retained.

NEW PLACE NAMES FOR NUBIA

New place names for regions of Nubia entered into the Egyptian lexicon during Dynasty XVIII—Genebteyew, Ikayta, Khenthennofer, Nemyew, and Tintto-emu—but their specific locations are matters of dispute, partly because their mention is habitually in contexts devoid of other geographic specifics. On the rare occasion, such as in the passage dealing with the forts of Tuthmosis I in Nubia, where geographic specificity appears intended, the information is presented in such a seemingly incomprehensible (to a modern, at any rate) manner, that academic debate continues about its precise interpretation. To wit,

... his southern boundary is as far as the frontier of this land, [his] northern boundary as far as that inverted water which goes downstream in going upstream.... (ARE 2: §73)

This particular passage bristles with difficulties of interpretation because the phrase, "that inverted water which goes downstream in going upstream" is a typically Egyptian idiom for stretches of the Nile River that actually flow south, due to its oxbows, as they travel northward. In this context the phrase may very well apply to the long bend at the fourth cataract in the Dongola basin. Some have taken this passage as evidence that Egyptians may have pioneered the desert route to this region, which began at Korosko in Lower Nubia and in so doing avoided the bend in the River Nile in the Dongola reach and the barrier in the region of the fourth cataract. But this remains uncertain.

PUNT

It is, therefore, within this context of geographic nonspecificity that one must consider Punt and its location, which is attested in ancient Egyptian records as a trading objective perhaps as early as Dynasty IV, but certainly by the time of Dynasty V and VI of the Old Kingdom. The most extensive account of any Egyptian expedition to Punt is found in the Mortuary Temple of Queen Hatshepsut at Deir el-Bahari in Western Thebes. One's interpretation of these scenes and their accompanying inscriptions has been hampered by damage, particularly in the form of looting, which has continued to this present day. The famous vignette, depicting Eti, the Queen of Punt, is now safely installed within the collections of the Egyptian Museum in Cairo, its plaster cast taking its place in Thebes, after having been successively ripped from the wall and repeatedly returned.

Knowledge about Punt appears not to have been wide-spread,

No one trod the Myrrh-terraces, which the people knew not; it was heard of from mount to mouth by hearsay of the ancestors.... (ARE 2: §287)

but this general ignorance about its existence may be regarded as propaganda, aimed at enhancing Hatshepsut's reputation and magnifying the accomplishment achieved by the successful return of the expedition. The same sentiments are expressed, but in this instance by the Puntites themselves in the inscriptions dealing with pharaoh Horemheb's (about 1319–1292 B.C.E.) expedition to Punt.

Speech of the great chiefs of Punt: "Hail to thee, King of Egypt, Sun of the Nine Bows!...We knew not Egypt; our fathers had not trodden it. Give us the breath which thou givest. All lands are under thy feet." (ARE 3: §38)

In keeping with other Dynasty XVIII missions into Nubia, the nominal head of Queen Hatshepsut's is an administrator, not a military commander, whose name, Nehesi, is related to one of the Egyptian place names for Nubia, but few have recognized this apparent coincidence or speculated about its significance. Was Nehesi himself a Nubian, because his name means "the Southern (i.e., the African, the Nubian) one"?

Behold, it was commanded, as follows: "They shall give...to the hereditary prince, count, wearer of the royal seal, sole companion, chief treasurer, Nehesi, to dispatch the army [to] Punt.... (ARE 2: §290)

The mission traveled by sea, and in fact, the sea features prominently in the inscriptions describing Punt.

Sailing in the sea...journeying in peace to the Land of Punt...in order to bring for him (the god Amun) the marvels of every country.... (ARE 2: §253)

But another passage seems to suggest a more circuitous route.

But I will cause thy army to tread them, I have led them on water and on land, to explore the waters of inaccessible channels, and I have reached the Myrrh-terraces.... (ARE 2: §288)

The internal inconsistencies regarding the route(s) taken, evident in these inscriptions from Deir el-Bahari, are compounded by a seemingly different set of directional clues preserved in the Punt expedition of pharaoh Rameses III (about 1183–1151 B.C.E.) of Dynasty XX, preserved in *The Harris Papyrus*.

I hewed great galleys with barges before them, manned with numerous crews...They were laden with the products of Egypt without number...they were sent forth into the great sea of the inverted water, they arrived at the countries of Punt...The galleys and barges were laden with the products of God's-Land, consisting of all the strange marvels of their country.... They arrived safely at the highland of Coptos. (ARE 4: §407)

The phrase "the inverted water" is an Egyptian circumlocution for the Euphrates River, whose flow from North to South was considered upside down by ancient Egyptian standards, which regarded the flow of rivers from South to North as normative, the Nile River being the exemplar. The Euphrates River flows into the Persian Gulf, but there is no reason to seek the location of Punt in any location this far to the East. It would appear that the phrase "the great sea of the inverted water" is a generic reference to all bodies of saltwater east of Egypt. The Egyptian sense of geography would appear in this context at least not to have considered the Red Sea and the Persian Gulf as separate, but rather as being part and parcel of the Indian Ocean.

The justly famous scene of the landscape of Punt, on the other hand, does appear to depict its fluvial environment shown as a river teaming with wildlife. But the known stylization imposed on the designs of all Egyptian depictions renders them unreliable as textbook illustrations of the flora and fauna depicted. Attempting to identify each in Linnean terms is virtually impossible, but the cumulative impression of the variety of species depicted has led some to identify this location as an estuary, reinforced, perhaps, by the location of the Egyptian camp.

Pitching the tent of the king's messenger and his army in the myrrh-terraces of Punt on the side of the sea.... (ARE 2: §260)

The inhabitants of Punt are captioned as such, including the chief of Punt, Perehu, and his wife, Queen Eti. These depictions were originally accompanied by representations of their two sons and a daughter, now stolen and their whereabouts unknown, but clearly present in early archaeological drawings of the scenes.

[The arrival] of the king's-messenger in God's-Land...before the chiefs of Punt.... the coming of the chiefs of Punt, doing obeisance...(ARE 2: §255)

Reception of the tribute by the chief of Punt
The coming of the chief of Punt (ARE 2: §261)

The chief of Punt, Perehu
His wife, Eti
The ass which bears his wife (ARE 2: §258)

In keeping with the observation made earlier with regard to the inappropriateness of demanding a literal interpretation of ancient Egyptian visual representations, there is nothing to distinguish the depiction of Perehu, the king of Punt, or those of his children and subjects, from the representations of the ancient Egyptians in this suite of relief decoration. If these figures were taken out of context and deprived of their accompanying labels, one would be unable to determine that Puntites, rather than Egyptians, were their intended subjects. Furthermore, careful study of early, modern drawings of these same scenes reveals that the houses of these Puntites are not erected on pilings, but that the pilings are posts covered with wicker.

The only anomalously designed figure in this entire suite of decoration is Eti, the Queen of Punt, but here again the imperatives of the design tenets governing all ancient Egyptian art precludes a precise pathological identification of her physical condition. Eti represents Punt, the exotic and the foreign. Her depiction must be recognized as a manifestation of ideology, a visual means by which the images of Queen Hatshepsut that abound in numerous other vignettes in this suite are contrasted. Indeed, Queen Hatshepsut is depicted in a bland and idealizing style, but it is the style adopted here in this suite for the depictions of Peheru, his children, his subjects, and all of the Egyptians. To borrow an analogy from the West, it would appear that the Egyptians in these instances preferred to view the world as an extension of self in much the same way as Italian artists of the Renaissance chose to depict either Biblical or mythological subjects as their contemporaries in the prevailing fashion of their day.

The depiction of Eti and her use as a visual device to contrast that which is Puntite with that which is Egyptian finds its exact correspondences in the virtually contemporary Botanical Garden of the Akh-menu in the Temples of Karnak erected under Tuthmosis III. The visual information from the Punt Chapel in the Mortuary Temple of Queen Hatsepsut at Deir el-Bahari is, therefore, of little assistance in identifying the location of Punt.

On the other hand, these same inscriptions forge an undeniable link between Punt and Nubia. This linkage of these two regions is emphasized in the captions accompanying the inventories of the products received,

The loading of the ships very heavily with marvels of the country of Punt; all goodly fragrant woods of God's-Land, heaps of myrrh-resin, with fresh myrrh trees, with ebony and pure ivory, with green gold of Amu, with cinnamon wood, khesyt-wood, with ihmut-incense, sonter-incense, eye-cosmetic, with apes, monkeys, dogs, and with skins of the southern panther, with natives and their children.... (ARE 2: §265)

Presentation of the marvels of Punt, the treasures of God's-Land, together with the gifts of the countries of the South, with the impost of wretched Kush, the baskets of the Nubian-land.... (ARE 2: §271)

as well as in the captions and depictions of the chiefs who present their tribute to Queen Hatshepsut, represented in four rows

Sailing, arriving in peace, journeying to Thebes...
...the chiefs of Nemyew
...the chiefs of Irem
...[kissing] the earth...by the chiefs of Punt.... the Nubian Troglodytes of Khenthennofer.... (ARE 2: §268)

The two rows of Puntites are not captioned, and only the chiefs of Nemyew are specifically depicted as Nubians, whereas those of Irem, a ubiquitous Nubian place name in Dynasty XVIII texts, are not, affording yet another example of the hazards of any literal interpretation of Egyptian visual images.

Wherever the ultimate location of Punt may be, it appears to have been reached in one instance by sea, in other instances by land. Its products, with the exception of the site-specific myrrh, are those also found in Nubia. And repeatedly in other inscriptions of Dynasty XVIII regions of Nubia and Punt are mentioned in the same breath, suggesting a geographic linkage between the two, as here in an inscription from Soleb from the time of Amenhotep III.

When I turn my face to the south...I cause the chiefs of wretched Kush to turn to thee...when I turn my face to thee the countries of Punt bring all the pleasant sweet woods of their countries.... (ARE 2: §891)

Within the geographical and political sphere of the Egyptians of Dynasty XVIII, Punt came to represent the point of the southernmost extent of Egyptian penetration of Africa, as reported on an obelisk from the reign of Queen Hatshepsut.

My southern boundary is as far as the lands of Punt. (ARE 2: §321)

The Egyptian phrase *"ta netcher."* "the god's land," was often applied to Punt. A literal interpretation of the phrase suggesting that Egypt's deities were native to Punt misses the force of the Egyptian designation. The phrase "ta-netcher" is habitually employed in ancient Egyptian texts referring to those lands or regions of the world that, to the Egyptians at any rate, were governed neither by pharaoh nor by any other recognized individual. The region was under the hand of a deity. And whereas the Punt reliefs do depict and caption a king and queen, recent investigations have suggested that the region of Punt lay farther afield and that the Egyptian encounter with the Puntites occurred at a convenient entrepot, or center for the collection and distribution of goods, far removed from the actual location of the region called Punt in these texts.

NUBIAN ARCHITECTURE DURING THE NEW KINGDOM

The almost total acculturation of the Nubians during the New Kingdom to pharaonic cultural norms virtually masked markers of their own ethnicity beneath a thick Egyptian veneer. As a result the temples erected in the region conform to Egyptian norms because they were commissioned by Egyptian pharaohs. Tombs of elite Nubians were designed and decorated in keeping with Egyptian decorum and would otherwise be mistaken as sepulchers of Egyptian elite if it were not for information about the deceased found in the autobiographical inscriptions in hieroglyphs on their walls. One is reminded that some of these inscriptions contain Egyptian attempts to render proper nouns existing in the spoken Nubian language, which was not written at this time.

NUBIAN COSTUMES OF THE EGYPTIAN NEW KINGDOM

Many Nubian cultural expressions were subsumed by Egypt's enveloping influence during the course of the New Kingdom with the result that elite Nubians, both in their own homelands as well as in Egypt, were often depicted in visual ways that are virtually indistinguishable from those employed for the depiction of their elite Egyptian contemporaries. On the other hand, Egyptian craftsmen of the period continued to depict Nubians in their traditional dress in both two-dimensional representations in tombs and temples as well as in the minor arts.

Before discussing such representations in detail, a few words must be addressed to ancient Egyptian pictorial conventions, particularly in two-dimensional depictions. The Egyptian craftsmen habitually rotated planes to provide their elite audiences with a comprehensible visual program. The most common of these rotated planes are encountered in depictions of the human figure. Here, for example, the human face is shown in profile, but the eye, and only one eye, of the head, is designed frontally; the torso is likewise depicted in front view with the breast, and generally only one breast appears in profile, which is also the view adopted for the depiction of the legs and feet. All of the fingers of both hands as well as all ten toes of the feet are normally shown in ways that defy modern anatomical explanation. Such visual conventions should caution all from attempting to explain ancient Egyptian art as an expression of reality. Egyptian art is not Western art, and one cannot look at a two-dimensional scene or vignette and explain the depiction as if it were designed in conformity with Western visual tenets. Furthermore, Egyptian art, created by and for the elite as a canonical enterprise, was symbolic, particularly with regard to palette. To argue, therefore, that certain depicted individuals are Nubians on the basis of the color used—blacks, browns, or any variations of these hues—is specious because women were habitually painted yellow indicative not of their ethnicity as Asians but rather of their status within sequestered, indoor environments.

Additionally, one must recognize that Egypt and Nubia were traditionally adversaries, and that depictions of Nubians in Egyptian art of the period may verge on caricature, because the Egyptians classified the Nubians among the Nine Bows, or their traditional foreign foes. As a result, each of these Nine were represented by an extremely stereotyped image, emphasizing almost to the point of caricature certain features that modern sensibilities might term racist.

These depictions must be regarded in the context of contemporary Egyptian designations of the Nubians. Some of these descriptives refer to their costume, others to generalized, stereotypical physical characteristics. These include "the pig tail wearers," "the scar bearers," "the animal skin wearers," "the Nehesiu with burnt faces," and "the fuzzy haired."

Several registers, or horizontal bands of figural decoration, in the Tomb of Huy, Viceroy of Nubia under the boy-king Tutankhamon, are again instructive. All depicted Nubians wear earrings, a unisex Nubian practice adopted by the Egyptians of the New Kingdom, and have a single feather in their hair. Behind are two women, wearing only long skirts of alternating stripes of leather, holding by the hand naked children and carrying infants on their backs in papoose-like conveyances. The combination of native and Egyptian dress and the appearance of shackled and unfettered Nubians suggests the ambivalence of the period. Nubians might select either habit, and the Egyptians might simultaneously be at peace with one Nubian tribe and at war with a second.

The one lasting contribution of the Nubians of the period to Egyptian fashion was the introduction of earrings. Contemporary with the C-Group culture were the Pan Grave Nubians whose members, during the course of the Egyptian New Kingdom, served as policemen in Egypt. Their practice of wearing earrings was soon adopted by the Egyptians so that during the course of Dynasty XVIII the wearing of earrings was a unisex fashion statement. Many of these were the shape of large, hooped rings inserted through pierced lobes.

The Nubians of the period in Egyptian representations are depicted with a limited number of coiffures. Chief among these is the so-called Nubian wig, often worn by the Egyptians themselves. The wig is characterized by pointed ends that fall toward the neck, often to the level of the collar bones. The strands of hair are arranged in a bipartite fashion. Those over the crown of the head and down the back are combed in vertical, regular rows. Those from the crown to the forehead and over the ears are arranged as a series of short locks arranged in rows that follow the contour of the skull. For reasons unknown, this was the fashionable coiffure during the reign of pharaoh Akhenaten for both sexes, elite and nonelite alike. Nubians are themselves depicted in such a wig, generally without indications of the bipartite arrangement of the locks of hair. Equally popular was a round, valanced coiffure consisting of small, tight curls arranged in ever larger rows, diagonally across the head from the crown to the level of the forehead and ears. This coiffure may be stylized in some representations so that it appears as a series of concentric, undulating lines over the skull. On occasion, Nubians are depicted with an escheloned coiffure that stands out, away from the head, and is designed in a way that recalls the cap of a mushroom. Very small, tight curls arranged in horizontal rows that conform to the contours of the head as if the individual were wearing a swimming cap represents yet another coiffure widely depicted during this time.

Of particular note is the depiction of Nubians in the Memphite Tomb of Horemheb, commander-in-chief of the Egyptian armies during the reign of Tutankhamon. Here some vignettes depict Nubian males wearing the same type of loincloth with its belt falling between the legs as worn by the elite archers from Assuit. These individuals may wear bracelets and large hoop earrings and wear their hair arranged in the round, echeloned coiffure, a variant of which, perhaps as a result of patterned baldness, is depicted far back on the skull, the rows of curls virtually vertical. In vignettes where the Nubians are either being led or presented to the general, they are taller in stature than their Egyptian escorts. This is significant, because the tenets of ancient Egyptian art allow for the more important figure in a scene to be taller in scale, regardless of the proportional relationship in nature. The reversal of this conceit, which renders the Nubian foe larger than his Egyptian captor, is significant and may not be based on reality.

It is visual, artistic propaganda suggesting that although the Nubian is larger, the smaller Egyptian was nevertheless able to prevail in battle over him. The Egyptian victory is enhanced by imbuing the foe with proportional advantage. Because of the artistic conventions, it is difficult to determine whether scarification, a Nubian practice by which the cheeks of the face were intentionally scarred, was practiced during the New Kingdom. Although it is difficult to distinguish between the conventions for skin folds and scars in Egyptian depictions, there do not appear to be any unequivocal depictions of Nubian scarification from the period. There is also no contemporary evidence for the cicatrix encountered in the one mummy of Middle Kingdom date.

THE DIET OF THE NUBIANS OF THE EGYPTIAN NEW KINGDOM

Although the Nubians must have maintained their dietary traditions and methods of preparing their foods, the apparent virtual assimilation of almost every facet of Egyptian culture by the Nubians in their homeland during the course of the New Kingdom suggests that they must have adopted or modified their diet to accommodate newly acquired Egyptian tastes. Because bread and beer were the staples of the ancient Egyptian diet, the Nubians, who had been importing these Egyptian beverages for quite some time, must have learned the recipes. Egyptian beer was made by fermenting bread baked from barley. In addition to barley, the Egyptians cultivated emmer; wheat was only cultivated on a large scale during the Ptolemaic Period, when it became the chief crop of the land. This was later imported in such quantities to Rome that Egypt became known as "the bread basket of the ancient world."

The vegetable oils that the Nubians once imported into Egypt came from a variety of sources, such as the seeds of lettuce, the castor-oil plant, the flax plant (for linseed oil) the radish, saffron, and sesame. Some of these were surely cultivated by the Nubians of the New Kingdom for their own use. The olive tree was cultivated successfully in Egypt only during the Ptolemaic Period when the crop was introduced on a large scale by the Ptolemies.

The Egyptians also raised a number of fowl, including ducks and geese, the latter force-fed, if one can trust the vignettes on walls of Egyptian elite tombs. The chicken does not appear to have been introduced until very late, but the pig gained wider currency earlier in time. One can suggest that the Nubian palette was introduced to these new food sources as well, perhaps with their accompanying Egyptian recipes.

8

Nubia during the Ramesside Period of the Egyptian Kingdom: Dynasty XIX and Dynasty XX

MILITARY CAMPAIGNS

The reign of Horemheb (about 1319–1292 B.C.E.), the last pharaoh of Dynasty XVIII, provides a convenient starting point for the discussion of the relationships between Egypt and Nubia in the Ramesside Period. As one learns from the previous discussions of his monuments, Horemheb was heavily involved in campaigns in Nubia. Upon becoming pharaoh of Egypt, he made fleeting reference to those events in his *Coronation Inscription*.

Behold, he [i.e., Horemheb] administered the Two Lands during a period of many years.... there came to him the chiefs of the Nine Bows, South as well as North (ARE 3: §26)

His account continues by mentioning his restoration of sanctuaries and their statues.

His Majesty sailed downstream...he organized this land.... he restored the temples [from] the pools of the marshes to Nubia...he shaped all their images...he fashioned 100 images with all [their] bodies correct and with all splendid costly stones...all the vessels of the temples were wrought of silver and gold.... (ARE 3: §31)

These architectural projects were doubtless inaugurated after a series of military sallies into Nubia, but the inscriptions in which these military activities are recorded are vague in the extreme, as these two examples from Gebel el-Silsileh in Upper Egypt reveal.

The Tomb of Penne. Courtesy of the Oriental Institute of the University of Chicago.

...he triumphs over the princes of every country. His bow is in his hand... [he] carries away the princes of wretched Kush.... [he] came from the land of Kush, with the captives which his sword had made....

... Hail to thee, King of Egypt...thy name is great in the land of Kush, thy battle cry is in their abodes.... (ARE 3: §42 and 44, respectively)

Like other pharaohs before and after, he likewise launched an expedition to Punt,

Bringing the tribute...being the tribute of Punt...Thou hast set their chiefs in tumult...by thy victorious might...bearing tribute upon their backs.... (ARE 3: §39)

but this account also lacks specificity.

The lack of significant detail in these accounts also characterizes the Nubian inscriptions of Egypt's Ramesside pharaohs of Dynasty XIX (about 1292–1185 B.C.E.) and Dynasty XX (about 1186–1069 B.C.E.). So, for example, Rameses I (about 1292–1290 B.C.E.), Horemheb's vizier who later became the founding pharaoh of Dynasty XIX, may have undertaken one military action against Nubia, but the theater of the campaign and its date are impossible to adduce with certainty from the evidence currently available. The meager data are contained in a series of stelae erected at Wadi Halfa, which may very well have been the location of the action described. Mention of this sally is perhaps implied in the second stelae of his son and successor Sety I (about 1290–1278 B.C.E.) at Wadi Halfa.

His Majesty…Menpehtire (the prenomen of Rameses I)…commanded to establish divine offerings for his father, [the god] Min-Amun in his temple, residing in Buhen…. (ARE 3: §77)

Sety I ordered at least one campaign, perhaps in his Regnal Year 8, against Nubia, judging from the slight evidence provided by data from Amara West and Sai. Its objective appears to have been the quelling of a revolt in Irem, which some suggest occurred in the vicinity of the fifth cataract, and the capture of six wells.

Other mentions of this campaign are equally laconic and of virtually no historical value, as demonstrated by the brevity and banal content of this record found at Karnak.

Utterance of Amun-re: I set thy terror…the Nubian Troglodytes are slain beneath thy feet. I bring to thee the chiefs of the southern counties, that they may make thee to receive the tribute, being every good product of their countries…. (ARE 3: §116)

The same brevity and banal content likewise characterize the following inscription, accompanying a relief in which Sety I is depicted slaying Nubians, from the temple Redesiyeh, five miles from Edfu in Upper Egypt.

Utterance of Amon: "Take to thyself the sword…in order to overthrow the chiefs of wretched Kush; in order to cut off their heads. Thy terror enters into their bodies…." (ARE 3: §164)

GOLD AND WELLS

The principal objective of such military action was to ensure the continuous importation into Egypt of the products of Nubia, but particularly of gold, which the Egyptian pharaohs of the Ramesside Period so specifically coveted. Sety I conducted a personal inspection of one such region,

On this day…as his Majesty inspected the hill-country as far as the region of the mountains…to see the mines from which the electrum is brought….

and exhorted his successors to maintain its control.

As for any king who shall be after me…may they overthrow…Nubia. (ARE 3: §170 and 180, respectively)

These forays launched to maintain Egyptian control over the rich gold-mining regions of Nubia were accompanied by grave concerns about wells, which received particular attention in these Ramesside inscriptions associated with gold mines and their activities. Pharaoh Sety I does not hesitate from reporting about one of his failed attempts to dig a well in association with his efforts to exploit the gold resources of the Wadi el-Alliqi.

His son and successor, Rameses II (about 1279–1213 B.C.E.), was equally preoccupied with wells in the gold-mining regions, as reiterated in passages from his Kubban stela, first here

Now when his Majesty was in Memphis…devising plans for digging wells on a road lacking in water, after hearing said that there was much gold in the country of Akita, whereas the road thereof was very lacking in water…. (ARE 3: §286)

and again later

…I will open a well there…. (ARE 3: §290)

The end result of these efforts was the reestablishment of an Egyptian presence on the Red Sea and in the gold-mining region of Gebel Zebara.

ARCHITECTURAL PROGRAMS

In keeping with the pattern established during Dynasty XVIII, these mercantile and military expeditions of the Ramesside Period were followed by architectural projects primarily in the form of temple building, references to forts being virtually absent. Sety I did erect a temple at Akasha and may have also begun the great temple at Abu Simbel. These construction activities were maintained through endowments, which often included Nubian slaves, as related in the second of his stelae erected at Wadi Halfa.

…[His Majesty commanded] to found [divine offerings for this father [the god] Min-Amun residing at Buhen…his storehouse was filled with male and female slaves from the captivity of his Majesty…. (ARE 3: §159)

As fate would have it, one is better informed about that pharaoh's building activities in Nubia from inscriptions in Egypt. At Abydos in Middle Egypt one learns about that pharaoh's architectural activity in Nubian Nauri.

The son and successor of Sety I, the long-lived Rameses II, was preoccupied throughout his reign with resolving conflicts in the Syria-Palestine region in territories of the ancient Near East, which had traditionally been under Egypt's influence, if not under her direct control. Those preoccupations centered around hostilities with the Hittites, which were in the end amicably resolved when the two warring parties signed a treaty, described as the world's first mutual, nonaggression pact. His campaigns earned him a reputation as the period's most seasoned warrior–pharaoh, and his unusually long reign afforded him ample opportunity either to build anew or usurp as his own earlier monuments on all of which he inscribed reports of his foreign exploits.

Of those architectural activities the Temples at Abu Simbel deserve special attention. Whether or not they were initially planned by Sety I is moot, insofar as all of their inscriptions seem to refer exclusively to Rameses II and to his chief queen, Nofertari. Both of these temples were erected, as were all of the Nubian sanctuaries of Rameses II with the sole exception of the Temple of Derr, on the west bank of the Nile River, Abu Simbel being located approximately midway between the first and second cataracts.

Both of these temples were cut into the living rock, or the mountain itself, but were designed as if they were free-standing structures. Imagine, for the sake of clarity, that one erected a typically free-standing Egyptian temple and then forced it into a mountain until its façade was flush with the mountain's slope. The impetus for erecting such a speos, or sanctuary cut into the living rock, has recently been associated with the cult of the god Nun. Briefly, Nun symbolized the watery abyss that existed from time immemorial and from which the primeval mound of creation arose. Whenever the Egyptians dug for water, as in the case, perhaps, of the wells associated with New Kingdom gold-mining activities, the operations could be characterized as searches for Nun. One must stress, however, that the inscriptions within the temples of Abu Simbel neither mention Nun by name nor make any allusion or reference to this deity. Furthermore, save for the fact that Abu Simbel was erected close to the water's edge, there are no cultic associations here with the watery abyss of Nun. The Great Temple was nominally dedicated to Horakhte, a hypostasis, or alternate manifestation, of the sun god.

Rameses II; he made [it] as his monument for his father, [the god] Horakhte, the great god, lord of Nubia. (ARE 3: §499)

In point of fact, the temples of Abu Simbel function in accordance with Egyptian temples in general as a pair, which rely on the interaction of the male and female principles of creation to achieve their cultic purpose. This model was adapted earlier by the Egyptians in Nubia for the cultic linking of the temple of Soleb, associated with Amenhotep III, and that at Sedeinga, associated with his chief queen, Tiye. In like manner, the Southern, or Great, Temple, dedicated to Rameses II deified associates him with the sun. The Northern, or Lesser, Temple is dedicated to Nofertari, his chief queen. The inscriptions of both temples clearly state that Rameses II rises daily as a manifestation of the sun god only as a direct result of the female principle, the ministrations of which are in the hands of Nofertari, characterized as "The one who causes the sun to shine." Because the religious conceit of pharaoh as sun god is a commonplace in Egyptian royal iconography, there is no reason to seek an astronomical basis for the erection of the Temples at Abu Simbel. The claims that the inner sanctum of the Great Temple are illuminated by rays of the sun on the solstices are exaggerations, and there is no hard and fast evidence to link either the birth date or coronation date of Rameses II with these solar occurrences because the ancient Egyptians habitually did not commemorate such milestone events. One simply does not know when Rameses II was born or when he was crowned pharaoh.

In addition to its religious function, Abu Simbel also served as a visual reminder of Egypt's might, the objective of which was to instill awe and perhaps even fear in the hearts of the Nubians who happened to chance upon these monuments. The intended effect is still experienced by visitors to the site today, who are completely overwhelmed by the visual impact of the Great Temple, which seems to appear suddenly and majestically as one walks down the desert path, working one's way to the left. The initial confrontation with the four seated colossal effigies of Rameses II on the façade is impressive, and they seem to grow larger and larger in size as one comes closer and closer to the structure. The same effect was doubtless experienced by ancient visitors as well, particularly those such as the Nubians traveling north on the Nile River, unaware of what lay ahead round its bend in this stretch.

The enormity of undertaking the construction of these two temples may be profitably gauged by considering the dimensions of the Great Temple, the pylon of which is 35 meters wide and 30 meters in height. The distance from this façade to the rear wall of the inner sanctum is 63 meters. It took modern architects, engineers, and workmen five years to dismantle and re-erect these temples at a cost of $36,000,000 U.S. dollars. And yet the temples at Abu Simbel articulate neither the foreign policy toward nor the campaign(s) waged by Rameses II against the Nubians, despite the fact that they are depicted larger than life as bound prisoners on the dais of the southern colossus and are occasionally smitten by pharaoh in other vignettes within.

THE NUBIAN ORIGIN OF THE SPEOS OR ROCK CUT SANCTUARY

One is ill informed about the specific religious beliefs of the ancient Nubians in the periods anterior to the Egyptian New Kingdom because of the lack of written records. Nevertheless a reassessment of monuments of later periods may shed some light on these early religious beliefs. The objective of the following paragraphs is, therefore, to argue that the ancient Nubians regarded living rock as an animate matrix within which a numen, or a deity believed to inhabit a particular object, resided.

The use of a complex of niches in the living rock together with a cave at Sayala, a Nubian site just north of Abu Simbel on the west bank of the Nile River, can be dated to the period of the Nubian A-Group culture on the basis of material excavated by the Austrian mission. During that period, the natural cave itself was modified with the addition of rudimentary masonry, the stones simply piled one on top of another without recourse to mortar to create a more prominent entrance. The ceiling of the cave and its walls were painted. The architectural and painted embellishments to this cave suggest that it was associated with ritual and that it was not simply a temporary shelter for nomads or hunters. The fact that this cave continued in use into the Roman Imperial Period further supports its function as a cult center. The nature of the godhead worshipped in the cave at Sayala has, however, not been identified, but the fact that the Nubians regarded its presence as existing within the living rock is significant.

THE NUMEN, OR INHERENT DIVINE POWER, IN THE MATRIX OF THE ROCK

The evidence provided by the cave at Sayala for the existence of a numen within the living rock gains confirmation from a raw, unworked piece of green feldspar in the collections of The Brooklyn Museum, which is inscribed with the name of the Nubian pharaoh Taharqa. This rock was purposefully shackled with a metal wire cord provided with a series of knots crafted in wax, a known magical material. Minute traces of gold leaf can still be seen adhering to the wax knots, suggesting that the object functioned as a deluxe amulet. The use of knots as restraints in magical praxis is well attested, and Taharqa's predilection for this particular stone is documented by the vast quantities of feldspar chips that litter the ground for hundreds of yards around a structure, identified as his storehouse, at the Nubian site of Sanam.

A second piece of rarer, blue feldspar in the same collection but without the knotted wire is inscribed for Psamtik. Whether this served the same function or was merely inventoried stock naming its owner is unclear, particularly because some of its surfaces had been purposefully cut. On the other hand, a third example in the form of an enormous chunk of unworked turquoise was engraved with an image of the ithyphallic Amun-Min and set into a gold armlet inscribed for Herihor, who eventually became the last pharaoh of Dynasty XX. Amun-Min was a creator deity within the Egyptian pantheon, and the color green as well as turquoise itself were imbued with fecund properties by the ancients.

It would appear from these examples that the ancient Nubians regarded unworked lumps of stone as talismans, within the matrix of which was resident a numen. The practice seems to have been extended to other materials, as the use of a natural nugget of gold, which served as a pendant, found at Gebel Barkal and now in Khartoum, suggests.

LATER MILITARY CAMPAIGNS

Despite the visual depictions of the Nubian military campaigns of Rameses II in the relief decoration and their accompanying inscriptions on his temples erected in the region, the data reported in the inscriptions is contained in such a nonspecific way so as to be virtually meaningless to a modern scholar attempting to determine theaters of operation, the peoples involved, or even the dates of the conflicts. Furthermore, these references to Nubia are often so intermingled with data about his campaigns elsewhere that it is difficult for a modern historian to distill data relevant for an understanding of Nubia from the opaque mixture of such events in different parts of the Egyptian world. At Abu Simbel, for example, one sees a vignette in relief of fallen Libyans, yet its accompanying inscription refers to the Nubians.

The Good God...crushing the countries...bringing the Nubians to the land of the north, the Asiatics to the land of Nubia.... (ARE 3: §457)

Furthermore, a cursory survey of this vast corpus of this material reveals that the minutiae that so characterizes his commemoration of the northern campaigns—here one takes the account of the Battle of Kadesh against the Hittites as the exemplar—is at variance with the scant reports about events connected with his southern campaigns against the Nubians. This is an unusual contrast, particularly because the enmity that the Egyptians may have felt toward the Nubians in this period seems to be reflected in the observation that the adjective "wretched/vile," generally appearing as a descriptive for the toponym Kush, is in at least one instance incorporated into the viceroy's title, as inscribed on his Kubban stela.

"As for the country of Akita, this is said concerning it," said the king's-son of wretched Kush.... (ARE 3: §289)

These accounts of his Nubian campaigns appear as perfunctory repetitions of hackneyed platitudes, as these two examples from Abu Simbel clearly demonstrate.

Good god...who smites the south...he causes the Nubians to say: "Away! His is like a flame, when it comes forth, and there is no water to quench it..." (ARE 3: §451)

The bringing of the tribute...after his arrival from the country of Kush, overthrowing the rebellious countries...the wretched chiefs of Kush, whom his Majesty brought from his victories in the country of Kush, in order to fill the storehouse of...Amun-re.... (ARE 3: §453)

The same obtains for the report inscribed on his granite statue at the pylon of the Luxor Temple, as these two excerpts reveal,

[The extent of his power extends to]...the southern countries of the Land of the Nubian as far as the marsh lands, as far as the limits of darkness, even to the four pillars of heaven.... (ARE 3: §480)

with a myriad number of civil administrators and military commanders

...coming with bowed head, bearing tribute of the impost of Nubia, every product of Asiatic countries.... (ARE 3: §484)

The data is no different in his stela at Aswan, regarded by many as a bombastic paean in celebration of all of his victories

...his battle cry is mighty [in] the land of Nubia.... (ARE 3: §479)

or in the banal character of a report in his temple at Abydos.

...His fame is mighty in...the land of the Nubia, with valor, slaying the Troglodytes of wretched Kush in the victories of his mighty sword.... (ARE 3: §490)

In those instances in which the data appear to be specific, such as found in a report dated to Regnal Year 44, Rameses II seems to have employed captives from his northern campaigns against the Tjemhu as construction workers on his temple erected on the site of an earlier one at Wadi es-Sebua in Nubia. A similar mention at Abu Simbel

...His might is in all lands; bringing for him multitudes of workmen from the captivity of his sword.... Afterwards he gave orders to the king's butler, Rameses-eshahab, to equip the land of Kush anew in the great name of his Majesty.... (ARE 3: §498)

would indicate that such slave labor was not uncommon during his reign. Such references doubtless support the contentious suggestion that Rameses II is to be considered the pharaoh of *The Exodus.*

When the data are specific, such as at Amara West, and to a lesser degree in his Temple at Abydos, one cannot be certain whether the information is historically accurate or appropriated from earlier sources. In this particular instance, the enumeration of 7,000 Nubian captives is identical to the Old Kingdom account, so that one suspects the earlier was employed as the model and simply copied. Nevertheless, it appears that Amara West served as one of the provincial capitals of Rameses II, and may have been renamed "Rameses-the-Town."

The real differences, in my view, between the Nubian and Asiatic campaigns of Rameses II can be inferred by examining the relief decoration of the entrance hall of another of his Nubian temples, that of Beit el-Wali, south of Aswan. This structure is another speos but on a less grand scale than the Abu Simbel temples. In keeping with ancient Egyptian design tenets of orientation, the Asiatic campaigns are depicted on the north whereas the Nubian campaigns are depicted on the south wall. The date of the Nubian action is not specified, but must have occurred early in the reign because Amenemopet, who is depicted and captioned,

King's son of Kush, Amenemopet, the son of Paser.... (ARE 3: §477)

served in this capacity early on.

In the vignettes of the north wall of the entrance corridor, five sequential vignettes depict (1) a train of bound Asiatics, (2) the king, battle ax resting on his shoulder holding another two Asiatics by the hair and standing atop other bound, prone Asiatics, (3) the king storming a citadel about to smite an Asiatic held by the hair, (4) the king in his chariot subduing a multitude of Asiatics shown in typical cavalier perspective, and (5) the king smiting with a scimitar-shaped weapon a single Asiatic, again held by the hair. These vignettes are clearly of a bellicose and bloody nature, doubtless reflecting the historical realities of such campaigns in the north.

These scenes are in contrast to the vignettes on the south wall depicting an incursion against the Nubians. In my view, these vignettes deserve an extended discussion of their own in another forum because they seem to form part of a rarely encountered continuous narrative. The wall is divided vertically into two episodes. The eastern half of the south wall depicts Rameses II in a chariot, loosing an arrow against a multitude of fleeing Nubians, again shown in cavalier perspective. And whereas it is true that some of these hapless foes are fallen, none are directly slain by pharaoh nor appear bound to his chariot. The inscription accompanying this vignette is laconic in the extreme. Over pharaoh's chariot one finds the same commingling of events encountered elsewhere in the Nubian inscriptions of Rameses II.

...powerful of horns, [smiting] the Southerners [and crushing the Northerners].... (BeWTR 11)

The Nubians at the head of the host, to the left-most side of the vignette, appear to have been able to flee into a heavily foliated environment, carrying their wounded. Beyond that appears to be the location of Nubian settlement or village toward which a child, to judge by the coiffure, runs while announcing the events to a woman engaged in cooking as she kneels at her pot. She appears to be saying:

...We have not yet known (such) raging of the Ruler.... (BeWTR 11)

The western half of the south wall is divided into two registers. The upper depicts Nubians bearing tribute in the form of an ox, a horned antelope (?), and a lion. They are preceded by a display of typically Nubian and African luxury goods. The lower register likewise depicts tribute bearing Nubians, including women with children carried in slings, and an array of beasts both wild and domesticated. This register also contains two groups, each of a single, bound Nubian and his Egyptian captor, the Nubians just slightly taller in stature. The visual impact of these vignettes is less bellicose and less bloody than any of the vignettes depicting the Asiatic theater of war in this temple.

On balance, then, it would appear that the evidence from Dynasty XIX through the reign of Rameses II is consistent with the view presented earlier. Namely, a military campaign of a certain dimension and perhaps punitive in nature, but certainly not of the size and scope undertaken in the Asiatic campaigns, was launched against the Nubians in order to secure the importation into Egypt of luxury products. The objective was not to slay and subjugate the Nubians, because they appear to bear their tribute in the two registers of the south wall at Beit el-Wali voluntarily and without military escorts.

This apparent wrist-slapping policy adopted by Rameses II toward the Nubians is horrifically reversed by his thirteenth son and successor, Merenptah (about 1213–1203 B.C.E.). His stela from Amada, perhaps still the provincial capital of Nubia during his reign, describes an uprising that is quelled savagely by the Egyptians. Prisoners were burned alive, their hands and ears having been cut off. These atrocities accompany this, the last Nubian revolt recorded to date for the New Kingdom.

THE WANING OF EGYPTIAN INFLUENCE IN NUBIA

The events subsequent to Merneptah's quelling of this revolt are unclear. Temples ceased to be constructed, and stelae are no longer raised, but viceroys of Kush are still attested, in graffiti. During the reign of Siptah (about 1194–1185 B.C.E.), apparently in his very first year as pharaoh, one Sety was appointed to that post and was conducted to his administrative seat by Neferhor.

[Regnal] Year 1 of.... Siptah...may he grant life...to...Neferhor...when he came with rewards for the officials of Nubia and to bring the king's son of Kust, Seti, on his first expedition. (ARE 3: §643)

African tribute apparently was still being imported into Egypt,

[Regnal] Year 3 under the Majesty of King Siptah...the fan-bearer...Piyay come to receive the tribute of the land of Kush.... (ARE 3: §644)

but, thereafter, the records cease, implying that the tribute did as well.

Some degree of normality appears to have occurred during the reign of Rameses III (about 1183–1151 B.C.E.) of Dynasty XX insofar as Nubian and

Egyptian relations were concerned, but it is another matter to define the nature of his glorified Nubian victories. The data derive from two sources, the first of which are contained in the relief decoration and its accompanying monumental inscriptions from Medinet Habu, the best-preserved pharaonic building found in Egypt today, which served as the mortuary temple of Rameses III in Western Thebes. Although these campaigns are visually represented, virtually no vignette is accompanied by an inscription or caption. The paucity of this evidence conforms to that from Beit el-Wali, and here, again, one finds a commingling of information. Namely, in the scenes devoted to his Syrian Wars, one finds a depiction of seven kneeling chieftains, one Nubian of which is lost. These are shown with their arms pinioned behind them and represented with stereotypical facial features indicating their ethnicity. The preserved three Nubians are captioned,

> The chief of wretched Kush
> The chief of Terses
> The chief of Terew (ARE 4: §114)

...they had no fear, [for] there was no enemy from Kush, [nor] foe from Syria. Their bows and their weapons reposed in their magazines.... (ARE 4: §410)

This activity presumably ensured the resumption of gold imports,

I come to thee, and I report to thee the statement of gold of the land of the Nubian. (ARE 4: §33)

the quantities of which are listed in the Great Harris Papyrus.

Gold of Kush 290 deben, 8 1/2 kidet (ARE 4: §228)

> fine gold 217, 5 kidet
> gold of the mountain, of Coptos 61 deben, 3 kidet
> total
> 569 deben 6 1/2 kidet (ARE 4: §228)

According to this inventory, approximately 50 percent of the gold came from Nubia!

The Nubian imposts continue to be dispatched to Egypt

Nubia and Zahi [came] to it, bearing their impost (ARE 4: §190)

as did captives, presumably slaves, enumerated using an aggregate figure.

Syrians and Nubians of the captivity of his Majesty...who he gave to the house of Ptah: persons 205 (ARE 4: §338)

These relations permitted the resumption of intercourse with Punt, mentioned both in the inscriptions from Medinet Habu and in the Great Harris Papyrus,

Utterance of Amon-Re…The South opens for thee the ways of Punt
   I led to thee Punt with myrrh, in order to encircle thy house every morning.…
(ARE 4: §209)

and a renewed interest in architectural endeavors in Nubia.

I made for thee an august house in Nubia, engraved with thy name, the likeness of the heavens, [named] House-of-Rameses-of-Heliopolis…Great-in-Victory…"
(ARE 4: §218)

The end of the reign of Rameses III is shrouded in mystery. Contemporary documents reveal that he was the intended victim of a harem conspiracy, but whether he was assassinated as a direct result, or died thereafter is moot. One of the conspirators, whose name literally means, "the evil which is in Thebes," obviously a pseudonym, was

The great criminal, Binemwese, formerly captain of archers in Nubia (ARE 4: §443)

His participation is taken by some as a harbinger of waning Egyptian influence in the south and a concomitant rise of Nubian power.

The presence of officials of the late Ramesside Period are attested at Soleb, and there is some evidence for the continued exploitation of Nubian quarries for stone. The last official attested for the late New Kingdom of any consequence in Nubia is Penne, governor of Aniba, suggested to have been the then-capital of Wawat, whose residence was at Derr. Penne belonged to a family influential in Nubia. His relatives held numerous positions of authority, serving as Lord of Miam, Treasurer of the Lord of the Two Lands, and mayor of Qasr Ibrim. The luxury products of Nubia and Africa further to the south continued to be imported into Egypt.

Said his Majesty to the king's son of Kush: "Give the two silver vessels of ointment of gums, to the deputy.
   May the ka of Pharaoh…who is satisfied with that which thou doest in the countries of the Nubians…thou causest to bring them as captives before Pharaoh.… (ARE 4: §476–477)

The elevated status of Penne may be gauged from his tomb, which was lavishly decorated in purely Egyptian style under the reign of Rameses VI (about 1142–1132 B.C.E.). With his interment, the archaeological and epigraphic records for a continued Egyptian presence in Nubia are spotty at best.

NUBIAN MERCENARIES

One realizes that Nubian mercenaries were in the employ of the Egyptian army, and that a chief of the archers of Kush was implicated in the harem conspiracy against Rameses III. So powerful had these Nubian mercenaries become that Rameses XI (about 1103–1069 B.C.E.) was apparently only able to suppress an uprising in Middle Egypt with Nubian troops under the command of Pa-nehesy, whose name literally means, "the Southern One," and by extension perhaps, "the Nubian," and provides the etymology for the modern personal name Phineas. In this context, however, the name cannot be taken as a marker of ethnicity. This revolt was a harbinger of the imminent collapse of royal central authority, the most striking example of which was the plundering of the royal tombs in the Valley of the Kings during the immediately preceding reign. The events are described in vivid detail in several preserved contemporary papyri and include an attempted cover-up and in-fighting among the thieves, which resulted in their successful prosecution.

THE END OF THE EGYPTIAN NEW KINGDOM

An attempt against pharaoh's life, a reliance on Nubian mercenaries to ensure domestic tranquility, and the callous, irreverent looting of royal tombs are indicative of the trends that so undermined central authority that the Ramesside Period collapsed. The ensuing Third Intermediate Period witnessed a return to smaller polities of competing elites.

One such polity was established at Thebes, where the leading religious position belonged to the High Priest of Amun. Over the course of time, this position eclipsed all others in the region with respect to status, privilege, and economic advantage. During the reign of pharaoh Rameses XI, the High Priest of Amun at Thebes was an individual named Herihor, who also managed to become Viceroy of Kush and commander of the army. Herihor was, therefore, able to control the reins of religious, secular, and military authority in his own hands and gradually assumed royal prerogatives traditionally reserved for pharaoh himself. He was also able to dictate the allocation of gold coming from the Nubian mines. As a result, the influence of pharaoh in Nubia was so weakened and undermined that his orders were not given priority, as is seen in this case that concerns the failure to execute in a timely fashion a royal directive.

Royal command to the king's son of Kush, Paynehesi...go forth after the majordomo...and cause him to proceed with the business of pharaoh...which he was sent to do in the southern region...thou shalt join thyself to him...and thou shalt look to this portable shrine...and thou shalt [complete] it.... (ARE 4: §597–599)

The subsequent history of the Third Intermediate Period in Upper Egypt is a vexing one for specialists not only in terms of the identifications and chronological positions of the competing elite families and their leading members, but also for events transpiring in Nubia. The situation in Lower Egypt is equally complex at this time, with its series of contemporary, competing dynasties, whose petty princes continued to refer to themselves as kings, despite the fact that they did not rule over a unified Egypt.

9

Nubia during the Third Intermediate Period: The Rise and Fall of Dynasty XXV

In order to place into sharper focus the emergence of the Nubians as pharaohs in their own right ruling from Egypt during Dynasty XXV (before 746–653 B.C.E.), one must briefly pass in review the salient features of the Egyptian Third Intermediate Period (about 1070–653 B.C.E.). This was once again an epoch during which there was no strong central authority. As a result, competing petty princes often ruled simultaneously in different parts of Egypt. Some of these dynasts ruled from cities in Lower Egypt; their counterparts ruled from Thebes. Their exact order in the sequence of rulers and their relative chronological positions within the Third Intermediate Period are often hotly contested, and the intricacies of these complex interrelationships are often bewildering. Rather than attempt to unravel this knotted skein, the following narrative will concentrate on three themes: namely, hostilities in Egypt in general and between Upper and Lower Egypt in particular, foreign relations between Egypt and Nubia within the context of the Asiatic campaigns, and the emergence of a Nubian theocracy at Thebes and its character.

CIVIL UNREST IN EGYPT

The civil disorder that may have prompted the looting of the royal tombs in the Valley of the Kings and the desecration of the royal mummies at the close of the Ramesside Period appears to have persisted at Thebes into the reign of Pinodjem I (about 1050 B.C.E.) at the beginning of Dynasty XXI. The exact nature of these disturbances, characterized by some as civil disobedience rather than a civil war, is difficult to determine because of the veiled language employed in their description in the so-called *Stela of the Banishment.* Its text makes clear that certain individuals appear to have been banished, for reasons not specified, and then recalled,

...thou shalt [relent] toward the servants, whom thou hast banished to the oasis, and they shall be brought [back] to Egypt.... (ARE 4: §655)

but the murderers among them were put to death.

...A slayer of living people.... thou shalt destroy him, thou shalt slay him.... (ARE 4: §658)

A full-scale civil war, characteristic of all of ancient Egypt's intermediate periods when there was no strong central authority, is described in *The Annals of Osorkon,* High Priest of Amun during the reigns of Takelot II (about 841–816 B.C.E.) and Sheshonq III (about 837–785 B.C.E.). The text as preserved links a prodigy, perhaps associated with a lunar eclipse, to a protracted civil war, specifically between Upper and Lower Egypt.

...before heaven devoured the moon, [great] wrath arose in this land.... they set warfare in the South and the North...years passed in hostility.... (ARE 4: §764)

In the end, Sheshonq III proved victorious.

MILITARY CAMPAIGNS AND THE WEALTH OF AFRICA

Such internecine warfare did not prevent the Egyptians from waging war outside their borders against traditional enemies, including the Nubians, but the data about these campaigns are quite sparse in the extreme, as seen, for example, in the information contained in the Great Karnak Relief of Sheshonq I (about 946–924 B.C.E.) of Dynasty XXII. This pharaoh's attention, like that of Rameses II, is focused on his Asiatic campaigns and an enumeration of the towns in the region over which he presumably triumphed. The limited references to Nubia are, as in the Ramesside Period, intercalated into those other campaigns so that distilling specific information about any Nubian campaign is impossible.

Smiting the chiefs of the Nubian Troglodytes, of all inaccessible countries, all the lands of the Fenkhu, the countries....

Thou has smitten the lands and the countries, thou hast crushed the Nubian Troglodytes.... (ARE 4: § 719 and 720, respectively)

Still, one gains the distinct impression that these raids were punitive, the objective of which was to ensure the continued flow of Nubian and

African luxury items into Egypt. Here at Karnak, the god Amun makes the following claim:

> I bring tribute to thee from the land of the Nubian … red cattle, thy firstlings … thy gazelles, thy panther skins. (ARE 4: §724)

One may assume that Nubian gold continued to be imported as well, an assumption perhaps supported by the aggregate weight of 560,297 pounds troy of gold and silver found in the record of temple gifts inscribed on the walls of a temple of his successor, Osorkon I (about 925–890 B.C.E.) at Bubastis, although admittedly this accounting does not specify the source of those precious metals.

The assumption is supported, nevertheless, by the information contained within The Annals of Osorkon, High Priest of Amun during the reigns of Takelot II (about 841–816 B.C.E.) and Sheshonq III (about 837–785 B.C.E.), cited earlier. After the victory was achieved, Sheshonq III witnessed the presentation of offerings that included products traditionally associated with Nubia such as gazelles, antelopes, and oryxes as well as "fine gold of Khenthennofer," a place name associated with Nubia.

The jubilee inscriptions of Osorkon II (about 875–837 B.C.E.) also suggest a normalization of relations because Nubia is not specifically mentioned among the subject nations.

> All lands, all countries, Upper Retenu, Lower Retinu, all inaccessible countries are under the feet of this Good God. (ARE 4: §749)

Furthermore, the stela of Harpeson, who served under Sheshonq IV (about 805–790 B.C.E.), traces his descent back 15 generations and includes one Namlot who was at least nominally charged with the administration of Upper Egypt and Nubia.

It is within this context that one turns to Thebes.

EGYPTIAN THEBES AND THE GOD AMUN

The theocracy established at Thebes by the High Priests of Amun during the Third Intermediate Period appears to have had a profound effect on the culture of ancient Egypt. The close bonds that traditionally tied the members of the elite to their deities appear to have become even stronger. One detects a sense of reverence in the treatment of the royal mummies that had been violated by the tomb robbers of the late Ramesside Period. Some of these were reverentially rewrapped and reinterred during the tenure of Pinodjem (about 1050 B.C.E.), who served as High Priest of Amun before his accession to the throne as another petty monarch of Dynasty XXI during the Third Intermediate Period. Here is the restoration text on the funerary equipment of Rameses II.

Regnal Year 17, third month of the second season, day 6, day of bringing Osiris, King Usermare-Setepnere (= Rameses II), life, health, prosperity, to bury him again, (in) the tomb...by the High Priest of Amun, Pinodjem. (ARE 4: §642)

These royal reinterments were continued by other members of the elite during this period.

From roughly the same time can be dated the Stela of Sheshonq, which established the primacy of Amun as the dispenser of justice. At issue are certain individuals, described as

...scribes, inspectors and administrators...who committed fraudulent acts in Thebes...who stole things from the offering-table of Osiris.... all the people who plundered from his divine offerings.... (ARE 4: §671 and 676)

These were condemned and duly punished.

The authority of the god Amun at Thebes was even solicited by members of this same Theban elite in the form of oracles delivered by the direction in which the divine barque, carrying the image of Amun, moved during the course of certain religious processions. The oracles were consulted for advice on a variety of personal issues, including the desirability of changing jobs.

...That man is my father, the wab-priest of your (Amun's) temple. Should Harsiese son of Peftjau, my father, serve Montu-Re-Harakhti? (SOPT 7)

The prestige, authority, and advantaged economic position enjoyed by the High Priest of Amun were also enjoyed by other elite members of the Theban administrative bureaucracy. Family members were able to establish virtual dynasties of their own with their offices passing down through the ages. It was not uncommon for these elite members to record lengthy genealogies in their autobiographical inscriptions; some of these family trees extend back in time for 15 generations, as was recorded by Harpeson.

THE GOD'S WIFE OF AMUN

In keeping with the observation that the position of elite women in ancient Egyptian society was relatively better than that of their sisters in either ancient Greece or Rome, the Theban clergy included the office of "God's Wife of Amun."

This title was originally bestowed on queens during the course of Dynasty XVIII and was revived during the course of the Third Intermediate Period, when, for example, this office was held by Shepenwepet I, a daughter of pharaoh Osorkon III (about 790–762 B.C.E.) of the collateral Dynasty XXII. Consistent with ancient religious tenets by which the male and female principles of procreation had to be in equilibrium for the desired maintenance of cosmic order, as seen earlier in the role of Nofer-tari at Abu Simbel, these God's Wives religiously contributed to the renewal of divine cycles by arousing the sexual appetite of Amun in very human terms. This role is explicit in the inscriptions on the statue of Ankhnesneferibre, daughter of Psamtik I (664–610 B.C.E.) of Dynasty XXVI, who was the last to hold this office.

> …the queen of beauty…the hand of the god…whose two eyes sparkle upon beholding him…the lady possessed of lovely, sweet charms, who pacifies Amun with her voice…. [author's translation]

The theological importance of the office of God's Wife of Amun placed her in the midst of political activities of the day because she was often called on to serve as a mediator between the priest kings of Thebes and their counterparts, the petty princes of Lower Egypt. Over the course of the Third Intermediate Period, the God's Wife of Amun became the supreme religious authority in Thebes, reflected by the fact that her name could be written in a cartouche, or royal ring, a convention otherwise generally reserved for the names of pharaohs and a very selected number of deities. The woman serving as the Divine Wife of Amun, therefore, was the real wielder of religious power at Thebes, and her prestige and authority eclipsed that of the High Priest of Amun.

PRELUDE TO DYNASTY XXV

One can summarize the preceding by making two observations. First, the ruling elite during the Third Intermediate Period appear to have maintained a policy toward Nubia established by the Ramesside pharaohs whereby punitive campaigns were occasionally launched to ensure the uninterrupted flow into Egypt of luxury goods traditionally coming from Nubia and Africa. Second, despite the eruptions of civil insurrection and war, the elite at Thebes developed a theocracy rooted in religious principle that may have served as an antidote for the nation's lack of a central, unifying political authority.

It is into this scene that the Nubians themselves now entered, but as was the case during the New Kingdom, so, too, during the early Third Intermediate Period the archaeological presence of the Nubians is difficult to detect, and one's focus has, therefore, to be directed toward Napata.

Control of the site of Napata, because of its geographic position at the middle of a large bend in the Nile River just before the fourth cataract, regulated both fluvial and overland travel and trade between Kerma and Kawa to the north and Meroe further to the south. It is for this reason, apparently, that the site served as the border between Egypt and Nubia. Napata became the southernmost frontier of the Nubians during the Kingdom of Kerma. It was doubtless this frontier status that was exploited

Gebel Barkal and its Yardang depicted in a vignette at Abu Simbel. Courtesy, Peter Der Manuelian.

by the Egyptian pharaoh Amenhotep II of Dynasty XVIII, who chose to
display the hapless head of his Asiatic captive on the walls of Napata to
serve as a warning against Nubian encroachments into his realm. Doubtless for the same reasons Tuthmosis III erected a fortress here. Aside from
the attractiveness of its geographic location, Napata was doubtless chosen
as the capital of one of Nubia's important cultural phases specifically
because it lies in the shadow of Gebel Barkal.

GEBEL BARKAL, THE HOLY MOUNTAIN

Rising majestically behind the town site of Napata to a height of some
300 feet, Gebel Barkal was anciently regarded as "the holy mountain"
associated with the god Amun. That association can be traced back to a
period as early as the reign of pharaoh Tuthmosis III of Dynasty XVIII. In
time the Nubians developed the site of Gebel Barkal into a cult center
regarded as the source of royal power, and "Amun of Napata who dwells
in the pure mountain" became one of that god's most popular epithets. It
is to that epithet that one must now turn.

Everyone who has ever visited Gebel Barkal attests to just how spectacular the natural setting of the site really is. Viewed from the west, this
tawny-colored majestic butte creates a lasting impression of beauty and

awe, with one's attention focused on a vertical section that seems to rise up independently as a yardang, defined as a naturally created formation seemingly crafted by human hands. The yardang at Gebel Barkal appears to be a gigantic cobra, issuing forth from the matrix of the butte itself. Already in a vignette in the Temple of Nofertari of Dynasty XIX at Abu Simbel, Amun of Napata who dwells in the holy mountain is in fact depicted as just such a serpent issuing forth from the butte. Later the Nubian pharaoh Taharqa added his name to the top of this yardang, which his sculptors may have enhanced so that its appearance as a cobra could not be doubted.

Whereas one cannot associate specific rulers with the history of Gebel Barkal and Napata at the beginning of the Third Intermediate Period, it is, nevertheless, clear that the Nubians were possessed of a worldview that transcended the confines of their narrow geographic homeland in the upper reaches of the Nile River. The Egyptian pharaoh Osorkon I engaged Nubian mercenaries in his military operations against Judah, and trade, doubtless between Egypt and Napata, may help explain the appearance of traditionally Nubian and African products in Assyrian records of the ninth century B.C.E. It has also been demonstrated that the Greeks on the Aegean island of Samos, off the coast of the modern nation-state of Turkey, learned the technique of casting bronze via the lost wax method at this time. The numerous bronze statuettes of distinctly Nubian types excavated on that island's sanctuary of the Goddess Hera raises the distinct possibility that the Nubians were in part responsible for this transference of technology, perhaps as a result of trade.

The extent of this trade may be gauged by noting that Egyptian luxury goods are attested in Nubian elite graves at el-Kurru together with imported stone vessels associated with the Phoenicians. It is, therefore, to the archaeological evidence from this royal cemetery to the southwest of Gebel Barkal and on the same bank of the Nile River, that we now turn to document the rise of what was to become Egypt's Dynasty XXV, or Nubian Kushite Dynasty.

DYNASTY XXV

Although each successive phase of ancient Nubia's cultural horizons do differ in many ways from one another, certain traditions appear to be maintained, as is only to be expected. So, for example, the earliest graves at el-Kurru have rough stones arranged in a circle over which the deceased is often cramped into underground niches, sometimes, however, on beds reminiscent of funeral practices known from the Kingdom of Kerma. With the passage of time, these circular sepulchers were transformed into square chambers, architecturally enhanced with the addition of an offering chapel constructed of fine masonry accompanied by a pyramid. The burial chambers below are no longer pits but spacious chambers, the deceased sometimes mummified and placed into coffins recalling Egyptian practice.

ALARA

Subsequent Nubians regarded Alara as the founder of their Napatan Dynasty, whom scholars suggest ruled some time between 785 and 760 B.C.E. He appears to have been a grand uncle of Taharqa, one of his successors, and owed his elevation to the crown to the fact that he had placed his trust in the god Amun, thereby establishing Amun's recurrent role in the subsequent history of Dynasty XXV and the Napatan Period as king maker. Alara is depicted on a stela, now in Copenhagen, on which he presents offerings to Amun. This stela, found at the Nubian site of Kawa, is an early example of the Nubian artistic appropriation of Egyptian norms and should be considered an initial step in the formulation of a typically Nubian iconographic repertoire rather than as a crude approximation of its more accomplished Egyptian model.

The political primacy enjoyed by Alara must be understood in terms of his peers' acceptance of his supreme authority. Throughout the history of Dynasty XXV and the subsequent Napatan Period, the rulers administered their realm via a bureaucratic system whose ranks were filled with members of their own family as well as with members of an elite, perhaps forming a priestly class whose members were literate and whose number comprised, according to one estimate, not much more than 1 percent of the total Nubian population.

Despite his primacy among the elite and his nascent appropriation of certain ancient Egyptian modes of display, Alara, according to the evidence presently available, never referred to himself as *nesu*, "king [of Upper Egypt]." There is presently no image in which he is depicted with the cobra at his brow on the model of Egyptian pharaohs. On the other hand, Alara habitually referred to himself as *wer*, "the great one," a title also employed by some of Egypt's own petty princes with royal pretensions during the course of the Third Intermediate Period. Little is known about the investiture rituals of this early period, but one can suggest that coronation ceremonies consisted of a progressive journey during which Alara probably traveled from one key urban area to another, stopping at each to be confirmed in his rank by the elite members of the population. The model for such a coronation crawl may have been the diurnal journey of the sun god Re across the heavens, each hour of his ascent and descent perhaps associated with specific sites visited during the king's journey.

As ruler, Alara was obliged to embellish his realm with architectural activities and did embark on several architectural projects at Nubian sanctuaries including the construction of Temple B at Kawa, a mud-brick structure, and Temple B 888 at Gebel Barkal for Amun to whom he ostensibly owed his reign. Scholars have argued for the identifying Tomb Number 9 at el-Kurru as that of Alara. This tomb contained a bed burial and a pyramidal superstructure, surmounted by a cast bronze *ba-bird*, representing the deceased as a human-headed avian. Such a composite figure, representing the deceased, is often depicted in two dimensions in illustrated papyri and on vignettes on tomb walls during the course of Egypt's New Kingdom and Third Intermediate Period, but its plastic expression appears to have been developed exclusively by the Nubians with a seemingly specific Nubian significance.

Because of his ancestral position within the posthumous history of the Nubians, Alara is often described as the Nubian Menes, the original unifier of the realm. Indeed, there is evidence to suggest that he did in fact consolidate the kingdom from Meroe in the south to the vicinity of the third cataract.

KASHTA

The evidence for writing the biography for Kashta, Alara's successor, is in some respects more complete, although the equivocal nature of the evidence precludes one from definitively identifying him as either a brother or cousin of his predecessor Alara. During the course of his reign, Kashta (in the period around 746 B.C.E.) enlarged his kingdom to include all of Lower Nubia as far as its border with Egypt at Aswan. Here at Elephantine Kashta erected a stela in which he referred to himself as "the king of Upper and Lower Egypt," appropriating for himself the very title that certain contemporary Egyptian petty princes of the Delta also employed. Like Alara before him, he continued to expand the sanctuary of Amun at Gebel Barkal and is suggested by some scholars to have been the first to have taken up his royal residence in Napata. Kashta was buried in el-Kurru in Tomb 8, which is 3 meters in size larger than any earlier funerary monument in the necropolis and is closer in its design to Egyptian models than earlier sepulchers.

The lunette of the Piankhy Stela. Copyright, Institut français d'Archéologie orientale, Caire.

PIANKHY

Kashta's successor was an individual whose name can be recorded as Piankhy, not Piye, according to the most recent study of the complex philological issues involved. His relationship to Kashta has not been established with certainty, and the suggestion that Piankhy was a son of Kashta is moot. Piankhy preferred to identify himself as the bodily son of the god Amun, an identification that again helped to cement the bond between Amun of Napata and Nubia's rulers. Piankhy's devotion to Amun and his dedication to that god's national shrine at Gebel Barkal cannot be underestimated.

Although the sanctuary of Amun at Gebel Barkal was embellished during the Egyptian New Kingdom as late as the reign of Rameses II, the site, save for the mud-brick structure erected by Alara, was a virtual ruin by the time Piankhy ascended the throne. Piankhy's architectural campaign at the site is remarkable for its conception, which relied to a great degree on the appropriation of earlier monuments. Piankhy's motivation appears to derive from a deep-seated, pious respect for the antiquity of the site and the reverence due Amun. As a result, his architects reverentially encased the weathered stone of earlier buildings in revetments both to preserve and intercalate the older remains into the fabric of his structures. He ordered his construction gangs to travel to Soleb about 200 miles south of Gebel Barkal to ship back statues erected there earlier in the name of Amenhotep III. These included 10 statues of rams, an animal associated with Amun, with which Piankhy's processional way at Gebel Barkal was lined. Statues in black granite representing serpents and a vulture were erected in the forecourt of his sanctuary of Gebel Barkal. Other monuments shipped from Soleb to Gebel Barkal included the Prudhoe lions, red granite beasts originally inscribed for pharaoh Amenhotep III, together with other statues of officials of the New Kingdom.

The motivation for this usurpation, as such an appropriation is termed, may be explained in various ways. One motivation is, of course, practical. The inclusion of these former monuments enabled the national shrine to be wonderfully appointed in the shortest amount of time with a minimal expenditure of cost and energy. Secondly, this usurpation can be regarded within the context of archaizing, a practice whereby monuments of earlier ages serve as sources of inspiration for a contemporary age. Indeed, as the artistic vocabulary of Dynasty XXV developed, its indebtedness to the creations of earlier ages became more and more apparent. On a third level, Piankhy may have wished to intercalate himself into a glorious religious-political past for purposes of propaganda because such blatant display visually linked him to the tradition of great Egyptian monarchs of the past in whose number he was now to be counted. In this practice, he was following an example of certain Egyptian pharaohs of Dynasty XII, who dedicated in their sanctuaries statues of their putative royal relatives of

Dynasty III–V, including Djoser, Sneferu, and Sahure. Given the archaizing tendency of this dynasty, it is possible to suggest that the Nubians were well aware of this earlier practice.

Consider for a moment the two monumental stelae that Piankhy also commissioned in his name for erection at Gebel Barkal within the great temple to Amun. This pair was dedicated in the immediate vicinity of an earlier stela of pharaoh Tuthmosis III, which had been standing in the ruined national sanctuary. This trio of stelae celebrate Amun of Napata and Amun of Thebes, forging a link in a theological chain with which Piankhy was later to bind Egypt to Nubia. In the lunettes, or curved tops of his stelae, Piankhy received the crown of Egypt from Amun of Thebes and the cap crown of Nubia from Amun of Napata, regalia reaffirming his suzerainty over both realms.

Amun of Thebes and Amun of Napata represented different, but compatible, characteristics of one and the same deity. The polyvalent nature of ancient African religious tenets provided for such a compartmentalization where local manifestations of one and the same deity permitted priesthoods to identify, isolate, and capitalize on aspects of a deity's total characteristics, selecting from among the traditional repertoire those divine aspects that were most appropriate and suitable for articulating local religious requirements. The program composed by Piankhy for public display of his devotion to both Amun of Napata and Amun of Thebes intentionally avoided any bellicose overtones. Its message was couched exclusively in religious terms, terms that reaffirm the close theological connections between Amun of Napata and Amun of Thebes.

The theological justification for such political posturing is further demonstrated by a text of a fragmentary sandstone stela discovered at Gebel Barkal, which some scholars maintain is the earliest datable official inscription of Piankhy. Therein one reads,

> Amun of Thebes has made him (Piankhy) king of Egypt
> Amun of Napata has caused me to be ruler of all lands (BPENR 179)

The text continues to inform all that Piankhy controls the political destiny of every petty prince in Egypt and Nubia.

> He to whom I say, "You are a Chief," he shall be a Chief.
> He to whom I say, "You are not a Chief," he shall not be Chief. (BPENR 179)

Having carefully orchestrated the religious foundation of such a program, Piankhy then addressed the politically fragmented situation in Egypt proper. He recognized that there was no central authority and perhaps even realized that Upper Egypt was weaker, politically as well as militarily, than the Delta of Lower Egypt. With a calculated policy in place, he publicly acknowledged the legitimacy of the kinglets of Lower Egypt, but did so by stressing his own primacy among them. This was an extraordinarily bold move because Piankhy had, up to this time, never set foot into Egypt proper, nor had any of his two immediate predecessors.

A Suggested Egypto–Nubian Condominium One can only speculate about the circumstances that led Piankhy to issue this declaration of his suzerainty over the whole of Egypt. Although one lacks specific information, a possible explanation appears to reside in the overall Egyptianization of Nubia during the New Kingdom. If one can judge from the archaeological record, Nubians such as Penne, governor of Aniba, belonged to a family influential in Nubia. His relatives held numerous positions of authority, serving as Lord of Miam, Treasurer of the Lord of the Two Lands, and mayor of Qasr Ibrim. The elevated status of Penne may be gauged from his tomb, which was lavishly decorated in purely Egyptian style under the reign of Rameses VI (about 1142–1132 B.C.E.).

Members of the Nubian elite, therefore, appear to have been so thoroughly integrated into the fabric of Egyptian cultural norms that their lasting monuments, their tombs, completely mask their Nubian origins. It may very well be that the Nubian elite came to regard their symbiotic interrelations with their Egyptian counterparts as the basis for a political condominium in which power, initially on a local level, was shared between the Egyptian office of the Viceroy of Kush and the Nubians in his administration. That administration linked Nubia with Egypt, but more particularly with Thebes as the political events at the close of the Ramesside Period of Dynasty XX reveal.

One may, therefore, cogently suggest that a religious-political bureaucracy was firmly established between Egyptian Thebes and Nubia, and that this bureaucracy, while recognizing a frontier at Aswan between the two regions, was regarded, in the eyes of the administration, as a unified condominium. One can further suggest that the Nubians themselves began to assume successively higher and higher positions in the established bureaucracy of the region as the presence and the authority of both Egyptian pharaohs and their deputies waned in Nubia during the course of the Third Intermediate Period. The spectacular and rapid but bloodless consolidation of Nubian territory, vis-à-vis Egyptian interests, from Alara to Kashata, and the ability of Piankhy to extend that territory as far north as Aswan without recourse to military action is adequate demonstration of how effectively the Nubians were able to co-opt the existing administration for their own ends. The architectural program of Piankhy at Gebel Barkal reveals his ability to head a highly efficient bureaucratic administration, the mechanisms of which must surely have been in place well before his accession to the throne.

Piankhy in Egypt The special relationship that Nubia appeared to enjoy with Egyptian Thebes speaks volumes about Piankhy's announcement that he would undertake a journey to Thebes, envisioned not as a military campaign but as a religious pilgrimage by which he might venerate Amun of Thebes in person. This pilgrimage does not appear to have posed a threat to the Egyptians at Thebes, because Piankhy was apparently able to make the journey uncontested militarily.

The details of his journey and the political jockeying for position between Piankhy and Osorkon III, the Egyptian ruler of Upper Egypt, remain obscure, but the determination of Piankhy to establish himself in Egypt and to gain the advantage over Osorkon III is clearly revealed by the following unprecedented event. Piankhy apparently coerced Osorkon III and his daughter, Shepenwepet I, who was serving as God's Wife of Amun at Thebes, to adopt his Nubian sister, Amenirdis I, as her heir and successor. The name of Piankhy's sister, Amenirdis, reflects the religious role she was to fulfill because of Amun himself. Her name translates, "She whom the god Amun has given." By virtue of this one bold move, Piankhy bloodlessly arranged for the supreme religious, and by extension secular, power of the Theban clergy of Amun to pass peacefully from Egyptian into Nubian hands.

Piankhy, now in Egypt with Thebes and the Nile Valley nominally under his control, was prepared to deal with the Delta princes, led by Tefnakht of Sais, but military intervention was his only option. In the twentieth year of his reign, Piankhy launched a military campaign against **The Military Campaigns of Piankhy** the Delta, but he regarded the operation as the quelling of a rebellion rather than as a military invasion with foreign conquest as its objective. This is an important distinction to bear in mind particularly because Piankhy, prior to journeying to Thebes, did in fact recognize the legitimacy of the Delta petty princes, but demanded that they in turn recognize his primacy. Such an assumption on his part reveals that Piankhy, as the successor to the role of Viceroy of Kush, the chief administrator of the region, clearly regarded himself as the de jure ruler of the kingdom. The acquiescence of Osorkon III to Piankhy's demand for the adoption of his sister, Amenirdis, as Divine Wife of Amun, clearly suggests that there had to have been some basis in fact for this politically motivated religious act. The apparent universal acceptance and embrace of the adoption by Shepenwepet I of the Nubian Amenirdis by the Egyptians of Upper Egypt would also suggest that there may have been precedents for similar assertions of power and authority by the Nubians over the Theban Egyptians during the course of the late Ramesside and early Third Intermediate Periods. The career of Pa-nehesy and the Nubian troops under his command in the quelling of the uprising in Middle Egypt during the reign of Rameses IX (about 1103–1069 B.C.E.) demonstrates the fluidity of the boundaries between the two realms and suggests the acceptance of a Nubian presence in their land by the Egyptians.

Having secured and asserted his authority over Upper Egypt, Piankhy in his twentieth regnal year embarked on the military conquest of the remainder of Egypt. Certain details of the campaign are recorded on several monuments, including the *Victory Stela* of Piankhy erected in the twenty-first year of his reign. The major conflicts of this campaign and their resolution is summarized later.

The opposition to Piankhy was headed by Tefnakht, petty price of the Delta city of Sais, who orchestrated a military coalition of his regional contemporaries to challenge the Nubian threat. As the forces of Piankhy marched northward, cities such as Hermopolis in Middle Egypt were surrounded

He (Piankhy) has circled it completely, not letting comers-out come out, not letting goers-in go in (ARE 4: §833)

and besieged. An embankment was made to enclose the wall; a tower was raised to elevate both archers and slingers allowing them to gain an advantage while loosing their arrows and slinging their projectiles, respectively. Days passed. The town ultimately surrendered with its leader, Namlot, prostrating himself before Piankhy.

Then Hermopolis threw herself upon her belly, and pleaded before the king.... [Namlot] threw himself upon his belly..."I am one of the king's slaves, paying impost into the treasury...." (ARE 4: §843 and 846)

Piankhy entered Hermopolis in triumph and inspected both the palace of Namlot and his stables, where the condition of the horses appalled the Nubian.

When he saw that they had suffered hunger, he (Piankhy) said, "...it is more grievous in my heart that my horses have suffered hunger than any evil deed thou has done.... (ARE 4: §850)

In his march northward Piankhy encountered other cities that offered resistance, but some, like Herakleopolis, remained loyal and recanted their stand with the rebels:

The ruler of Heracleopolis Pefnefdibast came, bearing tribute.... He threw himself upon his belly before his majesty..."I was submerged in darkness, upon which the light has (now) shown...O mighty king, thou hast expelled the darkness from me. I will labor together with (thy) subjects and Heracleopolis shall pay taxes into they treasury...." (ARE 4: §852)

Pinakhy's ultimate military objective was Memphis, the religious center of Lower Egypt, and original capital city of the unified country.

Then he (Piankhy) sent forth his fleet and his army to assault the harbor of Memphis...His Majesty commanded his army (saying): "Forward against it! Mount the walls!" (ARE 4: §864)

The battle raged.

The siege ended when the Nubians successfully stormed the city. Piankhy was recognized as the legitimate ruler by Ptah, the creator god of Memphis. Soon the outlying regions surrendered to him in turn. Piankhy then continued northward and camped near the city of Athribis, to which an embassy of leaders of the Delta coalition came.

Then came those kings and princes of the Northland, all of the chiefs who wore the feather, every vizier, all chiefs, and every king's confidant, from the west, from the east, from the islands in the midst, to see the beauty of his majesty. (ARE 4: §873)

The embassy invited Piankhy into the Athribis, where they swore oaths of fealty and placed all of their resources at his disposal.

Still, opposition to his rule persisted, and several days later Mesed, perhaps located in the Western Delta, revolted against his authority. Piankhy was swift to act.

We have slain every man whom we found there. (ARE 4: §879)

Tefnakhte, a petty prince who was doubtless the leader of the coalition against Piankhy, recognized that Piankhy was for the present at least in control of the situation. He therefore initially indicated his submission to the Nubian by dispatching a royal messenger:

Then the chief…Tefnakhte…caused a messenger to come to the place where his majesty was.… "Be thou appeased! I have not beheld thy face for shame…Send me a messenger quickly, that he may expel fear from my heart.… (ARE 4: §880)

Piankhy in turn dispatched an embassy at the head of which were a ritual priest and a commander of the Nubian army. They extracted an oath of allegiance from Tefnakhte:

…I will do according to that which the king says, and I will not transgress that which he has commanded. (ARE 4: §881)

This posturing evidently satisfied Piankhy, and soon thereafter the agriculturally rich district of the Faiyum, southwest of modern Cairo, and other cities together with their leaders pledged their submission to Piankhy, who then returned to Thebes.

The most significant aspect of the campaign and its after- **The Piety of** math, as recorded in this *Victory Stela* of Piankhy, is the reli- **Piankhy** gious terms in which the actions of his military opponents are couched. Tefnakhte, the acknowledged leader of the coalition, ritually cleanses himself by means of a divine oath performed within a temple, stating,

Let me go forth before him to the temple, that I may cleanse myself with a divine oath. (ARE 4: §880)

On the other hand, many of the last leaders of the opposition who were late in ceasing hostilities and swearing an oath of allegiance to Piankhy were prohibited from entering into his presence within the palace because they were ritually unclean.

They entered not into the king's house, because they were unclean, and eaters of fish, which is an abomination for the palace. (ARE 4: §882)

Whether the connotation of the word translated "[ritually] unclean" is in fact "uncircumcised" or not and whatever the religious prohibitions of the Nubians of Dynasty XXV were against eating fish may have been, it would appear that the collective challenge of the Delta coalition to Piankhy's authority was deemed religiously motivated, which under- scores Piankhy's initial assessment of their opposition as a rebellion rather than as a foreign aggression. The entire campaign, in the preserved texts, relies on religious imagery to such a great degree that one cannot escape the implication that the opposition was anciently regarded as a threat to the divine order of Maat, cosmic harmony often personified as a winged goddess, which pharaoh was obliged to maintain. And although the *Victory Stela* has been the subject of extensive and numerous literary criti- cisms and commentaries, the fact remains that when its text is intercalated into the corpus of all of the Egyptian inscriptions dealing with Piankhy, this Nubian pharaoh is portrayed as a righteous, religious ruler who maintains the cosmic equilibrium as religiously mandated. Although one cannot gauge the depth of Piankhy's own personal religious convictions, there can be no doubt that his reign was publicly portrayed in conformity with ideal, religious paradigms of kingship. This impression, which pos- terity also gains from a study of the reigns of other Nubian rulers, may well explain the unsullied reputation Nubia and its rulers enjoyed in the Classical tradition as exemplars of moral and ethical rectitude.

In victory, Piankhy was merciful. He avoided further bloodshed by for- giving the rebels and paying homage to the local deities of the cities that had fallen to his forces. Magnanimous in victory and apparently con- vinced that further opposition to his reign was nonexistent, he refrained from furthering his consolidation of the entire Delta and eventually returned in triumph to Napata.

Mindful of the accomplishments of Tuthmosis III and Rameses II, whose military exploits were still vivid in the collective memory of the Nubians, and wishing to be perceived as their legitimate heir and succes- sor, Piankhy adopted their throne names as his own, Men-kheper-re ("The manifestations of Re are enduring") and Wesir-Maat-Re ("Maat [= truth] is the power of Re"), respectively, and used them interchangeably in his titulary throughout his reign. In his thirtieth year Piankhy, in accordance with Egyptian precedents set by those monarchs, celebrated a sed-festival, or ritual of renewing his power, at Gebel Barkal.

There are no contemporary documents to indicate the nature of the state organization that Piankhy was per-force compelled to administer after his conquest of Egypt. One assumes, however, that it perpetuated in broad strokes the nome, or province, system tradition-**The Administration of Piankhy** ally in place in Egypt where the land was divided into districts each with a capital, but this cannot be confirmed with any degree of certainty. Positions in the upper echelons of the government were filled by members of Piankhy's royal family, who together with elite members of Nubian society commanded the armed forces. In Egypt proper, particularly at Thebes with personnel demands on the office of the God's Wife of Amun, and perhaps also in Nubia proper, members of the elite Egyptian population were co-opted to serve in the administration in much the same way that elite Nubians had earlier been engaged in the Egyptian bureaucracy of the Viceroy of Nubia. And whereas the overwhelming percentage of Piankhy's subjects continued to be engaged in the traditional Nubian agricultural and pastoral activities, urban settlements such as Pnubs, Kawa, Sanam, Meroe, and Napata itself suggest a cosmopolitan outlook that included manufacturing and trade.

Piankhy was buried in el-Kurru Tomb 17. Accessed by a staircase, its design was innovative and served as a model, becoming the canonical form of the royal Nubian tomb for the next thousand years. Nearby were tombs for Piankhy's major and minor wives and four of his horses. These were buried nearby, all standing side by side and facing east. Such equine burials punctuate subsequent Nubian funerary practices, some containing as many as eight individual horses.

SHABAKA

With the accession of Shabaka to the throne, Nubian history and Egyptian history become one, although certain details remain opaque. These include the familial relationships among the members of the Nubian ruling family. So, for example, earlier scholars regarded Shabaka as Piankhy's younger brother, but he was more likely to have been the son of Kashta and brother of Amenirdis I, the God's Wife of Amun.

Piankhy's decision not to further his political interests in the Delta had dire consequences for Shabaka, who was confronted by a military challenge to his authority over Egypt by the new dynast of Sais, Bakenrenef by name. By **Rebellion and Residence in Egypt** the time of Shabaka's decision to invade Egypt in his second regnal year, Bakenrenef had already exercised his control over most of the Delta and had been acknowledged as ruler in Memphis. The details of

Shabaka's campaign are not recorded anywhere in contemporary texts, but the subsequent Graeco-Roman tradition credits him with victory, the installation of a Nubian governor over Sais, and the recipient of oaths of fealty from his opponents. In the face of victory, Shabaka elected to remain in Egypt, rather than return to Napata, and chose Memphis as the site of his royal residence. Because he was the first Nubian pharaoh to reside permanently in Egypt proper, some Classical authors accord Shabaka the credit for founding Dynasty XXV. Herodotus, the so-called Father of History, writing in Greek about 450 B.C.E., described him as a just ruler who sentenced prisoners to public service in the form of dyke building for irrigation projects rather than condemn them to death.

The Archaizing or Antiquariaum Interests of Shabaka's Reign
There is a marked antiquarian interest in certain cultural aspects of Shabaka's reign, typical of the archaizing trend that characterizes the material culture of Dynasty XXV as a whole. In his particular case, Shabaka and his advisors, doubtless influenced by the antiquity of Memphis, the royal residence, modeled his throne name, Neferkare ("The *ka* of Re is beautiful"), on that of the longest-lived of Egypt's monarchs, Pepy II of Dynasty VI of the Old Kingdom. Other elements of his titulary resonate with references to other Old Kingdom royal protocols.

The most remarkable literary monument of his reign is doubtless the Shabaka Stone, a basalt stela that purports to have been copied from an ancient, but damaged, document to the degree that the worm holes of the alleged original have been faithfully reproduced as intentional gaps in the text of this stela. Written in a style reminiscent of the *Pyramid Texts* of the Old Kingdom, sculpted into the walls of the burial chambers of the pyramids of the pharaohs of Dynasty V and VI to ensure their successful passage into the Hereafter, the text of the Shabaka Stone deals with the role of Ptah, the creator god of the Memphite pantheon, and that of the city of Memphis relative to the Two Lands of Egypt. Whether the Shabaka Stone is, as stated, a Nubian copy of an older document or, as some scholars suggest, an original Nubian composition in an intentionally archaic style, it nevertheless demonstrates the antiquarian interests of Dynasty XXV in general and the reverential piety of its kings toward their venerable religious past. Such uses of the past helped to legitimize the contemporary religious programs of the Nubian pharaohs and enabled them to cloak those programs in an aura of authenticity.

The Shabaka Stone is not an isolated literary example of the period's archaism. *The Tale of King Neferkare and General Sasenet* is considered a Nubian composition of Dynasty XXV as well, an attribution that gains further support from the fact that Shabako employed the throne name of Pepy II of Dynasty VI, Neferkare, as his own. The tale interestingly enough takes place in Memphis and may actually contain heretofore not recognized anecdotes about that older king's reign. A second papyrus of

The sack of an Egyptian city depicted in a wall relief of a palace of Assurbanipal at Nineveh. ALEA.

the period, *The Tale of a King and the Ghost of Senefer,* was probably composed at Thebes. It treats as its subject an unnamed pharaoh and an excellent spirit who identifies himself as pharaoh Senefer's son, Khenyka, of Dynasty IV.

Egypt and Nubia formed two halves of one domain under Shabaka. He continued to stand in special relationships to Amun of Thebes and Amun of Napata and to regard himself as the legitimate successor of earlier Egyptian pharaohs, as had his immediate predecessors.

The Assyrian Threat

The increased physical presence of the Nubians in Egypt at the royal residence of Memphis was but one vignette in the ever-changing picture of the ancient Near East as a whole at this time. Nubian consolidation of Egypt and Nubia into one polity enabled Shabaka's administration to gain a monopoly on luxury goods once passing from Nubian into Egyptian hands. Papyrus scrolls, finely woven Egyptian linen textiles, and even hides of elephants are listed as gifts received by petty princes of the Syria-Palestine region. Timber-poor Egypt continued to import cedar from Lebanon in exchange for Egyptian luxury goods.

The loss of these territories at the end of the Egyptian New Kingdom, rekindled an interest in reconquest during the course of the Third Intermediate Period, as the foreign campaigns of the period demonstrate. Egypt's imperial aspirations regarding these former territories did not wane during Dynasty XXV, as Shabaka himself attempted to establish a presence in the region. He could only achieve this objective at the expense of the Assyrians, who were simultaneously expanding their own territory in a westerly direction.

The history of the Syrian-Palestine region during Dynasty XXV is an exceedingly complex one, compounded by Assyrian-Egyptian relations. Seals originally associated with now-lost correspondence and found at the Assyrian site of Kuyunjik suggest an exchange of diplomatic correspondence between Shabaka and Sargon, king of Assyria. When Sargon was compelled to deal with military campaigns elsewhere in his kingdom, Shabaka seized the opportunity of establishing a foothold in the Syria-Palestine region. This presence inevitably placed Egypt in an adversarial position relative to Assyria, and caused concern among the petty rulers of the region as to the nature of their diplomatic alliances.

Shabaka died before these issues came to a head, and only returned to Nubia as a corpse, having lived his life since Regnal Year 2 in Egypt. He was buried at el-Kurru in a tomb that was lavishly supplied with funerary goods, including vessels of various stones and finely worked articles of ivory and gold. His horses were also buried at el-Kurru, draped in beaded blankets and silver trappings.

SHEBITQO

Shabaka was succeeded by Shebitqo, the most enigmatic of the Nubian pharaohs of Dynasty XXV. His relationship to Shabaka is uncertain. The suggestion that he was Shabaka's son and younger brother of Taharqa, his successor, cannot be absolutely demonstrated, but is generally accepted. It is also unclear whether Shebitqo ruled as co-regent in Napata during Shabaka's residency in Memphis. Whatever the resolution of these issues, it would appear that Shebitqo was in Memphis following the death of Shabaka and, after having been crowned pharaoh in that city, accompanied the body of his predecessor back to Napata for burial.

The historical events that unfolded during the reign of Shebitqo are equally vague, often confounded or confused with those of his successor, Taharqa. The Assyrian king Sennacherib's preoccupation with Babylon may have permitted Shebitqo to establish either diplomatic and/or mercantile relationships with various petty princes of the Syria-Palestine region, but such activities cannot be documented. Equally problematic is whether he mustered troops in Nubia for a military campaign into that region. Although such a mission is possible, it would almost certainly have attracted the attention of the Assyrians, but their records are silent on this matter.

Upon his death, Shebitqo's corpse, mummified, was interred in el-Kurru. His coffin was laid to rest on a stone bench, the recesses of which indicate it originally had legs recalling those of a bed. So, although

Shebitqo was both mummified and placed into an anthropoid sarcophagus, the ensemble was placed on a bed in accordance with a Nubian custom that extended back in time to the Kingdom of Kerma. Other aspects of his funerary panoply reveal a markedly Egyptian flavor, which suggests the gradual appropriation by the Nubians of typically Egyptian funerary practices. These included funerary equipment such as shabtis, or servant figures modeled on those common in Egypt, and fragments of Canopic jars in which his internal organs were preserved. Other articles included ivory carvings and an enormous quantity of pottery.

TAHARQA

Shebitqo was succeeded by Taharqa, perhaps the Nubian pharaoh of Dynasty XXV best known to a modern, popular American audience. His own monuments celebrate the fact that he was the son of Queen Abar, a niece of Alara, whom these same monuments credit as the dynasty's founder:

(For) his mother's mother was committed to him by her brother, the Chief, the son of Re, Alara, [justified], saying, "O beneficent god, swift, who comes to him that calls upon him, look upon my sister for me, a woman born with me in one womb, act for her (even) as you acted for him that acted for you...." (Amun) hearkened to all (Alara) said and did not (fail to) pay heed to his every word. He appointed for him his son, the son-of-Re: Taharqa, may he live for ever, a king.... (IOWANA 350–1)

Although Taharqa appears to pass over in silence any specific mention of his father in those same inscriptions, there is every reason to think that his father was Piankhy. Confirmation derives from the fact that Taharqa gave his own daughter, Amenirdis II, for adoption as heiress and successor to the incumbent God's Wife of Amun, Shepenwepet II, who is identified as a sister of Taharqa and known to be a daughter of Piankhy as well.

Inscriptions from the Nubian city of Kawa relate how the 20-year-old Taharqa was summoned to Egypt by the command of Shebitqo. Approximately five years later Taharqa was crowned pharaoh in Memphis.

I received the crown in Memphis after the Falcon (= the deceased Shebitqo) had soared to heaven and my father commanded me to place every land and country beneath my feet (BPENR 230)

Taharqa does not fail to mention that the occasion of his coronation at Memphis was witnessed by his mother, Abar, who traveled from Nubia in order to be present at the investiture.

[The queen-mother] was in Napata as King's Sister, amiable in love, King's Mother.... Now, I had been separated from her as a youth of twenty years.... then she went north to [the Northland where I was] after a long period of years, as she found me crowned [as king upon the throne of Horus]...she rejoiced greatly [when she saw] the beauty of his Majesty.... (ARE 4: §895)

It is, however, extremely unclear how Taharqa came to succeed Shebitqo, although some scholars opine that he may have usurped the throne. The reality may very simply be the discipline's ignorance regarding Nubian rules for succession, which make them difficult to quantify because, where familial relationships can be established, successors are known to have been brothers, sons, cousins, and nephews of previous kings, often nominated to the office by divine oracle. The most recent investigation on the subject suggesting that one's relationship to primary royal women may have played a more significant role in the right to succeed than the rule of primogeniture is open to question.

The kingdom ruled by Taharqa was initially characterized by peace at home and abroad, although he did not neglect the military. A stela discovered on the desert road in Egypt near Dashur, south of Giza, and dated to his Regnal Year Five, describes how Taharqa on horseback accompanied his army in training by running the course of some 50 kilometers in five hours. During the first half of his reign, the Assyrians were preoccupied with other matters. The death of Sargon, king of Assyria, during a military campaign, elevated his son, Sennacherib, to the Assyrian throne. His first priority was to suppress dissention and uprisings within Assyria proper. Only after having accomplished this objective, could Sennacherib turn his attention to the West.

TAHARQA, SENNACHERIB, AND THE OLD TESTAMENT

Thereafter, Senneracherib focused his attention on the West and did so as recorded in two of the most controversial Biblical references with regard to the Nubians in general and Taharqa in particular. The passage in question is first found in 2 Kings 19: 8–9 and repeated verbatim in Isaiah 37:8–9. In these passages Taharqa's name is rendered in Hebrew as Tirhakah and his kingdom is referred to as Cush.

The cupbearer turned about and rejoined the king of Assyria, who was then attacking Libnah, the cupbearer having learned that the king had already left Lachish on hearing that Tirhakah [=Taharqa] king of Cush was on his way to attack him. (NJB 856)

This Biblical account is also reflected in the *Annals* of Sennacherib.

At issue in this matter is whether the Kushite king, Tirhakah, mentioned in these two Biblical passages is in fact the historical Taharqa, and whether he engaged in one or two campaigns against the Assyrians. Traditionalists in advocating a literal interpretation of the passages in the *Old Testament* defend the presence of Taharqa himself in this conflict. They are supported by some Egyptologists and Assyriologists but challenged by others.

Sennacherib, nevertheless, was resolved to march against Judah and take Jerusalem, as outlined in his communications with its ruler, Hezekiah, in 2 Kings 18–19. It is assumed from the two Biblical passages just cited that the Kushites, led by Taharqa, came to the assistance of Judah in time to help defend Jerusalem against the impending attack of Sennacherib. The Assyrian host marched up to the city and pitched camp for the night, intending to attack the following day. The Biblical account in 2 Kings 19:35–36 records that

That same night the angel of Yahweh went out and struck down a hundred and eighty-five thousand men in the Assyrian camp. In the early morning when it was time to get up, there they lay, so many corpses. Sennacherib struck camp and left; he returned home and stayed in Nineveh. (NJB 377)

This miraculous destruction of the Assyrian host is interestingly enough also recorded by Herodotus (II, 141), who reports:

So presently came king Sanacharib against Egypt, with a great host of Arabians and Assyrians...and one night a multitude of field mice swarmed over the Assyrian camp and devoured their quivers and their bows and the handles of their shields likewise, insomuch that they fled the next day unarmed and many fell.

Historians attribute the cause of the defeat of the Assyrians mentioned in these Biblical and Classical references to plague, but as is to be expected, there is no mention of this defeat in the Assyrians' records. The subsequent murder of Sennacherib was anciently regarded as an act of divine retribution either in the Assyrian records for his destruction of Babylon or in the Biblical account for his attack on Jerusalem. In any event, the inability of the Assyrians to take Jerusalem, the subsequent murder of Sennacherib, and the ensuing dynastic struggles for the throne of Assyria doubtless enabled Taharqa to pursue numerous Egyptian interests in the Syria-Palestine regions.

THE ASSYRIANS AND THE EGYPTIAN DELTA PRINCES

In the pursuit of these interests, the cities of the Egyptian Delta must have played decisive roles because of their geographic proximity to the Levant. The temporary cessation of hostilities between Egypt and Assyria also promoted the political aspirations of the Delta princes, particularly because the attempts of Shabaka and his predecessor Piankhy to bring the Delta firmly into their control were not comprehensive. Pockets of resistance to Nubian suzerainty continued to thrive and were eventually to be concentrated in the hands of the petty princes of Sais.

Nubian interests in the Syria-Palestine region expanded and intensified at the expense of Assyria's with regard to Mediterranean trade in general and cedar from Phoenician Lebanon in particular. In attempting to maintain their control over the latter, the Assyrians instructed the Phoenician cities on the coast to refrain from selling timber to Egypt and Philistia. This explicit prohibition is an accurate reflection of Egypt's growing influence in the region. His earlier alliance with Hezikiah of Judah against Sennacherib was but one component of Taharqa's foreign policy. He subsequently gave military support to a coalition of Phoenician cities when they were attacked by Esarhaddon, one of Sennerachib's younger sons who succeeded him as King of Assyria. The Assyrians were victorious, but the Phoenician cities, supported perhaps by Egypt's promise of military aid, remained defiant. The city of Sidon shortly thereafter renounced its alliance with Assyria. In response, Esarhaddon not only captured Sidon but razed its walls. Esarhaddon's booty included a wealth of luxury goods such as ivory, elephant hides, and ebony, all Nubian products, which suggest strong mercantile links between Sidon and the Nubians.

TAHARQA AND ESARHADDON, KING OF ASSYRIA

The Assyrians now regarded Egypt as their principal foe and launched a series of campaigns aimed at regaining control of the Syria-Palestine region in order to secure a base for an invasion of Egypt. The events are muddled, partially because the defeat of the Assyrians by the Egyptians is not mentioned in their accounts of the events, but one Assyrian victory is graphically recorded in a monumental stela erected by Esarhaddon at Til Barsip, which is currently in the collections of the museum in Aleppo, Syria. Esarhaddon is here depicted on a colossal scale, dominating the composition. His left hand holds a leash attached to two smaller figures whose identities are hotly contested because they are not accompanied by captions. One of these figures is represented with distinctly Nubian features and wears a cap crown fronted by a uraeus, regalia specifically associated with Nubian royals. Alternately identified as either Taharqa himself or his son, whose name appears as "Ushanuhuru" elsewhere in Assyrian texts, the figure does not represent an historically identifiable individual. His stereotypical features in association with Nubian regalia serve as a generic image implying an Assyrian victory over the Nubian rulers of Egypt in general.

The stereotypical depiction of this Nubian is not without significance because the Assyrians have here created a striking ideological image to the effect that their enemy in Egypt is the Nubian pharaoh, rather than one or more of the petty Egyptian princes of the Delta cities. One can suggest that these Delta princes may have welcomed the hostilities as a means of freeing themselves of Nubian sovereigns with the assistance of the Assyrians. The rapid unfolding of subsequent events lends credence to this suggestion.

The imminent Assyrian threat encouraged the formation of a coalition among the principalities of Phoenicia, which effectively placed an embargo on goods to Assyria and stopped the payment of tribute. Esarhaddon marched against them and was ultimately victorious. He then resolved to invade Egypt.

The reticence of the Egyptians to record military defeats and the rather laconic record of the military confrontation and subsequent victory of Esarhaddon in the Assyrian annals is noteworthy. Both the *Esarhaddon Chronicle* and the *Babylonian Chronicle* pay scant attention to both Assyrian preparations and initial engagements. Esarhaddon, after traveling through the desert from Gaza to Raphia with the assistance of local tribesmen, whose camels transported water needed by his thirsty troops, rapidly advanced on Egypt. Thereafter Esarhaddon engaged Taharqa's forces three times in pitched battles over the course of the 15 days it took the Assyrians to reach Memphis.

The personal valor displayed by both kings cannot be underestimated:

I [Esarhaddon] fought...very bloody battles against Tarqu [= Taharqa], king of Egypt and Kush, the one accursed by all the great gods. Five times I hit him with the point of (my) arrows (inflicting) wounds (from which he should not) recover.... (BPENR 268)

THE FALL OF MEMPHIS

Realizing the hopelessness of a continued defense of his capital and royal residence, the wounded Taharqa abandoned his city and withdrew, some historians claiming to Thebes. Those left behind within the city fiercely resisted with such zeal that several days after the last battle, as Esarhaddon entered the city, the battle raged along its streets with a horrific toll of lives lost.

I defeated and killed them with my weapons...in the city square their corpses were heaped upon one another, I erected piles of their heads.... (BPENR 268)

Many members of Taharqa's royal family, including both his queen and other members of his harem together with their sons and daughters as well as Taharqa's brothers were captured. The Assyrians were overwhelmed with the riches contained within the city that now fell into their hands. These treasures included what may be described as the Nubian crown jewels, consisting of dozens of tiaras and assorted types of crowns as well as horses, cattle, and sheep without number.

The Assyrian accounts document these events and conclude with Esarhaddon's statement, seemingly implementing a long-standing plan, that he

Appointed anew kings, viceroys, governors, commanders, overseers, and scribes (BPENR 269)

many of whom were doubtless drafted from the ranks of the Delta petty princes and the elite members of their courts. These individuals may even have conspired against Taharqa. Evidence for this assertion derives from the observation that Esarhaddon vowed to remove "the root of Kush (i.e., Nubia)" from Egypt. To that end, he systematically targeted Nubians, but not Egyptians, for removal from office. Many of these targeted Nubians along with some quarrelsome Egyptians were deported to Nineveh.

EGYPT ANNEXED BY THE ASSYRIANS

Esarhaddon then incorporated what had traditionally been Lower Egypt, from the vicinity just south of Memphis to the Mediterranean coast, into the Assyrian empire, but was a pragmatist insofar as his assessment of the fragmented political nature of Egypt was concerned with its various nomes dominated by competing petty princes. He, therefore, styles himself:

King of the kings of Lower Egypt, of Upper Egypt, and of Kush (BPENR 267)

In contrast to the subsequent Persian annexation of Egypt in the late sixth century B.C.E., which left its mark on the arts and various other aspects of Egypt's material culture, the Assyrian occupation of the land is virtually absent from the period's archaeological record. That absence may, in part, be explained by the fact that the Assyrians did not seem to appoint their own high officials for postings within Egypt proper. Their administration of the newly annexed territory appears to have relied upon co-opting the local bureaucracy and retaining its native hierarchy.

Esarhaddon's control over Egypt was to be brief. Taharqa apparently seized an opportunity of returning uncontested to Memphis while Esarhaddon was compelled to deal with an apparent threat to his authority in Assyria itself. Having established his authority, Esarhaddon immediately resolved to reinvade Egypt, but became ill en route and died in the Syria-Palestine region. A potential struggle for succession in Assyria, which would have been advantageous to Egypt's newly rewon independence, was squashed by Assurbanipal, a son and the successor of Esarhaddon, who within two years of gaining the throne embarked on a military campaign against the Nubians.

TAHARQA AND ASSURBANIPAL, KING OF ASSYRIA

The petty princes of the Syria-Palestine region, who had earlier repudiated Assyrian authority and allied themselves with Egypt, reassessed their former policy in light of the fact that Esarhaddon had successfully invaded and annexed Egypt. As Assurbanipal's Assyrian forces marched through the region en route to Egypt, approximately two dozen rulers pledged to him their allegiance and were forced to contribute manpower and other resources to the war effort. In a two-pronged assault by which the land army was accompanied by a flotilla, Assurbanipal defeated Taharqa's forces at Karbaniti, the Assyrian name for the location of the battle, which remains difficult to identify otherwise.

Assurbanipal records how he recaptured Memphis and once again forced Taharqa to seek refuge by fleeing to Thebes. In order to secure his position, Assurbanipal reinstated the petty princes, whom his father had confirmed in their offices, despite the fact that they had, when faced with the Assyrian invasion, abdicated their collective responsibility toward him.

These kings, princes, and governors, whom my father had appointed in Egypt and who had deserted their posts before the advance of Tarqu [= Taharqa], and had scattered into the open country, I reinstated in their former offices. (BPENR 278)

Assurbanipal then resolved to pursue Taharqa and to continue the campaign in Upper Egypt, determining that a battle would perhaps have to be fought on the West bank of the Nile River where the Nubian forces had been concentrated. En route from Memphis to Thebes, Assurbanipal was informed that the petty princes of the Delta, whom he had just reconfirmed in their offices, regarded this as an opportunity for reasserting their autonomy. There is solid evidence that some of these Delta princes, whose long-standing antipathy toward Nubian overlordship was well known, nevertheless conspired with Taharqa against the Assyrian king Assurbanipal at this time.

Assurbanipal's revenge was swift and merciless.

They arrested these kings and bound them hand and foot with bonds and fetters of iron...they did not spare any among them. Their corpses they hung on stakes. They flayed their skins and covered the city walls with them. (BPENR 279)

It is, therefore, all the more remarkable to acknowledge the resiliency of the petty princes of the Egyptian Delta city of Sais throughout this period of Nubian–Assyrian military confrontation. It is a lasting tribute to their political acumen and diplomatic skills that they could retain a degree of independence within a local hereditary dynasty of their own making while instilling either Nubian or Assyrian ruler with absolute confidence about the sincerity of their allegiance. The extraordinary career of Necho of Sais reveals his ability to navigate these treacherous waters without foundering. Assurbanipal remarked,

Those kings who had planned evil against the armies of Assyria they brought before me alive to Nineveh. I had mercy only upon Niku [= Necho of Sais]. I spared his life and laid an oath, more drastic than the former, upon him...I sent him back to his post...where my father had set him up as king.... (BPENR 280)

Necho was apparently able to communicate these skills to his son and successor, Psametik, whom Assurbanipal also mentions by name and installs as ruler in Athribis, another important Delta city.

It remains moot whether or not Assurbanipal did pursue Taharqa to Thebes and engage him in a heated battle. The Assyrian record is vague on the matter

As for Tarqu [= Taharqa] in the place to which he fled, the terror of the sacred weapon of [the god] Assur, my lord, overwhelmed him and the night of death overtook him (BPENR 280)

and Egyptologists are still divided in their assessment of iron weapons excavated at Thebes and their association with an Assyrian assault on this Upper Egyptian religious capital.

If the forces of Assurbanipal did pursue the Nubians to Thebes, they were unable to capture Taharqa, who escaped to Nubia and eventually died there. If they did receive the submission of the local Theban elite and did extend their reach to the region of Aswan, the traditional border between Egypt and Nubia, their control of this region in general and of Egypt in particular was short-lived. Relying on the administration that he had just imposed in Egypt with Necho of Sais as the nominal head, Assurbanipal withdrew to Assyria.

TAHARQA'S LEGACY

Taharqa's rule of some 26 years has been characterized by many as the single most glorious age of Dynasty XXV. Monuments bearing his royal cartouches have been found throughout the length and breadth of the land from Tanis in the extreme northeastern Delta to the southernmost reaches, including Meroe. Nubia proper benefited from his numerous architectural projects, including his modification of the yardang at Gebel Barkal.

In death he departed from custom and became the first Nubian to be buried at Nuri, to the northeast of Gebel Barkal and on the Nile River's opposite bank. His tomb consisted of an impressive pyramid, the estimated height of which has been calculated to have been between 50 and 60 meters, ranking it as the largest pyramid ever erected in Nubia proper.

The massive tomb beneath is also unique and innovative and evokes in its details and religious associations the Temple of Osiris at Abydos erected by Sety I of Dynasty XIX. One suggests that this tomb had astronomical associations linked with the rising sun.

TANTAMANI

Tantamani succeeded Taharqa, perhaps his cousin, as king. The events surrounding his rise to power are recorded in the so-called *Dream Stela*, discovered at Napata and now in the collections of the Egyptian Museum, Cairo. The text of the stela implies a political relationship between Tantamani and Taharqa, but scholars are divided in their opinion about whether Taharqa merely nominated Tantamani as his heir or whether Tantamani was actually a coregent ruling in Upper Egypt. Upon the death of Taharqa, Tantamani was summoned to Napata,

...his Majesty went forth from the place where he had been...his Majesty went to Napata (ARE 4: §923)

and there was crowned king in his own right. These events were revealed to Tantamani by means of a prophetic dream:

...his Majesty saw a dream by night: two serpents, one upon his right, the other upon his left. Then His Majesty awoke, and he found them not. His Majesty said, "Wherefore has this come to me?" Then they answered him, saying, "Thine is the Southland; take for thyself also the Northland." (ARE 4: §922)

TANTAMANI RETURNS TO EGYPT

As the narrative of the *Dream Stela* recounts, Tantamani, modeling his actions on those of Piankhy, embarked on a religious pilgrimage to Egypt, stopping at Elephantine to sacrifice to Khnum, the ram-headed creator god, and then to Thebes, where he paid homage to Amun. The fact that Tantamani encountered no resistance suggests that Assyrian control of Upper Egypt, if it existed at all, was minimal, and that the region still regarded the Nubians as their legitimate sovereigns.

The situation at Memphis was different because it had been reoccupied by those loyal to the Assyrians and had to be taken by storm.

When his Majesty arrived at Memphis, there came forth the children of the rebellion, to fight with his Majesty. His Majesty made a great slaughter among them...His Majesty took Memphis. (ARE 4: §928)

Tantamani subsequently campaigned in the Delta but was initially unable to engage any in combat,

His Majesty sailed north, to fight with the chiefs of the North. Then they entered their stronghold [as beasts crawl into] their holes. Then his Majesty spent many days before them, (but) they came not forth one of them to fight with his Majesty (ARE 4: §930)

and retired to Memphis where he considered his options.

In the end, according to the *Dream Stela,* the petty princes of the Delta voluntarily traveled to Memphis and demonstrated their submission to Tantamani, who reestablished Memphis as the Nubian royal residence within Egypt, an act that was to provoke an Assyrian response.

THE RETURN OF ASSURBANIPAL AND THE FALL OF DYNASTY XXV

Assurbanipal returned, recaptured Memphis, and chased Tantamani to Thebes, which was stormed, burned, and pillaged. Tantamani escaped to Napata, but the great distance through regions thoroughly unfamiliar to its military dissuaded the Assyrians from giving pursuit. He died in his Nubian homeland and was buried at el-Kurru.

The Assyrians reviewed their options by evaluating the performance of their Egyptian administrators, some of whom they removed from office and replaced with others. The primacy of the city of Sais and the authority of its petty princes had long been cultivated and recognized by the Assyrians, who now confirmed Psametik, son of Necho, in his office as virtual king of Egypt, a position that Assurbanipal wholeheartedly supported, on condition that Psametik refrain from any belligerent action against Assyria. By means of this declaration, Psametik's position gained legal sanction. The subsequent fall and dissolution of the Assyrian empire gave him license to consolidate his realm at the expense of the Nubians.

Politics and Religion

One is imperfectly informed about governmental institutions, their administrative mechanisms, the nature of the deities of the land, and the specifics of religious practice and ritual for several reasons. The Nubians adopted literacy fairly late in their history, with the result that information about government and religion in the earlier periods must be inferred from the archaeological data and from the records of their neighbors, many of whom viewed the Nubians through non-Nubian lenses. Some of these sources are, perforce, prejudicial. The introduction of Egyptian hieroglyphs by the Nubians during Dynasty XXV enabled them to express themselves, but as one shall see later, there is considerable debate among scholars about the exact meaning, and hence interpretation, of numerous passages in those written records. The development of purely Nubian notational systems during the Kingdom of Meroe enabled the Nubians to express their own thoughts in their own language for the very first time. Nevertheless, scholars still have an imperfect command of Meroitic, and information about specific administrative mechanisms and cult praxis are subjects apparently not dealt with in those texts. Such discussions are further confounded by the lack of consensus among scholars about chronology, particularly for Dynasty XXV and the periods thereafter. As a result, a good deal of caution must be exercised in any discussions about the specifics of Nubian government and religion.

THE CASE OF KATIMALO

The elite Nubian woman, Katimalo, may serve as a case study illustrating the problems involved. Her Nubian name, *Kdi-mel(ye)*, literally means, "the beautiful" or "the good woman," like the Egyptian personal name, *Nofret*. Katimalo is attested in inscriptions written in hieroglyphs in so-called New Egyptian, which gained currency as a vernacular during the course of Dynasty XIX–XX. One such inscription from the temple at Semna is obscure in the extreme and contains numerous passages that defy explication. There is disagreement about her chronological position within Nubian history. Whereas other elite Nubian women may have their name written in a cartouche, or royal ring, the name of Katimalo is not. The absence of a cartouche disqualifies her as a queen ruling in her own right, despite the fact that she bears the title "nesut bity," which literally translates, "The (female) king of Upper and Lower Egypt." Scholars interpret this title as a reference to her relationship to a ruling king rather than as an indication of her own independent status. The case of Katimalo is one of many, but it points out the difficulties encountered when one attempts to make sweeping generalizations.

Based on cultural analogies with Egypt and a study of the data derived from elite graves and tombs, one can suggest that Nubian society was an oligarchy whose elite members, numbering about 10 percent of the total population, controlled all aspects of government and religion. Because of the nature of this evidence, all discussions are generalizations about the elite and the society in which they moved. There is virtually no evidence from which detailed descriptions of the vast majority of nonelite members of Nubian society can be adduced. In the later periods with the introduction of literacy, the elite members of this priestly ruling class may have numbered about 1 percent of the population. It is to this ruling elite in the periods from Dynasty XXV onward that we now turn.

THE NUBIAN THEOCRACY OF DYNASTY XXV

The Nubians regarded their king as simultaneously the supreme ruler of the land and chief priest of all its deities. **The Goddess** The relationship between the king and the god Amun **Isis** needs to be emphasized inasmuch as from a list of 57 names of Meroitic kings and queens, 26, or just under 50 percent, are names compounded with that of the god Amun. One has already discussed the polyvalent nature of ancient religion, which admitted nuanced differences between several deities, all of whom were named, for example, Amun. To this polyvalence must be added another consideration. Eurocentric approaches to antiquity often invoke models derived from ancient Greece and Rome, where an Aristotelian compartmentalization accustoms one to associate specific deities with other deities in seemingly straightforward relationships. In such a system, boundaries are never blurred, and an internal consistency is maintained.

The polyvalent nature of ancient Egyptian and Nubian religion, on the other hand, contributes to the association of deities, which such an Aristotelian compartmentalization would deny. The nexus between the cults of the Nubian Amuns and kingship has already been noted earlier. This relationship was furthered by anonymous Nubian theologians, who via a series of very sophisticated religious formulations additionally regarded both Isis and Re as conveyors of the legitimacy of kingship. The role of Isis in this relationship derived in part from her associations with Osiris, who posthumously engendered her with their son and heir, Horus. Egyptian religious tenets had long identified a deceased pharaoh with Osiris and his living successor as Horus, but it was the Nubian theologians who forged the link between her and Re in this regard, as the following passage inscribed on the walls of the Temple of Kawa for Taharqa reveals:

Thy mother is Isis
His mother is Isis
Thy father is Osiris
His father is Osiris
The son of Re, Taharqa, his mother Isis bore him. (author's translation)

Such religious expressions find their correspondence in any number of representations from the period in which a Nubian king is shown either in the embrace of Isis, or another goddess assimilated to her, as seen in a sandstone relief, uninscribed but attributed to the reign of Taharqa in The Brooklyn Museum, or in the minor arts in which a Nubian king, generally standing and of smaller scale, is nursed by a standing, taller figure of a similar goddess.

Concomitant with the rise of the cult of Isis during Dynasty XXV was the reestablishment of the site of Abydos in Middle Egypt to the north of Thebes, which was traditionally the most important Egyptian sanctuary of Osiris. Numerous high-ranking elite Nubian women were buried here, including Isisemkhebit, the daughter of Shabako. Some would attribute her burial here to pragmatism. The journey from Thebes, where she presumably died, to Napata, where she would have presumably been buried, would have consumed so much time as to be impractical. The body was, therefore, buried at Abydos as an expedient. This prosaic explanation fails to account for the demonstrable religious ardor of the Nubians. The princess's very name, Isisemkhebit, incorporates the name of the goddess Isis and alludes to her asylum in the marshes where, protected, she raised her son Horus. Possessed of such a cultic name, the princess was doubtless buried at Abydos for cultic reasons, foremost among which was to be united for eternity with Osiris, her nominal spouse. The popularity of the cult of Isis during this time appears to be a better explanation for the interment of a great many elite Nubians at Abydos during the same period.

The popularity of Isis and of Amun was responsible for the choice of Western Thebes at Medinet Habu as another burial site for elite Nubians of the period. The choice was motivated in part by the cultic relationships between Amun of Thebes and Osiris of Djeme, the ancient name of the region in Western Thebes. Via a complex religious conceit, the deceased interred within a tomb as Osiris became transformed into a celestial being identified with Amun on his resurrection, a process described in the discussion of the Lake Edifice of Taharqa. It would appear, therefore, both in life and in death that the Nubian elite of Dynasty XXV resident in Egypt understood and adopted as their own the prevailing politicoreligious tenets of the day.

The primacy of the goddess Isis in such formulations of legitimacy of kingship has been linked to the exceptional role of elite women in Nubian society. Precise definitions of that role are difficult to formulate because of the paucity of modern European lexica, in which the term *queenship*, as a pendant to *kingship*, is both unfamiliar and disquieting. Nevertheless, the role of elite Nubian women in both government and religion cannot be underestimated. Their prominence, however, has caused some scholars to proclaim the existence of a Nubian matrilineal institution.

THE QUESTION OF MATRILINEAL SUCCESSION DURING DYNASTY XXV

The prominence of elite Nubian women, whose role in the cults of the deities of the land was demonstrably more important than the commensurate role of Egyptian queens, and the primacy of the goddess Isis in Nubian society of Dynasty XXV have often been adduced as proof of the existence of matrilineal institution in Nubia, defined in broad terms as royal succession based on a relationship to the primary elite female member of society, rather than by primogeniture or descent from the incumbent male ruler. An examination of some of the contemporary terminology applied to the Nubian elite women is, therefore, required to test the validity of this suggestion.

Almost all of the terminology is derived from inscriptions written in ancient Egyptian hieroglyphs, and therein resides a difficulty. Because the Nubians are writing in a language not their own, they themselves did not coin words narrowly defining their native concepts. Indeed, they were forced to select from the contemporary Egyptian lexicon those words or phrases that best expressed the desired concept, however imprecise that equivalence may have been.

In terms of titles associated with religious cults, elite Nubian women in Egypt bore titles such as "divine wife," the use of which was restricted to those serving as divine consorts of the god Amun in Thebes. In Egypt, these women might serve as priestesses of a number of goddesses, including both Hathor and Mut, and might be attached to the cult of Amun as one of his sistrum-players. When the titles "musician" and "sistrum-player" appear in Nubian context, they are invariably not accompanied by the name of the deity of the cult to which they are attached. In these contexts, their epithets relate to their priestly functions and include "the one great of praise," "the one sweet of love," "the mistress (variation, the great one) of the *iamet*-scepter," and "the lovable possessor of charm." Their aulic, or courtly, titles might include the feminine version of an honorific male title commonly translated as "hereditary princess," as well as "the first (among) his Majesty['s entourage]," "the king's acquaintance," and "mistress of all women." Royal titles of elite Nubian women might include "Mistress of the Two Lands," "Mistress of Upper and Lower Egypt," "Mistress of foreign lands," "Mistress of Egypt," and "Mistress of Nubia." Oddly enough, however, no elite Nubian royal women simultaneously bore the titles of mistress of Egypt and mistress of Nubia. These titles could be accompanied by a number of epithets including, "the one who satisfies the heart of the king through that which she performs daily," "the one who causes the king's heart to rejoice on account of all that she says," "the one who is united to the limbs of the god," "the one beloved of her master," and "the sole ornament of the king." All of the titles and epithets are common to the repertoire of titles for contemporary Egyptian women. None of these designates any familial relationship and not one can be interpreted as connoting the legitimacy of kingship.

One is left, therefore, with a series of titles that incorporate familial terms, such as "the daughter of Re," "the daughter of the god," and "the mother of the god" together with other titles, such as "the mother of the king," "the sister of the king," "the wife of the king," and "the daughter of the king." The most important of these in terms of discussions of a matrilineal institution is that of "mother of the king", *mut nesu*. Although this phrase literally translates into English as "the mother of the king," the Egyptian noun *mut*, "mother," may also connote familial concepts such as grandmother. The imprecision of such nouns is also evident in the phrases used for son and daughter, the connotative meanings of which may include uncle. Any insistence on a single, literal meaning of the phrase "king's mother" to demonstrate the institution of matrilineal succession is as academically perilous as suggesting that the ubiquitous use of the noun *sister* in love sonnets of the Egyptian New Kingdom is demonstration of incestuous unions. The noun *sister* is divorced of familial associations and is there used simply as a term of endearment.

Any generalizations about the mechanisms by which elite Nubian male members of the oligarchy became kings during Dynasty XXV cannot be adduced from the inscriptional evidence as preserved, as revealed by the following synoptic genealogies of those kings.

The rise of Kashta is shrouded in darkness. The parents of Piankhy are presently not known. Shabako appears to be a son of Kashta. His daughter, Amenirdis I, served as a divine consort of Amun at Thebes. The identity of his wife, the mother of his daughter Isisemkhebit, is not known, and that of the mother of his son, Harmakhis, speculative. Only one source, a Greek one and rather late based on the history composed by Manetho during the Ptolemaic Period, names Shebitko as the son of Shabaka. Taharqa's mother is Abalo, but his father is not named; he may very well have been Piankhy. Assyrian sources claim Tanatamani was the son of Ahabako, but other evidence suggests that he was the son of Taharka's sister, perhaps to be identified as Qalhata. As one can see, the nature of this evidence is so imprecise that it would be foolhardy to make any generalizations whatsoever about the mechanisms of succession in Dynasty XXV. The evidence would not seem to support the existence of a matrilineal institution for succession during this period.

Furthermore, one must bear in mind the propagandistic nature of many official Nubian and Egyptian inscriptions. Historical and genealogical information contained therein is often skewed to reflect ideals, often fictitious, far removed from historical truth. A case in point is a renewal inscription of Taharqa inscribed in the walls of the Temple at Semna West, which was dedicated to both Sesostris III, the now-deified Egyptian

The satyric scene from Medamoud. From *Nubia: History of a Fabulous Civilization* by Silvio Curto (Novara, 1965), p. 57.

pharaoh of Dynasty XII, and the god Dedwen, "foremost of Nubia." In this inscription Taharqa claims Sesostris III as his father. The claim cannot be taken literally, but must be regarded as an attempt by Taharqa to integrate himself into the venerable succession of successful rulers of Nubia with a view toward asserting his own legitimacy.

THE NUBIAN EGYPTIAN TEMPLES

Dynasty XXV The very fragmentary state of Nubian temples attributed to various depredations over time has resulted in the loss of their entire upper courses. For this reason, a study of the temples of Nubian Dynasty XXV is often confined to a discussion of their ground plans, which by and large conform to the model described earlier.

The Great Temple of Amun at Gebel Barkal may be taken as an example. Begun by Egyptian pharaohs of Dynasty XVIII, it was continually enlarged and modified by Nubians. It was originally restored and successively enlarged by the Nubian pharaoh Piankhy, who found it in ruins. Piankhy added a hypostyle, or large columned hall to the edifice, as well as a later colonnaded court and pylons. In its final form, its appearance may have rivaled that of the main temple of Amun at Karnak.

The temple of Amun at Kawa was one of several commissioned by the Nubian pharaoh Taharqa, who was perhaps the greatest builder of temples in the region since Rameses II. This temple shares so many features in common with a second at Sanam and a third at Tabo on the island of Argo, which were likewise commissioned during the reign of Taharqa, as to suggest they were designed by the same architect(s) perhaps using the same plans, the existence for which seems confirmed in ancient Egypt. The massive pylon opens onto an open courtyard with six columns on its north and south sides and four on its east and west. A doorway gives access to the hypostyle hall, its central axis flanked by eight columns on each side. Beyond was the roofed pronaos with four columns, leading to the inner sanctum, and four ancillary rooms. With the exception of the ancillary rooms wreathing the pronaos and inner sanctum, the common ground plan of each of these three temples conforms to the basic rectangular design of Egyptian temples, described earlier.

The decoration and accompanying inscriptions, invariably in Egyptian hieroglyphs, of these temples may be regarded as Nubian versions of ancient Egyptian themes. In keeping with the theological tenets of the temple by which one of pharaoh's significant obligations was the maintenance of cosmic order, military themes dominate, as is to be expected, given the numerous military engagements both against the petty princes of the Delta as well as the Assyrians, against whom the Nubians of Dynasty XXV warred.

Some of these scenes are extremely important in understanding the dialectic between tradition and innovation not only in Egyptian but also in Nubian art. One such scene is found on the walls of Temple T at Kawa from the reign of Taharqa. It depicts Taharqa as a monumental, triumphant sphinx trampling the foes of his realm underfoot. The enemy named in the accompanying legends as the Libyans does not appear to have been a group of peoples against whom Taharqa fought. In fact, the entire scene is a religious artifice, based on a prototype current at Memphis during the Old Kingdom and first used by Sahure of Dynasty V. It was subsequently repeated, almost verbatim as here at Kawa, by Pepy II of Dynasty VI.

The appropriation of this earlier scene by Taharqa is not an indication of any lack of creativity on his part. The appropriation must be regarded within the context of the archaizing of the period, defined as the cultural phenomenon by which earlier models are purposefully pressed into service to address contemporary requirements. One has already seen how the names of some of the Nubian pharaohs of Dynasty XXV are the same as those of New Kingdom pharaohs who left their lasting mark on Nubia, and how, perhaps as an act of religious piety, Shabaka edited the Memphite theology, ostensibly from an ancient, worm-eaten original. By imitating an earlier, and hence venerable, monument, Taharqa reveals himself to be a champion of tradition, worthy of being intercalated into the ranks of legitimate Egyptian pharaohs. He is portrayed as the guarantor of cosmic harmony, whose actual military victories in the field have here been compared to the significant victories of Egypt's hoary past.

This appropriation of an Old Kingdom model by Taharqa may be compared to a more innovative depiction of victory, that in the lower courses of the relief decoration of the Great Temple of Amun commissioned by Piankhy. Although fragmentary, it has been convincingly reconstructed. The reconstruction depicts Piankhy to the extreme right, standing erect in Nubian regalia and designed so that his height is equal to the combined height of the two registers to his left, which complete the scene. Prostrate enemies, represented with their mouths "kissing the earth," kneel before Piankhy. They are followed by grooms leading their horses, animals that figure prominently as well in the figural lunette and the inscriptions of Piankhy's *Victory Stela*.

The fragmentary state of so many of the royal reliefs of Dynasty XXV is lamentable, particularly when isolated worked blocks from ensembles long since vanished present the scholar with tantalizing glimpses of just how creative the subject matter of those scenes must have been.

A case in point are two worked blocks from Medamud, now in the collections of the Egyptian Museum, Cairo. Associated with the Nubian God's Wives of Amun and generally dated to Dynasty XXV, their subject matter is virtually without parallel in temple relief. One block in particular depicts a scene set within a Nilotic marsh, indicated by the curtainlike vertical elements representing stalks of reeds or other aquatic plants. To the left, a crocodile with his head turned over his shoulder strums a stringed instrument, accompanied by a nude female figure standing on his back who plays a lyre. In the center in smaller scale is a heavily draped human figure, perhaps a servant of the mice shown at the right. One of them is enthroned and attended by a cat. The topsy-turvy world order represented here has been interpreted as an illustration of an ancient Egyptian fable, but such an interpretation fails in light of the single column of inscription at the left, which is funerary in nature and translates, " ...foremost of the kas of the living...." It would appear that the Nubians, perhaps as part of the archaizing tendencies of Dynasty XXV, had recourse to an entire corpus of so-called satires, most of the preserved examples of which date to the late New Kingdom, and recognized their funerary nature. The appearance of such a fable as a relief is unique because all other examples presently known are illustrations on papyri or drawings on ostraca, limestone flakes used a sketch-pads by skilled scribal artisans. These reliefs are again eloquent witnesses to the creativity of the craftsmen in the employ of the Nubian pharaohs of Dynasty XXV. Although it is assumed that such a relief may have once decorated a temple, the possibility exists, because of the funerary nature of its accompanying inscription, that these two reliefs are to be associated with a funerary monument, which may even have been a tomb.

As innovative as was the design and construction of the *deffufa* by the Nubians during the period of the Kerma culture, so, too, was the remarkable sanctuary, called the Lake Edifice, of Taharqa within the sanctuary of Karnak at Egyptian Thebes. Like the *deffufa*, it was also a two-story building, and the first floor was similarly designed without any windows. Destruction by time has destroyed both the upper story and façade, but the sanctuary may nevertheless be described as follows.

In ground plan the Lake Edifice measures about 25 by 29 meters. It was designed on a slope with its four sides rising up from ground level in imitation of a small hillock. This slope appears to associate this building with the primeval mound of creation as well. Its principal entrance was to the east, approached by a ramp. One suggests that the principal façade of the superstructure resembled twin shrines, one at each corner, provided with a door and crowned by a cavetto cornice. The architectural appearance of the space between them is open to debate, but because it appears that the second story was hypaethral, that is, unroofed and completely open to the sky, that area may have been closed off by a curtain wall. This eastern façade may have had its relief decoration confined to its north side. The remaining three sides of the Lake Edifice were apparently decorated with relief sculpture, to judge from the worked blocks, the subject of which is the king's interaction with deities. These depict the sequential episodes in the king's departure from his palace and the subsequently performed rituals leading up to his entry into this sanctuary, each couched in the conceit of *do ut des,* "I grant thee X in order that you may bestow upon me Y," a reciprocal relationship consistent with the pattern established for Egyptian temple scenes in general.

The better-preserved first story appears to have been deliberately designed as a dark, subterranean complex of rooms, some interconnected. The thickness of its walls of uniform sandstone blocks average about a meter and half in length. These have been arranged in regular courses, pointed with mortar. The interior walls of this subterranean complex, on the other hand, are constructed of new and reused worked blocks simply laid upon one another.

Because of its poor state of preservation, discussions about the ground plan of the subterranean complex are limited to the suite of rooms in its northern corner. These are reached by a stairway on the west side that descends from north to south and ends in a vestibule arranged at right angles to the landing. Ninety degrees to the north of the landing and arranged parallel to the north wall are three rooms running west to east. They were designed with flagstone floors, which are beneath the level of the earth, suggesting their identification as crypts. Such a designation, however, may be ill advised because the entire first floor may well have been intentionally designed as a warren of subterranean cultic rooms. These rooms each have ceilings constructed of large sandstone slabs. A chamber, approximately equal to the combined dimensions of the three rooms and sharing their parallel alignment along the north wall, terminates near the east wall. It resembles a closed rectangle and reveals no indications of portals communicating with any of the other rooms in this subterranean complex. It has, therefore, been described as a pit that, when excavated, yielded a number of bronze statuettes of the god Osiris, all of which had been broken.

A study of numerous worked blocks used in the construction of the present Lake Edifice display markings or were designed with dovetails, details that do not correspond to their present use in this structure. Because many of these bear the name of Shabaka, it is possible that Taharqa dismantled an earlier structure on this site erected by Shabaka and reused the usurped worked blocks to modify or complete the Lake Edifice. Such usurpations are not necessarily prompted by economic factors, because the reuse of earlier material in a subsequent structure intercalates the contemporary building into the religious continuum of the site.

The function of the Lake Edifice may be suggested by the relationship between the terrestrial and the celestial shared by Egyptian funerary and solar deities and the importance placed on the cyclic nature of natural cosmic phenomenon within the religious tenets of the ancient Egyptians. One of the principal leitmotifs of this periodicity is the rising, setting, and subsequent rising of the sun. This cycle is linked to the creation of the cosmos on the first occurrence with the emergence of the primeval mound from the watery abyss. It is for this reason, doubtless, that the sides of the Lake

Edifice were designed as slopes of a hillock. The polyvalence inherent in ancient Egypt's religious tenets enabled her enlightened theologians to interweave masterfully all these seemingly disconnected elements into a unitarian religious statement made visually manifest by the architecture, relief decoration, and inscriptions of the Lake Edifice.

This unitarian statement in the Lake Edifice revolves around the god Osiris. He was murdered by his brother Seth. His dismembered body was recovered by his sister-wife Isis, reassembled, and reverentially interred, but not before they consummated a posthumous union, which resulted in the subsequent birth of Horus, their son and heir. It may well be in commemoration of one of these episodes in the myth of Osiris that the bronze statuettes found in the "pit" were intentionally broken, an act that can be interpreted as ritually replicating the dismemberment of Osiris before the fragmented bronze statuettes were buried.

During the mythological journey of Osiris toward resurrection, he was transformed into a solar deity and was associated with the sun god Re, himself on occasion associated with Amun, the principal Egyptian deity of the Nubian pantheon. This transformation is mentioned and the subterranean aspect of the Lake Edifice suggested by the scenes and their accompanying hieroglyphic inscriptions in the building itself.

O Re, the one of the cavern, who calls the inhabitants of the cavern. O Re who is in his caverns. (ETSLK 31)

These continue with a description of the journey leading to resurrection:

Ah, give way to him, for he is passing.... Mayest thou lead him on the ways [of the West, mayest] thou make him [come to] the caverns of Nun. (ETSLK 32)

The reference to Nun links the divine rebirth to the creation of the primeval mound because Nun is the personification of the watery abyss. This reference reinforces the primeval mound aspect of the Lake Edifice rendered by its sloped slides. The terrestrial-celestial connection is then explicitly mentioned in the enumeration of the Osirian forms of Re in this same architectural area. The successful passage through the night and eventual resurrection of the godhead at the dawn of the next day is celebrated in the morning greeting, which is accompanied by the morning offering. The cycle is completed by scenes and texts revolving around the theme of the evening offerings and the hymn to the setting sun, followed by a description of its nocturnal journey and subsequent rebirth. The sequence is a reaffirmation of the cyclic nature of the Egyptian cosmos. The preserved scenes and inscriptions of the remaining rooms deal with sophisticated theological concepts, elaborating on the relationship between Osiris and Re. These are linked to ceremonials performed at Thebes requiring processions traveling from the East at Karnak to mortuary sites on the West Bank.

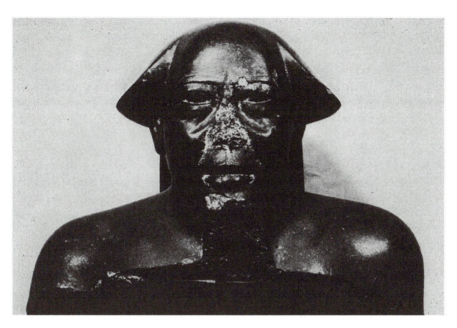

Portrait of Montuemhat. ALEA.

In keeping with the observation that ancient Egyptian sanctuaries served as the equivalents of theme parks in which the elite performed rituals made visually manifest by architecture, the Lake Edifice of the Nubian pharaohs at Karnak is an extraordinary accomplishment. Its subterranean warren of rooms cannot be described as crypts because they are concrete metaphors for the caverns of the underworld through which the interred Osiris was obliged to pass en route to his aspired resurrection at the dawning of the next day. That aspired resurrection was arguably performed in rituals celebrated on the now-destroyed second story, which appropriately lacked a roof so that the contrast between the hidden, mysterious nocturnal journey would not be mistaken with the passage of the solar deity across a wide open, visually unobscured sky.

THE SCULPTURE OF DYNASTY XXV

Although Nubians are represented in the arts of the Egyptian New Kingdom in both Nubia and Egypt, these representations are so Egyptian in their design, materials, and workmanship as to suggest that they were either the creations of Egyptian craftsmen or of Nubians so thoroughly schooled in Egyptian workshops that all traces of what one might define as a Nubian style are avoided.

The Egyptian Ateliers

Typically Nubian-designed and created sculpture again reappears with the ascendancy of the Nubian pharaohs of Dynasty XXV, but all discussions about its nature must follow a discussion of Egyptian art of the same period. And because that sculpture was indebted to prevailing, contemporary Egyptian norms, some attention must be paid to the Egyptian models to elucidate the nature of Nubian sculpture during this time.

It is a given that the sculptural repertoire of ancient Egypt was fairly limited, and although there are exceptions, by and large the Nubians restricted their creative output to a limited number of well-established types. The most frequently created royal image in stone was that of the striding king, wearing a kilt, with the left leg advanced. Smaller images of Nubian pharaohs, usually in bronze, were generally kneeling. Elite num-

Portrait of Amenirdis I in Egyptian style. ALEA.

Portrait of Amenirdis I in Nubian
style. ALEA.

bers of the Nubian royal family and its administrators would likewise be
represented as similar striding images, whereas the women of the period
were generally depicted wearing the tightly fitting sheath with their feet
together. There were, of course, other types such as the king or God's Wife
of Amun as sphinx, with human head and leonine body, or an administrator as mendicant, with the palm of one hand cupped under his chin, but
these also belonged to the repertoire. The block statue, in which the owner
was represented as a cube with protruding head and perhaps also hands
and feet, was also popular. Most of the statues of the Nubians found in
Egypt were excavated at Thebes, more specifically in the so-called
cachette of the Temples of Amun in Karnak located in front of the Seventh
Pylon in 1902. The cachette represents a typically Egyptian phenomenon
whereby over time the temple precinct became so cluttered with statues
that they had to be removed to accommodate more recent dedications.
However, the earlier dedicated statues, being sacred, could not be discarded as rubbish, but had to be disposed of ceremoniously. The most
expedient method was to dig a pit within the temple precinct and somewhat reverentially bury the statues in it. In such a manner, the statues,
although no longer visible, were still within the sacred precinct and
remained ritually charged.

Sphinx of Pharaoh Taharqa in Nubian style. ALEA.

Most of the statues of elite Nubians dated to Dynasty XXV were temple, rather than tomb, statues, and most of these are Theban. The statues found in Nubia were likewise temple dedications. In theory only pharaoh's statue might be erected within a temple precinct, and his authorization was certainly necessary before a statue of a member of his elite family or administration could be commissioned and there erected. Once erected within the temple precinct, the statue of pharaoh or of an elite member of society was magically incorporated into the praxis of temple ritual. Offerings to any deity, by virtue of having been made within the temple, would also, theoretically, be offered to individuals via their statues, which served as their surrogates.

THE NUBIAN ATELIERS OF DYNASTY XXV

Whether or not there were sculptural ateliers in which Nubians as opposed to Egyptians at Thebes were employed is a vexing issue. Certainly, statues of elite Nubians of the period are stylistically so similar to statues of individuals known to have been Egyptian as to suggest that prevailing Egyptian workshops were responsible for the creations. The image of Montuemhat, the head of which is in the Chicago Natural History Museum and the upper torso of which is in The Brooklyn Museum, is designed in keeping with the bland idealizing trends of the New Kingdom, and reveals nothing Nubian in its style.

Other images of the Nubian elite, primarily its pharaohs, were distinguished from earlier royal representations not only by the specifically Nubian character of the regalia, but also with regard to the design of their heads. In general, Nubians in sculpture of the period are shown with round skulls, and there is often a marked emphasis on the cheekbone together with a discernible wrinkle, the so-called naso-labial furrow, which runs from the nostril to the corner of the mouth. Whether this is an intentional stylistic device to indicate the ethnicity of the Nubians or whether this is an artistic device found in earlier representations, particularly in images of the pharaohs of the Middle Kingdom, reinterpreted for the design of images of Nubian pharaohs is a hotly debated issue. My stand on this point is that portraiture in the Western art historical sense did not exist in ancient Egypt, and that representation was a index of decorum. Whereas the native Egyptians, particularly at Thebes, regarded the Nubian pharaohs of Dynasty XXV as the legitimate rulers of the land and accepted the presence of the Nubians in their community and even intermarried without any discrimination, both Egyptian and Nubian elite realized that the Nubians were culturally distinct from the ancient Egyptians. In order to articulate these cultural differences, the craftsmen of the period could, via the phenomenon of archaizing, survey the entire history of Egyptian art. Proof of their ability to do so is afforded by the design of contemporary tombs in Western Thebes, some of which quote isolated vignettes and others elsewhere entire registers of tombs created during either the New or Old Kingdom. The alleged copy of the Shabaka stone, already stressed, is another manifestation of this tendency.

As a result, there was a preexisting repertoire of designs used by earlier Egyptian artisans, particularly during the Middle and New Kingdoms, with which to depict Nubians. Many of these designs, including those used to create objects for the Tomb of Tutankhamon, were stereotypical, emphasizing certain ethnic characteristics almost to the point of caricature, in order to articulate the cultural differences between the Egyptians and the Nubians. These stereotypes are part and parcel of the Egyptian depiction of foreigners in general, who were traditionally grouped together as nine ethnic complexes, the Nine Bows, each represented, on the model of the Nubian, as a stereotype.

The challenge for the Egyptian ateliers was the formulation of design principles by which the Nubian elite, now ruling their land, might be depicted in terms of traditional Egyptian representation of the Nubians, but in such a way that the stereotypical differentials with their pejorative connotations would be eliminated. To that end, the designs incorporated the round skull, the so-called Kushite fold, or pronounced cheekbone, and the naso-labial furrow. These design elements were then incorporated into a limited number of acceptable types within the repertoire of Egyptian statuary and accompanied by the appropriate attributes in the form of regalia specific to the Nubians, serving as indices of decorum both associated and commensurate with their actual prestige and authority. Other types of statuary within the repertoire were avoided. These included representations of the bound prisoner or the Nubian at the mercy of predatory animals, such as the lion, or the use of the Nubian as a decorative element in the minor arts. By innovatively working within an established tradition the Egyptian ateliers, particularly at Thebes, were able to develop distinctive, visual indices of decorum by which the elite would recognize images of Nubian pharaohs and administrators as imbued with status and authority.

The design of some statues depicting members of the Nubian elite are characterized by a degree of abstraction that seems to stand outside the traditions of contemporary Egyptian sculpture. This is best demonstrated by comparing two statues of Amenirdis I, a Nubian God's Wife of Amun. Her alabaster statue in Cairo, discovered in Karnak in the middle of the nineteenth century, is designed in conformity with Egyptian norms, well established by craftsmen of the late New Kingdom. The forms are organic and correspond to the Egyptian conventions for representing the female figure with a lily scepter. A second statue of the same individual in the Joslyn Memorial Art Museum in Omaha, suggested to have come from Thebes as well, is less organic. The contours of the stem of the lily scepter are rectilinear, and its flower is merely incised into the left shoulder. Similarly, the left wrist, hand, and fingers are conceived as a series of simplified, intersecting planes whose angularity is stressed. It would appear that these differences in style indicate two different sculptural schools: an Egyptian responsible for the image in Cairo and a Nubian responsible for the image in Omaha.

When divorced from all foreign stimuli, the Nubian tradition asserts its formal characteristics. This is best seen in a sphinx of Taharqa, found at Kawa, and now in London at The British Museum. The model for this sphinx is, of course, Egyptian, best exemplified perhaps by the sphinx of pharaoh Amenemhat III from Tanis now in the Egyptian Museum in Cairo. A stylistic comparison between the two has occasioned some commentators to remark that the London sphinx is a "provincial expression." Such an appraisal is inappropriate because the aesthetic achievement of the Nubian ateliers ought not be compared with those of native Egyptian ateliers. The tendency toward abstraction, evident in the image of Amenirdis I in Omaha, is full-blown in the London sphinx of Taharqa, and the Nubian aesthetic is fully exploited. This aesthetic became rooted in sculpture of the later Kingdom of Napata and continued to be developed in the Nubian statuary of the Meroitic Period.

10

Nubia during the Napatan Period

The retreat of Tantamani to Napata, the elevation to the throne of Egypt of Psametik I by the Assyrians, and the fall of their empire almost shortly thereafter, were to have lasting consequences for the Nubians. Whereas the Assyrians did recognize the Nubians as their avowed enemy in Egypt, the Nubian presence in the land was thoroughly accepted by the native Egyptians throughout the course of Dynasty XXV. At Thebes, where Nubian pharaohs successively confirmed their daughters and sisters in the position of God's Wife of Amun, and perhaps also at Memphis, where the royal residence of the Nubians in Egypt was located, members of the Nubian royal family and elite were enrolled in both secular and clerical positions of authority. These administrators relied on co-opted members of the native Egyptian elite, some of whom rose to extremely high positions in the government. Intermarriage was not uncommon between the two groups. Neither the couples nor their offspring were subject to discrimination based on their ethnicity.

THE DISMANTLING OF THE NUBIAN BUREAUCRACY AT THEBES

One of the first tasks confronting Psametik I, the first Egyptian pharaoh of Dynasty XXVI (664–525 b.c.e.) was the dismantling of the personnel in the Nubian-based bureaucracy of Upper Egypt, particularly at Thebes, and the appointment of loyal Egyptians to succeed those removed from office. Many of the individuals whom Psametik I elevated to positions of authority during his reign belonged to elite native Egyptian families of long standing, whose genealogies extended back in time over several generations, and whose immediate forebears had been aligned with the petty princes of Sais in their revolts against the Nubians. Drawing on a pool of these individuals, Psametik I was able to formulate a policy whereby he could effect personnel changes in his administration nonviolently and could follow precedents established by the Nubians themselves to achieve his objectives.

Psametik I apparently spent the first eight years of his reign consolidating his position in Lower and Middle Egypt. During that period of time, there is no indication to suggest that the Nubians attempted to reestablish themselves at Thebes, although the bureaucracy that they had established there was still functioning.

It was only in his Ninth Regnal Year (593 B.C.E.) that Psametik I turned his attention to Upper Egypt and Thebes. He enlisted the aid of Sematawytefnakht, whose father, Padeaset, had been an important ally and petty prince in Middle Egypt during the time of the revolts against Kushite rule. He charged Sematawytefnakht to orchestrate the transfer of divine power by overseeing the mechanics whereby Nitocris, a daughter of Psametik I, would be adopted as the successor of the Nubian Amenirdis II as God's Wife of Amun, just as Piankhy had earlier arranged for the Nubian Amenirdis I, to be adopted by Shepenwepet I, the daughter of the incumbent Egyptian pharaoh, Osorkon III. These events are recorded in the *Adoption Stela* of Nitocris, discovered at Karnak and now in the collections of the Egyptian Museum, Cairo. There one reads that Psametik I did not abrogate the existing rules of succession. He clearly states,

I am not one to expel an heir from his place...Hence I give her [= Nitocris] to her [= Amenirdis II] to be her eldest daughter as her [= Amenirdis II] father [Taharqa] (once) conveyed her to his sister [Shepenwepet II] (ARE 4: §942 [edited])

By means of this peaceful accommodation, the incumbent Nubian God's Wives of Amun would continue in office until their respective natural deaths, at which time Nitocris would assume the position.

This adoption ceremony was more than the performance of an empty ritual, because the *Adoption Stela* goes on to stipulate that the entire wealth of the Nubian bureaucracy was likewise transferred to the Egyptian heiress.

She conveyed to her the fortune which her father and her mother had conveyed to her and to her "great daughter," Amenirdis, king's daughter...It was put into writing concerning them, saying, "We have given to thee all our property in field and town. Thou abidest upon our throne, abiding and enduring forever and ever." (ARE 4: §946)

Thereafter follows a list of witnesses and a lengthy enumeration of the wealth and its sources. These included property and commodities controlled not only by Nubian royals, but also by elite members of their Theban bureaucracy, and even by temples and their estates. Montuehmat, fourth prophet of Amun and mayor of Thebes, who was a fixture in the Theban Nubian bureaucracy, together with his wife and son were obliged to convey to Nitrocris on a daily as well as monthly basis specific quantities of bread, wine, vegetables, oxen, and geese. The extraction of such extended payments was intended to place these former administrators of the land under economic duress with the intent of eroding their status and authority in the areas over which they were formerly masters. By such nonviolent, nonracially based policies, Psametik I effectively redistributed the wealth of the land and financially ruined those who served the former régime.

Psametik I had reunited Egypt and established its southern frontier at Aswan, the traditional border between Egypt and Nubia. Subsequent events suggest that the Nubians of Lower Nubia, south of that city, but more particularly those inhabiting the Dodekaschoinos, continued to interact amicably with their Egyptian neighbors. The only record of open hostility between the Nubians and the Egyptians during the course of Dynasty XXVI (664–525 B.C.E.) occurred during the reign of Psametik II, some half a century later in 593 B.C.E. The events surrounding that campaign are discussed later in connection with Aspelta, the Napatan king against whom he warred.

THE NUBIAN NAPATAN DYNASTY (ABOUT 656–300 B.C.E.)

The retreat of Tantamani and the subsequent reaffirmation of Napata as its political center witnessed the establishment of the Napatan Dynasty in about 656 B.C.E. The early kings of this dynasty, Atlanersa, Senkamenisken, and Anlamani, continued to perpetuate Egyptian cultural norms, including the erection of royal stelae inscribed in hieroglyphs, the sculpting of their statuary in traditional Egyptian types modified by the presence of typical Nubian regalia, and interments with such traditional Egyptian articles as shabtis, or funerary figurines. Nubian elite women continued to play significant roles in society and one, Queen Mother Nasalsa, succeeded Anlamani as ruler in her own right.

The rules of succession during the Napatan Dynasty are imperfectly understood and may not necessarily have been uniformly codified. According to the *Election Stela* of Aspelta and other documents, this Napatan ruler was elected king. The army convened at the death of the incumbent ruler so that a committee might be formed from their officers and other high-ranking members of the community with a view toward selecting a successor. In Aspelta's case the committee apparently nominated a slate of possible successors, referring to the candidates collectively as "the king's brothers," but that designation may have been honorific rather than familial. An inability of the committee to select a successor from among the group forced the matter to be submitted to the god Amun, who ultimately and via an oracle, proclaimed Aspelta the new king. Amun proclaims, on the stela,

He [Aspelta] is your king…His father is my son, the son of the Sun…the holy one, his mother is the king's sister and king's mother, Mistress of Kush, daughter of the Sun, Nasalsa, living forever.… (SAKN 212)

The priesthood via the oracle of Amun establishes Aspelta as the legitimate successor and associates his legitimacy with his mother, Nasalsa, his immediate predecessor. It is doubtless for this reason that Aspelta celebrates his mother's pedigree on another of his monuments in which Nasalsa is described as descendent from Amenirdis II. Such a suggestion would then imply that this God's Wife of Amun abandoned Thebes to return to Nubia, where she apparently married and gave birth to children.

The election of Aspelta by this extraordinarily unusual measure is remarkable because a similar committee was convened by which Irike-Amanote (about 425–400 B.C.E.), his successor, was immediately named and accepted by the military commanders and civil authorities as the next king. One suspects that the oracle of Amun was being manipulated by the priesthood, and that the events accompanying the succession of Aspelta may be regarded as harbingers of the progressively more authoritative posture of the Napatan clergy in matters of succession, which ultimately caused the eclipse of their power and relegation of their authority at the end of Napatan Period.

THE EGYPTIAN INVASION OF NUBIA IN 593 B.C.E.

There may be another factor involved in the association of Aspelta's mother, Nasalsa, with Amenirdis II, the former God's Wife of Amun of Thebes, because his reign witnessed the only recorded military action by Egypt against Nubia during the course of Dynasty XXVI. It may well be that the Nubians were already apprised of the impending attack and may have been preparing the way for an eventual return to Thebes by invoking the memory of an important religious office—that of God's Wife of Amun—which enabled Piankhy to secure a legitimate foothold in Egypt.

In 593 B.C.E. the Egyptian forces of Psametik II invaded Nubia, but the nature of the invasion and its immediate effects on Nubia remain opaque. Some scholars even question whether Aspelta was ruling Napata as king because the fluid nature of Nubian chronology cannot unequivocally establish the dates of his reign or whether those dates were contemporary with the Egyptian assault. Nevertheless, other scholars maintain that Aspelta and Psametik II were contemporary enemies and support that claim with the observation that the willful destruction of the monumental statues of the Nubian kings, the last of the series being that of Aspelta himself, at Gebel Barka, was caused by the Egyptian army, which reached and sacked Napata and the Holy Mountain. A reassessment of similar destruction levels at other sites in Nubia suggests that the devastation was subsequent to the reign of Aspelta, perhaps occurring during the fifth century B.C.E. In the end, all that one may state with certainty is that a military campaign against Nubia was launched by Psametik II in 593 B.C.E., but its effectiveness and effects remain open to debate.

Other documents would lend support to the hypothesis that the invasion had little impact on Nubian life, suggesting that Aspelta was occupied with the duties of ruling. A stela found at Napata mentions that he commissioned the construction and appointment of a tomb for a son of King Piankhy, and another from Sanam records his orders to fill vacant priestesses' offices. His successor, Irike-Amanote, was conducted to the royal palace immediately after being proclaimed king, an act that suggests that the Nubian capital was still properly functioning.

MARAUDING TRIBES THREATEN THE NAPATAN STATUS QUO

That there were other armed conflicts in Nubia proper during the period of the Napatan Dynasty is suggested by Classical texts, which make constant mention of clashes with enemies. These accounts are, however, too stereotypical and generic to be of historical value, and attempts to identify the peoples mentioned or the theaters in which these operations were conducted have proved frustratingly futile. It is, however, certain that some of these military confrontations involved the Blemmyes, a nomadic people whose marauding ways eventually contributed to the fall of ancient Nubian civilization at the end of the following Meroitic Period about 300 C.E. Contemporary accounts of the Napatan kings Irike-Amanote and Harsiyotef (about 400–365 B.C.E.) record repelling these troublesome peoples:

They sent to me the chief...who said, "You are my god. I am your slave. I am a wretch. Do not attack me." (SAKN 215)

Additionally Harsiyotef campaigned against rebellious servants in Lower Nubia on at least two occasions, but the status quo of Aswan as the frontier between the two realms seems not to have been affected.

Irike-Amantote records how he repelled one of these enemy tribes in the vicinity of the southern city of Meroe and apportioned the booty taken neither to the royal treasury or temples but rather to the local population, doubtless in keeping with local tribal obligations.

THE QUESTION OF MATRILINEAL SUCCESSION

During the course of the Napatan Period, elite Nubian women who served as queens were regarded as goddesses incarnated on earth. Nevertheless, this enhanced status is insufficient evidence for the existence of a matrilineal insti-

The Napatan Period

tution for succession. The theory that Nubian succession during this period could only be effected via the wife or mother can be documented in one and only one instance, that of Aspelta. The relevant passages from his *Enthronement Stela*, found at Gebel Barkal and now in The Egyptian Museum, Cairo, are:

His mother is the sister of the king, mother of the king, Mistress of Nubia, daughter of Re, Nasalsa by name, may she live eternally. Her mother is the sister of the king, attached to the cult of Amun-Re, king of the gods at Thebes.... (DFRK 31)

The fact that he marries a king's sister may be incidental to his ascendancy to the throne, and the fact that Amanitore, the widow of Natakamani, marries Shorkaror, his successor, may have another motive. These incidents may have been known to the Greek philosopher Aristotle who, writing in the fourth century B.C.E., obviously misunderstood their context and fantastically described the Nubians as a matriarchal society. Neither practice can be paralleled elsewhere, and should be used with caution in this regard. Succession might be effected in a number of other ways. So, for example, Harsiyotef sought legitimacy via the agency of two miraculous events, both associated with Amun of Napata, the divine Nubian king-maker. The events are complex but involve the communion of the cult of Amun at Kawa and that of Napata together with a mystic encounter with the godhead and the fulfillment of an omen in the form of a favorable inundation of the Nile River. These circumstances are far removed from any matrilineal institution and suggest that the mechanisms for Napatan succession were complex, often involving nuanced religious conceits.

In light of the evidence, Nubian legitimacy seems to reside, as indeed it does in Egypt, on the equilibrium of the male and female principals of procreation. Their union brings about the first time, namely, the creation of the world, and the beginning of the renewal of cosmic cycles. Without the female component and equal partner in the equation, the male component could not function properly. This theological underpinning, which regards the male and female principals as equals, provides the theoretical foundation on which an elite female member of either Egyptian or Nubian society might assume the purple in her own right. With regard to Nubian rulership, to coin a more neutral term, one is not justified in speaking either of a matriarchy or of a patriarchy.

THE FUNERARY ARCHITECTURE OF DYNASTY XXV
AND THE NAPATAN PERIOD

The Nubian kings of Napata were initially buried in the cemetery near el-Kurru. The earliest of these interments were designed as vertical shafts that communicated with a burial pit, generally to one side of the shaft, which was then covered over with a tumulus; its center was pebble filled. The design of such graves is so similar to graves of the Kerma culture that a degree of continuity in Nubian funerary practice over the millennia must be assumed. These pit graves were eventually modified by the addition of a funerary chapel on their west side and the inclusion of an enclosure wall, horse-shoe in shape. In time it appears that these burials approximated the appearance of Egyptian bench, or mastaba burials, which survive in numbers at both Giza and Saqqara. Shortly before the conquest of Egypt, the Nubians appear to have abandoned the placement of the corpse on the ground in favor of placing the deceased on beds, as was the case for elite burials of the Kerma culture as well.

Roughly contemporary in time with Kashta, contact with Egypt increased, and that intercourse resulted in the progressive adoption by the Nubians of Egyptian funerary equipment and practices. These included mummification and the placing of the deceased in Egyptian-styled sarcophagi rather than on beds. Typical Egyptian canopic jars, in which the soft internal organs were preserved, and shabti, or servant figures, now become dominant elements of Nubian funerary equipment. The Nubians in fact reintroduced the use of stone for the manufacture of shabtis, which were habitually made of faience during the course of the Egyptian Third Intermediate Period. The shabti ensemble created for Taharqa is extraordinary for the carving of the material and the accompanying inscriptions.

It was not long before the mastaba-style superstructures of these tombs yielded to pyramids. In fact, there are more documented pyramids in Nubia used as sepulchers than there are in all of Egypt, although this statistical superiority must be considered in conjunction with the greatly diminished size of the Nubian pyramids, none of which rival the mass of their Egyptian royal counterparts.

The tomb of Piankhy, now leveled, was thought to be marked by a pyramid. The burial chamber beneath was innovative and marks a departure from the design of the older tombs at el-Kurru. His burial shaft is reached by a long staircase, built into the east side of the superstructure from which one gained entry into the burial chamber proper via an arched doorway, which was carefully blocked up with worked blocks after the body had been interred. The burial chamber itself contained a bench cut into the living rock on which the sarcophagus was placed, although four depressions in the floor suggest that the Nubians did consider laying Piankhy's body to rest on a bed.

If later Nubian tombs may serve as examples, one suggests that the tomb chapels associated with these earlier burials were decorated with relief decoration depicting the deceased in some scenes, at least, enthroned as an index of his status. There might also have been a stela-niche in the rear wall for the insertion of a two-dimensional sculpted depiction of the deceased in the company of one or more deities. In front of this is suggested to have been an offering table on which presentation of foodstuffs and liquid libations would be offered for the well-being of the deceased in the Hereafter.

Taharqa decided to transfer the royal cemetery from el-Kurru to Nuri. Nuri was to serve as the Nubian royal cemetery for almost three centuries, with the sole exception of Tantamani, who was interred at el-Kurru. The transference of the cemetery was accompanied with changes in the design of Nubian royal tombs. Pyramids now become one of the most salient fixed features of ancient Nubia's material culture; they persist into the Meroitic Period until the fourth century c.e. It has been suggested that the impetus for the appearance of the pyramid in Nubian funerary contexts derived from the tombs of the Egyptian elite of the late New Kingdom in Western Thebes at Deir el Medineh. This may have been a contributing factor, but one cannot overlook as an important influence the royal pyramids of the Memphite region, where the Nubian residence was located. In keeping with the generally high status enjoyed by Nubian royal women, it should come as no surprise to learn that in many instances, the height of their pyramids is the same as the height of their respective kings.

The pyramid of Taharqa was originally designed with smooth, sloping sides but was modified into a stepped pyramid as a result of the subsequent increase of its height. Taharqa's tomb contains two rooms: an anteroom room and the burial chamber proper. The latter is rectangular in plan, its vaulted ceiling seemingly supported by six piers cut from the living rock, and its two long walls equipped with niches suggested to have held images of deities.

King Senkamanisken as a sphinx in Nubian style. ALEA.

It would appear that at some point early in the Napatan Dynasty, strict guidelines were issued governing the design and dimensions of royal pyramids of both kings and queens alike. From that time on, although there are exceptions, by and large the pyramids conform to a quantifiable set of standards. Scholars have not been able to explain why this should be so, and why exceptions to these standards were occasionally made. Among the standardized features are the height of the pyramid and the use of two chambers for a queens' tomb and three for those of kings. In keeping with the adoption of many of ancient Egypt's funerary practices beginning with the reign of Kashata, the Napatan kings continued to be interred in anthropoid sarcophagi based on Egyptian models. The Napatan kings Anlamani and Aspelta were, however, exceptionally interred in massive rectangular sarcophagi sculpted from granite obtained from the region of the third cataract. In keeping with the archaizing characteristics of Dynasty XXV, these two Napatan royal sarcophagi are inscribed with prayers compiled from the *Pyramid Texts* of the Old Kingdom and from the New Kingdom so-called *Book of the Dead.*

THE SCULPTURE OF THE KINGDOM OF NAPATA

The sculpture of the Napatan Period continues the aesthetic encountered in the Nubian ateliers of the immediately preceding period, as a comparison of the sphinx of Senkamanisken, from Gebel Barkal now in Khartoum, and that of Taharqa in London reveals. The sphinx of Senkamanisken with its human hands is a variation known from ancient Egypt. The musculature of the arms and of the rump are extremely stylized, rendered as deep grooves into the stone. The individual claws of the hind legs are not articulated, and the fingers of the hands are likewise without either joints or fingernails. The face of the king shares in its design with the head of the sphinx of Taharqa and has been described as "uncompromisingly 'African,'" in the way the former had been characterized as "brutal." Such assessments may reveal a bias on the part of the commentator, who prefers the bland, idealizing style of most images created by Egyptian ateliers to a style consistent with Nubian aesthetic principles.

A striding statue of Senkamanisken, likewise from Gebel Barkal and presently in Boston, is based on Egyptian design tenets that have here been modified in accordance with Nubian aesthetics. The entire image has been modeled in broad planes, the transitions between them glossed over. The legs are massive vertical elements, the toes of the feet hardly articulated. The same observation obtains for the massive arms and the balled fists, holding what are termed emblematic staves, but which are actually bolts of cloth here, as often in Egyptian art as well, stylized as cylinders. The head is round, in keeping with norms developed during Dynasty XXV, and decorated with the Nubian cap crown fronted by a double uraeus. A ram-headed lanyard, kilt, and sandals complete the costume. The rather rough-looking surfaces on the statue are intentional. This stippling served as a mordant for the gesso, or plaster, to which gold leaf was originally applied. The pervasive use of gold on this image bombarded the viewer's retina with the result that one gained an overall impression of status and authority. Attention to detail was, consequently, never the intent, and neatly explains why the atelier relied almost exclusively on a design that exploited unmodulated broad planes in the creation of the idol.

A statue of Queen Amanimalel, from Gebel Barkal now in Khartoum, is an extraordinary tour de force and ranks among the great masterpieces of African art, created in a Nubian atelier. The full-figured image of the queen, whose head has unfortunately not survived, is designed to conform to earlier images of elite Egyptian women in which the right arm is held alongside the body and the left arm, bent at the elbow, rests on the chest beneath the breasts, its hand holding an attribute. The feet of such images are generally parallel to one another, and the garment of choice is typically a tightly fitting sheath, generally without openings. Here, the queen wears what appears to be a Nubian variant of the sheath, because a discernible line, rendered in red, which is still visible, indicates a seam that runs along the left side of the garment and leaves the breast exposed. A second line, this time incised, indicates a fringed hem. In keeping with Egyptian depictions of elite males, the queen's left leg is unusually advanced. The entire surface is stippled to serve as a mordant, suggesting to have held the silver, which may have sheathed the statue, although the sandals may have been embellished with gold leaf.

The inscription on the back pillar of this statue mentions her role in the cult of Amun at Napata, which may be correlated with that of the God's Wives of Amun of Dynasty XXV. As a result, the identification of the two attributes held in each of her fisted hands ought to relate to the theology of that god. The attribute in her fisted left hand appears to be a child god wearing an Egyptian double crown and side lock. This image is habitually identified as the Horus the Child, the divine son of Isis and Osiris, but would be more accurately associated with Khonsu, the offspring of Amun at Thebes. Such an identification is consistent with the image of the deity on the aegis of the menat held in the queen's fisted right hand. A menat is a ceremonial, multistranded beaded cult object, resembling a necklace, the strings of which are attached to a terminal, termed an "aegis," which generally depicts a deity from the top of the head to the level of the neck, invariably represented as wearing a broad collar. Although damaged, the deity on the aegis may be Mut, the consort of Amun at Thebes. The back pillar inscription and the two attributes would therefore associate Queen Amanimalel with the divine triad of Amun, Mut, and Khonsu.

The design of this idol as a full-figured woman has occasioned some scholars to relate it to the seemingly corpulent images of the earlier periods, particularly the baked clay effigies of both the A- and C-Group

A Nubian pharaoh, perhaps to be identified as Taharqa, in
the embrace of a goddess. ALEA.

Nubians. But, as one has seen earlier, these images are androgynous, and
in the case of the figures of the earlier period, may in fact have been
intended as genderless, if not male. Whereas it is true that this corpulence
finds its correspondences in the relief representations of Nubian elite
women in the following Meroitc Period, one cannot exclude the possibility that the model of fecundity, doubtless connoted by the full-figured
female form, has its artistic antecedents in the Ramesside Period. Certainly, the images of Nofertari gracing the façade of the Lesser, or Northern Temple, at Abu Simbel, for example, were continually exposed to
sight, and these share to a remarkable degree the same general design
operative in the creation of this statue. In dealing with ancient art one
must habitually bear in mind that the objective of the ateliers was the creation of images as indices of decorum and not of images as allusions of
reality. The demonstrable abstraction and stylization of the sculpture created in Nubian ateliers should caution all against interpreting such
images as records of the actual appearance of living individuals.

THE RELIEF SCULPTURE OF DYNASTY XXV AND THE
KINGDOM OF NAPATA

With the fall of the Kerma culture and the ascendancy of Egypt, Nubian
cultural expressions appear to be subsumed by the thick stratum of
Egypt's material culture. The emergence of Dynasty XXV was accompa-

nied by a resurgence of the arts, the characteristics of sculpture in the round already having been presented earlier. As is to be expected, the relief style of the Nubians of Dynasty XXV is indebted to Egyptian norms and may have also been created by Egyptian artisans, if one can trust the statement made by Taharqa, who claims to have caused Egyptian artisans and their families to come to Nubia.

In general the relief sculpture associated with the Nubian elite at Thebes, particularly at Karnak, is decidedly linear. Subtle transitions between planes, which would be evident, for example, in the treatment of the face between the cheek, nose, jaw, and chin, are generally less well articulated than in traditional Egyptian depictions. The reliance on line, rather than plane, may explain why the relief is shallow, but also suggests that particular modulations may have been achieved by the application of paint, which has since disappeared. It is interesting, therefore, to compare this royal, Nubian relief style from Karnak with the relief style of highly placed Nubian administrators found in their tombs in the Asasif in Western Thebes, directly across the Nile River from the Karnak temples. Scholars have suggested that these tombs were designed with relief decoration appearing in each in both of these two styles, the perfunctory and a festive.

Nubian royal regalia including the double uraeus, cap crown, and lanyard with ram's heads as terminals. ALEA.

One has not satisfactorily explained why such two different styles should appear concurrently in one and the same monument, but economic imperatives suggesting that the perfunctory was less costly to execute do not satisfactorily explain this aesthetic dualism. One wonders whether this dualism is influenced by the Nubian penchant for abstraction, but one is simultaneously cautioned from pressing the case because the now lost paint might have effectively masked the less baroque sculpting of the perfunctory style and rendered it visually very different from its appearance today.

A sandstone relief in Brooklyn, retaining slight traces of paint, has been assigned to the early seventh century B.C.E. It depicts a mature, adult male Nubian king in reduced scale to indicate his cultic status as a child in the embrace of a much larger goddess, who cradles his head with her uplifted hand. Although the group composition would afford the designers ample opportunity to explore the effects of overlapping forms as seen, for example, in the treatment of similar scenes in relief in the Temple of Sety I at Abydos, the design avoids complex overlapping altogether. The figure of the

The corpulent Pekkerenkhonsu. The Metropolitan Museum of Art, Museum Excavations, 1911-12, Rogers Fund, 1928. (28.3.52) Photograph, all rights reserved, The Metropolitan Museum of Art.

king is merely superimposed on that of the goddess, and the fingers of her hand, which is likewise behind, merely come into contact with the edge of the top of his head. From this and other similar examples, it would appear that the Nubian relief sculpture aesthetic valued simplicity of design, in keeping with fundamental tenets of Egyptian art in general. It can be demonstrated that the Nubians of the period sought models of inspiration in more ancient creations of both the Old and Middle Kingdoms, and these compositions, by and large, are devoid of the kinds of design explorations that characterize the Egyptian art of the New Kingdom. One may summarize this discussion by stating that the material culture of the Nubians of Dynasty XXV is classic, based in part on an archaizing tendency, which, although acknowledging the New Kingdom, favored the cultural norms of earlier periods. Royal relief representations on stelae of both Dynasty XXV and of the Kingdom of Napata conform to these same Egyptian norms, but adhere to an attenuation resulting in tall figures, which are relatively thin. The fragmentary state of royal relief representations in Nubia proper and their habitual reproduction as line drawings rather than photographs precludes any substantive discussion of their design tenets.

THE COSTUME OF THE NUBIANS DURING DYNASTY XXV AND OF THE NAPATAN PERIOD

Because elite Nubians of the period elected mummification as their preferred burial practice, the bandages replaced earlier native costumes in the tomb. One is, therefore, ill informed about native costumes because virtually every depiction shows the Nubians in Egyptian dress with the exception of certain accessories, discussed later. Exceptional Assyrian representations, created during the time of their hostilities with Egypt, depict individuals identified as Nubians not only because of their facial features but also because of their characteristically Nubian short coiffures, appointed with a feather, which is held in place by a wide fillet, or band. There seems to be a degree of continuity in the costumes and accessories worn by elite Nubians of both Dynasty XXV and the immediately following Napatan Period.

In general, therefore, Nubian kings are shown wearing the kilt, secured with either plain or beaded belts. These belts are often inscribed with the name of the Nubian king wearing it, but whether this reflects a fashion of the day or is simply an artistic convention remains moot. Occasionally images of Nubian pharaohs are shown wearing the false beard of Egyptian pharaohs. The Nubian king might also be shown wearing a bretelle, or corslet, which resembles a woman's contemporary tank top. Nubian elite women wear the tightly fitting sheath. Both wear any number of crowns associated with Egyptian kings and queens or divine consorts of the god Amun.

Three types of regalia appear to be unique to Nubian kings of the period and continue to be worn as regal accessories in subsequent epochs. The first is the open-ended lanyard. This is draped around the neck in such a way that each of the loose ends rests on each side of the chest. The center of this lanyard and each of its loose ends is habitually decorated with a pendant in the form of a ram's head, often surmounted by a sun disk. Represented in sculpture in the round as well as in two-dimensional depictions, this ram-headed pendant is the one element that has survived in quantities. Most of these are crafted of gold, but examples in stone and other materials are also known.

A second element of royal regalia is the appearance of two uraei, or sacred cobras, on the brow of the Nubian rulers. Although this insignia appears earlier in Egypt, its appropriation by the Nubians of Dynasty XXV associates it from this time on almost exclusively with Nubian monarchs. Why these kings should have adopted this insignia is moot, and its significance hotly debated. In one view, the insignia must be regarded as emblematic of their legitimacy to rule two kingdoms, specifically Upper and Lower Egypt during Dynasty XXV. The continued appearance of this insignia by the kings of the Napatan Period may be ascribed to tradition and their harboring of the hope of returning to Egypt as that nation's sovereigns.

The double uraeus is often worn with a curious headdress, variously described as a skull cap or natural hair. The arguments in favor of one identification over the other rely on Western perceptions about how to read ancient Egyptian visual conventions. The surfaces of this puzzling motif are often articulated in ways that recall stylized natural hair or bosses added to material, further frustrating its identification. For several reasons, it is best to regard this element of the royal regalia as a cap crown, regarding it within the tradition of Nubian caps from the C-Group and Kerma culture through to modern times.

Certain depictions of kings of Dynasty XXV show them with four feathers as attributes atop their heads. This is a characteristically royal, Nubian headdress equating the king with Shu, the Egyptian god of atmosphere, whose cultic role in the myth of the eye of the Sun God relies on his interaction with Tefnut, a goddess associated with the Divine Consort of Amun at Thebes. This four-feathered headdress is associated with Taharqa and continued in vogue for the Kings of the subsequent Napatan Period.

It is within the context of Dynasty XXV that the question of Nubian eunuchs must be addressed. The evidence is sketchy at best, although there is one pointed reference to eunuchs in a Nubian context in one of the standard *Execration Texts* of Middle Kingdom date, where one reads:

[Every rebel of this land, all people, all patricians, all commoners, all males,] all eunuchs, all women, every chieftain, [every Nubian, every strongman, every messenger], every confederate, every ally of every land who will rebel in Wawat, Zatju, Iretit, Yam, Ianekh, Masit, and Kau, who will rebel and who will plot by saying plots or by speaking anything against Upper Egypt or Lower Egypt forever.

Every Nubian who will rebel in Irit, Wawat, Zatju, Yam, Kaau, Iankh, Masit, Mdja, and Meterti, who will rebel or who will make plots, or who will plot, or who will say anything evil. (MAEMP 139)

The practice of castration was abhorrent to the ancient Egyptians, and this reference intercalates such individuals within the number of every enemy and every ally of every land who plot with the Nubians against Egypt. Its mention in this particular magical context cannot, therefore, be adduced as evidence that eunuchs were either common or that castration was a widespread practice in ancient Nubia.

In point of fact, almost every other reference to eunuchs in either Egypt or Nubia derive exclusively from non-Egyptian textual sources, which are sited within the cultural contexts of the ancient Near East. One such reference is found in an Assyrian tablet (K 1577) mentioning two Nubian eunuchs, whose authority included the dispatching of royal body guards. The second is found in Jeremiah 38, 7–13, mentioning a Nubian eunuch in the service of Zedekiah, king of Judea. The third and final reference is in The Acts of the Apostles 37, where a eunuch, serving as an officer in the court of a Kandake, is described as the first Nubian to embrace Christianity. There is nothing particularly Nubian, or for that matter Egyptian, about the names of these eunuchs, and their association with the Nubian court is, in and of itself, not evidence that any of them were ethnic Nubians. In point of fact, there is no direct evidence from either Nubia or Egypt that either group practiced castration, a procedure that is, however, well attested outside Egypt in contemporary Near Eastern cultures. One might argue, therefore, that the eunuchs mentioned in these texts were foreigners in the employ of their Nubian monarchs.

In like manner, there is no good reason for interpreting the depiction of Irike-takana in his statue in The Egyptian Museum, Cairo, as a depiction of a Nubian eunuch. Such an interpretation is based on the application of Eurocentric artistic criteria to Egyptian and Nubian works of art. Such an application is methodologically unsound. The attempt to regard the fact that he is depicted both clean-shaven and corpulent and that he was attached to the Theban clergy of the Nubian divine wives of Amun does not provide a tautology for associating the corpulence of one in the service of the divine wife with being a eunuch. Corpulence is a visual index of decorum in ancient Egyptian art, fully exploited in the Old Kingdom as seen in the statues of such high officials as Hemi-unu, architect of the Great Pyramid at Giza, and Ka-aper, the so-called sheikh of his village. This index continued to be employed throughout the history of Egyptian art by subsequent ateliers. The corpulence of Irike-takana must be regarded within this tradition and can be neither isolated nor separated from it.

Irike-takana's titles appear to be honorific rather than concrete indices of actual offices held, so that his actual position within the hierarchy cannot be established with certainty. The sculptural design of his physiognomy is in keeping with artistic tenets established for the representation of Nubians, but those features also found in the faces of other officials, Montuemhat for example, whose ethnic background is Theban Egyptian, not Nubian. There is no reason, therefore, solely on the basis of artistically rendered physiognomy, for identifying any representation as an ethnic Nubian. It has been further suggested that Irike-takana was married and sired children, demonstration of which would certainly preclude his having been a eunuch.

The costume which Irike-takana wears has been described as exceptional, and the artistic conventions that have been employed for its design render an exact description of its component parts and means of putting them on obscure. Nevertheless, the costume appears to be similar to that worn by Pekkerenkhonsu, his contemporary, as depicted on a painted, wooden fragment from his sarcophagus now in New York's Metropolitan Museum of Art. The fashion of wearing wraparound skirts in association with short-sleeved garments very much resembling modern T-shirts and wraparound fringed shawls gained currency in Egypt during this period. The garments worn by these two individuals must be understood within this emerging fashion and seem to be reflected in the later costume worn by Queen Amanimalel in her granite statue in Khartoum. It is interesting to note in conclusion that the depiction of the physiognomy and corpulence of Irike-takana in his statue has been exactly duplicated in the two-dimensional depiction of Pekkerenkhonsu, suggesting that both representations are to be understood as generic depictions of corpulent, aged bureaucrats rather than as images of eunuchs.

Excavations of elite Nubian burials of Dynasty XXV and the following Napatan Period have unearthed a wealth of accessories in a variety of types and media. A selection of faience amulets from Dynasty XXV reveals that the lacelike designs of the mica appliqués of the Kingdom of Kerma still dominated design concerns. These amulets are often janiform, with designs on both front and back. Although uninscribed, their iconography suggests identifications with deities of the Egyptian pantheon. These include the dwarf god, Pataikos, associated with Ptah, the creator god of Memphis, falcon-headed deities, wadjet, or sacred eyes, and a host of composite images of human form with wings and additional attributes, which are described as pantheistic or all-encompassing deities. Amulets were also crafted in gold with suspension loops at their backs. Most of these are in the form of traditional Egyptian deities as well, that of Isis nursing her divine son, Horus, being popular.

Gold jewelry was extremely fashionable during this period. Crescent-shaped earrings and finger rings, resembling modern wedding bands, were common, and gold nuggets, suggestive of the animism inherent in the

The unusual headdresses of elite Nubian women. Courtesy of Angelika Lohwasser.

The fox tail accessory of elite Nubian women. Courtesy of Angelika Lohwasser.

Nubian cultural milieu, were not uncommonly incorporated into jewelry designs. Gold was also used for wadjet eyes serving as necklace elements together with paired Egyptian deities. Ram's heads, with or without sun discs, of gold and other materials are ubiquitous, suggesting the widespread use of lanyards so often depicted on images of royal Nubians.

Other types of jewelry include a variety of necklaces. One example consists of two strands of 750 tiny gold beads, whereas another uses elements of gold and carnelian, a combination known from earlier periods. Some articles of Nubian jewelry of the period are so abstract as to defy identification. These include amulets made of wire that superficially resemble human beings with two very stylized arms and legs.

ACCESSORIES UNIQUE TO ELITE NUBIAN WOMEN

The design tenets that govern two-dimensional compositions and the motifs depicted within them are intentional manipulations of reality that often confound modern attempts at defining their exact nature. As a result, it is exceedingly difficult for a modern commentator to define clearly and precisely the nature of the costumes and accessories worn by elite Nubians, and particularly elite female members of Nubian society.

Several two-dimensional depictions from both epochs reveal what appears to be the furry tail of an animal, projecting from the lower hem of the garment behind the ankles of the feet. The identification of this article is difficult to define, for the reasons just mentioned. It does not appear to be related to the Egyptian hieroglyph representing fox tails, as has been recently suggested, because these fox tails are always shown in a group of three, whereas the "tail" in the Nubian images is habitually a singleton. Nevertheless, the seemingly elective appearance of this "tail" in association with specific depictions of elite Nubian women suggests that it is an index of decorum connoting an elevated status. As enigmatic as this tail is as an accessory, so, too, is the nature of a particular Nubian elite woman's headdress. This accessory is depicted as one or more curving lines, rising from the crown of the head and arching backwards. It may consist of as few as one to as many as four elements, variously described as feathers or streamers. Here again the design tenets preclude any precise description, but this unique headdress is doubtless yet another index of decorum symbolizing an elevated status.

Elite Nubian women of the periods may be depicted in a panther skin, but only during instances when they perform cultic rituals for Nubian kings. The wearing of sandals also appears to be elective. In general, female costumes of both the Egyptian and the Nubians are devoid of closures and fasteners. The garments of an elite woman's wardrobe were generally wrapped around the body and secured in place by knotting. It is interesting, therefore, to identify certain accessories on garments worn by elite Nubian women of the periods as fibulae, or ancient versions of the safety pin. The use of the fibula as a fastener for garments is Greek, and the appropriation of this accessory by elite Nubian women of the period suggests that they were both aware of and appropriated for themselves the current Greek fashion statement.

11

Nubia during the Kingdom of Meroe

The events precipitating the transfer of the Nubian capital from Napata to Meroe further to the south revolve around the priesthood, which asserted its right to control the process of succession. The *Election Stela* of Aspelta may be regarded as a harbinger of the assertion to this right, but there is other evidence to suggest that the Napatan kings did not always countenance the decisions of its priesthood. The *Banishment Stela,* attributed to Aspelta, but perhaps earlier in date, records the exile of certain priests from Napata for behavior described, but not more narrowly defined, as illegal. The periodic clashes between the authority of the king and that of the clergy culminated, according to tradition preserved by Diodorus Siculus writing in Greek in the third century B.C.E., when the priesthood could unilaterally remove a king from office by ordering his death, as if the execution had been willed by a deity. The Napatan king who took issue with this position has been identified in the Classical accounts as King Ergamenes, who was a contemporary of the Macedonian Greek pharaoh of Egypt Ptolemy II Philadelphus (285–246 B.C.E.). This Ergamenes has been equated with the Nubian ruler Arkamani I. Whether or not this identification obtains, it is clear that the capital of the Nubians was transferred at about this time from Napata to Meroe and that in fact Arkamani I was the first of the Nubian kings to be buried in the newly founded royal cemetery there. The transfer of the capital signaled the beginning of the Meroitic Period (about 275 B.C.E.–300 C.E.).

MEROITIC—THE NUBIAN LANGUAGE

It is a given that the Nubians possessed a language, perhaps dialects of a common language, and quite possibly several different languages that were current in the periods before the Egyptian New Kingdom, but these languages appear to have been exclusively oral. To date, there are no indications to suggest that the earliest spoken language or languages of the ancient Nubians were ever rendered in a written, notational system.

During the course of the New Kingdom when most of the external, visible indices of Nubian ethnicity were subsumed beneath the thick veneer of Egypt's material culture, elite members of Nubian society appear to have become literate in the ancient Egyptian scripts. From that period on, certain proper nouns, written in Egyptian, can be identified as attempts to render a handful of purely Nubian proper and place names in the ancient Egyptian language. In order to understand the subsequent development of writing in Nubia, it is necessary to explain the nature of the ancient Egyptian language and its three scripts—hieroglyphs, hieratic, and demotic.

The Meroitic alphabet. Courtesy of K.H. Priese.

THE NATURE OF THE ANCIENT EGYPTIAN LANGUAGE

The principal script of the ancient Egyptians for monumental inscriptions is hieroglyphs. The word *hieroglyph* is derived from the ancient Greek phrase meaning "sacred [thing] sculptured," referring to inscriptions sculpted into either the stone of sacred temple walls or other public monuments. Hieroglyphs are basically images of objects found in the real world that have been designed as stylized, generic pictograms. These can be divided into two major categories, namely ideograms, or sense signs, and phonograms, or sound signs. To the first category belong a number of hieroglyphs that represent specific words, such as a sun disk, which is literally taken to indicate the actual sun itself. On occasion, an ideogram may be written at the end of one or more immediately preceding hieroglyphs to indicate the sense of the word as a visual clue. To that end, the sun disk could be written after the signs meaning "day." Phonograms are hieroglyphs, which may serve as ideograms, but were soon assigned specific sound values that are used to spell out words. Hieroglyphs serving as phonograms may represent one or more sounds, but these are always in the nature of consonants because the Egyptian system of writing did not employ vowels. Vowels were pronounced when speaking, but were never written.

An offering table inscribed in Meroitic in the Ägyptisches Museum und Papyrussammlung, Berlin.

As time passed, the writing of hieroglyphs proved to be too cumbersome for rapid composition of administrative records and other bureaucratic documents. As a result, the ancient Egyptians developed what the Greeks called hieratic, from their word for the priestly class, whom they associated with the scribes. Hieratic was, initially, nothing more than the summarily rendered rounded forms of the hieroglyphs, which could be easily written with a reed pen and ink on papyrus. If one wishes to press a modern analogy, hieroglyphs would be to printing what hieratic is to script. In time hieratic departed more and more from the hieroglyphs upon which it was initially dependent.

The final script employed for the writing of Egyptian is demotic, from the Greek adjective "popular," because during the Graeco-Roman Period this script was generally used for everyday correspondence. Demotic is a very rapid form of hieratic and may be compared, to continue the analogy, with shorthand. Demotic first appeared as a script in Egypt during Dynasty XXV, when the Nubians were pharaohs of Egypt, but its development appears to be independent of their presence in the land. Demotic was apparently developed to meet the administrative needs of the petty princes of the Delta, who required a more expeditious notational system to compete with increasing use elsewhere of the Greek alphabet. The Egyptian language, primarily in its hieroglyphic script, continued to be employed for official Nubian documents until the transference of the capital from Napata to Meroe at some time in the third century B.C.E., at which time Meroitic, the earliest, native written language of the Nubians was introduced.

THE MEROITIC LANGUAGE

At some point in time almost contemporary in date with the transference of the ancient Nubian capital from Napata to Meroe, but certainly by the second century B.C.E., the Nubians of the Kingdom of Meroe developed their own notational system, termed Meroitic. Meroitic writing displays two scripts, namely the hieroglyphs and the cursive. The individual characters appear to be derived in part from certain signs current in both Egyptian hieroglyphs and demotic, but that is where the similarities end. Unlike ancient Egyptian, which relied on both ideograms and phonograms, the two scripts of the Meroitic language employ 23 characters that incorporate vowel notations. As a result, this Nubian language may be described as a syllabic system because every one of the 23 signs potentially represents a consonant plus a vowel, which in most cases is an *a*, except when followed by another symbol used to indicate the vowels *i, o,* and *e*. There are, consequently, 15 consonantal signs, four syllabic signs, notably *ne, se, te,* and *to,* and four additional signs for vowels, *i* and *o/u,* and *e*, the latter of which takes a different form when it is in an initial position. Within this notational system there is also a sign that serves not only as a divider between words but also separates, on occasion, grammatical elements. The use of this sign is similar to a dot used in the Egyptian language in a limited number of contexts, generally reserved to separate verses in some types of literary compositions.

Attempts to link Meroitic to ancient Greek fail because of its syllabic nature. This Nubian language is, however, similar in many respects to the old Persian cuneiform script in the way both are syllabic with respect to their use of vowels and in their utilization of a special character to separate words. These resemblances may be gratuitous and coincidental because scholars have been unable to argue for the mechanism by which aspects of the old Persian cuneiform script could have been adapted and utilized by the Meroites. It should further be noted that the Meroitic scripts seemed to appear suddenly in their fully developed form without a gestation period.

Linguists have attempted to classify the Meroitic language, but such attempts have proved futile. Meroitic is not a Hamito-Semitic language, as is ancient Egyptian. The two are, therefore, not related. Other attempts to relate Meroitic to well-known groups of African languages are equally frustrating, but the suggestion that Meroitic may belong to a group of northern Sudanese languages is worthy of consideration inasmuch as the recognizable rules of their linguistic structure appear to be common.

From the second century B.C.E. on, Meroitic, which had been one of the spoken languages of the Nubians, continued to be written, particularly in Lower Nubia, into the fifth century C.E. A graffito of the Meroitic *qore*, Kharamadoye, celebrating his victory over an enemy, suggested to have been the Blemmyes, on the walls of the Temple of Mandulis at Kalabsha is perhaps the last inscription ever written in the Meroitic cursive script. During this period of over six centuries Meroitic was the exclusive notational system employed by the ancient Nubians with the one exception occurring during the reign of Natakamani (about 50 C.E.) when, perhaps influenced by Egypt's impact on the culture of Rome, inscriptions were carved in both Egyptian hieroglyphs and Meroitic. With the fall of the Kingdom of Meroe, the Nubians adopted another notational script, termed Old Nubian, which was an African adaptation of the Greek alphabet, with the notable inclusion of three signs taken directly from Meroitic.

F. Ll. Griffith was the pioneer in the decipherment of Meroitic. The strides in furthering one's understanding of this language made since his time and the appearance of bilingual inscriptions from the reign of Natakamani have been important, but there are still numerous Meroitic texts that frustrate modern attempts at their comprehension. As a result, scholars have made less progress in their decipherment of Meroitic royal inscriptions, particularly those dealing with historical events, than they have with funerary inscriptions. The following discussion of an offering table in Berlin reveals the state of affairs with regard to the deciphering of Meroitic.

The offering table, erected for the performance of rituals on behalf of the deceased, is crafted of sandstone and measures approximately 17 by 20 inches. It is dated to the period around 250 C.E. The main scene shows a goddess to the left and a jackal-headed god to the right pouring liquid libations from situlae, or ritual buckets, onto a table piled high with offerings. The spout on one side would metaphorically conduct these liquids to the deceased. The border is inscribed in the Meroitic cursive script, a tentative translation for which appears to be:

O Isis, O Osiris, [King] Tamelordeamani, born of Araqatanmakasa, and created by Teritanide, a rich...?...may...become. A good Nile may...become...may..." (SAKN 259, no. 218)

In inscriptions of this sort, one can recognize personal, divine, and on occasion geographic names, together with an adjective or two and the presence of the verb "to be." However, the meanings of many other words are so difficult to decipher that an exact translation of the prayer expressed remains obscure.

There is evidence that as late as the fifth century C.E. Meroitic continued to be used, however sparsely, as a written language, but the number of Meroites literate in the scripts was drastically diminishing with the passing of time. It has, therefore, been cogently suggested that Meroitic's late survival indicates its status as a dead language, analogous with the decline of Latin in the West. It was replaced, at least in northern Nubia, by both Greek, the vernacular of the Byzantine Empire, and Coptic, the language of contemporary Egypt.

THE NATURE OF MEROITIC GOVERNMENT

The transference of the capital to Meroe was accompanied by other significant transformations in Nubian culture and society, foremost of which was the development of a uniquely Nubian notational system, just described. This language, termed Meroitic, enabled the Nubians to write in their own language, without recourse to the ancient Egyptian hieroglyphs, which were gradually abandoned as more and more Nubians became skilled in the practice of their own language.

These Meroitic inscriptions reveal that the upper echelon of Nubian power was shared on apparently an equal basis by three individuals, who are habitually represented in Nubian royal relief sculpture of the period often in the presence of the Nubian gods. The dominant male member of this oligarchy is called the *qore,* a title current in Nubia during the course of the New Kingdom, which may be translated something on the order of "commander." The dominant female is a woman, often depicted as a corpulent, full-figured female, whose title is *kdke,* rendered in the Classical sources as Candike. Those Classical sources often mistake the Meroitic title *kdke* for a personal name of the reigning queen, although this Meroitic Nubian word is in fact the etymological origin of the modern personal name Candice. The *qore* and *kdke* shared an equal status with a third, male member of the oligarchy whose title was *pqr*. It is unclear about how power was shared among these three and whether or not each was responsible for specific aspects of the bureaucratic administration of the realm. Nevertheless, the scenes and inscriptions indicate that the *qore* did exercise powers analogous to those of a king and that at times, a *kdke* might rule the Meroites in her own right as a female pharaoh, evocative of the power wielded by the Egyptian queen Hatshepsut of the New Kingdom, who likewise ruled alone as pharaoh. It has been suggested that one might regard these three titles in the English sense of "king," "queen," and "prince." Additionally, Lower Nubia was administered by an official whose Meroitic title is recorded as "petaso," perhaps meaning something on the order of "viceroy [of Lower Nubia]."

THE QUESTION OF MATRILINEAL SUCCESSION

It is only during the Kingdom of Meroe that one has direct evidence for elite Nubian women ruling as absolute monarchs in their own right. These women were anciently called "kdke" or "ktke," from the root "kd," "woman," compounded with "ke," assumed to be either a title or index of status. Those subscribing to any matrilineal institution theory erroneously regard this ruler as a king's sister, but such a suggestion is without foundation. There is no compelling evidence to suggest that royal succession in the Meroitic Period was dependent upon a successor's relationship with an incumbent *kdke*.

MEROITIC AGRICULTURE AND ANIMAL HUSBANDRY

By and large the majority of the Meroitic population continued to be engaged in traditional agricultural and animal husbandry pursuits, which remained little changed over the millennia. Contact with the Greek-speaking world and later with the Romans resulted in the introduction of new crops, notable among which was cotton. Date palm cultivation appears to have been limited, restricted initially perhaps to royal gardens within temple precincts, if the evidence from the reign of the Napatan king Harsiyotef can be trusted. How extensive the cultivation of the grape and the industry of wine making were in the Kingdom of Meroe remains a contentious issue. Oxen, sheep, and goats, as well as horses, continued to be bred and raised, but there is little evidence for the extensive use of the camel.

THE MEROITIC ECONOMY

One is imperfectly informed about the mechanics of the Nubian economy, which continued to rely on barter rather than on currency exchange.

One assumes that the *qore, kdke,* and *pqr* individually and perhaps collectively were responsible for the resources of the kingdom as a whole and might have controlled their own sources of wealth, possibly modeling the office of the Kushite God's Wife of Amun and her bureaucratic staff of Dynasty XXV. The same holds true for other members of the royal family and members of the Nubian elite, as well as perhaps the priesthoods of temples, which habitually seem to have controlled the resources within their domains. This picture appears to be confirmed by evidence from Meroitic Lower Nubia, which suggests that members of large, nuclear families established virtual hereditary fiefdoms in specific areas, which were administered by their family members as officials who were able to pass their offices onto their heirs over extended periods of time. The status of women in these families was relatively high, reflecting, perhaps, the status of the Meroitic *kdke.*

Classical sources describing the wealth of the Ptolemaic court in contemporary Alexandria contain so many references to deluxe products from Africa that one cannot escape the conclusion that the Meroitic oligarchy controlled the procurement and exchange of all of these products from Africa into Egypt.

That exchange was facilitated by the generally peaceful relationships that the Nubians of the late Napatan and Meroitic Period generally enjoyed first with the Ptolemies and later with the Romans. During the tumultuous period in the second half of the fourth century B.C.E., when Egypt was invaded for a second time by the Persians, the last native pharaoh, Nectanebo II, of Dynasty XXX fled to and was successfully granted asylum in Nubia.

EGYPTIAN PROCESSIONS

One of the fundamental characteristics of ancient Egyptian ritual was the procession performed to celebrate a cyclic event. Temples were placed into the landscape, and those in Egypt and Nubia were symbolically transformed into sacred topographies. At Thebes, for example, the Opet Festival was a rite expressly linking the pharaoh to his putative father, Amun. The reigning pharaoh would travel to the Luxor Temple, where Amun would bestow on him the powers of kingship confirming him as the living Horus. This festival linked aspects of the mythology of Osiris to that of Amun. By the time of the Egyptian New Kingdom Amun's role as the conveyor and guarantor of kingship was well established, and this association was perhaps the motivation for the Nubian appropriation of the same relationship between their own kings and Amun.

At other times an Egyptian religious procession might celebrate the coming of the Nile flood and the beginning of the Egyptian New Year. This festival, celebrated at Philae and in the Dodekaschoinos, is worth describing in some detail. The Egyptians regarded the stench and afflux accompanying the Nile flood as the eviscerated body of Osiris whom Isis reassembled. On another level, the fructifying waters of the flood, which deposited the rich alluvium from which Egypt's crops seem to so effortlessly spring was regarded as the semen of Osiris. These ancient, nuanced interpretations of the Nile River and its associations with Osiris occasioned the Egyptian theologians to credit the ministrations of Isis as the cause of the Nile's annual flood. These same theologians correlated the rising of Sothis with the oncoming flood. By the Late Period, the Greek identified Sothis as the dog star. The proliferation of numerous baked clay figurines of a goddess riding sidesaddle on the back of a dog is a visual allusion to Isis, the rise of Sothis, and the Nile flood.

In order to prepare for the flood and to alert the population of the impending event, the priests, particularly those attached to the cult of Isis at Philae situated at Egypt's southern frontier near the first cataract, would ready for display one or more boats associated with the goddess Isis and the deities in her entourage. These portable vessels would be on view on the podium, or special viewing area, such as seen at Aswan in the vicinity of the Temple of Khnum and at Kalabsha at the Temple of Mandulis. As the day approached, the vessels of Isis would begin a pilgrimage from Philae to each of her major temples in the Dodekaschoinos where requisite rites would be performed. So ingrained had this procession become that it was still being performed, perhaps in modified form, in the late Meroitic Period.

THE CORONATION JOURNEY

The importance of these processions was not lost on the Nubians. Their theologians adapted this Egyptian practice, particularly the procession of Isis as harbinger of the flood with its stations, for the legitimacy of kingship. In Nubia the king's investiture and coronation were not confined to one city, but consisted of a series of ceremonies, each localized and somewhat independent of one another, performed during the coronation journey. The sites visited adhered to a prescribed canonical itinerary, each station of which consisted of a temple to a form of Nubian Amun in the vicinity of a palace. At least three sites were visited, namely Napata, Kawa, and Pnubs (in the vicinity of ancient Kerma), but others were doubtless incorporated into the procession. The journey of coronation paralleled the visit of Isis prior to the flood but took on an added cosmic dimension. The procession could also be understood as a reaffirmation of the king's authority over his unified realm, equating his journey with that of the sun god's diurnal journey across the heavens. A similar journey is described on a shrine of Aspelta's suggesting that the practice had long been established in Nubia. The rites performed at the pilgrimage site of Musawwarat es-Sufra may be a late manifestation of this Nubian practice. The requisite ceremonies having been performed, the Nubian king might then fulfill his ideal role, as described in the so-called *Myth of State*, inscribed in Regnal Year 6 of Taharqa on his Kawa Stela V:

> Now His Majesty is one who loves god,
> So that he spends his time by day and lies by night
> Seeking what is of benefit for the gods,
> Rebuilding their temples if they have fallen into decay,
> Giving birth to their statues as on the first occasion,
> Building their storehouses,
> Presenting to them endowments of every kind,
> Making their offerings of fine gold, silver, and copper.
> Well, then, because His Majesty's heart is satisfied
> By doing for them what is beneficial every day.
> This land has been overflowed (with abundance) in his time
> As it was in the time of the Lord-of-all,
> Every man sleeping until dawn,
> Without saying, "Would that I had!", at all,
> Maat being introduced throughout the countries,
> And inequity being pinned to the ground. (IOWANA 349)

THE KINGDOM OF MEROE AND THE EGYPTIAN PTOLEMAIC DYNASTY

The subsequent capitulation of the Persians to the demands of Alexander the Great, which resulted in the peaceful transference of Egypt from Persian control to that of Alexander, witnessed the continuance in office of many bureaucrats, some of whom served the Persians and even the last native pharaohs. It can be argued that Nubians were among their ranks as well, although Alexander the Great does not appear to have been personally preoccupied with any Egyptian district to the south of Memphis. In the aftermath of his death and the struggle among his successors for kingdoms, Ptolemy, one of Alexander's older generals, eventually proclaimed himself pharaoh of Egypt and in so doing in 305 B.C.E. inaugurated a Macedonian Greek dynasty, the Ptolemaic named in his honor, whose descendants were to rule Egypt uninterruptedly until the death by suicide of Cleopatra VII in 30 B.C.E. The relationships between the Ptolemies of Egypt and the Meroites of Nubia were, on the whole, peaceful for the three centuries of Macedonian rule, as the constant flow into Alexandria of African luxury products suggests. The grand procession of Ptolemy II Philadelphus, as recorded by Athenaeus of Naukratis, included 12 chariots drawn by antelopes, 7 by oryxes, 15 by hartebeest, 8 by ostriches, and 7 by onelaphoi. The Nubian tribute bearers in the procession carried 600 elephant tusks, 2,000 logs of ebony, and 60 vessels filled with gold and silver and gold dust. There were, in addition, 130 Nubian sheep, 20 Nubian cows, 14 leopards, 16 cheetahs, 4 caracals, 3 cheetah cubs, 2 giraffe, and a Nubian rhinoceros. The Meroites, like other Nubians before them, fostered a slave trade that continued to be a feature of the Meroitic economy, the hapless bartered individuals captured as prisoners of war in the increasing conflicts between the Meroites and neighboring marauding tribes. So ensconced had the Nubian slave trade become that many of its norms were appropriate wholesale, as seen by their survival in the Medieval Islamic system of the slave trade, the *baqt*.

The agreed-upon boundary between the Kingdom of Meroe and that of Ptolemaic Egypt was at Aswan, but the region, anciently termed the Dodeckaschoinos, stretching for about 90 miles from Aswan as far as Hiera Sykaminos (Maharraqa) to the south, became a condominium of sorts in which both Ptolemaic and Meroitic interests intersected. The Temples of Isis on the island of Philae were to become the most important religious and pilgrimage sites for subjects of both kingdoms, and its priesthoods were to dominate the region until the establishment of Christianity. Although there are scant references to military confrontation between the two kingdoms during this period, a degree of competition did exist within the Dodekaschoinos between the Meroites and Ptolemies, particularly with regard to religious patronage of its temples. This is most evident in the introduction by the Ptolemaic priesthood of Philae of a new deity, Thoth of Pnoubs, Lord of Pselkis. This deity is in fact a conflation of the Nubian deity worshipped at Pnoubs with the Egyptian deity Thoth as Lord of Nebes. The motivation was doubtless to erode the authority and status of the Meroitic priesthood attached to those cult centers in the Dodekaschoinos while promoting the authority of Philae. At the same time, there was an effort to move the administrative capital from Elephantine, adjacent to Philae, to Kom Ombo, several miles further to the north, thus distancing the administrators from their Lower Nubian constituents. Despite these periodic attempts by the Ptolemaic priesthoods to assert their authority in the region, the Meroitic rulers habitually honored their obligation of sending the requisite tithes regularly and without interruption to the temples of the Dodekaschoinos in general and to Philae in particular throughout the history of the Ptolemaic and Roman Periods. At Dakke in the Dodekaschoinos, Ergamenes II/Arkamani II commissioned the interior of the temple whereas his contemporary, Ptolemy IV, commissioned its exterior. As a result, Lower Nubia, that region of the Meroitic Kingdom close to the common Nubian-Ptolemaic border at Aswan, appears to have become more affluent than the Meroitic regions further to the south. The material culture reveals a plethora of Graeco-Roman imports, principal, among which were bronzes.

ERGAMENES OF MEROE AND PTOLEMY II PHILADELPHUS

The earliest documented case of political cooperation between the Kingdom of Meroe and the Ptolemaic Dynasty of Egypt occurred during the reign of Ptolemy II Philadelphus (275–246 B.C.E.). Ergamenes, as he is called in the Classical texts, has been equated with the Meroitic king, Arkamani I, the traditional founder of the Meroitic Dynasty. It is difficult to separate fact from fiction regarding his biography, but the assertion that Ergamenes received a Greek education and was well versed in Greek philosophy is significant. Ergamenes/Arkamani I possessed a titulary composed of five royal names, on the model of traditional ancient Egyptian pharaohs. That titulary included his throne name, *Khnum-ib-re*, which was also the throne name of Amasis, a pharaoh of Dynasty XXVI, who was himself a philhellene, a lover of things Greek. The choice of such a name was conscious, emphasizing Ergamenes's ties to the Ptolemaic Court of Alexandria. These close ties are further reinforced by the observation that Ergamanes supplied Ptolemy II with African elephants, which were imported to serve in the Egyptian army. This is the first documented instance of the use of those elephants for that purpose, the older claim that Taharqa also used elephants in war now being dismissed as erroneous.

THE SECESSION OF THE THEBAID

During the reign of Ptolemy IV Philopator, a revolt of the Thebans in Upper Egypt resulted in the temporary secession of Upper Egypt from the Ptolemaic kingdom. The reasons for the revolt are not clear but appear to be related to issues of nationalism, social and economic inequities, and an unfavorable view in general toward the Ptolemaic court by the native Egyptians. Two counter kings, presently identified as Ankhwennefer and Horwennefer, succeeded one another as self-styled pharaohs of Egypt. A study of contemporary accounts suggests that at least one of these counter kings, Horwennefer, was himself a Nubian. A graffito from Aswan asserts that Nubians were among the rebels and that they fortified themselves within a temple precinct. Clearly, the Nubian priesthoods of the Dodekaschoinos were complicit in the revolt. All of the rebels were doubtless aided and abetted in the struggle by the leadership of Meroe, perhaps in the person of Ergamenes II/Arkamani II, an observation supported by a contemporary text that states that Nubian troops in the Sixteenth Regnal Year of an otherwise unspecified Ptolemaic king attacked and destroyed the region around Aswan. One scholar has even suggested that the Meroitic *qore* Adikhalamani, suggested to be the successor of Ergamenes II, opportunely seized control of the Dodekaschoinos during this time, although that ruler's position in the chronology of Meroitic rulers is not firmly established.

The Thebaid revolt, one of at least 10 documented for the Ptolemaic Period throughout Egypt, was eventually suppressed. In keeping with a long-standing policy of maintaining the status quo, the Ptolemies were inclined to offer amnesty after the cessation of hostilities rather than to continue to exact reprisals. Upper Egypt appears to have returned to nor-

Model of the Temple of Dendur in situ. ALEA.

malcy, and the symbiotic relationship between the Ptolemies and the Meroites was soon resumed.

THE ROMAN CONQUEST OF EGYPT AND THE REVOLT OF A MEROITIC CANDAKE

Roman involvement in the affairs of Africa progressively increased during the course of the first century B.C.E., particularly after Ptolemy XII Auletes secured financial and military support from Rome in his successful bid to reestablish himself as pharaoh of Egypt, having been forced into exile by a rival faction. Upon his death in 51 B.C.E. he bequeathed his kingdom to his daughter, Cleopatra VII, and her much younger brother, Ptolemy XIII. Of Cleopatra's direct ancestors, only the identity of her maternal grandmother remains unknown, and there is no compelling evidence to suggest that she was either an Egyptian or a Nubian. All of Cleopatra VII's other forebears were of Macedonian Greek descent. The account of her spectacular rise to power and her relationships with Julius Caesar and Marc Antony are beyond the scope of this narrative, but her ultimate confrontation with Octavian at the Battle of Actium in 31 B.C.E. and suicide a year later enabled the Romans to gain possession of Egypt. Octavian, now named Augustus as the first emperor of Rome, fearing that Egypt might mount another challenge to his authority, declared the country his personal property rather than a province of the empire and forbade immigration except by those with specially issued imperial visas.

Between 28–21 B.C.E., his administrators were confronted with disturbances in the Arabian peninsula directly across the Red Sea from Egypt. Wishing to address the situation as expeditiously as possible, the Romans decided to dispatch legions already stationed in Egypt to the troubled area. Once the legions had departed, the Nubians of Lower Egypt appear to have revolted and stormed the frontier at Aswan, sacking the area and toppling official monuments, including recently erected statues of Augustus himself. The head of one of these bronze images of Augustus was severed from its body and carried off to Meroe, where it was intentionally buried beneath the threshold of one of the palaces so that each time the Meroites entered and exited, they would be symbolically trampling the head of their foe underfoot. The Classical authors credit a Candake as the leader of the Meroites. As one has seen earlier, they had mistaken the title, *kdke*, for the personal name of the female ruler of kingdom of Meroe. Her identity remains unknown, although there are attempts to identify her with the Queen Mother Amanirenas, who is suggested to have ruled during this period of time. She apparently shared power with the *pqr*, Akinidad. If one's reading of the monuments is correct, Akinidad continued to rule after her demise with another *kdke*, Amanishakheto by name. Akinidad exercised personal control over both Upper and Lower Nubia, as his titles attest. He is to date the only Meroite known to have held the office of *pqr* and *pesato*, "viceroy [of Lower Nubia]," simultaneously.

In order to address this insurrection, the Romans dispatched new legions to the region in anticipation of a military confrontation and began their march into Lower Nubia. The Meroites, in an attempt to meet the Roman challenge, mustered their own forces and marched north. Both forces marched into the vicinity of Qasr Ibrim (Primis). A pitched battle was avoided when representatives from both sides agreed to discuss the matter. The Meroites indicated that their revolt against Rome was prompted by certain grievances that had not been remedied. The Roman geographer, Strabo, writing in Greek shortly after the actual events, is decidedly prejudiced in his account, incredulously posing a question to the Meroites inquiring as to their reason for not bringing their concerns to the emperor Augustus. As if to portray the Meroites as individuals ignorant of current affairs, Strabo records their reply by stating that the Meroites did not know where to find Augustus. In point of fact, the Meroites were correct because Augustus himself had been on the move as a result of his inspection tour of the East.

It was then resolved that an embassy of the Meroites would be granted safe conduct to the Greek island of Samos, where Augustus was temporarily headquartered. This was perhaps the first recorded instance in the entire history of Africa when diplomats representing a Black African ruler independent of Egypt traveled to Europe to effect a diplomatic resolution. The Meroites and Romans signed a peace treaty that not only remitted their tax liability to Rome, but also established the Dodekaschoinos as a buffer zone. In order to gain the favor of the inhabitants of this region, Augustus directed his administrators to collaborate with the priesthoods of the region in the erection of a temple at Dendur. In its relief and inscriptions, Augustus himself appears as the chief celebrant of the local deities but there pays particular homage to two youths, whose deaths had elevated them to the status of divine intercessors. They are enrolled among the local deities in this temple and are the recipients of a cult. The temple of Dendur also served as their cenotaph.

THE EGYPTIAN SPEOS

Earlier in this volume, we demonstrated that the Egyptian rock cut temple, or speos, was of Nubian origin, the earliest example of which was the cave sanctuary at Sayala. This particularly Nubian architectural expression was adopted by the Egyptians of the New Kingdom, whose pharaohs commissioned several speoi in Upper Egypt and in Nubia. The earliest of these, at Speos Artemidoros, is dated to the reign of Queen Hatshepsut of Dynasty XVIII, and the most famous are the paired Northern and Southern Temples at Abu Simbel. Here, Rameses II, to whom the Greater, or Southern Sanctuary is dedicated, is equated with male solar deities but can only dawn via the ministration of the female principal, ascribed to his chief queen Nofertari, to whom the Lesser, or Northern Sanctuary is dedicated.

THE TEMPLE OF DENDUR

The temple that Augustus commissioned at Dendur is to be regarded within the context of such Egyptian speoi. Ostensibly depicting Augustus worshipping the local deities, the relief decoration and accompanying inscriptions pay particular homage to brothers, Pahor and Pedese, who are believed to have been sons of a local Nubian elite ruler and who seem to have met their fate by drowning in the Nile River, apparently resulting in their being deified. The temple of Dendur celebrates these two brothers and contains within the thickness of its rear wall, which abutted the hillside into which the temple was constructed, a chamber serving as their cenotaph. This temple appears to have replaced an earlier rock cut shrine, or speos, in which the cult of these two brothers was apparently celebrated. The rituals celebrated at Dendur in the name of Augustus on behalf of these two brothers were contemporary with other rituals performed at Sayala in the vicinity of Abu Simbel. Nubian religious praxis in speoi, therefore, persisted into the Roman Period at both Sayala and Dendur alike.

THE TEMPLE ARCHITECTURE OF THE MEROITIC PERIOD

It may be fairly stated that the plan of the typical Egyptian temple continued to serve as the model on which temples erected in Lower Nubia, and more specifically in the Dodekaschoinos, were based. This is certainly the case for the Temples at Dendur, just discussed, as well as those at both Dakka and Kalabasha. Some of these temples have already been described as joint efforts by the kings of Meroe and their contemporary pharaohs of Ptolemaic Egypt. That such temples should also be constructed in Nubia farther to the south should come as no surprise because these are usually reserved for the worship of Meroitic deities closely associated with members of the Egyptian pantheon. So, for example, temples to Amun at such southern Meroitic sites as Meroe, Naqa, and Amara are virtually indistinguishable in their ground plans from Egyptian temples, although, admittedly, they are on a much smaller scale. The scenes in relief that decorate such temples are also indebted to Egyptian norms.

On the other hand, the Meroites appear to have pioneered the development of the single- or double-chambered sanctuary that, in light of one's present knowledge, appears to have been dedicated exclusively to Nubian deities. Such sanctuaries appear to derive from simple shrines erected in Nubia during Dynasty XXV by the order of Taharqa at both Kawa and Sanam, but may in fact ultimately derive from the one-room funerary chapels associated with the great tumuli of Kerma.

The temples of the god Apedemak at both Meroe and Musawwarat es-Sufra share many of the same features. As a result, one can describe this type of chambered Meroitic sanctuary, sometimes erected on a plinth and usually oriented toward the southeast, as a temple entered in most cases via a pylon with the same two-tower design encountered in Egyptian gateways. The sanctuary may be partitioned into a pronaos and naos, or sanctuary proper, at the rear. Often its roof is supported by columns, either four or six in number, and the naos itself may have been wreathed with an additional colonnade. Because of the general uniformity revealed by their orientation in an east-southeast axis, these chambered sanctuaries are thought to have been astronomically aligned on one and the same fast-moving star or planet. In keeping with the rigid regulation of the royal funerary pyramid tombs, these sanctuaries seem to have been constructed in accordance with a canon of proportions, which appears to have employed the diameter of a column drum as its module.

The most unique sanctuary in either Egypt or in Nubia is doubtless the complex at Musawwarat es-Sufra. Its confusing ground plan led earlier scholars to reach erroneous conclusions about its function, claiming that this complex in its distinctive enclosure was either a Meroitic queen's summer residence, a theater for the training of elephants, a secular, educational complex, or a seminary for Meroitic priests. One now realizes that the complex in its present state is the result of the rebuilding and modification over time of a pilgrimage center. The focal point of the center consists of at least seven temples, three of which are located within the Great Enclosure, one of these having been erected on a terrace. These are surrounded by a maze of courts and individual rooms of varying size, some of which are connected by a network of corridors.

The so-called Great Temple within the enclosure at Musawwarat es-Sufra was erected on an elevation. Its principal façade abandons the twin towers of the pylon in favor of a shrine-shaped entrance, crowned with a series of cavetto cornices, each decorated with its own winged sun disk, which is set into a long, proportionately not very tall wall. Its design appears to recall that of the façade of the second story of the Lake Edifice of Taharqa at Karnak. This was fronted by a series of remarkably designed columns, the shafts of which feature sculpted decoration erected on bases in the form of animals. Monumental statues of Meroitic gods, suggested to have been Arensnuphis and Sebiumeker, flanked the entrance on the model provided by ancient Egyptian temples. A unique detail was a wall projection depicting an elephant. Behind the colonnade of the façade was a one-chambered sanctuary surrounded by a columned ambulatory. Its roof was supported by four interior columns, and its interior walls were provided with niches, perhaps for statues. Its façade and two lateral walls contained doorways as well, but the rear wall did not. Its ground plan, although unusual, appears to have been specifically designed to accommodate efficiently the circulation of pilgrims. There is no indication, however, of the deity to whom this innovative sanctuary was dedicated.

FUNERARY ARCHITECTURE OF THE MEROITIC PERIOD

The Meroites continued the practice of the immediately preceding Napatan Period of incorporating a pyramid into the design of their royal tombs. The pyramids of both eras are virtually indistinguishable from one another, and the height of the tallest rarely exceeded 30 meters. The pyramid cemetery was located at Meroe, but for reasons unknown, the royal cemetery was reestablished at Gebel Barkal for a short interval during the first century C.E. Whereas the earlier royal tombs were designed with entrances into the burial chamber for the performance of rituals benefiting the deceased, such portals were eliminated during the course of the first century C.E., indicating that the pyramids could only have been constructed after the interment. Thereafter in time, the pyramids show a rapid deterioration in the care with which they were constructed, which is commensurate with their ever-decreasing size.

Members of the Meroitic elite seem to have continued to bury their deceased in rudimentary sepulchers, which consist of a narrow shaft, enlarged at one end to form the burial chamber proper. No superstructure for any of these elite tombs has survived, but one assumes that they did exist either in the form of a mastaba or a pyramid.

MEROITIC ARCHITECTURAL MATHEMATICS

There is virtually no mention of Nubia's scientific achievements in either the inscriptional or literary traditions as preserved to this day. Their success in other fields of endeavor is passed over in silence as well in these same records. And yet a survey of their rich material culture throughout the ages suggests that the Nubians possessed scientific knowledge and that the elite placed the knowledge at their disposal into the hands of their craftsmen. An engraving, discovered at Meroe, provides a tantalizing glimpse into the nature of Nubian mathematics during the late first century B.C.E. and suggests that continued excavation will provide additional information about Nubian science.

This engraving measures 1.68 meters in height and has been interpreted as a representation of a pyramid, such as those still standing at Meroe, reproduced in such a way that only its left-hand half is shown in elevation. Its floor and platform are also indicated. Although not provided with any ancient key to indicate dimensions, we can calculate from its details that this anonymous Nubian architect employed a scale of 1:10 for his architectural plan. The dimensions of the pyramid may then be calculated to be approximately 11.58 by 16.80 meters in length and height, respectively. More remarkable still is the inclusion of several lines set running diagonally up the engraving from the base of the pyramid. These lines are inclined at approximately a seventy-two degree angle, and were doubtless intended to represent the steep sloping slide so characteristic of Meroitic pyramids in general. Further modern calculations utilizing the details shown on this engraving reveal a sense of relative proportion of the pyramid's height to the length of its base in the ratio of 8:5. The mathematical data yielded by a study of this engraving was then compared to the actual dimensions of pyramids at Meroe. The comparison revealed that this engraved architectural plan corresponds to the pyramid identified as belonging to the Meroitic King Amanikhabale, whose reign is tentatively placed into the second half of the first century B.C.E.

The engraving demonstrates the existence of a sophisticated understanding of mathematics and suggests a Nubian appreciation of the harmonic ratios which mathematics can impart to architecture.

MEROITIC SECULAR ARCHITECTURE

At the height of their power, the kings of Meroe ruled over a population of an estimated 500,000 individuals. Many of these subjects continued to live in simple reed huts and shelters; others lived in more durable houses of mud brick, the rectangular floor plans of which usually contained two or three rooms.

There is little evidence for town planning. The settlement at Karanog, which covered a maximum surface area of 80,000 square meters, was home to an estimated 4,000 residents. A description of the town does not seem to differ from that of contemporary rural villages in Roman Egypt, such as Karanis (Kom Ouchim). The streets were not laid out in any perceptible, predetermined pattern, but meandered as if at will and resembled narrow alleys. The houses were constructed of a variety of materials, the use of which was doubtless a reflection of wealth and status, which included mud brick, stone, and rubble, with an occasional mud-brick veneer. Mud-brick houses consisting of three stories are still regarded by the inhabitants of the region as castles or palaces but were, in all probability, the residence of the most elite member of society, whom some identify as a "governor."

Larger settlements, such as that of Kawa with its 8,000 inhabitants, are worthy of designation as towns, and the 24,000 residents of Meroe justify its designation as a city. Despite the size of these last two urban areas, the archaeological remains are not sufficient for one to present even a cursory description of the dwellings.

Cult image of a Meroitic king in the National Museum, Khartoum.

Occasionally a site such as Wad Ban Naga provides sufficient remains of a royal complex to warrant comment. Here was found the residence of Queen Amanishakheto and several temples. Her mud brick palace is one of the largest identified to date. It measures some 61 meters in length and covers an area of some 3,700 square meters. The ground floor contained over 60 rooms for various purposes. This palace originally had a second story as the remains of columns found on the ground floor indicate, and this may have contained an atrium, a design feature paralleled elsewhere.

One can conclude this section with a mention of the Baths of Meroe. Although assuredly based on Classical models derived from Alexandria, no definitive description can be offered here because of the insufficient data available to date. The presence in the baths of Classically inspired sculpture demonstrates the adaptability of Nubian artisans who were able to use Classical models for the creation of sculptures in an indisputably Meroitic idiom.

THE SCULPTURE OF THE MEROITIC PERIOD

The Continuance of Napatan Aesthetic Concerns

The transference of the capital of the Nubians from Napata to Meroe was accompanied by innovations in the material culture of the Meroites, but also signaled the perpetuation of some older Nubian traditions. One of these was certainly artistic, as seen in the magnificent bronze and gilded statue of a Meroitic archer-king from Tabo on the island of Argo, now in the National Museum of Khartoum, which perpetuates traditional Nubian aesthetic concerns expressed in the striding idol of Senkamanisken, discussed earlier.

The statue is just under two feet in height and cast in bronze. It represents a striding male figure, wearing sandals, a kilt with central flap, the Nubian cap crown fronted by the double uraeus and encircled by a diadem, a ram-headed lanyard, a broad collar, armbands, and earrings. Earrings as a male fashion accessory are first documented among the Nubians of the Pan Grave culture, from whom the practice was adopted by the Egyptians of Dynasty XVIII. Thereafter earrings might be a unisex accessory. The male figure is also equipped with a thumb ring on his right hand and a forearm guard on his left forearm, equipment used by archers. One can, therefore, confidently restore a bow in his fisted left hand, and perhaps a clutch of arrows in his right.

In keeping with the design tenets employed for the creation of the striding statue of Senkamanisken, the modeling of the legs and arms as well as the torso are massively conceived broad planes with virtually no articulated detail. The entire image is stippled, serving as a mordant for gesso, or plaster, traces of which still remain where gilding was applied and which has survived to a great degree principally on the face and neck. The resulting idol conveyed the same impact as did the statue of Senka-

A ba-statue of an elite Meroitic woman. ALEA.

menisken and served as an index of the authority and status of Meroitic kingship. Because it functioned as an ideological statement, rather than perhaps as a depiction of a specific king because it is not inscribed, the statue is thought to have been continually displayed from the time of its creation, suggested to have been in the second century B.C.E., for over six centuries until the tumultuous period at the end of the Meroitic Period. The statue then seems to have been ceremoniously buried, perhaps to secrete it from an enemy, with the intention that it would be later retrieved so that it could continue to serve its cultic function. The ultimate fall of Meroe precluded its ancient recovery.

THE BA-STATUES AND NUBIAN FORMALISM

There are several different, but contemporary design tenets current in Nubian sculptural ateliers of the Meroitic Period. These include an adaptation of Classical naturalism, the perpetuation of Egyptian norms in modified form, and a Nubian formalism. It is that formalism, which is the linear descendant of the Nubian aesthetic discussed earlier, to which one turns first.

This formalism receives its fullest and longest-lived expression in the Meroitic creation of the ba-image. The ba is a difficult ancient concept to define, but is one of the five integral components of a human being, consisting of the body itself, its shadow, the individual's name, and his/her ka, or life force, and the ba. For convenience, the ba is often equated with an individual's personality, but such a simplification masks the fact that the ancient concept of the ba encompasses all of those nonphysical characteristics that contribute to the uniqueness of each and every individual. Human beings as well as divinities have a ba, a divine ba often representing a different hypostasis, or physical manifestation, of the divine. So, for example, the Apis bull worshipped at Memphis was anciently regarded as the ba of the god Ptah.

In ancient Egypt, the ba of a human being was traditionally depicted as a human-headed bird. Such representations were generally confined to two-dimensional representations, either on papyri or in tomb painting, but might also on occasion be depicted in two-dimensional relief representation. The ancient Egyptians seem never to have created three-dimensional sculptures of the human ba, except in small scale for use as amulets or funerary jewelry and small wooden statuettes.

The pioneering of depictions of the elite deceased, both male and female, as large, free-standing ba-statues is an innovation of the Meroitic Period, which seems to have been developed first in Lower Nubia. These images appear to have evolved independently of both official sculpture of the court at Meroe and outside stimuli. These elite images are often, but not exclusively, associated with individuals bearing the Meroitic title, *petese*, high-ranking officials in the Meroitic administration.

As an autochthonian, Nubian creation the ba-statue continues the tradition of Nubian formalism encountered earlier in the sphinx of Taharqa in London, which represents for convenience a beginning of this artistic tradition. The ba-statue of a woman, perhaps to be identified as Malitakhide, is representative. It is a consummate expression of Nubian formalism. The entire body is designed as a rectangular volume within which feet, arms, hands, and breasts are defined. These anatomical details are simplified planes, often rectilinear in contour. A unique feature of this abstraction is the 90-degree rotation of the breasts. The head is an orchestration of lunette forms that balance and enhance the overall abstract design. Each half of the bilaterally symmetrical face echoes the contour of each ear. This interest in the lunette is reinforced by the wide-open eyes, which recall the hairline on the brow. The vertical orientation of the statue as a whole is emphasized by the bridge of the nose and the parallel lines of scarification on each cheek.

The design of the heads of both male and female ba-statues is remarkably alike, as we compare the head of a male ba-statue excavated at Karanog, now in Philadelphia, with that of the ba-statue of Lapakhidaye depicted on a stela from Serra West, now in Khartoum. The faces are generally framed by two vertical incisions, which generally separate the ears from the checks. That incision may be continued horizontally to indicate the hairline. The face thus framed is then designed with eyes, nose, and mouth, occasionally with a second horizontal line on the brow, evocative of a wrinkle caused when frowning. The coiffures are habitually closely cropped and unisex because the gender of heads of all ba-statues, but particularly those separated from their bodies, appear to lack gender-specific indices. This is a significant observation, reinforcing the earlier suggestion that the baked clay effigies of the C-Group culture are ambivalently asexual, because the design of their heads is remarkably akin to the aesthetic employed in the design of the heads of these ba-statues of both sexes.

The style of such ba-statues is non-Egyptian, non-Western; it might almost be termed "Primitive," in the sense once applied by art historians to the artistic creations of the sub-Saharan cultures of Africa. What links there are between the Nubian formalism of the Napatan and Meroitic Periods and those productions are, due to the present state of one's knowledge, highly speculative, particularly because diffusionist theories are difficult to support and because studies regarding the art history of East Africa in general and that of the Sudan and Ethiopia in particular are in their infancy. Nevertheless, the formalism of certain wood carvings of the Bongo Tribe from Bussere (Dongurungu) share an affinity with the Nubian formalism of certain ba-birds in the simplified, rectilinearity of the body. The same interests in the linear abstraction of the head, evident in the ba-statue, reappear in this example as well. The tenets of this Nubian formalism appear, therefore, to have spanned the millennia and to have survived in certain works from The Republic of the Sudan.

These same stylistic characteristics are apparent in the standing male figure, attributed to the Dinka Tribe, although they have more in common with the oeuvre of the Bari Tribe, who inhabit the south of modern Ethiopia. The rectilinearity of the body, pronounced verticality of the figure, and linear abstraction of the balanced forms of the face are all similar to the general aesthetic of the Meroitic ba-statue and Bongo figure.

These apparent cultural survivals are even more striking in the head of a Meroitic ba-statue from Argin now in Khartoum. Measuring almost 11 inches in height, this sculpture is unique in the repertoire of Meroitic art because it was purposely designed as an independent sculpture in the form of a head and neck. It has not been broken or separated from a body, because it was never intended to join a sculptural body. Its design is in keeping with the design of heads of ba-statues in general. The hair, resting on the head as a raised plane, articulated with a reticulated pattern of incised lines, is short. It serves to define the face framing it at the level of both ears and across the brow, which is itself scored by a deep horizontal line, and perhaps a fainter second one below. The abstract rhythm of the sculpture is evident in the use of lunette forms, two joined to form the oval-shaped eye brows and sockets, the eyes themselves depicted as slits, and one each serving as a vertical ear. The nose and mouth are sculpturally designed in virtually the same way as are some of the heads from the baked clay effigies of the C-Group Period.

Africanists additionally find correspondences between this particular head and works of art created in the region of present day Nigeria around the time that Christianity was there adopted. Not withstanding the observation that modern Nigeria and the Kingdom of Meroe are situated on about the same latitude in eastern and western Africa, respectively and are separated by a distance of about 2,500 miles, the seemingly similar design tenets and aesthetics of particular artistic creations invites further investigation with regard to influences.

A glass chalice from Sedeinga. Courtesy of the Pisa Egyptological Museum, Catalogue number 436, Pisa-Cattedra di Egittologia-Università di Pisa.

If one now accepts the working hypothesis that the Nubian formalism of the Napatan and Meroitic Periods is related to similar phenomena in certain Black African sculptures, the ethnographic works that influenced Gauguin and the Postimpressionists and that led Picasso to the formulation of Cubism have a pedigree reaching across three millennia. As a result, the Black contribution to modern Western painting would be as deeply rooted in the traditions of the African peoples as is the Black contribution to Western music. It remains the task for Africanists to seek the necessary links in this chain.

MEROITIC SCULPTURE AND ART IN AN EGYPTIANIZING IDIOM

The long-standing relationships between Nubian and Egypt continued to find visual expression during the Meroitic Period by the creation in Nubian ateliers of sculpture based on Egyptian design elements. These creations may exhibit degrees of Nubian formalism.

A good example is a sandstone head from Meroe, now in Khartoum, which is generally identified as a depiction of the god Sebiumeker. The head is based on Egyptian models, with its almond-shaped hieroglyphic eyes and paint-striped brows, but relies on broad, unmodeled planes for its sculptural effect in keeping with the tenets of Nubian formalism. The double crown fronted by a uraeus exhibits a characteristic bulge, which is common to Nubian depictions of Sebiumeker, and suggests the identification of this uninscribed image.

The same synthesis of Egyptian norms and Nubian formalism is evident in a crouching, sandstone ram from Naga, also in Khartoum. Based on Egyptian models for its attitude, it was one of a dozen monumental rams that were associated with the Temple of Amun. Although its muzzle is destroyed, the treatment of its fleece as a series of snail-shell spirals is decorative in the extreme and conforms with the abstract quality of the treatment of hair of other mammals in Meroitic art.

Less imbued with Nubian formalism are statuettes in steatite representing the god Amun, examples of which abound in collections worldwide. Many of these may very well be mistaken by scholars as creations of Egyptian ateliers, such as the headless example in Munich of unknown provenance. Other examples, such as one from Meroe, now in Khartoum, share the same baroque treatment of its costume and accessories, which are rendered in very bold relief and may be identified as Nubian creations, perhaps, on the basis of the design of the faces, which in this instance approaches that of the sandstone image identified as Sebiumeker.

The creativity of these Meroitic ateliers is again in evidence in their creation of figural protomes, such as the triad found at Musawwarat es-Sufra, now in Berlin. These were placed into walls of temples from which they projected, and may in fact be a Meroitic innovation, as was the creation of the ba-statue. There is no reason, therefore, to suggest that the impetus for the design and development of the characteristically Meroitic protome was the lion-headed water spout of pharaonic Egypt because of their different placement within the walls of Meroitic temples and because they are often group compositions as opposed to single heads of lions serving as water spouts in Egyptian architecture.

The central figure of this protome is a ram, whose headdress consists of double plumes, a sun disk, and spiraling ovoid horns, fronted by a double uraeus. The animal is doubtless a manifestation of the god Amun, guarantor of Nubian kingship, by virtue of the double uraeus, which is the Nubian royal regalia par excellence. The two lions which flank Amun as a ram ought to be identified in terms of Nubian deities in his entourage, rather than in terms of deities of the Egyptian pantheon.

MEROITIC SCULPTURE IN A HELLENIZING IDIOM

The material culture of the Kingdom of Meroe is replete with metal artifacts, both of bronze and of silver, which are assuredly of Graeco-Roman manufacture and which arrived into Nubia as imports. These include a deluxe silver goblet with relief decoration of Roman manufacture, found at Meroe and now in Boston. The skill of the Nubian ateliers as metalsmiths, evident in the bronze figure of the archer-king from Tabo and in the Treasure of Amaniskakheto, enabled their craftsmen to create wonderfully mimetic works in metal. Several bronze oinoichoe, or pitchers, such as one from Karanog, now in Philadelphia, is likewise a Roman creation and import, but a second, found at Meroe and now in Khartoum, is a Nubian variant of this Roman form. Its profile is tall, more slender, and more attenuated than its Roman model, and its handle, while evocative of Roman prototypes, relies on a head of the goddess Hathor as its principal decorative device. In like manner, a footed, bronze bowl with loop handles, found at Gamai and now in Khartoum, is a Meroitic artistic response to another Roman model. The exaggerated loops of the handles on this particular vessel, which extend well into the interior of the bowl, is well attested from similar vessels from Meroitic contexts, revealing that it is a creation of a Nubian atelier.

The difficulties in describing the architectural complex conveniently called the Baths of Meroe do not mask the fact that Alexandrian models may have served as its prototypes. Within the complex were excavated several statues, of which the so-called Venus of Meroe, now in Munich, is an example. This statue was one of several erected on a series of stepped balustrades surrounding the water basin below. The pose of this statue is indebted to the repertoire of Aphrodite figures created in the preceding Hellenistic Period, which were widely copied during the Roman Period. As preserved the figure is nude, and her coiffure, indicated by a network of incised lines, is in imitation of the fashionable melon-coiffure popular in

Alexandrian artistic depictions of women. The modeling of the body in broad planes, the simplification of the transitions between them, most evident perhaps in the design of the face, and the treatment of the fingers without joints are well within the traditions of the Nubian aesthetic. Dismissed by some as retarditaire in comparison with contemporary creations of the Roman Imperial Period, the Venus of Meroe together with the statues of Amun in steatite reveal the technical dexterity of the Nubian ateliers and their craftsmen. They fully understood the prevailing aesthetic concerns of neighboring civilizations and could appropriate those norms transformed to serve their specific needs.

There is perhaps no greater testament to this chameleonlike character of the Nubian ateliers of the Kingdom of Meroe in their technical mastery of materials and mimetic ability to copy motifs than in a pair of footed blue glass and gilded goblets discovered at Sedeinga, one of which is now in Pisa. They are identical in manufacture and of approximately the same size, measuring some 8 inches in height. Each is decorated with figures, framed top and bottom by four horizontal bands, beads dominating the one and alternating beads and dotted/circled rectangles the second. Each has a four-leaf clover like floral frieze below, separated by dots, and a Greek inscription above, which translates, "Drink and you shall live," an exhortation frequently encountered in early Christian texts. The fact that there are errors in the spelling of the Greek words in this exhortation has been taken as additional evidence for the Nubian manufacture of the vessels.

That evidence is consistent with the eclectic selection of the four figures that appear on each vessel. They depict three offering bearers, one female and three male, in the company of an enthroned Osiris. Their orientation around the vessel is not consistent with traditional Egyptian iconographic programs in which the figures in a procession bearing offerings would all be facing the principal deity of the scene. In contrast, the design of this procession of offering bearers departs from this program because the single female figure and only one of the male figures is so aligned. The third offering bearer is oriented with the figure of Osiris.

The female figure wears a tripartite wig with sun disk and a reticulated sheath, which leaves the breasts exposed. She carries aloft a tray of offerings on which is a votive statuette and holds a horned African animal—an oryx or antelope. Her male companions wear kilts, corslets perhaps with shoulder straps and a broad collar. Their heads are covered with the Nubian cap crown, devoid of any serpents, which are similarly topped with a sun disk. The one holds a disproportionately large *hes*-vessel, used for liquid libations, in one hand and grasps the forepaws of a deer with the other, whereas his companion bears a similar horned African animal on his shoulders and a brace of fowl in his extended hand.

The pair of vessels appear to have been created in order to be destroyed, because they were found smashed into 80 pieces within the tomb at

Sedeinga, as if deliberately broken as part of a specific Meroitic funerary rite, the details of which are not known.

The deluxe quality of this pair of chalices is perhaps exceeded only by the Treasure of Queen Amanishakheto, now shared between Munich and Berlin. The circumstances of the find have been romanticized to the point of fiction and revolve around the colorful career of Giuseppe Ferlini, an Italian physician who traveled to Nubia around 1830 with the army of Mohammed Ali, the founder of Egypt's modern monarchy, whose last member, King Farouk, was forced to abdicate in 1952 by a military coup led by Nasser.

Intent on finding treasure and believing in the tales still current in Egypt and The Sudan that the ancients secreted treasures in the most extraordinary places within their monuments, Ferlini was convinced that treasure lay beneath the summits of the pyramids of Meroe. Tradition maintains that he then decided to hack off their summits in the hopes of finding treasure. Later, archaeologists required the assistance of armed battalions to dissuade subsequent treasure hunters from similarly destroying other pyramids in hopes of the same success. In point of fact, Ferlini's treasure appears not to have been found in the pyramid's summit, but rather in the burial chamber beneath the pyramid, which Ferlini did enter from above. Some of the treasure was apparently wrapped in cloth and placed in a bronze bowl. Other pieces apparently lay on the floor, including fragments of a wooden bed, doubtless associated with the Nubian bed burial rite.

ROYAL RELIEF SCULPTURE OF THE KINGDOM OF MEROE

A survey of the sunk, royal relief sculpture of the Kingdom of Meroe reveals an interest in detail unparalleled in the royal relief of the preceding two periods, and this interest was continually explored from the first century B.C.E. to the first century C.E. One may take as an early example a remarkable two-sided votive tablet in Baltimore, inscribed for King Tanyidamani and dated to the early first century B.C.E. The depiction of the king on the obverse is minutely detailed and includes the rams' heads of the earring and lanyard, and intricate pleats and folds of the costume. The better-preserved reverse features the lion god Apedemak, which is similarly detailed with an interest in generating space by designing elements of the attributes that pass in front of or behind the staff held by the god. The fact that monuments such as this one, which are generally small in scale, are sculpted from either schist or steatite is significant. The general homogeneity of the physical structures of these stones is inherently able to provide the craftsmen with sharp, crisp lines. They appear to have functioned as votive plaques, erected, it has been suggested, in walls of temples. Each is a technically highly accomplished and completed work of art.

There are no compelling reasons, therefore, to classify them as sculptors' models or trail pieces.

For the most part, the style of relief sculpture encountered on Meroitic temples generally relies for its effect on line, in much the same way that the royal relief images of Dynasty XXV at Karnak did. This appears to obtain for representations created over almost the entire course of Meroitic art from the third century B.C.E. to the first century C.E. For example, the preserved monumental image of King Arnekhamani, from the south, exterior wall of the Temple of Apedemak from Musawwarat es-Sufra, dated to the third century B.C.E., has been sculpted in the space of 10 vertical courses of dressed stone, excluding his headdress, with a linear precision worthy of an engraver. The amount of detail evident in a line drawing is remarkable, from the terminal of his staff over his far shoulder to the motifs on his cuff bracelets, armlets, ram-headed lanyard, earrings, uraeus-fronted cap crown, and the amulet, which is attached to that headdress's streamers. He also wears an archer's thumb guard. The same attention to detail is evident in the depiction of the Kandake Amanitore on the rear, exterior wall of the Temple of Apedemak at Naqa, which is dated to the early first century C.E., and in the image of that deity himself, which accompanies hers. To the lasting credit of the Nubian ateliers of the Kingdom of Meroe is their domination of their chosen material; the fact that these reliefs were sculpted in friable sandstone was no obstacle to their technical ability to create exacting linear detail in these impressive temple reliefs.

Raised, royal relief sculpture of the Meroitic Period can be divided into two categories, the first of which exhibits a bold, three-dimensional quality. A stela inscribed for King Amanikhabale, now in Khartoum and dated to the middle of the first century B.C.E., is designed in such a way that the sculpted figures actually rise three-dimensionally from the background plane. One gains the distinct impression that representations of members of the Meroitic royal family depicted in bold relief are imbued with a particular significance, perhaps as an added index of decorum. This certainly seems to be the case for the vignette in which King Tanyidamani, in Boston, is shown astride the back of a prostrate enemy in such bold relief that the image plastically projects from the background in contrast to the depiction of the accompanying deities, which are designed as incised, sunk-relief linear images.

A second category of raised, relief sculpture may be distinguished from the first in the treatment of the contours. In the examples just cited, the contours of the figures are well rounded and exhibit a sculptural plasticity. The contours of the raised, royal relief of this second category consist of contours that may generally be described as having been sculpted in such a way that their edges are approximately perpendicular to the background plane, and consequently are devoid of the sculptural plasticity of the first category. This aesthetic interest is evident in a votive table inscribed for Prince Arikankharer, now in Worcester, Massachusetts, and dated to the early first century C.E. The scene depicts the prince bending forward at the waist in the time-honored attitude, about to brain a group of captives whom he holds by their hair. A dog, its snout rendered in three-quarter view, gnaws at the head of a fallen prisoner behind the prince, while the goddess, Talakh, smaller in scale and unprecedentedly shown with her wings deployed, is depicted in the field to the right.

The negative stone defining the contour of the king's image has been deeply cut into the plane of the tablet so that his figure emerges from the background in high relief. Nevertheless, the contours of the king's image have neither been modeled nor articulated in the way that the raised relief of the first category has been. The impression of such sunk, royal relief is that of a circle cut by a cookie cutter into a thickly rolled, but uniformly thick sheet of dough. The imperative of this design-driven composition is, however, not uniformly applied throughout, because certain passages are more plastically rendered than others. These passages include details of Talakh's costume and attributes, the tail of the mauling canine, and the fanned-out faces of the prisoners.

More characteristic of the raised, royal relief style, which appears to eschew all sculptural, plastic modulation of the contours and a negation of rich, linear detail is a repository stone for a divine barque, used in religious processions, from Wad Ban Naga, now in Berlin. The four sides are decorated with alternating images of King Natakamani and Kandake Amanitore of the early first century C.E., who raise their hands with palms open over their heads in an attitude of supporting the heavens, artistically represented by a star-spangled sky-sign. Here, the cookie-cutter analogy can be evoked, and applies not only to the contour and details of the figures but also to their accessories. The ram's head, for example, so consummately rendered in certain sunk, royal relief images, is here reduced to an amorphous globular form. One must again stress, however, that the addition of paint may have fundamentally altered the appearance of such relief and masked the absence of modulated contours that characterize such creations in their present state.

The same design concerns are evident as well in a relief depicting King Amanitenmemide, enthroned, protected by a winged goddess from his pyramid chapel in Meroe, dated slightly after the middle of the first century C.E. The goddess is undeniably designed in accordance with the cookie-cutter analogy, whereas portions of the king's costume and accessories are relatively more detailed. Because this stylistic discordance is also observable in the Worcester votive table inscribed for Prince Arikankharer, one can suggest that design imperatives were being invoked in deliberately determining which passages in any vignette were worthy of articulation. Selections thus articulated must have been possessed of special significance or symbolic value.

One can suggest that this particular relief style was indebted for its design tenets to Egyptian relief, particularly that created in Upper Egypt and in the Dodekaschoinos during the Ptolemaic Period. An unusual sand-stone stela, not inscribed, of unknown provenance currently in Brooklyn, may serve as a representative example. It depicts two identical archers with two minute canines at their feet on the ground line. There are additionally five divine and/or royal images distributed within the composition. The suggestion that the two archers are depictions of the brothers who are commemorated in the Temple of Dendur requires demonstration.

Nevertheless, this relief shares stylistic affinities with a number of like relief images of similar date with known Egyptian provenances now in the Egyptian Museum in Cairo. Together they form a coherent group. The design of the principal figures relies on a bold contour and the avoidance of all interior detail. One may, therefore, suggest that such Egyptian reliefs served as models for the Nubian ateliers of the Meroitic Period in the cre-ation of this particular style of relief decoration.

In certain instances one can justifiably speak of a uniform, Meroitic royal style of sculpture. The sunk, royal relief sculpture just described finds its exact correspondence in certain sculptures from the Meroitic Period. The colossal, granite statue of a god from the island of Argo and the sandstone statue, identified as the god Sebiumeker, from Meroe now in Copenhagen, appear to be nothing more than translations into the round of the royal, relief just described. The bodies are rendered as a series of very abstracted planes with little or no modulation; the details of the costume and accessories are rendered as linear adjuncts and, like those on the royal relief, are devoid of careful detail. It would appear, therefore, that the same Nubian ateliers of the Kingdom of Meroe that were respon-sible for the design of certain temple reliefs were also responsible for the creation of certain stylistically similar statues in the round.

Occasionally, sunk royal relief representations rely exclusively on the incised line. This is clear from the funerary stela of Taktidamani, from Meroe now in Berlin. The main scene depicts the owner, thought to be a prince of the Meroitic family, to the left adoring an enthroned god, behind whom stands a goddess, her wings deployed in a gesture of protection. The entire scene was sculpted as if it had been engraved with a stylus. The fact that the winged sun disk in the lunette is plastically rendered in an uncommonly Meroitic fashion suggests that the stela was originally part of an Egyptian atelier's partially completed inventory of materials, which was subsequently appropriated by the Nubians. An offering table of Aryesbokhe, from Meroe and now in Khartoum, was sculpted in exactly the same manner so that the resulting figures likewise appear as line drawings.

Raised relief is encountered on offering tables such as that of Atedokeye, again from Meroe and likewise in Khartoum. The design-concept is that of the cookie-cutter analogy, with contours perpendicular to the background plane of the table and the general avoidance of interior detail. On the other hand, there is a group of stelae on which the deceased is depicted frontally

Vessel attributed to the Antelope Atelier. ALEA.

as a ba-bird. These representations conform in general to the analogy of the cookie-cutter, but occasionally exhibit an interest in more sculptural plasticity. This interest can be seen in a stela of an anonymous individual of unknown provenance now in Boston. The image is exceptional in a number of ways, including its design that incorporates simultaneous views (the feet appear in profile), suggesting that the Nubian atelier in which it was created was imitating Egyptian design tenets. The same plasticity and Egyptianizing design tenets appear to be operative as well in a door jamb from Sedeinga, now in Khartoum, depicting a libating, jackal-headed deity.

Those compiling a corpus of Meroitic sculpture have included several objects that deserve closer examination because these works of art appear either to have been created by non-Nubian, Meroitic ateliers or were imported. A sandstone funerary stela from Meroe, dated to the late second century C.E. and now in Khartoum, is a case in point. It depicts two deities, both goddesses (?) designed in the Egyptian fashion of simultaneous views, flanking a central, frontally designed figure. Although effaced, the plasticity of the richly three-dimensional figures together with certain details, such as the hand of the goddess to the left holding the ritual pail, are so close to contemporary portrayals from Egypt as to suggest that this

Detail of a vessel depicting a lion felling a Nubian. ALEA.

is an import, rather than a local product. Such a conclusion is not surprising, given the general peaceful mercantile relations that were maintained during the period and the quantity of known foreign imports appearing within the material cultural record of the Kingdom of Meroe.

THE POTTERIES OF THE KINGDOM OF MEROE

We now turn our attention to the potteries of the Kingdom of Meroe, mindful of the fact that there is virtually no corpus of identifiably Nubian pottery in the intervening millennia after the Kingdom of Kerma, when pottery, like so much of the material cultural expression of the Nubians, was subsumed beneath a thick veneer of Egyptian cultural norms. The sudden emergence of potteries during the Kingdom of Meroe is remarkable, because their creations appear without any demonstrable antecedents in much the same way that Meroitic scripts seem to have appeared out of nowhere. Neither the potteries nor the scribal institutions have any gestation period for their respective creations. A survey of the entire range and breadth of the creation of the Nubian potteries of the Kingdom of Meroe reveals these ateliers were well aware of developments in Egypt, Greece, and Rome. The extensive use of the potter's wheel, the up-draught kiln, and finely levigated clays indicates a complete understanding and masterful manipulation of ancient Egyptian technologies by the Nubians. The appearance of shapes and other techniques, common to the potteries of the Graeco-Roman world, attested in the Meroitic pottery repertoire, demonstrate that the Nubian potters were equally adept at understanding and manipulating those extra-Egyptian ceramic traditions. Their resulting creations are not inferior approximations of any foreign model. On the contrary, they are quite accomplished aesthetically and technically, and so distinctively Nubian that they cannot be confused with the production of any other ancient culture. These same Nubian potteries inexplicably vanish from the stage of history almost as abruptly as their sudden debut.

Although the pottery of the Kingdom of Meroe is visually attractive and appeals to modern aesthetic sensibilities, there is a great deal about the potteries that remains unknown. Whereas scholars would agree that the most accomplished potteries were probably located in Lower Nubia, there is evidence for potteries further to the south, particularly at Meroe, but it is unclear about whether the presumed ateliers of the south were independent or whether the wares discovered there were imported from the north. Some vessels, found at sites widely separated from one another, are so similar in their shape and in the style of their decoration that scholars have suggested the vessels shared a common origin, from which they were shipped.

This suggestion raises several significant issues, the first of which addresses the actual transport of the vessels. Whereas it is true that many of these vessels are very fragile, by both modern and ancient standards, that fragility cannot be used as an argument to suggest that these vessels were not transported over even greater distances within Nubian proper for fear of breakage. The art of transporting even the most fragile of materials, intricate glass vessels included, from one end of the Roman Empire to the other, had advanced to such a degree that fragility was a non-issue. These packing and transport advances had to have been known to the Nubians. After all, their potteries were conversant with and competent in all other contemporary aspects of the potter's craft. As a result, one cannot invoke the transportation issue in claims suggesting Nubian pottery of the

Meroitic Period was restricted to relatively small geographic areas. Whether the transportation was arranged directly by potteries or by agents is moot, but the degree of specialization found in other mercantile spheres of the contemporary Roman world would favor the employ of shipping agents.

Secondly, the suggested common origin of some of the vessels found at different sites miles apart argues in favor of potteries having developed signature wares, specific to their ateliers that are quantifiably different from the wares of other production centers. One further argues that this distinctiveness can be associated with individuals, the craftsman himself rather than the collective of the atelier in which he may have worked. The absence of signatures does not negate the premise because ancient Nubian art in general was never signed. The greater issue, however, is to define the craftsman's participation. Some scholars argue that such craftsmen were both painter and potter, whereas others would argue that painter and potter were two different individuals. The issue is far from being resolved, but the evidence would seem to support the suggestion that the vases were thrown by one individual and painted by a second, although the painting style should be ascribed to an atelier and not to an individual painter. It would, therefore, be more correct to refer to the idiosyncrasies of individual groups of decorated vases as characteristics of a particular school rather than of a painter.

To the questions concerning the location of the Nubian potteries and of the role of the individual in the creative process must be added that of chronology. There is virtually no agreement among scholars on even so basic a subject as a relative chronology for Nubian vessels of the Meroitic Period. In keeping, therefore, with traditional assessments of Meroitic pottery, the following discussion will focus on wares, suggested potteries, and/or individual craftsmen, as the nature of the evidence permits.

The Meroitic potteries created thick-walled, black white-incised wares, recalling earlier types. An example from Faras, now in Munich, is an ovoid vessel with a relatively tall, cylindrical neck. Its decorative scheme, confined to the shoulder and upper belly, relies on conjoined bow-tie-like forms, crosshatched and arranged vertically. A second example, somewhat larger and more gourdlike in shape, without provenance but also in Munich, features an iciclelike motif of five fingers cascading down the belly of the vase from a horizontal element at the shoulder. It is interesting to note that the designs of both of these motifs incorporate the negative space of the vessel itself into the patterns, which appear, therefore, to be bichromatic. A vessel, similar in profile to the last, from Wad Ban Naga, features the same bichrome scheme. On the neck are rectangular, sail-like elements, and below a rich, relatively wide border of a dotted lines from which are suspended elements recalling tapestry swags. This frames a herd of long-horned cattle accompanied by a single herdsman. The composition recalls both the herds on the bowls of the C-Group culture from

Adindan and the herdsman in relief on one of the teapots from the Kerma culture.

These same potteries also created a series of vessels in which the brick-red fabric served as an effective foil for the banded decoration of white and black. Relatively tall, with most examples measuring over 12 inches in height, the banding on these vessels was applied with the pot still rotating on the potter's wheel. They may very well have served as storage jars, analogous with Romano-Egyptian imported storage jars found in Nubian contexts. These imports may well have served the Nubian potteries as sources of inspiration in the banded decorative schemes of the vessels as well, but once again, the bold use of color in limited, wide bands reveals the creativity of the Nubian ateliers, which avoided a slavish imitation of the more pencil-thin and less visually arresting banding of the Romano-Egyptian model.

Hand-made pottery continued to be manufactured in two distinctive styles, one each associated with Lower Nubia and the southern reaches of the Kingdom of Meroe. These wares are of less interest to an art historian than are one classification of rather unsophisticated, wheel-made, undecorated ware also created in the south, with an important center for its manufacture apparently located at Musawwarat es-Sufra. It is, therefore, the more aesthetically accomplished wheel-made wares to which one now turns.

These are generally divided into two distinctive groupings, which some scholars suggest ought to be called families because of their many shared characteristics. Both groupings, or families, represent the apogee of Meroitic pottery production, and this production is on a par with the very best ceramics ever created by any culture on the African continent.

The first classification consists of bowls, beakers, and cups, all examples of which qualify as Meroitic fine ware and each of which is characterized by such thin walls as to be termed eggshell. The geographic extent and temporal range within Nubia of these Meroitic fine ware vessels suggest diverse ateliers throughout the kingdom, which were operative for prolonged periods of time.

To the second category are assigned various other shapes of somewhat larger dimension and of different fabrics that are often termed Meroitic ordinary ware. The potteries are suggested to have been located in northern Nubia and have often been adduced as evidence for the creative genius of the Nubians. Imitations of these vessels suggested to be of southern manufacture appear only later in date.

Differences between potteries located in the north and those in the south have been noted and may be summarized as follows, with the understanding that these comments are generalizations. The potteries of the north, of medial Kerma, and the south all share in the use of a white or light-gray colored slip, whereas the northern potteries of Lower Nubia preferred an additional palette ranging in hue from reddish-brown to yellow. Vessels created in the north are more likely to have figural scenes as their principal decoration, whereas the south's predilection was for ornament, modernly judged to be more delicate and carefully executed in keeping with a perceived aesthetic superiority said to be imposed by the tastes of the ruling elite in the capital city of Meroe. In this regard the motif of either serpent or square, although occasionally encountered in works of the north, are more common as decorative elements on vessels created in the south. In like manner, tall beakers with impressed geometric patterns have been attributed to royal potteries at Meroe, particularly because its fabric's characteristic brick-red color and unique profile have only been unearthed at Meroe.

Continued excavations in Nubia may change these generalizations, and continued research may suggest a relative chronology, but such advances are unlikely to alter the picture of the unique quality of each decorated Nubian pot. Of the literally thousands of examples known, no two are identical, and this unique quality is yet further evidence of the unfettered creativity of the Nubian potteries of the Meroitic Period. Following are discussions of the more interesting individual vessels and related groups.

The accomplished precision of the draftsmanship and the mastery of linear forms arranged in single, tall registers, or horizontal bands around the vessel, characterize the works associated with the academic school of Meroitic potteries. The bottoms of the vessels are generally devoid of all decoration. Their carefully executed motifs often include a ball-bead motif on the upper shoulder of these vessels just before the juncture of the neck. Spherical vessels with flaring, truncated conical necks are a favorite shape. One from Faras, now in Berlin, relies on vertically composed, repeated stylized floral images that include a lotus flower of seemingly Egyptian inspiration. A second, in Khartoum, is decorated with four registers, three registers decorated with a horizontally designed crescent and the fourth designed with a ball-bead motif.

The ubiquity of the vine leaf as a decorative motif has led to the identification of the Vine Leaf Atelier, whose members decorated a limited number of vessel shapes. In general, the decorative scheme is designed to accommodate itself to two main zones, often including colored stripes around the neck and body. These major zones may be subdivided into additional registers. The combination of decorative elements varies, but the motif of tendrils encircling the shoulder is invariable on creations of this atelier, despite the fact that no two tendril designs are ever identical. A number of these vessels are decorated with the motif of a horned-altar, so-called because of the pointed, U-shaped form of each of its four sides. These have been assigned to "the Horned Altar Painter." Although the identification is tempting, the fact that the vine motif on the vessels is never the same suggests rather that these are products of an atelier. In assigning works to individuals, the idiosyncratic characteristics of style and technique in addition to the selection of specific motifs are fundamental to the identification of individualism. One can, however, only speak of a particular painter if a Morellian consistency of similarly treated motifs, style, and technique can be demonstrated, as seen, for example, on Attic Greek pottery of the late sixth and early fifth centuries B.C.E. in which individual identities are revealed by the application of this method.

The same applies to the Antelope Atelier, the work of which is characterized by a springing antelope, seen, for example, on a series of vases in Brooklyn, Cairo, and Philadelphia. The scenes depict a single or group of antelopes, often in combination with floral images in the same register, the leaves of which whimsically point, like arrows on street signs, toward the direction in which these animals run. The atelier also specialized in birds, either in combination with the coursing antelope or alone.

The vessels decorated by the Prisoner Atelier include jars and vases on which the prisoner, habitually facing left, is drawn with hands bound behind the back and chest in front view. These images are all rendered in a fluid, linear manner, evocative of a drawing by Ingres, or another academically trained individual. The variations in detail, however, suggest that the production was due to several different individuals because of the inconsistencies evident in the calligraphic style of the drawings. What is even more remarkable is the apparent artistic freedom of the draftsmen. The prisoners, in some instances, have been drawn onto the body of the vessel without respect for any of its banded decoration, their legs and heads often intersected by the horizontal, decorative bands.

A similar calligraphic style is evident in the figural decoration of a two jars, only one of which is handled. The human figures are rendered as outlines, much more cursory in the example from Faras, now in Oxford, than in the example from Karanog, now in Philadelphia, but these contours are filled in, resembling a completed coloring book drawing, either completely in the example in Philadelphia or simply restricted to the hair in the Oxford jar.

A tantalizing shard from Meroe now in Liverpool is likewise rendered in a calligraphic style but with a degree of naturalism not found in the preceding examples. The scene depicts three, stylized lotus flowers alternating with a male figure, left, and a female, right, both apparently nude, their nakedness concealed by a fabric, which both seem to be holding, although only one hand of the female figure is preserved. The significance of the scene is elusive, its erotic intent speculative. Nevertheless, this scene appears to resonate with stylistic overtones of contemporary, Roman Alexandrian painting and may suggest the ultimate origin of all of these linear calligraphically dominated scenes on Meroitic vessels.

Indicative as well of the Meroitic potteries' awareness of other developments in the Roman world beyond is the creation in their ateliers of barbotine ware. Here small lumps of clay are applied to a vessel's surfaces as a form of decoration. Barbotine vessels were created as far afield as England during the Roman Period, but the contemporary barbotine ware found in the

Kingdom of Meroe is the exclusive product of native Nubian potteries. These same ateliers appear to have surveyed the history of African pottery and reintroduced shapes of bygone ages. The ring flask represents a Meroitic reintroduction of an ancient Egyptian form popular during Dynasty XVIII, almost a millennium and half earlier. Tradition and innovation, therefore, characterize these productions. Innovative also is the appearance of the barrel-shaped vase, which seems to be without antecedent in the ancient world as well as the use of openwork for a variety of shapes.

The appearance of winged cobras or serpents, *ankh*-signs (the Egyptian hieroglyph for "life"), lion masks (the god Apedemak?), and the like suggest an appropriation by the Nubian potteries of royal and divine motifs for nonroyal and nondivine contexts. Vessels decorated with such motifs are known from elite graves without other royal or temple associations. The frequent use of a human head, its face seemingly caricatured, as a decorative motif has been noted as a unique Meroitic decorative element and should be considered in association with these other divine and royal elements. Its design and frontality recall the Egyptian hieroglyph *her*, "face," which had acquired a cultic significance in contemporary Egypt representing the visage of a deity kindly disposed to the entreaties of a supplicant.

The most modernly endearing of all of the designs on Meroitic pottery are the figural scenes, some of which evoke royal images, but all of which are imbued with a sense of whimsy, characteristic of other aspects of ancient Nubian art. The narrative quality of some of these compositions suggests that they reflect a rich folkloric tradition of tales or fables that have, regrettably, not survived in either written form or oral tradition.

The shoulder of one vessel from Faras, now in Oxford, is decorated with a pair of images in which a lion fells a kilted Nubian. The motif is known from Egypt of the New Kingdom, where it served to symbolize pharaoh's domination of the land. Here, however, the scene is rendered somewhat innocuous by the lion, which seems to cradle the Nubian's head with his chin and forepaw. Equally humorous is the scene on a wine vessel from Karanog, now in Philadelphia. It is decorated with four muscular male figures, three shown dancing as indicated by their one raised foot. The fourth plays a double flute. They are fauns, identified by their tufts of hair and manes, short horns, tails, and animal-shaped ears. The festive scene is consistent with the vessel's use as a container for wine and demonstrates that the Meroitic potteries were well aware of Classical myths and iconography, the cavorting of fauns being a mythological staple of their northern neighbors. The fauns are, however, rendered in a distinctly Meroitic idiom, suggesting this is an illustration of a local tale.

NUBIAN CERAMICS—A QUESTION OF CONTINUITY

The disjunctive cultural record of the ancient Nubians, which is characterized by seemingly great gaps in one's knowledge for epochs of signifi-

cant lengths of time, has contributed in no small way to the compartmentalization of Nubian studies. There is a certain reluctance on the part of
scholars, therefore, to entertain the possibility of the transference of one feature of the ceramic production of an earlier Nubian culture to a subsequent
culture. This seems to be the case in the appraisal of ceramic interconnections involved with black-topped red ware. During the earlier A-Group culture the Nubian potteries created technically accomplished wares in this
fabric. This perceived degeneration of the technique evident in the C-Group
examples has led some scholars to question their relationship to the production of the A-Group culture; these scholars suggest that each is an independent creation. On the other hand, the appearance of a very similar fabric
in the ceramics of the contemporary Kerma culture would tend to support
the suggestion that there is a relationship. It would appear, therefore, that
one ought to argue in favor of continuity rather than disjunction, because
continuity appears to characterize other aspects of Nubian potteries.
Indeed, the remarked similarities among the painted wares of the Kerma
culture, represented by the painted vase in the form of a lidded basket, and

The costume and regalia of the
Meroitic *Qore* Arnekhamani.
Courtesy of Steffen Wenig.

those of the C-Group culture suggest a strong tradition rather than a local transference between contemporary cultures, particularly because bichrome ware, relying on white-filled incisions, was created by the potteries of all of the Nubian cultures discussed up to this point.

The production of hand-made domestic wares is perhaps the best indicator of the continuity of the Nubian potteries. Such vessels for everyday use were already being created by the Nubians of the Neolithic Period and continue to be produced in The Sudan today. These particular wares have affinities with productions of wares of both the C-Group and Kerma cultures, indicating that intermediate stages in this continuum can be identified. One should, therefore, entertain the possibility of a Nubian continuum with regard to the wares that the Nubian potteries created over time along different cultural horizons.

THE COSTUME OF THE KINGDOM OF MEROE

The move of the capital from Napata to Meroe, the initial suppression of the priests, and the introduction of writing were cultural transformations of Nubian society that were accompanied by changes of fashion and accessories, the most noticeable occurring in the habits of kings and queens.

The king of Meroe was called "*qore*" by his Nubian subjects, a word that was current during the Egyptian New Kingdom presence in Nubia and may be translated "commander," or the like. The state regalia of the Nubian *qore* of the Meroitic Period was very elaborate and detailed. It consisted of a pleated overgarment, identified by some as a coat and by others as a long gown that reached the ankles. Deities wore the same costume, but the divine gown is characterized by a long train that is not found on the garment worn by mortals.

Around this a sash was draped diagonally across the right shoulder and torso. The width of the sash serves as a chronological indicator, because it becomes wider over time. Long, tasseled streamers hang from the level of the shoulders in both front and back and reach to the level of the calves. This cord has been linked to a primeval Nubian hunter-god with whom the rulers were identified. A long staff was included as an index of decorum, recalling the sheyba carried by the Nubians of the New Kingdom. This costume appears to be worn by all royals, kings, queens, and princes and may be regarded as the descendant of the Egyptian three-piece costume introduced earlier that relied on the asymmetrically draped shawl for its effect.

Commentators suggest that the wearing of the royal kilt and of the corselet or bretelle went out of fashion, but these garments continued to be depicted in statues of Meroitic kings in Nubian style. The magnificent gilded bronze statue of a king from Tabo on Argo island was designed with the Nubian cap crown of Dynasty XXV fronted by the double uraeus, the lanyard with three ram-headed pendants, a broad collar, earrings, armlets, and sandals. He is depicted with the royal Egyptian kilt complete with a central flap to which is attached a bull's tail at the rear. He wears an archer's thumb ring and forearm guard.

The gods and goddesses depicted in two-dimensional relief decoration on offering tables and other works of art of the period are habitually shown wearing typically Egyptian fashions. These include the kilt for gods and the tightly fitting sheath for goddesses. The stela of Amikikha-bale, from Meroe now in Khartoum, depicts him with a composite Egyptian crown on his closely cropped hair bound by a fillet fronted by a uraeus. His costume includes a broad collar and armlets, sandals, a corslette, and pleated skirt over which may be an apron decorated in relief with the image of a falcon(?). Such decorated aprons characterize Egyptian two-dimensional relief depictions of Roman emperors, as seen in the exterior screen walls of the mammisi, or birth hall, at Dendera inscribed for Tiberius.

Statuettes identified as images of the god Amun, although not inscribed as such, depict the deity wearing a broad collar together with a choker-length necklace of ball beads, the longevity of which in Nubian culture has already been stressed. The pectorals, or pendants in the form of plaques suspended from necklaces, are exceptionally large on these figures and carved in bold relief, perhaps to stress their symbolic power. The belts around the waist are adorned with streamers, which may relate to the tassels of the royal Meroitic costume.

Representations of ba-birds form a special category of Meroitic sculpture in the round and two-dimensional representations. The coiffures of these composite soul figures are generally unisex and exhibit closely cropped hair framing the forehead and checks. Skirts appear to be the garment of choice for men as well as women, both sexes appearing topless.

A granite statue of Queen Amanimalel from Meroe now in Khartoum depicts her in an unusual garment that may derive from a fashion current during Dynasty XXV among the elite Nubian court at Thebes. Although difficult to describe in detail, this garment appears to be close-fitting, one seam of which, depicted in red, seems to run from the left shoulder in the direction of the right arm pit, which leaves the breast free. Another seam appears to be visible over the feet and wrists, while a third is in the form of a vertical line at the left passing over the left toward the left breast. The number of garments involved is moot, because of the design tenets used, but fringe seems to be integral to its creation.

Two-dimensional representations of these royal Nubians depict them as ornately accessorized. The jewelry represented includes necklaces and broad collars, anklets, bracelets, and armlets.

The latter may be intricately designed with various scarablike composite beasts. A common motif is one with four ram's heads and two frog's legs. The repertoire of crowns is full, and these are derived from Egyptian types. A diadem with wide streamers at the back fronted by two uraei is often found in association with a number of these crowns. With very rare exceptions, only images of gods are shown wearing the false beard.

The Meroitic ateliers appear to have pioneered the development of an exclusively Nubian gesture, seen for example in the temple reliefs of Meroe. This gesture consists of a standing figure reaching out and touching the elbow of an enthroned figure. This contact is a symbol of legitimization and indicates that the figure whose elbow is being touched is the rightful ruler of the kingdom.

NUDITY AND SCARIFICATION

The ancients, both Egyptian and Nubian alike, did not seem to share the embarrassment some modern sensibilities ascribe to nudity. Children in general went about naked, and women were habitually depicted topless, as a matter of course. Carnally erotic representations are virtually unattested in the Nubian cultural record. The nudity of the baked clay figurines of the earlier periods has been linked to religious precepts explained on the model of human procreation. Even the tattoos of Amunet and her contemporaries must be regarded within the cultic context of the cult of the goddess Hathor in which they served.

It should come as no surprise, then, to learn that clay images with similar intent were created by the Nubians of this period as well. Some, such as that found at Meroe and now in Khartoum, are designed as flat, unbaked clay plaques when viewed from the front, on which the eyes and nose as well as breasts and pubic triangle are depicted. Others, such as that from Karanog now in Philadelphia of baked clay, are simply rectangular plaques without any indication of limbs or head on which emphasis is given to the breasts, navel, and pubic mound. These may be related to fecundity rites and rebirth, as the Karanog example from a grave would indicate. The example from Meroe is associated with an iron foundry and may well have a cultic significance culturally analogous with the Egyptian practice of smelting metal, which was linked to rituals involving the god Sokar.

A pot shard with an enigmatic scene of a nude male and female figure holding a textile in front of them, from Meroe now in Liverpool, finds its closest Nubian parallel in a graffito from the Great Enclosure at Musawwarat es-Sufra, in which an ithyphallic male figure cradles the head of a seemingly nude female figure, who likewise holds a textile stretched out between her spread hands. These two scenes represent virtually the only known examples of Nubian erotica, but their exact meaning is elusive. The graffito may in fact refer to a divine birth, episodes of which were commemorated in a series of gold rings of the period.

Some heads of Meroitic representations of the ba-bird are designed with geometric patterns on the forehead. These may take the form of incised lines or, less often, one or more rows of incised dots drilled into the sur-

A shield ring from the Meroitic Treasure of Queen Amanishakheto. ALEA.

face. Often these patterns are horizontal in orientation, but in other exam-ples the design curves upward in a lunette-like arch. Although some may take these designs as artistic abstractions for furrows of flesh on the brow, others relate them to other incisions, generally grouped in threes, found on the cheeks of some ba-representations of the Meroitic Period. These cheek incisions do not appear to conform to anatomical reality and have consequently been identified either as body painting or scarification, the academic consensus favoring the latter identification. Ancient scarifica-tion appears to have been a typically Meroitic, Nubian practice, which survives in parts of the Sudan today and in other parts of Africa, particu-larly in Nigeria where individual designs appear to be specific to particu-lar tribes. Here the practice was unisex. The cultural record of the Kingdom of Meroe reveals that such scarification was widespread and neither gender nor status specific. Men as well as women, royal as well as nonroyal individuals might exhibit these markings. The significance of scarification remains to be satisfactorily explained, but its specific pres-ence within the culture of Nubia during the Kingdom of Meroe is certain.

THE TREASURE OF MEROE

Folk legends still circulating in Nubia and Egypt speak about untold trea-sures lying secreted in ancient tombs and temples waiting to be discovered by individuals willing to face jinni and other guardians. The discovery of the treasure of Meroe was a response to just such a legend, but the account of the discovery and its importance were soon questioned. It is only with the passing of time that the true significance of this treasure was understood.

Giuseppe Ferlini, an Italian physician born in Bologna, was appointed as a military doctor for the troops of Mohamed Ali, the man who proclaimed himself the ruler of Egypt, breaking the country away from the Ottoman Empire. The Egyptian army had occupied The Sudan, and Ferlini served first at Sennar and Kordofan before being transferred to Khartoum. While on duty, he had heard many of these fantastic folk legends, which apparently inspired him to resign his commission in order to seek permission from the Egyptian military governor of the Sudan in 1834 to excavate. The permission was granted, and Ferlini began his career as a dismal excavator, motivated more by the hopes of finding treasure than by promoting scholarship. He eventually arrived at the city of Meroe and, according to some versions of what ultimately transpired, resolved to find a treasure purportedly buried beneath the summit of one of the pyramids. The pyramid he selected for decapitation is that currently identified as belonging to Queen Amanishakheto, which at the time was just about 100 feet in height. Ferlini's own account records how his team had to restrain the Nubians with the threat of their guns from getting to the treasure first. He goes on to describe the find and continued to dismantle the pyramid in hopes of finding more. The account gained such wide currency that years later, R. Lepsius, the famed Prussian Egyptologist who was working at Meroe, was obliged to dissuade Egyptian troops in the area from further vandalism because they, too, wanted to try their luck at treasure hunting by attacking the tops of remaining pyramids in the area.

Ferlini was able to sell slightly fewer than 100 articles from the find to Ludwig I of Bavaria, despite the fact that some critics declared the lot to be forgeries. Lepsius disagreed and via agents in London was able to acquire several articles from the treasure for the Berlin museum. As late as 1913, four additional pieces were acquired by that museum from Ferlini heirs, and in 1929 some of the pieces acquired by Ludwig I, which eventually entered the collections in Munich, and others in Berlin were exchanged so that both Munich and Berlin might have more representative examples of the treasure as a whole. The Berlin articles, like other art treasures in the city, were packed and shipped to different locations for safekeeping during the course of World War II. One crate disappeared, and with it some of the objects from the treasure, one of which reappeared on the art market in 1965. The museum in Berlin was able to acquire it. Continued interest in the Meroitic Treasure of Queen Amanishakheto has shown that Ferlini's account of the discovery was sheer nonsense. The treasure was in fact found in the burial chamber beneath the pyramid. This is confirmed by Ferlini's own statement that he found fragments of a bed with the treasure. One realizes that bed burials were a feature of Nubian funerary rites.

The treasure itself is remarkable for the variety of types and materials used. It contained 10 bracelets, 9 so-called shield rings, 67 signet rings, 2 armbands, and an extraordinary number of loose amulets and elements belonging to necklaces and other articles. Most of the articles were created especially for Queen Amanishakheto, although a few were heirlooms, and almost all of the jewelry appears to have been created by Nubian ateliers in the Kingdom of Meroe.

The techniques employed included gold granulation by which tiny beads of gold are fused to the surface, glass inlays, the use of semiprecious stones, and enameling. The appearance of enamel reminds everyone of just how extraordinarily talented the Nubian ateliers of the period were. The mastery of this technique is attested in Egypt in the late fourth to third century B.C.E. and must have been adopted by the Nubians shortly thereafter. The process is sophisticated and requires the jewelers to fashion small cells of thin gold into which crushed, colored glass is then placed. The entire article is then fired in a kiln, the heat of which causes the glass to fuse into enamel. The proficiency of the Nubian ateliers in the creation of enamel accords well with their manipulation of glass, as the goblets from Sedeinga attest.

The motifs selected for the designs of the jewelry in this treasure also reveal the dexterity of the Nubian ateliers in adapting foreign motifs for their needs. One sees Nubian appropriations of both pharaonic Egyptian and Graeco-Roman elements together with motifs that are purely Nubian in origin. The treasure, unfairly compared with contemporary jewelry from the Graeco-Roman world, bears witness to a queen and her court that are aware of the world around them, and ateliers whose artisans were up to the task of creating crown jewels worthy of any ancient monarch.

Among the articles are the shield rings, so-called because the large hinged plaques attached to the loop are so broad that each plaque spans the width of the knuckles of several adjacent fingers when worn. The plaque is often in the shape of an aegis except in one instance. The aegis is represented as a broad collar to which is attached the head of a deity, often in animal form, such as that of a ram symbolizing Amun or that of a lion identified as Apedemak. The heads are accessorized with a variety of composite crowns drawn from the repertoire of Egyptian divine regalia. In one instance the aegis is designed in such a way that it includes the façade, giving the illusion that the deity is within a shrine within a temple's inner sanctum.

Several of the armlets also rely on an aegis design as the central motif of their respective compositions. One such also relies on the shrine façade, which was cleverly added to conceal the hinged joint of the two separate curved elements from which the armlet was crafted. The fact that these armlets have holes at their outer edges indicate that they were placed on the arm and tied in place with string or leather thongs which have not survived. The fact that the same motifs appear on different types of jewelry in the treasure would suggest that Queen Amanishakheto wore jewelry with similar motifs in rituals for celebrating particular deities. It is for this reason, perhaps, that the ensemble as preserved today includes a grouping of Amun as a ram, Apedemak as a lion, and Sebiumeker as human-headed.

Other shield rings, bracelets, and armlets are adorned with images of typically Egyptian deities, foremost among whom is a female goddess often represented with an Egyptian double crown and paired wings. On the jewelry worn on the arm, this goddess again covers the joint of the two elements, which are decorated with the same repeated images of a second goddess, either standing and wearing a different headdress or as a face within a series of metopes, or windowlike boxes. Without accompanying inscriptions it is difficult to determine which goddess is here represented, but the range of choices seems to be limited to Isis, Mut, or perhaps Hathor.

The signet rings are perhaps the most interesting from an iconographic point of view. Designed as loops with round bezels, these finger rings are decorated with raised relief vignettes. A group from among the total of 67 examples form a discrete group of their own because each vignette on the bezel represents a scene in the narrative of the divine birth of a monarch. The myth is known from monumental temple scenes of Egypt's Dynasty XVIII both at Deir el-Bahari in Western Thebes and across the Nile River in the Luxor Temple. In both, the god Amun is portrayed as the divine father, cohabitating with a mortal queen, whose divine offspring is Hatshepsut in the former and Amenhotep III in the later case. In the Meroitic bezels, a ram-headed deity, doubtless to be understood as Amun, is depicted as the father of a divine child, after having known a Meroitic queen, who should perhaps be identified as Amanishakheto herself.

Two points need to be emphasized. The first is that the narrative sequence represented by the scenes on this bezels is unique. There are no known parallels in the entire history of Egyptian or Nubian jewelry up to this point. Such an observation is a fitting witness to just how creative and innovative the Meroitic ateliers were. Secondly the narrative sequence invites one to speculate about the model(s) or means of transmission. One wonders whether the Nubian jewelers actually visited Thebes in order to consult the originals as models or whether they had recourse to pattern books, which seems the more likely of the choices.

The treasure also includes countless other elements that were once part of larger, strung compositions, the strings of which have long since been destroyed by time. As a result, it is difficult to suggest how these disparate elements may have been combined into their original designs. These elements include at least one modernly restrung broad collar consisting of beads made of white, red, green, dark blue stones as well as faience beads and amulets in yellow, green, and both light and dark blue. Hathor heads, wadjet-eyes, ankh-signs, scarabs, lotus flowers, small pendants as workable bells, and the like represent some of these elements. In addition, there are braided chains of gold, spiral-formed gold finger rings, earrings of various designs, and a collection of beads of jasper and sardonyx around which either gold bands have been placed or separately made plaques attached. The principal motif of these additions is the wadjet-eye, and each is crafted of gold, to which enamel may be added.

THE NUBIAN DIET AND CUISINE IN THE PERIODS SUBSEQUENT TO THE EGYPTIAN NEW KINGDOM

It has been cogently suggested that as late as the Kingdom of Meroe, the types of animals domesticated and the crops cultivated by the Nubians would not have differed significantly from those of the earlier periods. The diet of the Nubians appears not to have changed drastically over time. Classical sources contemporary with the late Napatan and Meroitic Periods (about 575–300 B.C.E.) record the cultivation of traditional cereals with an emphasis on the importance of millet and barley. Other Classical authors report that the Nubians had no oil but relied instead on suet and butter. Many of these same authors maintain that the Nubians had no fruit, except the date palm.

This traditional Nubian diet and cuisine were, nevertheless, modified by the acculturation to Egyptian norms by the Nubians during the course of the New Kingdom. This acculturation had its impact on diet as a result of the specific agricultural and animal husbandry practices adopted by the Nubians. The types of crops grown and animals raised were, however, dependent on local ecological conditions. These are unknown because the preserved records stress the ancient interest in Nubia's natural resources such as ebony, ivory, myrrh, the ostrich, and other exotic beasts rather than the local ecology.

Still, one can observe that the Nubian encounters with Egypt during the course of the New Kingdom created an avenue along which foods and their preparations traveled back and forth freely. New items subsequently added by either the Nubian or Egyptian culinary repertoire would soon be enjoyed by both. So, for example, there is evidence for the introduction of new crops. These include the cultivation of the grape and, perhaps, also wine production during Dynasty XXV in Nubia proper, particularly during the reign of Taharqa of Dynasty XXV, who reportedly enlisted the advice of Syrian vintners. There is also evidence for royal gardens in which palm trees were planted, if we can trust the Classical sources and a royal inscription of King Harsiyotef, who claims to have planted six palm trees each in royal gardens associated with the sanctuaries of Amun of Napata and Amun of Meroe. The evidence from the Kingdom of Meroe suggests that the Nubians began the cultivation of sesame and cotton during the latter part of this epoch.

How extensively the Nubians relied on irrigation is difficult to gauge. In those regions, such as Meroe and its surrounding areas, with their large annual summer rainfalls, the Nubians apparently channeled water through natural wadis to help irrigate their crops. Doubt has been cast on the use of hafirs—large, circular basins with raised earthen walls—in which rainwater is collected and stored. Because of their habitual location in proximity to settlements, the capacity of these hafirs would seem to satisfy the domestic needs of the inhabitants with little surplus for the demands of agriculture. The saqia, or water wheel, did not see widespread use until the post-Meroitic Period. The prominence accorded cattle by the Nubians persisted until the very end of the Meroitic Period and is featured as a rare genre scene on a bronze bowl now in the Egyptian Museum, Cairo, which depicts milking.

Scholars studying Greek papyri from the Roman Period found in Egypt remark that the continuing presence of Greeks in Egypt from the time of Alexander the Great in the late fourth century B.C.E. had a profound effect on the cuisine of the native Egyptians, which witnessed them eating proportionately more Classically oriented dishes as time went on at the expense of traditional Egyptian cuisine. One can suggest that this dietary transformation occurred, but perhaps to a lesser degree, during the Meroitic Period as well.

It is interesting to note in passing that the rare mentions of Nubian cuisine in ancient Egyptian texts of the Late Period (after 664 B.C.E.) are unflattering in the extreme, but must be placed into the context of ancient Egyptian attitudes toward foreigners in general. The poor opinion about Nubian cuisine expressed in these temple inscriptions and echoed by the Greek historian Herodotus are but one of the many cultural criteria by which the Egyptians attempted to differentiate themselves from their neighbors and promote their own nationalism.

THE KINGDOM OF MEROE DURING THE ROMAN IMPERIAL PERIOD

The treaty signed by Augustus and the Meroites inaugurated an era of peace between the two realms. Thereafter, military campaigns waged by the rulers of the Kingdom of Meroe would be exclusively directed against marauding tribes of Africans and the incursions into Meroitic territory by other African groups.

Passages in both Seneca, the Stoic author, and Pliny, the encyclopediast, suggest that during the reign of the Emperor Nero at least two Roman expeditions were launched into the heartland of Meroe. Whereas some regard these as military assaults, it seems more probable that their objective was exploratory in an effort to reach the source of the Nile. In 61 C.E. one of these expeditions did reach the White Nile. The Romans themselves would doubtless have never ventured into such a hostile, remote region without the full consent and support of the Meroites, who certainly knew, as they did at least as early as the reign of Taharqa, that the rains in Africa were responsible for the flooding of the Nile River in late summer.

The waves of Egyptomania that inundated Rome during the course of the first century C.E. and the close contacts shared between Roman administrators and the rulers of the Kingdom of Meroe may help to explain why there was a return to the use of Egyptian hieroglyphs in monumental inscriptions during the reign of Natakamani (about 50 C.E.). Some of these inscriptions were carved in both hieroglyphs and Meroitic with the result that such bilingual texts help to serve as aids in deciphering the latter. Shorkaror, a successor of Natakamani, commissioned a rock-cut monument at Gebel Qeili on which he celebrated a victory over one or another of the marauding tribes. In keeping with the iconography of Roman victory monuments, Shorkaror is depicted in typical Meroitic costume and regalia, striding over bound prisoners, assisted by the Roman sun god, Helios, depicted with radiant nimbus who grasps a shackle tied to a group of standing, bound prisoners. The sun god additionally offers Shorkaror a floral motif that is suggested to be durra. If this identification can be maintained, this relief documents the earliest datable depiction of that grain in a Nubian context.

The events that transpired in the Kingdom of Meroe after the middle of the first century C.E. remain largely unknown. Monumental construction projects for temples and other buildings appear to have halted, if the absence of any names of any rulers subsequent to the reign of Shorkaor is any indicator. In like manner similar building activity in Lower Nubia appears to cease after the reign of the Roman Emperor Augustus.

This absence of official projects should not conceal the observation that the Meroites continued to observe their rituals, particularly in Egypt at Philae, where one of the last delegations of the Meroitic rulers record their pilgrimage to the island sanctuary to fulfill their obligatory tithe, this time to the goddess Isis, who had become the principal deity of the region as a whole.

THE FALL OF THE KINGDOM OF MEROE

Changing Patterns of Trade

The defeat of Cleopatra VII, and the treaty between Rome and the Candake of the Kingdom of Meroe shortly thereafter concluded the Roman conquest of the East, and transformed the mercantile picture of the ancient world in the following ways.

Roman control of North Africa appears to have opened up new avenues for the procurement of African beasts for use primarily in gladiatorial combats throughout the Roman Empire. The sheer number of two-dimensional representations in both wall painting and floor mosaics in both North Africa, Sicily, and elsewhere suggest that during the course of the Roman Empire the Nubians were no longer serving as the primary middlemen in this trade. The importance of Africa as a source of luxury products was also eroded by Roman exploitation of other luxury goods from the Orient.

The Roman subjugation of Syria and the establishment of forts along the Euphrates River enabled the Romans to control the termini of goods from the East traveling along what was to become the Silk Routes. The presence of Roman Imperial coins in lands as far east as Vietnam indicate a degree of trade and an awareness of desirable articles heretofore unavailable, but which during the Roman Imperial Period now stood in direct competition with the deluxe natural resources of Africa. The degree of competition was acerbated by the progressive increase in the volume of maritime trade, particularly via the Red Sea, which was pioneered in the region as early as the Persian domination in the fifth century B.C.E. Awareness and understanding of monsoons, combined with the absence of any substantial naval threat, contributed to the increased number of Roman merchantmen plying these waters. They were apparently able to establish viable ports of call for cargo that had previously been transported overland and on the Nile River. Toward the end of the Meroitic Period, control of the African trade seems to have passed into the hands of the rulers of Axum (see following), whose rulers waged war against the Kingdom of Meroe and who appear to have sacked the capital in the middle of the fourth century C.E.

MARAUDING TRIBES

The shift in these mercantile patterns of trade was coincident with the ever-escalating assaults on the Meroites by marauding tribes. These conflicts were not new. They may be regarded historically as endemic of the tribal nature of Africa south of Aswan. The Egyptians of the New Kingdom and earlier, and the Nubians themselves throughout their long history, were forced to confront other African tribes on any number of occasions. The Roman presence in Egypt and in the Dodekaschoinos initially had a moderating influence on these attacks. Indeed, the presence of the Roman legions in the area can be compared to the presence of the Egyptian garrisons in Nubia during the Middle Kingdom. Although securing the frontier was certainly a paramount concern for both pharaoh and emperor alike, the protection of the trade routes and the economic advantages of the uninterrupted flow of luxury goods assumed primacy in their respective policy decisions. When, therefore, the Roman Emperor Diocletian at the end of the third century C.E. realized that this empire was threatened elsewhere by foreign military aggression and that the luxury trade of both Africa and the East might continue without disruption independent of a secure Meroitic Kingdom, the decision to withdraw Roman garrisons from Upper Egypt and the Dodekaschoinos was indeed a very pragmatic one. That decision effectively left the Meroites abandoned, and the condominium that they had earlier enjoyed suddenly was no more. Without the military strength to procure and securely transport the coveted natural resources of Africa to foreign markets, the history of the ancient Meroitic of Nubia begins to come to a close.

THE KINGDOM OF AXUM

The erosion of Meroitic control over Africa's desirable natural resources can be attributed in part to the rise of the Kingdom of Axum. Culturally tied to peoples of the Arabian peninsula across the Red Sea, the Axumites gradually established themselves in the highlands of what is now the modern nation-state of Ethiopia during the course of the first millennium B.C.E. By the time of the Roman conquest of Egypt during the first century C.E., the Axumites were the principal suppliers of African ivory and somewhat later also of gold, resources over which the Nubians had earlier exercised exclusive control. In addition, the trade in precious stones, notably emeralds, which had not heretofore been generally exploited by any ancient peoples, became a virtual Axumite trading monopoly.

Whereas the Meroites were literate in both their own scripts and in ancient Egyptian hieroglyphs, Greek was the international language of the region because of the impact of Hellenism on the East resulting from the campaigns of Alexander the Great in the late fourth century B.C.E. Greek was to remain the official language of Roman Egypt until its conquest by the forces of Islam in the seventh century C.E. It comes as no surprise, therefore, to learn from a fragmentary Greek inscription found at Meroe that a still to be identified Axumite ruler captured that city in the early fourth century C.E. Meroe seems to have recovered only to be captured once more by the Axumite king Ezana about 350 C.E., after which it rapidly declined in importance.

THE BLEMMYES

The rise of the Kingdom of Axum occurred simultaneously with the incessant assaults against the Meroites by marauding tribes, foremost among whom were the Blemmyes. These tribal peoples are now considered ancestral to the modern Kushite-speaking Beja living in the eastern desert of the modern nation-state of The Republic of the Sudan. A principal theater of attack was the fertile Butana, an expansive plain between the Atbara River and the Blue Nile on which the Nubians habitually grazed their cattle. The constant conflicts in this region depleted the herds and consequently diminished the wealth, prestige, and status of the Meroitic elite for whom extensive herds of cattle served as a social index of decorum.

THE NOBADAE

In addition to the assaults of the Blemmyes, a Nubian-speaking people identified as the Nobadae (not to be confused with the modern Nuba) continued to migrate into lands once controlled by the Meroites to perpetuate

Graffito on a wall of the Temple of Mandulis
depicting King Silko. ALEA.

their pastoral way of life, which included the raising of their own cattle. In
time, the Nobadae abandoned their pastoral-nomadic life style and began
to live in settlements, some of which were in towns once ruled by the
Meroites over which the Nobadae now exercised control. It was not long
before the Blemmyes and the Nobadae were engaged in power struggles
of their own.

KHARAMADOYE, *QORE* OF THE KINGDOM OF MEROE,
AND SILKO OF THE BALLANA CULTURE

In light of this constant state of unrest, it is all the more remarkable that
isolated pockets of Meroitic rule and culture continued to survive, particularly in Lower Nubia as late as the fifth century C.E. A graffito on the
walls of the Temple of Mandulis at Kalabsha has been identified as the last
known inscription ever written in the Meroitic cursive script. Ordered by
one Kharamadoye, who bears the venerable Meroitic title of *qore*, the text
goes on to evoke the god Amun, who even at this late date remained

supreme in the Meroitic pantheon, and commemorates that king's victory over an enemy, suggested by some to have been a ruler of the Blemmyes.

Kharamadoye's victory was short-lived, as demonstrated by a subsequent graffito on the walls of this same temple commemorating a King Silko, who must have lived in the middle of the fifth century C.E. and is now known not to have been a Christian king, as earlier surmised. This inscription is written in Greek and states that Silko is "King of the Noubades and all the Aithiopians" and mentions three campaigns against the Blemmyes, whom he claims to have defeated in each instance.

Confirmation of Silko's claim comes from a letter written on papyrus, which has been excavated at the site of Qasr Ibrim (Primis). Therein one learns that the Blemmyes were themselves enemies of Silko, who is specifically named, and that Silko repudiated their terms of a treaty whereby the Blemmyes negotiated the return of lands conquered by Silko in return for a payment of sheep, cattle, and camels. Silko accepted the payment, but treacherously retained the land, slew one of the opposing leaders, and imprisoned a number of priests. The ascendancy of the Ballana culture occurred at the expense of the rulers of the Kingdom of Meroe, but the history of that culture lies beyond the scope of the present volume.

THE PERSISTENCE OF NUBIAN CULTURAL NORMS

And yet, it is significant to observe that the presence of the Meroites in the land was to have a lasting influence in the regions, an influence that survived despite the eclipse of Meroitic political authority. One manifestation of this survival is to be found in the material culture of the kings of the subsequent period such as Silko, who was probably buried at Ballana, the site of the cemetery after which the Ballana culture (to which the Nodadae belong) is named. Among the rich grave goods found in their tombs at the sites of Ballana and Qustul, the most notable are their silver crowns, described elsewhere. These crowns demonstrate the persistence of ancient Nubian cultural norms and their appropriation by the Nodadae themselves who regarded the Meroites as their enemy.

At some point in the second half of the fifth century C.E. a Roman administrator from Alexandria traveled to Aswan with the objective of normalizing relationships between Rome and both the Blemmyes and Nodadae. The treaty was ratified among the venerable temples on the island of Philae. The terms of that treaty granted to both the Blemmyes and Nodadae permission to cross the border in order to visit Philae as pilgrims for the performance of millennia-old rituals in honor of the goddess Isis. A further provision permitted her statue to travel by water to all of the cult stations in the Dodekaschoinos on the occasion of her annual festival. With the fall of the Kingdom of Meroe, the ancient Meroitic language of the Nubians ceased to be the vernacular of the region. It was replaced by

Old Nubian, an African language based on the Greek alphabet. Neverthe-less, three signs of the Old Nubian language are adaptations of signs cur-rent in the Meroitic language.

Such survivals of ancient Nubian manners and customs persisted into the nineteenth century, particularly in Lower Nubia. Cultural anthropolo-gists recorded the visits to cemeteries by family and friends on the anniversary of the burial of a family member in order to offer the deceased a liquid libation, evocative of the ritual performed by the ancient Meroites on some of their stelae and offering tables. Such survivals are the clearest indication of the impact that ancient Nubian civilizations continue to make on subsequent African cultures. In this regard one is reminded of a remark made during one of the plenary sessions during an international meeting in London convened to determine the feasibility of an exhibition on the art of the entire continent of African continent. "The art and culture of Africa is so much more than simply the art and culture of ancient Egypt." It is in response to such observations that the previous chapters on the material culture of the ancient Nubians are to be understood.

POST SCRIPT

The fall of the Kingdom of Meroe has been discussed, but the rise of subsequent Nubian cultures in the region lies beyond the scope of this book. Nevertheless, in order to conclude the narrative about Nubian cos-tume and accessories with a view toward arguing, once again, for the longevity of Nubian cultural norms and against cultural dislocations, one turns to the so-called Ballana treasure.

The 13 Ballana Crowns have been divided into three groups, four asso-ciated with kings, six with queens, and three with princes. This division assumes that the triumvirate characteristic of the Kingdom of Meroe was being perpetuated in death by the Nubians of the Ballana culture. These crowns were, according to their means of manufacture, intended for the burial and were not worn in life. Their construction consists of simple bands of two silver sheets over a plaster core formed into a circlet that fits over the head. Their decoration was designed as embossed designs inset with semiprecious stones, such as beryl and carnelian together with glass. One such circlet has a ram's head in three dimension, to which is attached a large, horizontally designed lunette from which four stylized plumes flanked on each side by a uraeus. The design of this crown, and at least one other, reflects Nubian models recalling not only the design of Meroitic shield rings but also the four-feathered Nubian headdress of kings associ-ating them with the god Shu. Such survivals are not uncommon. The rep-resentation of Silko at Kalabsha depicts him wearing the Nubian cap crown with streamers surmounted by a typically Egyptian composite headdress. Despite the eclipse of their power and the disappearance of their last empire, the cultural norms of the ancient Nubians continued to survive in the material culture of subsequent epochs. Such survivals demonstrate the impact of the ancient elite Nubians and the longevity of some of their cultural expressions on the subsequent development of the cultures on the African continent.

Glossary

Androgynous   Possessed of both male and female characteristics.

Animal husbandry   The science of caring for domesticated, usually farm, animals.

Artifact   A noun employed for objects created in early societies by human beings.

Asiatic, Asiatics   By convention, the adjective and noun applied by Egyptologists to the peoples living in the ancient Near East. In this context, such designations have nothing whatever to do with individuals living in modern Asian nations.

Ba-Bird   A composite figure consisting of a human head on the body of a bird.

Barbotine   An adjective applied to certain types of pottery in which the applied decoration protrudes from the surface.

Bichrome ware   Pottery whose decoration is limited to two colors, generally black and white.

Bronze age   By convention, the second millennium from about 2000–1000 B.C.E.

Burnish   To polish pottery to make it appear bright and shiny by rubbing its surfaces with water and a pebble, or other tool.

Cataract   An obstruction in the bed of the Nile River caused by the geological intrusion of granite into the prevailing sandstone, which wears away at a lesser rate of erosion, forming rapids that impede navigation.

Centimeter   In the metric system of linear measurement, 1 inch is the equivalent of 2.54 centimeters.

Circumvallation   Any wall surrounding a building, fort, or an entire settlement.

Deben   A unit for measuring the weight of metals such as gold, silver, and copper in ancient Egyptian culture, one *deben* being the approximate equivalent of 93.3 grams. See also *Kidet.*

Deffufa   A noun, etymologically derived from an ancient Nubian word for any fortified structure erected of unfired brick and applied in a limited context to the two massive mud-brick structures at Kerma.

Do et des   A Latin phrase, "I do [this unto you] in order that you may do [this unto me in return]," expressing the reciprocal relationship enjoyed by pharaohs and the deities of the land.

In situ   A Latin phrase commonly employed in archaeological reports to indicate the very place in which an object has been found.

Indigenous   An adjective used to describe groups of individuals who are native to a specific geographic area and who did not arrive as settlers from elsewhere.

kdke   The title of the dominant female of Nubian society during the Meroitic Period.

Kidet   A unit for measuring the weight of metals such as gold, silver, and copper in ancient Egyptian culture, one *kidet* approximating 9–10 grams. See also *Deben.*

Kilometer   In the metric system of linear measurement, 1 kilometer consists of 1,000 meters, the equivalent of either 3,280.8 feet or 0.621 miles.

Lower   Employed as a geographic term to indicate the direction of the flow of the Nile River, Lower Egypt and Lower Nubia being located in the respective northern regions of these countries, that is, downstream.

Mace heads   A clublike weapon of war consisting of a stone head, either disk or pear shaped, attached to a handle.

Matriarchy   A society ruled by women.

Meter   In the metric system of linear measurement, 1 meter consists of 100 centimeters, the equivalent of 39.37 inches.

Millennium   A period of 1,000 years.

Mother-of-pearl   A hard, iridescent substance forming the inner layer of certain seashells, such as that of the pearl oyster.

Nine Bows   A designation developed by the ancient Egyptians, each representing one of their traditional enemies, among which the Nubians were one. See also **Troglodyte**.

Nome An ancient geographic area with defined boundaries into which the country of ancient Egypt was divided and which may be regarded as equivalents of states or provinces.

Palette A noun employed for a flat object, generally worked by human hands, on which substances used for cosmetics can be ground to prepare them for application.

pesato The title of a high-ranking Meroitic official, traditionally male, who exercised his authority over Lower Nubia. The title is sometimes translated, "Viceroy [of Nubia]."

Petroglyph An image, usually without accompanying written inscription, carved or painted by human beings into the living rock; also known as rock art.

pqr The title of one of the three dominant members of Nubian society during the Meroitic Period, thought to be of somewhat less elevated status than either that of the *qore* or *kdkt*.

Provenance A noun employed to indicate the precise geographic location from which an object originally came.

qore The title of the dominant male member of Nubian society during the Meroitic Period.

Semitic languages An important subgroup of Afro-Asiatic languages, which includes modern Arabic and Hebrew.

Silo A noun given to any architectural structure primarily employed for the storage of grain.

Sistrum A noun used to describe a sacred rattle used in ancient Egyptian religious ceremonies.

Stela (Stelae, plural) Any stone monument, generally with a rounded top, in which an inscription with or without an accompanying figural scene is carved. Stelae might serve to record official decrees or mark the spot of a burial.

Terra-cotta Clay that has been fired in a kiln.

Troglodyte A noun employed to translate into English an Egyptian noun serving as a generic, pejorative designation from the time of the Old Kingdom for several of Egypt's neighbors. See also **Nine Bows**.

Tumulus The noun applied to an artificially created mound heaped up over a grave or burial.

Upper Employed as a geographic term to indicate the direction of the flow of the Nile River, Upper Egypt and Upper Nubia being located in the respective southern regions of these countries, that is, upstream.

Uraeus From the ancient Greek, this noun refers to the sacred cobra that often adorns the brow of depictions of ancient Egyptian pharaohs in order to protect them from harm.

Wattle-and-daub   A phrase used to designate an architectural method of construction that relies on covering, or daubing, straw or other pliant plants or twigs with mud as a kind of plaster.

Yardang   A noun derived from the Turkish language describing a naturally created formation, generally of rock, which gives the appearance of being a sculpture made by human beings.

Zoomorphic   An adjective generally applied to an abstract form or shape that recalls that of a particular animal.

Abbreviations

AEL   Mirian Lichtheim. *Ancient Egyptian Literature.* Berkeley:
             University of California Press, 1975.

AHAE   N. Grimal. *A History of Ancient Egypt.* Trans. I. Shaw.
             Oxford: Blackwell, 1992.

ALEA   Archive of Late Egyptian Art. A photographic and biblio-
             graphic archive maintained by Robert Steven Bianchi.

ARE   James Henry Breasted. *Ancient Records of Egypt.* Chicago:
             University of Chicago Press, 1906. Each citation is followed
             by the volume number and the corresponding paragraph
             indicated by the symbol §.

B.C.E.   Before the common era. Here used as the equivalent of B.C.,
             before Christ.

BeWTR   H. Ricke, G. R. Hughes, and Edward F. Wente. *Campagne
             internationale pour la sauvegarde des monuments de la Nubie.
             The University of Chicago Oriental Institute Nubian Expedition,
             Volume I. Joint Expedition 1960/61 with the Schweizerisches
             institut für Ägyptische Bauforschung und Altertumskunde in
             Kairo, The Beit el- Wali Temple of Ramesses II.* Chicago: The
             University of Chicago Press, 1967.

B.P.   Before the present. Customarily used for chronological
             references of the earth's remote past.

BPENR   Robert G. Morkot, *The Black Pharaohs. Egypt's Nubian Rulers.*
             London: The Rubicon Press, 2000.

C.E.   Common era. Here used as the equivalent of A.D., anno
             Domini.

DFRK   Angelika Lohwasser. *Die königlichen Frauen im antiken Reich
             von Kusch. 25. Dynastie bis zur Zeit des Natasen.* Wiesbaden,
             Germany: Harrassowitz Verlag, 2001. [= *MEROITICA* 19].

ETSLK   R. A. Parker, Jean Leclant, and Jean-Claude Goyon. *The
             Edifice of Taharqa by the Sacred Lake of Karkak.* Providence, RI:
             Brown University Press, 1979. [= *Brown Egyptological
             Studies* VIII].

IOWANA   László Török. *The Image of the Ordered World in Ancient
             Nubia: The Construction of the Kushite Mind, 800 BC–300 AD.*
             Leiden: Brill, 2002.[= *Probleme der Ägyptologie* Achtzehnter
             Band].

MAEMP   Robert Kriech Ritner. *The Mechanics of Ancient Egyptian
             Magical Practice.* Studies in Oriental Civilization No. 54.
             Chicago: The Oriental Institute of the University of
             Chicago, 1993.

NJB   *The New Jerusalem Bible.* Standard edition. New York: Dou-
             bleday, 1999.

SAKN   Dietrich Wildung. *Sudan: Ancient Kingdoms of the Nile.* Exhi-
             bition catalogue. Trans. Peter Der Manuelian. Paris: Flam-
             marion, 1997.

SOPT   R. A. Parker. *A Saite Oracle Papyrus from Thebes in The Brook-
             lyn Museum [Papyrus Brooklyn 47.218.3].* Providence, RI:
             Brown University Press, 1962.

Suggestions for Further Reading

Abu Simbel News 1, no. 2 (n.d.).

Adams, W. Y. "The Invention of Nubia." In Berger, Clerc, and Grimal, 2:17–22.

———. "Some Doubts about the 'Lost Pharaohs.'" *Journal of Near Eastern Studies* 44 (1985): 185–92.

Aldred, C., F. Damas, C. Desroches-Noblecourt, and Jean Leclant. *L'Egypte du crepuscule.* Paris: Editions Gallimard, 1980.

Andrews, C. *Ancient Egyptian Jewellery.* London: British Museum Publications, 1990.

Berger, Catherine, Gisèle Clerc, and Nicholas Grimal, eds. *Hommages à Jean Leclant 1–4* [= *Bibliothèque d'Étude* 106/1–4]. Cairo: Institut français d'Archéologie orientale, 1994.

Bevan, E. R. *The House of Ptolemy. A History of Hellenistic Egypt under the Ptolemaic Dynasty.* Chicago: Ares Publishers, 1968 [reprint of the 1927 edition].

Bianchi, R. S. "Egyptian Metal Statuary of the Third Intermediate Period (Circa 1070–656 B.C.), from its Egyptian Antecedents to Its Samian Examples." In The J. Paul Getty Museum, *Small Bronze Sculptures from the Ancient World: Papers Delivered at a Symposium Organized by the Departments of Antiquities and Antiquities Conservation and Held at the J. Paul Getty Museum, March 16–19, 1989,* 61–84. Malibu, CA: The J. Paul Getty Museum, 1989.

———. "An Elite Image." In *Chief of Seers. Egyptian Studies in Memory of Cyril Aldred,* edited by E. Goring, N. Reeves, and J. Ruffle, 34–48. London: Kegan Paul International in association with National Museums of Scotland, Edinburg, 1997.

———. *In the Tomb of Nefertari. Conservation of the Wall Paintings.* Santa Monica: The J. Paul Getty Trust, 1992.

———. "Napatan and Meroitic Sculpture: An Art Historical Reappraisal." In *Nubian Studies. Proceedings of the Symposium for Nubian Studies,* edited by J. M. Plumley, 41–44. Warminster, England: Aris and Phillips, 1982.

———. *The Nubians. Peoples of the Ancient Nile.* Brookfield, CT: The Millbrook Press, 1994.

———. "Tattoo in Ancient Egypt." In *Marks of Civilization. Artistic Transformations of the Human Body,* edited by A. Rubin, 21–28. Los Angeles: Museum of Cultural History, University of California, 1988.

———. "The Theban Landscape of Rameses II." In *Ancient Egypt, The Aegean, and the Near East. Studies in Honour of Martha Rhoads Bell* I, edited by J. Phillips. San Antonio: Van Siclen Books, 1997.

Bothmer, Bernard V. "Block Statues of Dynasty XXV." In Berger, Clerc, and Grimal, 2:61–68.

Breasted, J. H. *Ancient Records of Egypt I-5.* Chicago: University of Chicago Press, 1906.

Caminos, R. A. (posthumous). "Queen Katimala's Inscribed Panel." In Berger, Clerc, and Grimal, 2:73–80.

Camps, G. "Amon-Re et les beliers à sphéroïde de l'Atlas." In Berger, Clerc, and Grimal, 4: 29–44.

Caneva, I. "Prehistoric Hunters, Herders, and Tradesmen in Central Sudan." In *Egypt and Africa. Nubia from Prehistory to Islam,* edited by W. V. Davies, 6–15. London: British Museum Press, 1991.

Červíček, P. "Archaische Orantendarstellung auf ägyptischen und nubischen Felsbildern." In Berger, Clerc, and Grimal, 2: 97–104.

Coppens, V. "L'ambiguité des double Vénus du Gravettien de France," *CRAIBL* (July-December 1989): 566–71.

Curto, S. *La satira nell'Antico Egitto.* Turin, n.d.

Dawson, W. R., and E. P. Uphill. *Who Was Who in Egyptology.* 3rd rev. ed. By M. L. Bierbrier. London: The Egypt Exploration Society, 1995.

Depuy, C. "The 'State of the Art.' The Rock Art Engravings of the Adrar des Iforas (Mali)." *International Newsletter on Rock Art* 3 (1992): 7–13.

Emery, W. B. *Archaic Egypt.* Baltimore: Penguin Books, 1963.

Gibson, M. F. "Reading the Mind before It Could Read," *The Sunday New York Times,* 21 April 2002, AR 33.

Godley, A. D. *Herodotus with an English Translation* I. The Loeb Classical Library. Cambridge: Harvard University Press, 1960.

Goedicke, H. Review of *Studies in Honor of John A. Wilson. The Journal of the American Research Center in Egypt* 8 (1969–70), 85.

Gratien, B. "Le céramique à décor figure du village fortifié du Groupe C à Ouadi es-Séboua est." In *Artibus Aegypti. Studia in Honorem Bernardi V. Bothmer a colleges amicis discipulis conscripta,* edited by H. De Meulenaere and L. Limme, 63–77. Brussels: Koninklijke Musea voor Kunst en Geschiedenis, 1983.

Grimal, N. *A History of Ancient Egypt.* Translated by I. Shaw. Oxford: Blackwell, 1992.

———. "Le roi et la sorcière." In Berger, Clerc, and Grimal, 4: 97–108.

Hawkes, J. Review of *Women in Prehistory,* by M. Ehrenberg. *Antiquity* 64 (1990): 424–25.

Herodotus. *The Histories.* Translated by Aubrey Selincourt. Baltimore, MD: Penguin Books, 1961.

Hinkel, F. W. *Exodus from Nubia.* Berlin: Akademie-Verlag, 1978.

Hoffmann, E. *Lexikon der Steinzeit.* Munich: C. H. Beck'sche Verlagsbuchhandlung, 1999.

Jung, M. "Rock Art of North Yemen." *Rivista degli Studi Orientali* 54 (1990): 255–73.

Kadish, G. B. "Eunuchs in Ancient Egypt?." In *Studies in Honor of John A. Wilson.* Chicago: University of Chicago Press, 1969.

Kitchen, K. A. *The Third Intermediate Period in Egypt 1100–650 BC.* 2d ed. with supplement. Warminster, England: Aris and Phillips, Ltd., 1986.

Kyzyaniak, L. "Dakhleh Oasdis Project: Research on the Petroglyphs 1990." *PAM* 2 (1991): 60–64.

Leclant, J., and G. Clerc. "Fouilles et travaux en Egypte et au Sudan, 1984–1985." *Orientalia* 55 (1986): 236–319.

Lichtheim, M. *Ancient Egyptian Literature. III. The Late Period.* Berkeley: University of California Press, 1980.

Lohwasser, Angelika. *Die königlichen Frauen im antiken Reich von Kusch. 25. Dynastie bis zur Zeit des Nastasen.* Wiesbaden, Germany: Hassassowitz Verlag, 2001.[= *Meroitica* 19].

Malamat, A. "Foot-runners in Israel and Egypt in the Third Intermediate Period." In Berger, Clerc, and Grimal, 4: 199–201.

Marshack, A. *The Roots of Civilization: The Cognitive Beginnings of Man's First Art Symbol and Notation.* New York: McGraw-Hill, 1972.

Martin, G. T. *The Memphite Tomb of Horemheb, Commander-in-chief of Tutankhamon. I. The Reliefs, Inscriptions, and Commentary* [= Egypt Exploration Society, *Fifty-fifth Excavation Memoir*]. London: Egypt Exploration Society, 1989.

Midant-Reynes, B. "Egypte prédynastique et art rupestre." In Berger, Clerc, and Grimal, 4: 229–36.

Millet, N. B. "The Narmer Macehead and Related Objects" *Journal of the American Research Center in Egypt* XXVII (1990): 53–60.

Morkot, Robert G. *The Black Pharaohs. Egypt's Nubian Rulers.* London: The Rubicon Press, 2000.

Moussa, Ahmed Mahmoud. "A Stela of Taharqa from the Desert Road at Dashur." *Mitteilungen des Deutschen Archäologischen Instituts Abteilung Kairo* 37 (1981): 331–37.

Muzzolini, A. "Les beliers sacrés dans l'art rupestre saharien." In Berger, Clerc, and Grimal, 4: 247–72.

The New Jerusalem Bible. Standard Edition. New York: Doubleday, 1999.

Parker, R. A. *A Saite Oracle Papyrus from Thebes in The Brooklyn Museum [Papyrus Brooklyn 47.218.3].* Providence, RI: Brown University Press, 1962.

Parker, R. A., Jean Leclant, and Jean-Claude Goyon. *The Edifice of Taharqa by the Sacred Lake of Karkak* [= *Brown Egyptological Studies* VIII]. Providence, RI: Brown University Press, 1979.

Parkinson, R. B. *Poetry and Culture in Middle Kingdom Egypt. A Dark Side to Perfection.* London: Continuum, 2002.

Pestman, P. W. "Haronnophris and Chaonnophris. Two Indigenous Pharaohs in Ptolemaic Egypt (205–185 B.C.)." In *Hundred-Gated Thebes. Acts of a Colloquium on Thebes and the Theban Area in the Graeco-Roman Period* [= *Papyrologica Lugduno-Batava* 27], edited by S. P. Vleeming. Leiden: E. J. Brill, 1995.

Pharaonen und Fremde. Dynastien im Dunkel. Exhibition catalogue. Vienna: Eigenverlag der Museen der Stadt Wien, 1994.

Phillips, J. "A Note on Puntite Housing." *Journal of Egyptian Archaeology* 82 (1996): 206–7.

Phillips, T., ed. *Africa. The Art of a Continent*. Exhibition catalogue. Munich: Prestel, 1995.

Pomerantseva, N. "Composition and Iconographical Structure of Reliefs in Lion Temple A in Naga." In *Etudes nubiennes. Conférence de Genève. Actes du VIIe Congrès international d'études nubiennes, 3–8 septembre 1990. Volume II. Communications*, edited by Ch. Bonnet Chêne-Bourg, 159–69. Geneva, Switzerland: Médecine + Hygiene, 1994.

Priese, K. H. *The Gold of Meroe*. Exhibition catalogue. Mainz, Germany: Verlag Philipp von Zabern, 1992.

———. *Museuminsel Berlin. Ägyptisches Museum. Staatliche Museen zu Berlin. Stiftung Preussischer Kulturbesitz*. Mainz, Germany: Verlag Philipp von Zabern, 1991.

Redford, D. B. *Akhenaten: The Heretic King*. Princeton, NJ: Princeton University Press, 1984.

Ricke, H., G. R. Hughes, and Edward F. Wente. *Campagne internationale pour la sauvegarde des monuments de la Nubie. The University of Chicago Oriental Institute Nubian Expedition, Volume I. Joint Expedition 1960/61 with the Schweizerisches institut für Ägyptische Bauforschung und Altertumskunde in Kairo, the Beit el-Wali Temple of Ramesses II*. Chicago: University of Chicago Press, 1967.

Rilly, Claude. "Une nouvelle interpretation du nom royal Piankhy." *Bulletin de l'Institut français d' Archéologie orientale* 101 (2001): 369–92.

Ritner, R. K. *The Mechanics of Ancient Egyptian Magical Practice*. Studies in Oriental Civilization No. 54. Chicago: The Oriental Institute of the University of Chicago, 1993.

Satzinger, H. *Funde aus Ägypten. Österreichische Ausgragungen seit 1961*. Exhibition catalogue. Vienna: Kunsthistorisches Museum, 1979.

Schulman, A. R. "The Nubian Wars of Akhenaten." In *L'Egyptologie en 1979. Actes prioritaires de recherches* 2, 299–316. Paris: Editions du Centre National de la Recherche Scientifique, 1982.

Shaw, I., and P. Nicholson. *British Museum Dictionary of Ancient Egypt*. London: British Museum Press, 1995.

Smith, H. S. "The Princes of Seyala in Lower Nubia in the Predynastic and Protodynastic Periods." In Berger, Clerc, and Grimal, 2: 261–376.

Török, László. *The Image of the Ordered World in Ancient Nubia. The Construction of the Kushite Mind, 800 BC–300 AD* [= *Probleme der Ägyptologie* Achtzehnter Band]. Leiden: Brill, 2002.

———. "Upper Egyptian Pottery Wares with Hellenistic Decoration and Their Impact on Meroitic Vase Painting." In Berger, Clerc, and Grimal, 2: 377–87.

Trigger, B. G. *Early Civilizations. Ancient Egypt in Context*. Cairo: The American University in Cairo Press, 1993.

Van Dijk, J. "The Nocturnal Wanderings of King Neferkare." In Berger, Clerc, and Grimal, 4: 387–93..

Vatikiotis, P. J. *The History of Modern Egypt from Muhammad Ali to Mubarak*. 4th ed. London: Weidenfeld and Nicholson, 1991.

von Beckerath, J. *Handbuch der ägyptischen Königsnamen*. Mainz, Germany: Verlag Philipp von Zabern, 1999.

Wegner, J. W. "Interaction between the Nubian A-group and Predynastic Egypt—The Significance of the Qustul Incense Burner." In *Egypt in Africa*, edited by T. Celenki, 98–100. Indianapolis: Indianapolis Museum of Art in Cooperation with Indiana University, 1996.

Wenig, S., (ed. *Africa in Antiquity: The Arts of Ancient Nubia and the Sudan I. The Essay and II. The Catalogue*. Exhibition catalogue. Brooklyn: The Brooklyn Museum, 1978.

Wildung, Dietrich. *Sudan. Ancient Kingdoms of the Nile*. Exhibition catalogue. Translated by Peter Der Manuelian. Paris: Flammarion, 1997.

Wilkinson, A. H. *Early Dynastic Egypt*. London: Routledge, 1999.

Wilkinson, C. K., with a catalogue by Marsha Hill. *Egyptian Wall Paintings. The Metropolitan Museum of Art's Collection of Facsimiles*. New York: Metropolitan Museum of Art, 1983.

Williams, B. "Forebearers of Menes in Nubia: Myth or Reality?" *Journal of Near Eastern Studies* 46 (1987): 15–16.

———. "The Lost Pharaohs of Nubia." *Archaeology* 33, no. 5 (1980): 12–21.

Index

About the Author

ROBERT STEVEN BIANCHI served as curator in the Department of Egyptian, Classical, and Ancient Middle Eastern Art at the Brooklyn Museum of Art. He has written several articles about Nubian art in general and one young reader's book on the subject, *The Nubians: People of the Ancient Nile* (1994).